Equality and Inequality in Education Policy

Equality and Inequality in Education Policy

This Reader is part of an Open University Course (E826) Gender Issues in Education: Equality and Difference, forming one module in the MA in Education programme. The selection is related to other material available to students. Opinions expressed in individual articles are not necessarily those of the course team or of the University.

Other volumes published as part of this course by Multilingual Matters Ltd in association with The Open University:

Identity and Diversity: Gender and the Experience of Education
    M. BLAIR and J. HOLLAND, with S. SHELDON (eds)
Debates and Issues in Feminist Research and Pedagogy
    J. HOLLAND and M. BLAIR, with S. SHELDON (eds)

For information about books of related interest, please contact:
Multilingual Matters Ltd,
Frankfurt Lodge, Clevedon Hall, Victoria Road,
Clevedon, Avon BS21 7SJ, England

Gender Issues in Education: Equality and Difference

Equality and Inequality in Education Policy

A Reader edited by

Liz Dawtrey, Janet Holland
and Merril Hammer,
with Sue Sheldon

at The Open University

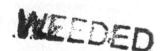

MULTILINGUAL MATTERS LTD
Clevedon • Philadelphia • Adelaide
in association with
THE OPEN UNIVERSITY

The Open
University

Library of Congress Cataloging in Publication Data

Equality and Inequality in Education Policy: A Reader/Edited by Liz Dawtrey [et al.]
(Equality and Difference)
Includes bibliographical references and index.
1. Education and state–Great Britain–History. 2. Women–Education–Great
Britain–History. 3. Educational equalization–Great Britain.
I. Dawtrey, Liz. II. Series.
LC93.G7E78   1995
379.41–dc20   94-28786

British Library Cataloguing in Publication Data

A CIP catalogue record for this book is available from the British Library.

ISBN 1-85359-250-1 (hbk)
ISBN 1-85359-249-8 (pbk)

Multilingual Matters Ltd

UK: Frankfurt Lodge, Clevedon Hall, Victoria Road, Clevedon, Avon BS21 7SJ.
USA: 1900 Frost Road, Suite 101, Bristol, PA 19007, USA.
Australia: P.O. Box 6025, 83 Gilles Street, Adelaide, SA 5000, Australia.

Selection, editorial matter and commissioned items (Articles 13 and 15)
copyright © 1995 The Open University.

Cover design by Bob Jones Associates.
Index by Meg Davies (Society of Indexers).
Typeset by Action Typesetting, Gloucester.
Printed and bound in Great Britain by WBC Ltd, Bridgend.

CONTENTS

PREFACE

This is the second in a set of three Readers which have been prepared for the course E826, *Gender Issues in Education: Equality and Difference,* a module in the Open University's taught MA in Education. The two companion Readers for the course are *Identity and Diversity: Gender and the Experience of Education* and *Debates and Issues in Feminist Research and Pedagogy.* The articles in this Reader provide a review of the history of education policy in relation to issues of equality and inequality. They also offer an overview and critique of specific areas of policy, and a glimpse of the ways in which policies operate in practice. Part 1 constitutes a history of education policy from 1800 to the mid 1990s, with the focus on class and gender inequalities. Part 2 contains some comparative material on equal opportunities policies, and also articles concerned with equal opportunities in relation to race, gender and special needs. The final part of the book deals more explicitly with the themes underlying much of the earlier material: the implications of policy in practice. A range of perspectives are covered in these articles, and the opinions expressed are not necessarily those of the editors or of the course writers or of The Open University. The Reader will be particularly useful for those with an interest in the history of education policy and issues of equity.

Further information about the MA in Education can be obtained by writing to: Central Enquiry Service, PO Box 200, The Open University, Milton Keynes MK7 6YZ.

SOURCES

We would like to thank the authors and publishers concerned for kindly granting permission to reproduce copyright material in this Reader. Every effort has been made to trace the correct copyright owners, both authors and publishers, as listed by article below.

1. **J. Purvis** Women and Education: A Historical Account, 1800–1914
   From: Purvis, J. (1984) E205 *Women and Education,* Unit 25 (pp. 14–28). Milton Keynes: The Open University.

2. **D. W. Dean** Education for Moral Improvement, Domesticity and Social Cohesion: The Labour Government, 1945–1951
   From: *Oxford Review of Education* (1991) Vol. 17, No. 3, pp. 269–86. Carfax Publishing Company, P.O. Box 25, Abingdon, Oxfordshire OX14 3UE, England.

3. **R. Deem** State Policy and Ideology in the Education of Women, 1944–1980
   From: *British Journal of Sociology of Education* (1981) Vol. 2, No. 2, pp. 131–43. Carfax Publishing Company, P.O. Box 25, Abingdon, Oxfordshire OX14 3UE, England.

4. **M. Littlewood** Makers of Men
   From: *Trouble and Strife* (Spring 1985) Vol. 5, pp. 23–9.

5. **M. E. David** The Education Policy Context: The Idea of 'Parentocracy', 1976–1992
   From: David, M. E. (1993) *Parents, Gender and Education Reform* (pp. 53–74). Cambridge: Polity Press.

6. **L. Paterson** Social Origins of Under-achievement Among School-Leavers
   From: Maguiness, H. (ed.) (1992) *Educational Opportunity: The Challenge of Under-achievement and Social Deprivation* (pp. 4–16). Local Government Centre, Paisley College.

7. **E. Edwards** Educational Institutions or Extended Families? Women's Colleges in the Late Nineteenth and Early Twentieth Centuries
   From: *Gender and Education* (1990) Vol. 2, No. 1, pp. 17–35. Carfax Publishing Company, P.O. Box 25, Abingdon, Oxfordshire OX14 3UE, England.

8. **J. Arends and M. Volman** Equal Opportunities in Education in the Netherlands and the Policy of the ILEA.
   From: *Gender and Education* (1992) Vol. 4, No. 1/2, pp. 57–66. Carfax Publishing Company, P.O. Box 25, Abingdon, Oxfordshire OX14 3UE, England.

9. **S. Miles and C. Middleton** Girls' Education in the Balance: The ERA and Inequality.
   From: Flude, M. and Hammer, M. (eds) (1990) *The Education Reform Act 1988: Its Origins and Implications* (pp. 187–206). Basingstoke: Falmer Press.

10. **S. Middleton** Women, Equality and Equity in Liberal Educational Policies, 1945–1988: A Feminist Critique
    From: Codd, J. and Jones, A. (eds) (1990) *New Zealand Education Policy Today* (pp. 68–93, 218–20). Wellington, New Zealand: Bridget Williams.

11. **M. Arnot** Feminism, Education and the New Right
    From: Arnot, M. and Barton, L. (eds) (1992) *Voicing Concerns: Sociological Perspectives on Contemporary Education Reforms* (pp. 41–65). Wallingford, Oxfordshire: Triangle Books.

12. **H. Mirza** The Myth of Underachievement
    From: Mirza, H. (1992) *Young, Female and Black* (pp. 10–31, 197–98, 206–30). London: Routledge.

13. **H. Daniels, V. Hey, D. Leonard and M. Smith** Gendered Practice in Special Educational Needs. Commissioned article.

14. **P. Broadfoot and M. Osborn, with M. Gilly and A. Paillet** What Professional Responsibility Means to Teachers: National Contexts and Classroom Constants.
    From: *British Journal of Sociology of Education* (1988) Vol. 9, No. 3, pp 265–87. Carfax Publishing Company, P.O. Box 25, Abingdon, Oxfordshire OX14 3UE, England.

15. **I. Siraj-Blatchford** Racialized and Gendered Discourses in Teacher Education
    Commissioned article.

INTRODUCTION

Deem (1980, p.1) has suggested that 'The development of mass education in England and Wales since the beginning of the nineteenth century has been marked by three crucial divisions: social class, ability and sex'. In reading historical analyses we can see class and gender as crucial divisions long before the advent of mass education (Gardiner, 1929; Kamm, 1965) and since the 1960s there has been increasing awareness of 'race' and disability. In this book we have put together a selection of articles that discuss the history and gendered nature of education policy and the impact of policies on practice in education. The articles represent a range of views and approaches to education, demonstrating the complexity of educational experience and the influence of class, race, culture and gender. Education emerges from many of these articles as being far from a radical and liberating experience for many pupils, but rather restraining, and a means of legitimizing dominant ideologies of state and society. We have chosen some well-known and some new pieces which contribute to ongoing debates.

The articles in Part 1 outline the history of education policy, largely in relation to class and gender divisions. Covering the period 1800 to 1914, Purvis (Article 1) describes the divisions between and within the education of the middle class and the working class through the nineteenth century and the introduction of the possibility of mass schooling in the 1870 Education Act. She argues that up to 1870, the middle class organized education for the working class through charity, religious groups and philanthropy, or some combination of the three, and that girls were schooled for an ideal of 'useful' domestic work, as domestic servants in the homes of the bourgeoisie, or unpaid domestic labour in their own future homes. Middle-class girls were also educated for their roles as wives and mothers, but trained in the 'useless' ideal of ladylike accomplishments, schooled to attract husbands. For each, their education was inferior to boys in their own class.

Dean pursues the theme of the domestic role of women through an analysis of the social welfare and education policies of the Labour Government 1945–51 (Article 2). Since 'acute fears were growing in postwar Britain that established networks of family and friendships were being disrupted in the painful rebuilding of devastated Britain', the emphasis was on strengthening the family and the domestic role for women within it for the construction and rehabilitation of social cohesion. For Dean, these concerns help to explain the attitudes taken by the Labour administration in this period to issues such as equal pay, nursery education and forms of schooling.

In the period from the 1944 Education Act to 1970 there was growth in the UK economy, in the participation of women in the labour market, and in welfare state provision including education in an attempt to eradicate some of the grosser inequalities of the society. There was a shift to comprehensive schools and an apparent consensus about educational provision within a social democratic framework. But the 1970s saw the decline and fall of the consensus and of social democracy in an increasingly harsh economic environment. Deem (Article 3) charts the fate of women's education through this period in the light of changing state policies and ideologies about women's role in society, which serve to mask the structural sources of their oppression and inequality.

David, in Article 5, picks up the story at the point of collapse of social democratic policy and the swing to the right. By the end of the 1970s 'British educational policy was no longer officially debated in terms of its ability to aid in the process of, and achieve, equal opportunities on the basis of reducing differences in socio-economic family backgrounds'. She discusses the educational reforms of the government since 1979 in the context of the parent–school relationship, and compares the processes of educational reform in the UK and the USA. Although these processes differ (increasing centralization for the UK, decentralization for the USA) David argues that they each contribute to diversity and difference in education provision which is liable to exacerbate social divisions, rather than produce equal educational opportunities.

Paterson asserts that 'the Scottish education system has had the reputation of being open to children of any social background' (Article 6). While charting in detail the points in their educational career at which class differences in the proportion of school leavers who enter higher education are generated, indicating the fallacy in that statement, Paterson none the less has an optimistic view of the long-term effects of the social democratic educational reforms of the 1960s and 1970s. Change may be slow, but in Paterson's view there are opportunities for higher education institutions to expand the class base of their students within an underlying situation of reduction in the size of the working class and improved educational standards since the 1960s.

In contrast to the broad sweep of many of the articles in Part 1, Edwards (Article 7) and Littlewood (Article 4) each concentrates on particular aspects of women's experience in the education system in higher education and as teachers. Edwards draws on the insights of feminist post-structuralism to analyse the way in which discourses of social practices and family organization in the Victorian middle-class home were translated into the institutional context of women's colleges. She continues to discuss the difficulties faced by women principals to meet the requirements of a dual gender role as father and mother in these familial institutions, and ways in which they dealt with the problems of expressing their own femininity within these constraints through homoerotic relationships.

Littlewood's contribution throws light on the history of the National Association of Schoolmasters (NAS) which broke away from the National Union of Teachers in 1922 forming a separate union for men, to protect them from an upsurge of 'militant feminism' within the profession. Based on an analysis of NAS publications in the 1920s and 1930s, Littlewood argues that this period saw the emergence of a group of men organized on the principle of male domination in school and family life, with an ideology and teaching practice more patriarchal than that of the state, and that this element has been institutionalized and has remained in schools and teaching unions.

The articles in Part 2 contain comparative material on equal opportunities policies, and discussions of equal opportunities in relation to 'race', gender and special needs. Arends and Volman (in Article 8) compare what they see as the anti-sexist approach of the Inner London Education Authority (ILEA) with the equal opportunities approach of the Dutch Government. The first is more radical since it focuses on the structures which produce difference and inequality, while the second, combining an equal opportunities approach with a difference/equivalence approach, focuses on individual rather than structural change.

Miles and Middleton (Article 9) provide an analysis of the potential impact on equal opportunities of the Education Reform Act (1988) and the introduction of the National Curriculum (NC) at the time it became law, as it might be debated by different strands within the liberal-feminist tradition. For those operating with a liberal individualistic perspective the NC could be seen as offering leverage for implementing equal opportunities as an entitlement curriculum, making areas where girls are underrepresented compulsory for all pupils. For those within the social democratic tradition who place emphasis on social bases of disadvantage, the formal structural reforms of the NC seemed unlikely to herald any drastic change. The authors stress the importance of looking beyond the liberal-feminist agenda if the educational needs of all girls (rather than merely the brightest) were to be addressed. This would involve a commitment to anti-sexist and anti-racist work, and a funding policy which would seek to redress social inequality through education. Their 1994 postscript to the article indicates that the future of girls' education remains, as it was in 1988, in the balance.

In examining education policy in New Zealand since the Second World War and contrasting the 'liberal-left, social-democratic ideals of the first Labour government with the liberal-right (or market-liberal) assumptions . . . of the fourth' the article by Middleton (Article 10) enables us to take a broader, comparative perspective on policy. Two key education policy texts from 1945 and 1987 are analyzed from a feminist perspective. The major philosophical differences between the two liberal positions exemplified are drawn out, and their inadequacies for the realization of gender ('race' and class) equality are illustrated in relation to the educational and social history of postwar New Zealand.

With the articles by Arnot (Article 11), Mirza (Article 12), and Daniels *et al.* (Article 13) in this section, we are firmly back in the UK educational context with incisive descriptions and trenchant critiques of recent policy and practice in relation to gender, 'race' and special needs. Arnot describes the work of the 'sociology of women's education', which began to emerge in the early 1970s in the context of increasing disillusion with the social democratic principles underlying education and social policy, and which has seen since 1980, a phenomenal growth in feminist educational analyzes and research, at a time when paradoxically the pursuit of equality was increasingly challenged by central government initiatives. Her intention here is to analyze the significance of New Right ideology for women in the UK, and to take the feminist critiques in the work she describes in this article into the sociological analysis of current education reforms.

Mirza reviews the literature on race and education in the UK since the 1950s, arguing that the phenomenon of black female scholastic success has been consistently neglected in the study of black 'underachievement', since gender was seen as irrelevant and the terms of reference and key concepts in the debate were 'race' and culture. She charts the invisibility, the pathologizing or even romanticizing of black women through various policy and race research moments, highlighting the theoretical inadequacies of the approaches taken, which include the low self-esteem 'self-concept' and that of resistant subcultural forms.

The numbers of black children, particularly boys of African-Caribbean descent, identified as having special needs, requiring separate educational provision, has been a political issue since the mid 1970s. The 'under-representation' of girls in provision for special educational needs (SEN) and the consequent lower level of resourcing of girls' needs is a more recent concern. Daniels *et al.* argue that explanations for gender inequality in special needs provision come from three areas of academic study—the nature of special educational provision, the conceptualization of special educational needs, and analyses of gender inequalities—which have to date been assiduously kept apart. What is required is empirical work which covers all three areas simultaneously, and a conceptual model which holds on to a material analysis of the macro structures of class and gender which frame educational endeavours. This integrated model is yet to be achieved.

The articles in Part 3 deal with equality issues in primary schools, teacher education, local government, and in relation to sexuality. Broadfoot *et al.* (Article 14) compare English and French primary school teachers' conceptions of their work, in order to reveal the relative significance of policy directives, as opposed to features of teaching and learning inherent in the classroom itself, as determinants of teachers' practice. Their work highlights the importance of ideology and tradition in affecting the way in which teachers respond to central directives and use them in their teaching. Writing at the time of the 1988 Education Act they draw implications from their work, arguing that if 'policy changes ride roughshod over such ideologies ... the result is likely to be widespread resentment, a lowering of morale, and reduced effectiveness'.

Siraj-Blatchford (Article 15) reviews the main theoretical approaches for explaining the reproduction of 'race' and gender inequalities in schooling and education, following through the implications for Initial Teacher Education (ITE). She asks for an analysis of 'race' and gender together, incorporating structural, cultural and political dimensions, recognizing and illustrating how difficult this task is, and suggesting routes forward.

Halford (Article 16) examines attempts to introduce policies and practices which promote positive alternatives for women in the context of local government, drawing out the implications for other state organizations and bureaucracies. Using material from an extensive empirical study of Women's Initiatives, she illustrates the ways in which bureaucracies in general, and local government bureaucracies in particular, can resist, oppose and impede change.

'Sex is a contested zone, a moral and political battle field' (Weeks, 1985) and Thomson (Article 17) enters the battle zone on the key site of school sex education. She traces through the intersection and shifting configuration of two institutional discourses which address sex and sexuality in the public sphere—public health pragmatism (exemplified in the approach of the Department of Health, particularly in the light of the AIDS 'epidemic') and moral authoritarianism (exemplified in the approach of the Department for Education).

These articles afford an examination of the place of education policy in the production, reproduction and transformation of the major dimensions of social inequality.

References

Deem, R. (ed.) (1980) *Schooling for Women's Work*. London: Routledge and Kegan Paul.

Gardiner, D. (1929) *English Girlhood at School: A Study of Women's Education Through Twelve Centuries*. Oxford: Oxford University Press.

Kamm, J. (1965) *Hope Deferred: Girls' Education in English History*. London: Methuen.

Weeks, J. (1985) *Sexuality and its Discontents*. London: Routledge and Kegan Paul.

Note

1. The articles in this book have been edited: significant wording additions are shown in square brackets, and substantive deletions of text are indicated by ellipses (three points); however, minor changes are not flagged.

Part 1   History of Education Policy

1 WOMEN AND EDUCATION: A HISTORICAL ACCOUNT, 1800–1914

JUNE PURVIS

BEFORE 1870

Nineteenth-century society was clearly stratified by social class. This is encapsulated in some lines from that well-known nineteenth-century hymn, *All Things Bright and Beautiful*:

> The rich man at his castle
> The poor man at his gate
> God made them high and lowly
> And ordered their estate.

As these lines illustrate, social class differentiation was often supported by the belief that this was a part of the divine order. The education of children in the nineteenth century reflected this differentiation. Elementary education, which mainly involved the teaching of the three Rs, was associated with the working class, and such education was often offered free by philanthropic organizations or obtained for a few pence a week. Secondary education, on the other hand, which introduced a much wider range of subjects and which necessitated a much longer time at lessons, was associated with the middle class. Secondary education, especially that offered at the prestigious boarding schools, could be expensive.

Middle-class girls

When they were young, both middle-class boys and girls were usually educated within the home. They might be taught by a governess, a parent, or some combination of the two. However, whereas the boys would be sent away to school as soon as they were old enough, their sisters usually continued to receive their education at home, though sometimes they might attend a small private school. This separate education that middle-class girls received was inferior to that of their brothers, who were to be prepared for the public world of salaried work and financial responsibility for a future wife and children. Middle-class girls, on the other hand, were to be

Source: Abridged from Purvis J. (1984) 'Conflict and change in education: a sociological introduction', E205 *Women in Education*, Unit 25 (pp. 14–28). Milton Keynes: The Open University.

TABLE 1.1 Education of girls, 1800–1914

	Working-class girls	*Middle-class girls*
Before 1870		
Forms of schooling	Dame schools Sunday schools Factory schools Voluntary day schools	Home education by governess Small private school
Content	Three Rs Plain needlework	Snatches of wide range of subjects, e.g. English, geography, history Practical accomplishments such as piano playing
Aims espoused by providers	Making of good practical wives and mothers Training of domestic servants	Making of household organizers who employ servants Accomplished ladies
1870 Education Act—state system of elementary education[1]		
Forms of schooling	State elementary Dame schools Sunday schools Voluntary day schools	Outside state provision, e.g. home education by governess Small private day schools Prestige private boarding schools Fee-paying high schools
Content	As before, plus history, geography and a range of domestic subjects, such as cookery, laundry work, domestic economy	Primary emphasis upon ladylike accomplishments, but, for first time, high schools offered more academic curriculum that could lead to entry into professions
Aims espoused by providers	As before	As before, plus making of educated women who could enter professions
Forms of femininity upheld	Practical housewife Competent domestic servant	The lady Household organizer Educated lady Professional worker

1. After 1870, class divisions maintained, though some lower middle-class girls did enter state sector.

prepared for the private sphere of home and family, and financial dependency on a man.

Middle-class girls were schooled in 'useless' ladylike accomplishments that would make them more attractive in the marriage market. In other words, they were given knowledge that would confer social status, rather than knowledge that would give them vocational skills for use in the labour market. The epitome of ladylike accomplishments was found among the wealthiest of the middle classes who sometimes sent their daughters to very expensive boarding schools. Other wealthy families provided nurseries and schoolrooms at home where girls were taught by resident or visiting governesses. Even less prosperous middle-class families employed governesses to teach girls till they were about ten years old, when they were often sent to local day schools (Dyhouse, 1981, pp. 40–1).

Overall, it would appear that the home education offered by a governess was generally of a low standard. Bryant (1979, p. 40) suggests that governesses were miserably qualified and miserably paid teachers who gave their middle-class female pupils snatches of disconnected information and trivial accomplishments which educated them not for marriage, but to get husbands. Even when a middle-class girl was sent to a local day school, it was no guarantee that the standard of her education would be improved. [. . .]

Working-class girls

Before the 1870 Education Act, working-class children could attend a variety of educational institutions such as Sunday schools, dame schools (small private schools usually run by one woman, or 'dame', in her own home), ragged schools (free schools provided by philanthropists to teach children considered too dirty and poor to be acceptable elsewhere), industrial schools, factory schools and day schools organized by religious voluntary societies. It is difficult to estimate the proportion of working-class children who received the basic elements of education, such as the capacity to read and write, before 1870. The working class was particularly active in the organization of dame schools and Sunday schools, and it is highly probable that the vast majority of working-class boys and girls attended either or both of these organizations at some time during childhood. Laqueur (1976, p. 89), in a scholarly study of Sunday schools 1780–1850, suggests that Sunday school attendance was almost universal among the working class. However, Sunday school was only part-time schooling, and though reading might be taught there, the teaching of writing was a controversial issue. Attendance at a dame school, where reading and writing might be taught, could be intermittent and short-lived too, especially for those working-class families on low incomes who needed the money that their children could earn in waged labour. The proportion of working-class boys and girls who could, by 1870, read and write as a result of attending Sunday or dame school is debatable. One of the main problems is the difficulty of defining and measuring literacy and illiteracy. One source suggests that in

1839, 33.7% of adult males and 49.5% of adult females were illiterate, but that by 1861, these figures had fallen to 24.6% and 34.7% respectively (Porter, 1912, p. 147). Illiterate people were likely to be working class and more working-class females than working-class males fell into this category.

Dame schools were not, however, the only day schools that working-class children might attend. The day schools organized by the two main middle-class religious organizations (the British and Foreign School Society and the National Society for Promoting the Education of the Poor in the Principles of the Established Church) were the most important since these schools offered over 90% of the voluntary school places (Hurt, 1979, p. 4). Within such day schools, fewer places were offered to working-class girls than to working-class boys. Sometimes pupils were segregated on the basis of sex and sometimes they were educated together. It would appear that co-educational schools were much more likely to be found in rural areas where the catchment population was not large enough to support separate schooling. But whether together or separate, the sexes received different kinds of education. For example, the National Society's two main schools in London instructed both boys and girls in prayers, ciphering (arithmetic), religious exercises, writing and reading in the morning but, while the boys continued with ciphering, writing, reading and arithmetical tables in the afternoon, the girls were taught knitting and needlework until half-past four and then arithmetical tables until five o'clock. This sort of curriculum for working-class girls was justified in terms of their preparation for a future life in domestic service and in marriage.

Though there was considerable regional variation in the kinds of education offered to working-class girls, it would appear that the common pattern was that cited above, i.e. a basic grounding in the three Rs and plain needlework. By 1861, for example, the Newcastle Commission on Popular Education (a government body) said that, in girls' elementary schools, most of the afternoon was devoted to needlework. In 1862, when needlework became an obligatory subject for girls, as 'compensation' for this extra time devoted to sewing, they were permitted to attain a lower standard in the annual arithmetic examinations (Digby and Searby, 1981, p. 46). It seems that the middle-class organizers of the education of working-class girls had firm ideas about what this education was for. Working-class girls were to be schooled for an ideal of 'useful' domestic work that would prepare them for paid work as domestic servants in the homes of the bourgeoisie or for unpaid domestic work within their own future homes when they would be wives and mothers. This 'useful' domestic ideal was in direct contrast to the 'useless' ideal of ladylike accomplishments that was upheld for middle-class girls.

The 1870 Education Act made possible the gradual development of a national state system of elementary schooling. The aim of the Act was to provide elementary schooling for children then lacking it through establishing school boards in districts where there were no efficient and suitable schools. School boards could charge any child who attended one of their schools a weekly fee of up to ninepence [9d], and they also had the power to remit fees and pay the fees of poor children who attended schools other than board schools. Such 'public elementary schools' were intended primarily for working-class children, though some lower middle-class children later came to benefit from them, and these board schools were largely 'self-contained' and not preparatory for any form of secondary education (Lawson and Silver, 1973, pp. 317–18). The new board schools were soon offering superior facilities to the voluntary societies' schools.

School attendance was not made compulsory until 1880 and not provided free, in most schools, until 1891. The social class divisions in education provision for girls were stoutly maintained:

> Most middle-class girls were still educated outside the newly emerging state sector since they were mainly educated by governesses within the private sphere of their parents' home. It was the working-class girl who might attend the emerging board schools. As H.G. Wells was to comment in his autobiography, the 1870 Education act was not an Act to provide a common universal schooling for all social classes but an Act to educate lower-class children for employment in lower-class occupations. For working-class girls, however, the provision of a state system of national education meant a renewed emphasis on education for motherhood rather than education for employment, a renewed emphasis that was especially pronounced in the latter decades of the century when grants were made for the teaching of cookery and laundry work.
>
> (Purvis, 1981a, p. 111)

After 1875, optional subjects in state maintained schools were divided into 'class' subjects and 'specific' subjects. Class subjects were taken by classes above Standard I and specific subjects were taken by pupils above Standard IV. In 1878, domestic economy was made a compulsory specific subject for girls and between 1874 and 1882 the number of pupils studying this subject in board schools rose from 844 to 59,812 (Dyhouse, 1981, p. 89). In 1882 and 1890, respectively, the government gave grants for the teaching of cookery and laundry work and the number of girls studying these subjects rose rapidly towards the end of the century. For example, the number of girls qualifying for the cookery grant rose from 7,597 in 1882–3 to 134,930 in 1895–6. For the same years, the number of girls studying in recognized laundry classes rose from 632 to 11,720 (Dyhouse, 1981, pp. 89–90).

In the first two decades of the twentieth century a movement grew to expand the teaching of domestic subjects and to introduce lessons in childcare for working-class girls. Davin (1979), Turnbull (1980) and Dyhouse (1981) link these developments in the curriculum for girls in state elementary schools to fears about the future of the British race and the decline of the British Empire. The number of recruits declared unfit for call-up in the Boer War (1899–1902), for example, revealed the poor physical condition of many adult working-class males. In addition, the falling birth rate and a high infant mortality rate aroused fears about the quantity of potential recruits to defend the Empire and about the quality of maternal care in the rearing of children. The issue of 'national efficiency' became much discussed:

> Around the beginning of this century infant life and child health took on a new importance in public discussion, reinforced by emphasis on the value of a healthy and numerous population as a national resource ... population was power. Children, it was said, belong 'not merely to the parents but to the community as a whole'; they were 'a national asset', 'the capital of a country'; on them depended 'the future of the country and the Empire'; they were 'the citizens of tomorrow'.
>
> (Davin, 1979, pp. 9–10)

The issue of so-called 'ignorant' working-class mothers, unable to cook and care 'adequately' for their families, an issue that had been much discussed in the nineteenth century, assumed new proportions.

WHY DID MASS SCHOOLING ARISE?

By the early twentieth century, a state system for mass elementary school had evolved—but why? How can we account for it? Histories of education tend to offer two main explanations for the rise of mass schooling, explanations that largely refer to the 'needs' of British society and are therefore functionalist in orientation. The first is that Britain needed an educated electorate after the extension of political enfranchisement (in the late 1860s) to working-class men. The second is that Britain needed an educated, skilled workforce, a workforce that would be able to produce goods not only for home consumption but also to compete internationally. However, Davin has argued that while such explanations may help to account for the schooling of working-class boys, they do not for working-class girls since women were not given the right to vote in the nineteenth century and neither could they enter the range of skilled jobs which (it was believed) would bring prosperity:

> The political explanations relate most directly to the growing labour movement, in which women played no part at this time, and to the 1867 Franchise Act, which created a million or so new voters, none of them women; while the economic context concerns the development of a new skilled and literate workforce (including a whole range of minor technicians significant in the expansion of empire and commerce as well as industry—telegraphists, sappers and signalmen as well as the more obvious draughtsmen, engineers and clerical workers) from which women (to begin with at least) were again absent. If such political and economic grounds had been the only reasons for introducing general elementary education, one might ask why girls were included at all.
>
> (Davin, 1979 p. 89)

Functionalist explanations are not the only ones that have been advanced. At least two others that owe much more to Marxism, even though they may have functionalist overtones, can be identified. So a third explanation relates the rise of mass schooling to social control. (The control of the working class was often openly and explicitly the purpose of those advocating mass schooling—even if it may not have been achieved.) Richard Johnson has argued that the early Victorian obsession for the education of the poor can be interpreted as an attempt by the bourgeoisie to reform and civilize a decadent working class who posed the threat of a 'spiralling crime-rate or even bloody anarchy' (Johnson, 1970, p. 104). Schools for the poor, it was hoped, would bring about a new moral order amongst the working class: working-class children would be taught aspects of allegedly bourgeois morality, such as self-reliance, self-respect, deference to authority, that would help to civilize society. In his discussion of education and social control, however, Johnson does not consider the issue of sex differences. The fourth explanation does. It states that mass schooling was intended to impose upon working-class children a middle-class family form of a male breadwinner and an economically dependent, full-time wife and mother. In an illuminating analysis of textbooks provided for children in the London board schools, Davin illustrates the prevalence in them of this family form and how girls' domestic role is valued above their scholastic role as pupils:

> It is interesting that few of the stories are about school situations: home and the family loom much larger. The family as presented (even in the animal world) almost always has a breadwinning father and a housekeeping mother. Occasionally, however, reality impinges, and it is admitted that mothers (especially widowed ones) may have to go out to work.
>
>> Household management ... is, or may be, your business any day. Do not many of your mothers go out to work, leaving you to manage the house, and the baby as well? Are not your mothers ill sometimes, and in bed, and unable to see to anything downstairs? Some of you have had the misfortunes of losing your mothers, and have to mind the house and keep things comfortable for your father ...
>
> Such contingencies merely reinforce the over-riding importance of the girl's domestic role, which in one story is even put before achievement at school. The 'best scholar in the class', full of self-confidence in her scholastic prowess, looks down on her humble quiet sister, who is no good at school. But when their mothers fall ill, the older sister has to stay at home to look after her, and learns that she is useless as housewife or nurse, whereas her sister is a marvel of unobtrusive efficiency. Her father is quite firm about which kind of knowledge is more to be valued: 'school could not be the right place for Alice if it made her so useless at home', and he told her to learn by her mother, who all her life had 'thought nothing

of herself, only to do her duty by God and man.' Alice learnt her lesson, and the mother recovered at last to find her eldest daughter a different person, humble and thoughtful, and affectionate, and though not neglecting her home lessons, always making much more effort to do her home duties.

(Davin, 1979, pp. 97–8)

The quotations Davin uses are from the fifth book (written by A.R. Grant) of the 'School Managers Series of Reading Books', published in 1871.

As Davin herself warns, it is impossible to assess how far the assumptions and presumptions of such reading books influenced the children who read them. Similarly, Williamson (1981), in an analysis of two schools in Northumberland in the late nineteenth century points out some of the difficulties of trying to test the 'social control' thesis. He notes that in the two schools he studied, the attendance of working-class boys and girls was very irregular and their level of scholastic achievement very low. Williamson's work alerts us to the fact that we cannot assume that *the intentions* of the providers of education matched what occurred in *practice*. And of course in historical work it is often difficult to find documented the kinds of opposition that working-class children offered to those who attempted to educate them. Nevertheless, it is worthwhile reiterating the point that Davin made, that in those textbooks she analyzed, the behaviour advocated for girls—unselfishness, compassion, devotion to housewifely industry and family duty—and the situations presented as 'natural' to women, directed girls towards an exclusively domestic role, even at the expense of scholastic ability (Davin, 1979, p. 98).

The mass elementary education system that developed after 1870 continued to stress 'useful' domestic work as the ideal form of femininity for working-class girls, useful domestic work that mainly related to a future state of wifehood and motherhood, but which could also be useful in paid work in domestic service. Within a patriarchal society, girls were encouraged in values of submission and service to their future families, especially future husbands.

Writers such as Dyhouse claim that the family and the school interlocked to stress such values for women of *all* social classes:

> Women were expected to occupy themselves in providing an environment—a context in which *men* could live and work ... Closely related to this emphasis on the idea of women creating a context for men to live and work in was the ideal of femininity as representing self-sacrifice. Women of all social groups were encouraged from childhood to consider it selfish to become wrapped up in their own interests, for the ideal was to serve others, and always to consider the interests of their menfolk first.

(Dyhouse, 1981, p. 26)

We can find this theme of service and domesticity too in the education provided for middle-class girls from 1870–1914. It was evident, for example, in those useless accomplishments which girls still learned, which supposedly made them more attractive to potential husbands. Over the period 1870–1914, girls of the most prosperous middle class were still mainly educated at home by governesses, though in the early twentieth century an increasing number (but still very much the minority) attended the prestigious private schools such as Roedean (founded in 1885). Further down the social scale, it was still common for the daughter of a prosperous middle-class father to be educated at home by a governess and perhaps sent to a 'finishing' school (Dyhouse, 1981, p. 41). [. . .]

Girls in the lower-income levels of the middle class were often educated first at home and then at a small local day school. This pattern appears to have remained 'fairly stable' until the First World War (Dyhouse, 1981, p. 42). Once schooling was over, these girls, like most in the middle class, usually stayed at home until they married, though, of course, much depended upon the economic circumstances of the family—in particular, whether the income a daughter might earn from paid work was necessary to the family.

One of the early historians of women's education, Alice Zimmern, estimated that by the beginning of the twentieth century approximately 70% of the total number of girls receiving secondary education were being educated in small private boarding schools (Zimmern, 1898, p. 167). In other words, the vast majority of girls receiving secondary education in the nineteenth century were from middle-class families who could afford to pay the private schools' fees. The major challenge to these schools came from new, academically oriented schools, such as the North London Collegiate School, established by Miss Frances Mary Buss and her mother in 1850; the Cheltenham Ladies' College (founded in 1854), of which Miss Dorothea Beale became principal in 1858; and the schools (sometimes known as 'high' schools) established by the Girls' Public Day School Company (GPDSC), which was founded in 1872.

The aim of the GPDSC schools was to give a 'first-class education' at fees placed as low as was compatible with the schools being self-supporting (Kamm, 1971, p. 46), and Miss Buss's North London Collegiate was taken as the model school. Once again, the future domestic vocation of girls, as wives and mothers, was used to justify the existence of the new schools, but this time the education considered necessary for this included academic and intellectual subjects. Digby sums up these changes in the following way:

> The domestic vocation of the middle-class girl was used as a conservative
> rationale for improving her schooling. Writing on the education of girls,
> that formidable headmistress of Cheltenham Ladies College, Dorothea
> Beale, argued, for example, that improved schooling meant that 'a wise
> and right-minded woman will be less likely to make a foolish, an incon-

siderate marriage' and 'that if girls were more accustomed to weigh
and consider, there would be less of extravagance and folly, homes
better ordered, servants more honest and contented, children happier'.
However, it is important to notice that the moral and intellectual education that she and like-minded 'progressives' had in mind was not the
'cookery and needlework and arithmetic enough for accounts' which tra-
ditionalist headmistress such as Elizabeth Sewell thought appropriate for
girls' domestic vocation. Thus the Beales and Busses of the second half
of the nineteenth century diversified content rather than fundamentally
restating customary social objectives of female education.

(Digby, 1982, p. 3)

The curriculum included compulsory academic subjects, which were studied
usually in the mornings since most high schools demanded only morning
attendance. In 1884, for example, Brighton High School offered Latin,
grammar, mathematics, chemistry, geography, art and music (GPDST, 1972,
p. 39) while, by 1900, Shrewsbury High School offered a range of languages
(Latin, French and German), mathematics (including algebra, geometry, and
trigonometry), science (including physiology, biology, chemistry and physics)
geography, history, English, divinity and physical education (Bates and Wells,
1962, pp. 33–6).

However, the inclusion of such subjects often caused battles. These schools
were fee-paying schools to which parents *chose* to send their daughters. The
middle-class parents who did send their daughters to such schools did not want
an education that would 'unsex' their daughters and make them unladylike
through studying subjects that were usually offered to boys. At the Cheltenham
Ladies' College, for example, Dorothea Beale encountered a number of such
problems and devised a number of solutions:

> Then the curriculum, simple as it was, was considered too advanced and
> complicated. A mother, who removed her daughter at the end of one
> quarter, complained bitterly that it was all very well for the girl to read
> Shakespeare, 'but don't you think it is more important for her to be able
> to sit down at the piano and amuse her friends?'
>
> Neither science nor mathematics was taught in the early days; and
> Dorothea, who had wanted to start Euclid straight away, desisted, real-
> izing that had she done so she might have ruined all prospect of success.
> Instead, after a cautious beginning, she introduced scientific teaching under
> the name of physical geography; and as few boys learned geography, the
> subject was considered unexceptionable for girls.

(Kamm, 1958, pp. 55–6)

Such fears about the 'unsexing' of middle-class girls were voiced too by critics
of the practice, begun in 1865, of entering female pupils for public examinations

taken by their middle-class brothers—the Junior and Senior Local Examinations of Cambridge University. Some schools solved the dilemma of combining an intellectually demanding education with the more traditional ladylike accomplishments by offering subjects such as music, art and languages as optional extras in the afternoon. As Delamont has noted, both the educators and educated in these new schools for middle-class girls were caught in a 'double bind' situation. Their dependence on fees meant that headmistresses had to be sensitive to the desires of parents and insist upon ladylike behaviour for their pupils, while at the same time insisting that their pupils should study those intellectually demanding subjects that were a part of the dominant male cultural and educational system (Delamont, 1978, pp. 140–1).

As I have already mentioned, around the turn of the century, fears were expressed about the survival of the British race, the decline of the Empire and the importance of healthy mothers who would rear healthy children. The emphasis upon education for motherhood and wifehood that was evident in the state elementary schools had an impact upon *some* of the fee-paying schools for middle-class girls but the form it took was rather different. Rather than emphasizing the practical skills of housekeeping, some of the new schools for middle-class girls emphasized the 'scientific principles' underlying domestic management. Sara Burstall, for example, headmistress of Manchester High School, claimed that science for women, 'especially biological science, must be the foundation of their work for the family, for hygiene, and for housecraft' (Burstall, 1933, p. 144), and in the session 1900–1901 a housewifery course was established for girls who were 'going home and had no intention of following a profession' (Burstall, 1933: 149). But the kinds of subjects offered in this housewifery course included a much wider range than the subjects offered to working-class girls in state elementary schools—the course included English, history, French, 'household arithmetic', science, as well as cookery, laundry work, hygiene, household management and needlework (Burstall, 1933, p. 149). But not all of the new high schools followed this course. Miss Gardiner, for example, headmistress of Blackburn High School, represented the opposing view when she warned that 'the intellectual birthright must not be sold for skill in making puddings' (quoted in Digby, 1982, p. 6).

The vocational value of the education offered in these private schools was rarely stressed though *some* schools did offer a direct vocational training for some paid jobs, for example in preparing pupils for the competitive examinations for entry into clerical grades of the Civil Service. Since the Post Office Examinations for entry into the lower clerical grades demanded proficiency in maths, English, geography and a foreign language, girls were prepared for these too (Digby, 1982, p. 13).

The Technical Instruction Act of 1889 enabled counties and county boroughs to make grants to secondary schools, such as the high schools, and to provide scholarships for able boys and girls whose parents could not afford secondary school fees. Though such scholarship girls formed only a small number of a school's population, the scheme did provide an opportunity for able girls whose parents could not afford school fees to study the more academic curriculum provided in the secondary schools. Such parents included those from working-class as well as impoverished middle-class backgrounds. However, the number of scholarships available for girls was often well below the number available for boys. Even if a girl did pass a scholarship, her parents might well not support her attendance at a secondary school, such as a high school. Working-class girls generally were not promoted up the educational ladder in the same way as working-class boys. In a patriarchal society, where it was assumed that men would be the major breadwinners and women the major homemakers who would be financially dependent on their husbands, priority was given to working-class boys.

   Though secondary schools aimed mainly at middle-class girls were the most important institutions providing education beyond the elementary stage for females, they were not the *only* institutions at this time to do so. Within the state-aided elementary sector, largely attended by working-class pupils, quasi-secondary education was being provided, mainly through evening classes and so-called 'higher grade' schools. The 1902 Education Act helped to stop this overlap in provision by maintaining a stricter division between secondary and elementary schooling. The Act designated local education authorities which were to 'take such steps as seem to them desirable ... to supply or aid the supply of education other than elementary, and to promote the general co-ordination of all forms of education'. Both Robert Morant, a key government figure in drawing up the Act and the regulations to implement it, and A. J. Balfour, the Prime Minister at this time, had doubts about the abilities of working-class children to benefit from secondary education. Secondary education was seen as belonging within the fee-paying school sector, which included the grammar schools. It was this sector which received a boost, following the 1902 Act, in terms of various government grants to aid the development of secondary schooling. Lawson and Silver (1973, p. 373) suggest that the effect of the 1902 Act was to make secondary education a more stable element in a coherent pattern of education. The story of secondary education from 1903 to the First World War is, they continue, a combination of two main themes—the building up of a system of schools and the introduction, in 1907, of the 'free-place' system in the secondary grammar schools. The free-place system selected pupils on the basis of an attainment test, taken at 11 years old. Such a system enabled high-ability girls and boys whose parents could not afford the necessary fees to attend grammar schools. However, it is highly likely that more children from middle rather than working-class backgrounds, and more boys than girls, were free-place scholars. For example, of the holders of scholarships in London in 1920–21, 42% were described as having parents who were of 'lower middle-class status, 41% of 'skilled working' and 17% of 'unskilled working': the areas in which fewest children attended grammar schools tended also to be those areas with greatest poverty, overcrowding and infant mortality (quoted in Lawson and Silver, 1973, p. 382). By the outbreak of the First World War, then, the educational system of England was clearly stratified according to class and gender.

BY 1914

Let us pause for a moment and consider the condition of education for girls by 1914. By then, as we have seen, class and gender had helped to structure both the form and content of education for girls, and it is useful for us to reflect upon this under the following headings.

Working-class girls—unequal and inferior

By the First World War, working-class girls were mainly educated in elementary state schools which were usually, but not always, co-educational, i.e. they included both boys and girls. However, even though girls and boys might be educated under the same roof this does not mean that they shared all school activities equally. The mixing of working-class boys and girls was often controlled in some way, for example through separate entrances, separate playgrounds, separate departments for boys and girls, and different teachers. By the turn of the century, female elementary schoolteachers were mainly concentrated in the low-status sectors of girls' and infants' departments and in the lower grades of boys' departments: the advanced work in the boys' departments was nearly always undertaken by men (Partington, 1976, p. 2). Partington goes on:

> Mixed classes for older children were declining in numbers before 1914 mainly because it was widely believed that co-education created unnecessary difficulties in the teaching of laundry work, carpentry and other skills thought suitable for one sex only.
>
> (Partington, 1976, p. 2)

Working-class girls were, therefore, more likely than their brothers to be taught solely by women for the duration of their school lives. These women usually had lower academic qualification than male teachers and were often uncertificated. From 1875, a new large group of uncertificated female teachers became available as 'supplementaries' or 'additional' teachers or, under the 1890 Code, as 'Article 68s', and the number of such uncertificated teachers grew rapidly towards the end of the nineteenth century since they were cheaper to employ than certificated teachers (Horn, 1978, p. 112). By 1914, 12% of the male but 41% of the female elementary schoolteachers were uncertificated. The expansion of the state system after the 1870 Education Act was largely made possible, therefore, by the supply of lowly paid, uncertificated women teachers (Purvis, 1981b, p. 367). In addition to the fact that working-class girls were more likely to be taught by such teachers, it was mainly girls, and not boys, who were taught courses such as cookery, laundry work and domestic economy—courses that stressed their future location in life as poorly paid domestic servants/future wives and mothers. As we have seen from the analysis of the content of textbooks used in state schools, a particular form of family life was upheld—the middle-class form of a male breadwinner and an economically dependent wife and mother. This stress on a future domestic role must have depressed educational aspirations and ambitions. And any aspirations that a working-class girl might have held in regard to secondary schooling and possible university education were severely handicapped because scholarships and grants were much less available to women than those for their working-class brothers. Overall then, during the period 1870–1914, we can say that the schooling of working-class girls was shaped by both their social class location and their gender. As members of the working class they were given an education which was separate and inferior to that of middle-class children, and as females they were given an education which was different and inferior to that of working-class boys and men.

Middle-class girls—separate but prestigious

Up to the First World War, middle-class girls were largely home-educated by governesses and/or sent to small private schools or the more academically oriented 'high' schools. Though home education might involve joint lessons with brothers, the private schools that middle-class girls were sent to were usually single-sex. Whatever variant of the home/private schools scheme was followed, such forms of education were regarded as superior to those attended by working-class girls. Whereas working class girls were usually educated within the low prestige state elementary schools, middle-class girls were largely educated in high prestige forms of education *outside* the state system.

For both working-class and middle-class girls, femininity was linked with domesticity. But overall, the rhetoric justifying education for girls and the education offered were class-specific. Over the period 1870–1914, whereas working-class girls were schooled to be domestic servants and practical housewives, middle-class girls were schooled to attract husbands. The dominant ideal of femininity upheld for working-class girls in state schools was that of practical housekeeper, while for middle-class girls a number of different and competing ideals of femininity were presented—such as accomplished lady of leisure, educated woman and scientific household manager. However, the education offered to middle-class girls was usually inferior to that enjoyed by their brothers. Thus while middle-class girls might enjoy certain privileges from their social location, they too experienced the burden of their gender. As girls, rather than boys, they were primarily prepared for the separate sphere of the home.

References

Bates, H. and Wells, A.A.M. (1962) *A History of Shrewsbury High School*. Shrewsbury: Shrewsbury High School.
Bryant, M. (1979) *The Unexpected Revolution: A Study in the History of the Education*

of Women and Girls in the Nineteenth Century. London: University of London Institute of Education.

Burstall, S. (1933) *Retrospect and Prospect: Sixty Years of Women's Education*. London: Longmans, Green and Co.

Davin, A. (1979) 'Mind that you do as you are told': reading books for board school girls. *Feminist Review* 3, 89—98.

Delamont, S. (1978) The domestic ideology and women's education. In S. Delamont and L. Duffin (eds) *The Nineteenth Century Woman: Her Cultural and Physical World*. London: Croom Helm.

Digby, A. (1982) New schools for the middle-class girl. In P. Searby (ed.) *Educating the Victorian Middle Class*. London: History of Education Society of Great Britain.

Digby, A. and Searby, P. (1981) *Children, School and Society in Nineteenth-Century England*. London: Macmillan.

Dyhouse, C. (1981) *Girls Growing Up in Late Victorian and Edwardian England*. London: Routledge and Kegan Paul.

GPDST (Girls Public Day School Trust) (1972) *1872—1972: A Centenary Review*. London: GPDST.

Horn, P. (1978) *Education in Rural England, 1800—1914*. New York: St Martin's Press.

Hurt, J. S. (1979) *Elementary Schooling and the Working Classes 1860—1918*. London: Routledge and Kegan Paul.

Johnson, R. (1970) Educational policy and social control in early Victorian England. *Past and Present* 49 (November), 96—119.

Kamm, J. (1958) *How Different from Us: A Biography of Miss Buss and Miss Beale*. London: Bodley Head.

—(1971) *Indicative Past: A Hundred Years of the Girls' Public Day School Trust*. London: George Allen and Unwin.

Laqueur, T. W. (1976) *Religion and Respectability: Sunday Schools and Working-class Culture 1780—1850*. New Haven: Yale University Press.

Lawson, J. and Silver, H. (1973) *A Social History of Education in England*. London: Methuen.

Partington, G. (1976) *Women Teachers in the 20th Century in England and Wales*. Windsor: National Foundation for Educational Research.

Porter, G.R. (1912, revised edn by F.W. Hirst) *The Progress of the Nation*. London: Methuen (first published 1836).

Purvis, J. (1981a) The double burden of class and gender in the schooling of working-class girls in nineteenth century England, 1800—1870. In L. Barton and S. Walker (eds) *Schools, Teachers and Teaching*. Lewes: Falmer Press.

—(1981b) Women and teaching in the nineteenth century. In R. Dale, G. Esland, R. Fergusson and M. MacDonald (eds) *Education and the State: Politics, Patriarchy and Practice*. Lewes: Falmer Press.

Turnbull, A. (1980) Home economics—training for womanhood? In C. Love, D. Smith and A. Turnbull (eds) *Women in the Making*. South Bank Sociology Occasional Paper 2. London: Polytechnic of the South Bank.

Williamson, B. (1981) Contradictions of control: elementary education in a mining district 1870—1900. In L. Barton and S. Walker (eds) *Schools, Teachers and Teaching*. Lewes: Falmer Press.

Zimmern, A. (1898) *The Renaissance of Girls' Education in England*. London: A.D. Innes.

2 EDUCATION FOR MORAL IMPROVEMENT, DOMESTICITY AND SOCIAL COHESION: THE LABOUR GOVERMENT, 1945–1951

D. W. DEAN

Writing on the 1945 election Labour victory had concentrated heavily on the success of its leadership in exploiting issues raised in the war debates on peacetime reconstruction (see Morgan, 1984, pp. 1–44; Addison, 1975; the defeat of more radical trends is described in McCulloch, 1985). In a prolonged election campaign the party had finally reached a wider section of the population and became a national rather than a class-based movement. [...] In the new climate there would still be an emphasis on strengthening the family within the community, insisting on the domestic role for women, widening the cultural horizons of the mass of the population and preaching a gospel of deferred rather than immediate pleasure. There was even the underlying note of crisis for according to Mass Observation (1947, p. 159), a barometer of this strand of opinion in the era, 'In the political sphere the election of a Labour Government in 1945 ... represents for many a last hope within the whole range of political parties and programmes'.

[...] Sympathy went back to the earlier part of the century for campaigns waged by 'welfare feminists' for the protective legislation or financial aid to assist working-class mothers. These could be incorporated easily into the broader welfare programme of the Party. Other demands, even those for equality of pay or career opportunities, were regarded as preoccupations of a minority of women who had rejected either marriage or motherhood. They came far down on the list of priorities of a reforming government.

Attlee's apppointments to Cabinet demonstrated this narrowness. Only one woman with a feminist background, the fiery Ellen Wilkinson, was included in the Cabinet. Her arrival at Education was greeted with surprise. [...] She was appointed because, 'again nowadays, if you can you should have a woman in, and there are certain jobs like Education or National Insurance where a woman would fit in better than others' (Williams, 1961, p. 150). The

Source: Abridged from 'Education for moral improvement, domesticity and social cohesion: expectations and fears of the Labour government', Oxford Review of Education (1991) Vol. 17, No. 3, pp. 269–86.

Labour leader thus revealed his conventional attitude to women politicians. It was much more acceptable to the general public for women to be placed in 'softer', caring positions. He had cleverly anticipated the warmth of the response to the news. A congratulatory letter to the new Minister summed this up: 'May I say how glad I am that a woman is Minister of Education. A woman naturally knows more about children than a man'.[1] She was to become immersed in the Education ministry where she exhausted herself in the task of reconstructing the nation's schools. It left her with little time to play a role in Labour or feminist politics.

The Labour government's approach to women shifted in its period of office. Its stance depended on the state of the economy and the overall demands of the labour market. At the close of the war the major concern was that a rapidly demobilizing military machine, predominantly male, should find employment in peacetime Britain. It was important that sources of labour, temporarily recruited for wartime purposes, made way for those returning. The immediate task was to lure women back from the workplace to the home. What seemed to be required was a mixture of persuasion, education, rewards and warnings. First of all it was necessary to explore the mood of working women. Ministers possessed surveys of the impact of war on women's attitudes to work, family and marriage. Geoffrey Thomas's investigations had detected that war experience had not fundamentally changed attitudes. Most married women wanted to withdraw from the labour market provided that the male breadwinner was given secure employment with a reasonable wage. Nevertheless there was a recognition that women in the home had suffered too long from restricting isolation:

> If wages were good enough to enable a man to marry and support his wife on what she considers to be a reasonable standard of life (and this has been influenced by the money she has earned during the war) she will not on average want to work while the children are young and could only be prompted to do so by boredom and lack of company at home.[2]

Younger women presented a contrasting picture. They were more likely to be career orientated, less fearful of combining work at home and outside and less responsive to appeals to accept a life of domesticity and child-rearing. Governments had to be aware of these varied responses when making their plans. [...]

The housewife was to be surrounded by sympathy and understanding. Male breadwinners had to be educated to be made aware of the problems in running a home and bringing up the family. Claims were made that a younger generation of fathers were becoming more receptive, a Ministry of Education (1949a) pamphlet claiming: 'The popularity of the courses known as Handyman and Householders among the men in the Forces in the Released Period education services is sweeping evidence that for most Englishmen "helping Mum" is not a distasteful or derogatory term.' Young males were encouraged to take courses in child-care or domestic management ensuring they would know 'of the important and often neglected part that can be played by the men and the boys in the household' (Ministry of Education, 1949b). Male assistance was to remain quietly in the background. Marriages would ultimately benefit by giving wives respite from household tasks and women would broaden their horizons and become more interesting companions.

Acute fears were growing in postwar Britain that established networks of family and friendships were being disrupted in the painful rebuilding of devastated Britain. Courses multiplied in which psychological and child-care experts trained home advisers to serve local community centres. This supply of trainees was to be recruited largely from those previously engaged in voluntary organizations, and it was anticipated that once armed with knowledge 'they would give whole or part-time service in Home Advice Centres in which women would be able to come with any sort of problem relating to home and family affairs'[3]. The authority of the expert, usually male, would be transmitted by a network of advisers, often middle-class female, to working-class mothers and their families. [. . .]

Threats to family and community influenced debate in the early years of the Labour government about the value of nursery education. A broad coalition of interests attacked limitations placed on its expansion (for an insider's view of the whole campaign, see Allen and Nicholas, 1975, pp. 150–96). Many trade-unionists argued that nursery education was a right and that the children of the wealthy were already cosseted by an army of trained nursery staff. The government was warned that 'the policy of partial closing of day nurseries is naturally enough being subjected to severe criticism in many parts of the country' (*Tribune*, 22 March 1946). Other advocates supported provision as important in the socialisation of the youngest children. Its purpose did not end there. One important pressure group, proclaiming that it 'stands for family life and in all its work takes the view that the nurseries are an extension of the home and not a substitute for it'[4] went on to explain why postwar Britain needed a more extensive nursery service:

> The average young wife is not skilled in housecraft, her cookery is learned by a process of trial and error. When the first baby arrives she is not fortified by any real knowledge of how to care for it and therefore lacks confidence in herself. In the absence of any domestic help not only is her work never done but she is never off duty.[5]

Attendance at nursery classes with their children promised to provide relief from constant home pressure and opportunities to reinforce much needed infant care lessons for mothers.

The promotion of nursery schools was strongly opposed by 'pronatalist' officials within the Ministry of Health who viewed the wartime expansion of crèches and nursery classes as an emergency measure. It was in this light that they approached nursery provision in peacetime. Only those families facing crisis could be furnished with this safety net. 'Normal' families were to be persuaded that the only possible place for youngest children was with their mothers. As labour shortages grew the Ministry of Labour increasingly challenged this view by turning attention to the possibility of recruitment among married women. Local employment committees insisted that without an expansion of crèches near to factory sites recruitment efforts would fail. Thus the Health Ministry was warned: 'one of the subjects on which the committees have recently displayed the most active interest has been the need for providing child care facilities on labour supply grounds'.[6] This was precisely the kind of service that the Health Ministry feared would undermine family life. The Ministry of Education took a middle stance. It certainly shared many of the fears and endorsed limitations on the age of entry to nursery education. A joint circular drawn up with the Health Department stated:

> The Ministers concerned accepted the view of medical and other authorities that in the interests of health and development of the child and no less for the benefit of the mother the proper place for a child under 2 is in the home with the mother. They are also of the opinion that under normal peacetime conditions the right policy would be positively to discourage mothers of children from going out to work.[7]

Within the Ministry there was more sympathy for the educational aspiration of nursery provision provided that the needs of children received wholehearted consideration:

> We are primarily concerned to promote nursery classes for the educational value to the children and their normal future development might not be on the soundest educational lines if we were moved by a desire to help mothers (for example the need to help mothers might lead us to provide larger nurseries than we think suitable).[8]

On later occasions warnings were given that nursery education might be endangered by linking it with labour supply arguments, HMI Miss Bell insisting, 'I do not think we could agree that on a long-term basis the nursery school should make provision for child minding'.[9]

The issue of birth control information had to be handled with caution. This was a subject that had dogged the labour movement throughout the century and great care was taken by party managers to avoid divisions among traditional supporters. Increasingly it was accepted that mothers ought to be made aware of the benefits of 'spacing' their children. Large families were not singled out for criticism but pregnancies too close together were seen as harmful to the mother's health, and consequently to the family and the community. In examining some of the implications of child neglect one influential group took a careful line about large families but warned, 'there is abundant evidence that pregnancies too close together are a more important cause than

the size of family'.[10] It was widely accepted that in the provision of information on this delicate subject great progress had been made since the 1930s.
At a conference held under the auspices of the Family Planning Association
it was claimed, 'the provision advice on contraception by LEA and private
clinics has become a generally accepted part of the medical services'.[11] Quiet
diffusion and avoidance of conflict was preferred to a more substantial educational programme which was demanded in progressive and feminist circles.

If sharp divisions occurred about ways of sustaining women in their domestic
role there was little disagreement that if a young mother failed to establish a
bond between herself and her child in infancy severe character maladjustments
could emerge. This would lead to ever-rising juvenile delinquency figures. The
finding of the disturbing Curtis Report, on the plight of children in care, was
used extensively to hammer home more general lessons about the vital role of
ordinary mothers:

> Looking at these families there emerges one dominating factor, the capacity
> of the mother. It is she who stands out predominantly as the person to
> give the 'temper' to the household. Frequently the family can survive in
> spite of a weak or vicious father but it is only rare that it can survive
> with an incapable mother for it is she who is the coping stone of the
> structure.[12]

Thus, in the case of deprived children, evidence was gathered that the mothers
had been forced into crisis because of ignorance or sheer exhaustion rather
than through cruelty. This was the image thrust before the 'normal mother'.
If the worst households demonstrated that mothers tried instinctively to
behave properly, it was inferred that there was something very unnatural
about women desiring to pursue a career before a proper bonding with a
child had been made.

From 1947 the economic situation created an intense search for new sources
of labour. Women were regarded as an easier source of recruitment than displaced Europeans or West Indians provided that the needs of the family were
not neglected. This continued to be judged of importance because influential
voices condemned the employment of mothers outside the home. At a Home
Office conference on Juvenile Delinquency the Archbishop of Canterbury
warned of the dangerous consequences to society: 'He questioned the pace
at which the country was encouraging mothers to enter industry'.[13] Women
were asked to respond as a patriotic duty in an hour of crisis just as they
had done in war. They were urged to 'fill the gaps' particularly in a range
of ancillary or service industries. Married women were not expected to turn
to occupations that enhanced their career prospects. Boundaries between the
household and the world of labour were being redrawn but lines of division
remained. It was made abundantly clear that the world of outside work could
never become the major concern for married women.

Nothing demonstrated this more dramatically than the government's cool attitude to the publication of the very guarded and far from unanimous Report of the Royal Commission on Equal Pay. This had been set up at the time of the passage of the Butler Education Act when a rebellion of Labour and Conservative backbenchers seriously endangered the future of the wartime Coalition. Chuter Ede recalled the circumstances: 'The Labour Party have helped to defeat the Government in the Commons on this issue and was clearly pledged to the prospect of equal pay for equal work.'[14] In its deliberations the Royal Commission concentrated on demands of groups such as women teachers and civil servants whose discontent was singled out for comment:

> There is no doubt in our minds about the extent and identity of the present discontent although it is most naturally marked among those who envisage their work as a career and not as an interim activity to be terminated on marriage and consequently it is most marked with the higher grades of women workers i.e. teachers and civil servants.[15]

An emphasis on these sections allowed the charge to be made that agitation came from an unrepresentative group of women such as teachers, who were ambitious, single, and out of touch with public opinion. George Isaacs assured his colleagues that 'the matter has been raised at particular conferences which he attended but there was no pressure from trade unionists'.[16] In the Cabinet Committee set up to examine the implications of the Equal Pay Report most ministers chose to measure equal pay against broader family concerns. Arthur Greenwood spoke for the male breadwinner: 'If equal pay was initiated by itself the result could be that the married man with the family would be left in a worse position than any other member of the employed community.'[17] Attlee's conventional streak made him a strong supporter of this viewpoint and he urged consideration of the feelings of the housewife: 'When you get into questions of this sort I would like to see whether you are absolutely sure that you will not have a certain amount of feeling among women in the home if you find the girl next door getting as much as their husbands.'[18] Thus the advocates of equal pay found themselves increasingly represented as endangering the economy, threatening the spread of welfare measures and jeopardizing labour and family relations. [...]

Until the close of the government's life Gaitskell at the Treasury continued to resist even limited moves to secure equal pay in areas such as teaching, maintaining 'a decision can only be taken in the light of general policy since any move towards equal pay would not be confined to the public service'.[19] The Minister of Labour, facing embarrassment at the International Labour Organisation, was instructed to block resolutions put forward for the adoption of equal pay.[20] What this approach ensured was that although women were to be encouraged to undertake employment outside the home for the sake of the nation's productivity they were to be confined mainly to low status and less well paid work. [...]

For Labour feminists the government's position caused much heart-searching. The Party Conference in 1947 was used by the most angry of them to show dismay at the hostile response to their demands for equal pay. A critical resolution was moved by Eirene White:

> This conference, convinced that discrimination in salary and wage rates on grounds of sex whether in the professions or in industry affects adversely their position in all walks of life including the home, reminds the government it has signed the United Nations Charter which denounced discrimination on grounds of sex.[21]

While continuing to attack the government for its refusal to listen to their case, Labour feminists and their supporters sought to root out those elements within party and trade union circles who were sympathetic to the government's stance. [...]

Jennie Lee attempted to make a reappraisal of the Labour feminist setback. She chose to use the language of priorities which was much favoured in the postwar world. Her audience was assured that it was only a matter of time before the issue of equal pay was resolved. One precondition of women attaining full equality was the continued survival of a Labour goverment. At all costs tensions between male and female, housewife and careerist, trade-unionist and feminist, must be avoided. Her advice to Labour feminists was to remember these wider needs:

> Every woman of integrity must be prepared to look at the whole problem and not just at those parts of it which affects herself and her sex. It has been a long grim fight to win through to our present status. But there will be most decidedly reaction against the women wage and salary earners if we behave in such a way that it will seem to imply that ours is the only fight or the only worthwhile cause that has not yet won complete victory. [...]   (Lee, 1947)

Major pieces of education legislation have been followed by reappraisals of content and aims and intense speculation on the likely impact of the changes. The 1944 Act was no exception and raised issues about social cohesion. In many of its circulars the Ministry of Education strongly encouraged schools of all kinds to create within their walls an image of the idealized home. When submitting development plans local authorities were urged to pay particular attention to size and avoid the construction of massive complexes. Thus the Ministry warned:

> In a large community even an adult tends to have a feeling that his personal contribution is of little value to the whole body and it is still truer of children if they belong to a school they cannot comprehend as a unit. The development of a community spirit in these large schools will not be easy.[22]

A family atmosphere would be further encouraged by activities bringing all pupils together. Ellen Wilkinson described the midday meal in near religious terms: 'By its very nature this daily act is necessarily part of the corporate life of the school and is regarded as such by those in most secondary schools and many others and its traditions most deeply affect the attitude of the child and the love of the school.'[23] Senior officials at the Ministry of Education, reflecting their own educational experiences, praised the clubs, societies and sporting teams of public schools and urged them to be fostered in the new system of local authority schools. Total involvement in the daily round of school life would develop in the pupils a sense of responsibility and concern for others. Inside the Ministry fears were raised that proposals for comprehensive secondary schools would result in very large institutions. The ability of a headteacher and staff to establish this close community would be nullified. An equally powerful feeling, often expressed in debates about the correctness of streaming in schools, was that pupils ought to relate to each other and this meant identification with groups in the school who had similar attitudes and aptitudes. The presence of fragmented and isolated subgroups, very different from the majority in the school, ought to be avoided. Thus the Inspectorate issued a warning 'that a one stream grammar school within a multilateral school was not satisfactory'.[24]

In the postwar period progressive circles pressed strongly for an end to single-sex schooling arguing that co-education was more appropriate for less formal relationships between the sexes. Evidence was gathered from a range of surveys that teachers and parents had moved in this direction (Moreton, 1946). Significant opposition remained to co-education. Within the old Board of Education fears had been expressed that its widespread introduction would have a detrimental effect on the schooling of boys (Ministry of Education, 1945).[25] The highly criticized *Nation's Schools*, issued in the dying days of the European War, was sympathetic to some periods of co-education for social and educational reasons and concluded, 'in the fields of primary and further education it is to be preferred'. When the secondary stage was discussed the pamphlet came down heavily in favour of separate schools and spacing insisting: 'it is in the secondary field that the real advantages of separation make themselves most apparent. At this stage boys and girls must be separated for physical training and major games and there are many other aspects in which their needs and interests will run further apart.' Opponents raised the untried nature of extensive co-education at this level which was 'so rare in this country that it was difficult to obtain any vital evidence on which to base reasonable conclusions'.[26] It was left to associations representing women teachers in secondary education to supplement the case for single sexed schooling. They used highly conventional arguments.[27] Mixed schooling, often dominated by male teachers, was likely to be less concerned about the dual nature of the education of girls. Health lessons, biology teaching and courses on domestic management were more certain to flourish in schools set aside specifically for girls.

[. . .] The new secondary schooling came under intense scrutiny. In 1945 the only clearly recognizable secondary school was the academic grammar school. These schools, as the model for wider secondary education for girls, were seen to display shortcomings. John Newsom's (1948) influential book, *The Education of Girls*, criticized them because they placed too much stress on public examinations and success in obtaining professional careers. He condemned an attitude of mind in which 'a school is said to be a good school because the headmistress can recite an impressive list of academic successes at the annual prize giving' (p. 13). As a result of the Butler Act larger numbers of clever academic girls from all classes were more likely to be involved in this extended educational process. The implications needed watching:

> A 'clever' girl at school is encouraged to give up domestic subjects for the academic areas. She leaves school to take a job and few mothers expect their working daughters to help in the home. Because of her financial independence the girl of today can dress better and enjoy more pleasure with her friends but her activities—dancing, games, cycling, going to the cinema or even public affairs, are all outside the home.[28]

The full egalitarian spirit of a socialist Britain was used to warn these 'clever' girls how disadvantaged they would be in their future lives if they ignored domestic skills in their early education. Courses in child-care or household management were deemed appropriate for all girls, 'and this probably applies whatever the school they attend and whether on leaving school they are to enter a shop, an office, a hospital, a training college or a university career' (Ministry of Education,1949b). The experiences of war were used to hammer home valuable lessons. Many young women had been situated in barracks and lodgings distant from their homes and lost an informal home domestic education. As they settled into marriage they recognized their shortcomings and clamoured for practical courses. The Ministry of Education was informed: 'as you will probably be aware it is the demand for instruction in the home crafts which is in the forefront at the present time—a demand coming from all part of the country and hitherto unprecedented in our experience'.[29] Scientific advances in knowledge of nutrition, health and good design ensured that 'clever' girls could be provided with domestic courses of a more demanding nature. The stress on the dual aspects of an academic girl's education was not new. Indeed the Association of Headmistresses, in attempting to deflect implied criticism, pointed out: 'Domestic Science rightly forms part of the ordinary school course in secondary school and to the majority it is particularly congenial'.[30] Official opinion shifted its ground and insisted that since the struggle for equal educational opportunities had been apparently won, it was now more important to consider separate needs:

> It seems that for too long the content of education generally has been based on the requirement of boys, and criteria particular to girls have

hardly been considered in all their aspects. A girl's school must not forget that it has to prepare the girl for home-making and motherhood and at the same time prepare her for a way of life which may not offer either of these.[31]

The case was put that 'the time has come when we ought to consider whether it takes into account two facts; one that all girls, whatever else they may do, will have at some time to run a home, and secondly that most girls will find their fulfilment as individuals in having children'.[32]

The spinster schoolmistress, traditionally the backbone of the academic grammar school, faced the kind of attack that had begun in the 1930s. The charge was made that these women lacked 'feminine graces' and presented an unfortunate model for older, impressionable girls. A progressive journal described these women: 'It means to be badly dressed, to look prim, not wear make up, to be old fashioned' (*The New Era*, 1947). Boys were considered to be more fortunate since they were able to identify with male staff:

> The boys can see their master as a man who like their fathers goes to work whereas the girl sees her teacher differing from her mother. As a general rule she is not married, has no children of her own, sometimes she is younger and more fashionably dressed or else she is older and less attractively dressed.[33]

John Newsom, pressing for a family model in all schools for girls, demanded that a staff must consist of a mixture of unmarried and married teachers. He urged the exclusion of either unhappily married teachers or those of 'strong homosexual impulses'. His advice was that, 'teachers in girls' schools should for the most part be attractive, and even when unmarried look as if they could be married if they liked' (Newsom, 1948, p. 149).[34] Ironically evidence from government surveys indicated that in spite of fears that schoolwork, hobbies and reading divorced grammar school girls from the household, they continued to support their mother in the home.[35]

For the 'unintellectual' majority (a Ministry of Education description of the young female population leaving school at the statutory age) social and domestic training received great attention. There was much anxiety over the behaviour of both males and females in this category. John Wolfenden commented on the hostility present in young working-class males: 'The aggression and the self-assertiveness so often seen in the newly emancipated group (so often no more than whistling in the dark to keep up one's spirit in unfamiliar surroundings) are symptomatic of a maladjustment which it is the community's business to diagnose and cure'.[36] Local authority youth clubs, increased participation in sports teams and even a period of National Service were presented as the answer to this male restlessness. As their maladjustment lasted longer, and on occasions, ended in violence, it attracted most attention. A survey on youth organizations accepted that this resulted in less provision for girls 'for the police had less trouble with girls so that even the claim that organizations stave off delinquency weakened the cause of the weaker sex' (Jephcott, 1954, p. 154). Young female adolescents were seen to possess qualities needed to promote civilized living in society. John Newsom urged that their schooling should constantly make them aware of this role:

> It may be well to stress the importance to a whole civilization of ensuring that women of all classes receive the very best preparation for adult life that can be given to them; not because of their inalienable rights as individuals but because they are of the two sexes the most influential for the future well-being of mankind. Women nurture men and women; they do so physically, mentally, spiritually as mothers, wives and teachers.
>
> (Newsom, 1948, p. 108)

[. . .] Much has been made of the aspirations that swept Labour to power with commitments to full employment, better housing and education, a revolution in health-care and the creation of a fairer society. What has been overlooked was that Labour benefited also from growing fears about marriage, population fall, decline in family and community cohesion, all of which rose to the surface in the latter stages of war. These anxieties shaped what the government was prepared to do in providing better housing, full male employment, fairer education and improved welfare facilities. These policies were believed to be essential to improve the quality of family life. On the other hand underlying fears were at the heart of reluctance to promote other causes. Comprehensive nursery services or equal pay might threaten the family playing its full role in the well-being of the nation and were thus discouraged.

Many of the alarms emerging in the last period of the war did not materialize. The institution of marriage did not lose its hold on the population, and after 1945, the boom in families caused successive Education Ministers to revise their forecasts on teacher supply, buildings and other priorities. Nevertheless, a strategy had been evolved to present the home and family as the agents of social cohesion in a world of chance. This was promoted in schools, cinemas and magazines. Even when women sought outside employment it was for the 'extras' that would make households more appealing and comfortable. [. . .]

Fabian social engineers increasingly pinned their hopes on the forces of economic change slowly shifting hardened class attitudes. Nothing must be done to hinder this process and those who could best engage in this work must be given maximum encouragement to do so. It was a signal for universities and grammar schools to search out talent that would ultimately furnish the necessary scientists, technologists, administrators and managers who would be in the forefront. Social improvers, for their part, grew disillusioned at the slow progress made by scientific socialism. Donald Macrae, while accepting that some advances had been made to ensure a population 'better educated, better supplied with the materials of culture and demonstrably more successful,' expressed his reservations about a society in which 'the great majority of boys and girls emerge unread, unqualified, semi-skilled and semi-barbarous with little training in the arts of civil life and none in the understanding of society' (Macrae, 1949). In this mood this opinion fell easy prey to the voices of cultural conservatism which had grave reservations about the spread of a common culture in an age of mass civilization. [. . .]

Notes

1. Hon. Cordelia Leigh to E. Wilkinson, PRO ED 147/39, 17 August 1945.
2. Geoffrey Thomas Survey, PRO CAB 24/765, June 1944.
3. Panel of HMIs in Further Education, PRO ED 46/650, 20 October 1947.
4. National Society for Children's Nurseries, PRO CAB 124/1037, April 1945.
5. Ibid.
6. Ministry of Labour to Ministry of Health, PRO MH 55/1673, 9 September 1947.
7. Ministry of Health and Ministry of Education, Circular 75, 14 December 1945.
8. HMI Miss Bell, PRO ED 136/821, August 1949.
9. Ibid.
10. Women's Group on Public Welfare, PRO MH 55/1644, undated 1946. The Royal Commission on Population (1949) CMD7965, XIX, p. 148 (London: HMSO) was certain that the mood of most women had changed fundamentally:
    From this evidence it is clear that in general women today are not prepared to accept as most women in Victorian times accepted a married life of continuous housework and care of children, and that the more independent status and wider interests of women today, which are part of the ideals of the community as a whole are not compatible with repeated and excessive childbearing.
11. Doctors' Conference of the Family Planning Association, PRO MH 55/1503, 24 November 1946.
12. Women's Group on Public Welfare, PRO MH55/1644, undated 1946.
13. Archbishop of Canterbury, PRO HO 45/2406, 2 March 1949.
14. J. Chuter Ede, PRO CAB 134/209, 8 January 1947.
15. Royal Commission on Equal Pay (1946) CMD 6937, XI, p. 12 (London: HMSO).
16. G. Isaacs, PRO CAB 134/209, 8 January 1947.
17. Arthur Greenwood, PRO CAB 129/19, 20 May 1947.
18. C.R. Attlee, PRO PREM 8/1394, 6 June 1947.
19. H. Gaitskell, PRO CAB 129/46, 1 June 1951.
20. A. Robens, PRO CAB 129/46, 26 June 1951.
21. Mrs E. White, Labour Party Conference Report, 28 May 1947.
22. Ministry of Education, Circular 144, 16 June 1947. The earlier Ministry of Education Circular 73, issued in December 1945, had been even more strongly phrased: 'On the other hand each individual secondary school should be suitable in size to permit a satisfactory social and corporate life and there is not sufficient experience at present to justify a general reversal of past practice which does not favour very large schools.'
23. Ministry of Education, Circular 97, 2 April 1946.
24. Secondary Education Panel of HMI, PRO ED 158/18, 9 July 1946.
25. See Earl de la Warr's reply to J. Moore Brabazon, PRO ED 12/462, 7 November 1939: 'As a matter of fact the personal view of our Senior Chief Inspector coincides with your view that it is not so good for boys as for girls.'
26. Principles of Education Panel of the HMI, PRO ED 158/14, 19 September 1947.
27. Association of Headmistresses, PRO ED 146/12, undated 1946.
28. Memorandum of the National Society of Children's Nurseries, PRO CAB 124/1037, April 1945.

29. Women's Group on Public Welfare to J. Maud, PRO ED 146/13, 13 March 1946.
30. Association of Headmistresses, PRO ED 146/12, undated 1946. See also the strong assertion of the Assistant Mistresses Association, PRO ED 146/12, undated 1946, that 'the aims of girls' secondary education had never been limited to the purely academic.'
31. HMI Miss Dodds, PRO ED 146/13, undated 1946.
32. Ibid.
33. Ibid.
34. Even the Women's Co-operative Guild Memorandum, PRO ED 146/12, undated 1946, joined the criticism arguing: 'Much psychological harm may be done to girls especially in the adolescent stage of motherhood if they were to recognize marriage and motherhood as undesirable because it is usual for the teaching staff which they admire to be wholly celibate.'
35. Children Out of School Leisure Activities, PRO CAB 124/639, November/December 1947.
36. Notes prepared by John Wolfenden, PRO ED 146/19, undated 1947.

References

Addison, P. (1975) *The Road to 1945*. London: Jonathan Cape.
Allen, M. and Nicholas, M. (1975) *Memoirs of an Uneducated Lady*. London: Thames and Hudson.
Jephcott, A. P. (1954) *Some Young People*. London: Allen and Unwin.
Lee, J. (1947) Are women a priority? *Tribune*, 13 June.
Macrae, D. (1949) Domestic record of the Labour Government. *Political Quarterly* 20, 1–11.
McCulloch, G. (1985) Labour, the left and the British general election 1945. *Journal of British Studies* 24, 465–89.
Mass Observation (1947) *Some Puzzled People*. London: Gollancz.
Ministry of Education (1945) *The Nation's Schools*. London: HMSO.
—(1949a) New secondary education, pamphlet. London: HMSO.
—(1949b) Citizens growing up, pamphlet. London: HMSO.
Moreton, F. (1946) Attitudes of teachers and scholars towards co-education, pamphlet. *British Journal of Educational Psychology*. London.
Morgan, K. (1984) *Labour in Power*. Oxford: Oxford University Press.
The New Era (1947) The woman teacher's problem. *The New Era* 28, 9 January.
Newsom, J. (1948) *The Education of Girls*. London: Faber.
Williams, F. (1961) *Memories of a Prime Minister*. USA: Viking Press reprint.

3 STATE POLICY AND IDEOLOGY IN THE EDUCATION OF WOMEN, 1944–1980

ROSEMARY DEEM

In this article I shall be arguing that changes in the education of women since 1944 have usually also been accompanied by changes in general social policy, and that those changes have been closely linked to the needs of the economy and to prevailing ideologies about women's role in society. Ideologies about women are important because they have usually facilitated the masking of not only capitalist social relations but also patriarchal relations of male dominance, so that most women have been unable or unwilling to see the structural sources of their oppression and inequalities.

THE ROLE OF THE STATE IN CAPITALIST SOCIETIES

It is important to recognize that the state itself is not a monolithic actor but consists of a number of apparatuses—government, civil service, judiciary, armed forces, local state, public bodies—any or all of which may be in contradiction with other state apparatuses. The main focus in this paper is on state policy and ideology as evidenced in government and the local state.

As Scase (1980) has noted, the state in any capitalist country must try to meet the needs of capital and to provide conditions which are not inimical to the process of capital accumulation. But this does not necessarily mean that there is a close 'fit' between the functions of capital and those of the state, since capital is also heterogeneous, and what appeases one faction will not do so for another. So we cannot see either state policies or ideologies about women as directly or only fulfilling the needs of capital, although there is a strong indirect connection. O'Connor (1973) and Gough (1980) argue that the state in capitalist society, as part of its attempt to help the accumulation of capital, must assist in the reproduction of the labour force. This is done in a variety of ways: through

Source: *British Journal of Sociology of Education* (1981) Vol. 2, No. 2, pp. 131–43. A version of this paper was originally given to the British Educational Research Association 1980 Conference at the School of Home Economics, University College, Cardiff, 4th September 1980.

education, housing, welfare provision and the social services. Women play an important role in that social reproductive process not just because they bear children but because, to varying degrees in different historical periods they are expected to take on the responsibilities of caring for and socializing children, performing free domestic labour for paid workers and caring for the sick and elderly. In certain periods since 1944, however, the apparatuses of the state and occasionally of capital have been prepared to take on some of these burdens.

The state must also legitimate its activities, and for this purpose the use of ideology is important, although not *all* ideology emanates from the state. Ideologies about women (which say things about the nature of femininity; women's intellectual quality; their place at home and in the labour market) have supported various social policies concerning women, including educational policies. For instance, in the 1960s there was a need for clerical, manual and professional labour which could only be fully met by using female employees. So state and non-state ideologies about women in that period stressed dual roles (work and family) and encouraged women into higher education and training courses, whilst social and welfare services were extended to enable women to participate more fully in the labour market, even though only in segregated sectors of it. With the contraction of the need for female employment, and with more political emphasis on the disadvantages of a welfare state, expenditure on welfare and the social services have been reduced and limited or reduced resources provided for women's educational opportunities. There has also been a return to ideologies of women which emphasize their role in the family. The state not only has to legitimate its activities, but also to repress opposition to those activities, and in periods (as at present) when state policies are likely to be unpopular, there are attempts both to reassert traditional modes of social control (for instance, strengthening of the family by encouraging mothers to stay at home) and to strengthen repressive apparatuses (for example the police). Scase (1980) also points out that states in capitalist societies have tended to become more centralized; this is evidenced in recent educational policies (for example, the APU, the weakening of teacher representation on the Schools Council, the 1980 legislation on school meals and parental school choice) so that more power passes from elected representatives to civil servants. This process encourages the development of forms of direct action which bypass established political procedures, and the Women's Movement may be seen as one group which has adopted this procedure. However, where considerable power is held by civil servants, changes of policy become more difficult to bring about, so that, for instance, those who wish to alter the situation facing women in education now have a much harder task, and one which is not easily tackled through the formal political procedures (these are also problematic, of course, because they are predominantly patriarchal, in character and social relations, as well as ideology). Much of what has happened in the education of women and social policy affecting women since

1944 can be seen as a reflection of the gradual shift after the Second World War to a social democratic ideology and policy.

Social democracy made possible the extension of social policy and the welfare state giving many gains and benefits (for example in education, housing, social services, health-care) to women and the working classes as a whole, not only because of its emphasis on a more equitable distribution of goods and resources but also because from the mid-1950s onwards, the British economy enjoyed relative prosperity. The welfare state in Britian has, however, not simply offered gains to women or to the working class generally; those gains have usually been offset also by an increased amount of social control by apparatuses of the state. For instance, as Hilary Land (1978) has pointed out, most social policies are based on certain sets of assumptions about the family and relationships between the sexes and different generations. Hence, in a particular piece of social policy a 'normal,' family might be considered to consist of a working man, plus dependent wife and children; anyone who falls outside this (single parents or people cohabiting, for example) are disadvantaged in relation to the benefits and services to which they are entitled. Furthermore, since 1945 although concessions in welfare provisions have been made to women and the working class as a whole, these have usually been in an attempt to preserve political rule by the dominant classes and may be withdrawn if they are seen to be too beneficial to the working classes or to women, rather than to capital or apparatuses of the state (Corrigan, 1977). So, the Conservative administration of 1979 onwards has withdrawn many welfare provisions and reduced the social wage ('paid' through things like housing policy, health-care, social services) on the grounds firstly that too much welfare 'softens' people's initiative and independence and secondly that massive public expenditure is a major factor in the economic recession. So although it cannot be argued that all welfare provision and social policies are directed only at the benefits for capital and the state rather than for the working classes, where any section of the working classes (including women) is conceived by the dominant classes to be gaining too much benefit, or too much control over welfare provision, then the gains won may be lost or their system of allocation changed.

The process of extending the welfare state and expenditure on social policy which began in the late 1950s and was consolidated during the 1960s on the basis of a social democratic platform, began to decline from 1970 onwards. It was from this point that some of the contradictions brought about by social democratic policies (increased welfare provision, for example) began to affect both the state and capital, through high public expenditures, increased production costs, and falling profits. And it was these conditions which set in motion the rise to dominance of a new ideology—authoritarian populism. There are however inevitable time lags at work between the dominance of certain ideologies, the social conditions favourable to certain policies, and the establishment of those policies. Furthermore, different apparatuses of the state may themselves be in disagreement. So, for example, legislation on sex discrimination came at the very point where social democratic ideologies were being challenged. Consequently, it now faces minimal implementation in an unfavourable climate of authoritarian populism, an ideology which puts the national interest above either class or gender divisions and which ideologically masks the nature and very existence of those divisions.

IDEOLOGY AND EDUCATION

I am using here an adapted version of Larrain's (1979) concept of ideology, which is drawn from Marx. Larrain writes: 'For ideology to be present, the two conditions which Marx laid down should be present: the objective concealment of contradictions and the interest of the dominant class' (Larrain, 1979, p. 210). It should be remembered, however, that patriarchal relationships of male dominance over women articulate with capitalist social relationships (Beechey, 1979). Hence ideologies about women are also based on the existence of patriarchal relations of dominance by men over women, and attempt to conceal also the contradictions of those patriarchal relations. These contradictions include the belief that male dominance over women is 'natural', which hides the socially constructed power relations and capitalist economic and social relations which underly male dominance. They also extend to the notion that women should carry out domestic work and childcare on the basis of the love and affection present in the marriage relationship, which masks the benefits accruing to both men and to capital from the free performance of those tasks. To declare that women's place is in the home rather than in the (paid) workplace disguises the concern of some male trade-unionists to prevent 'dilution' of their skills and pay-levels by the presence of women in their hitherto male-dominated occupation; equally, it also means that employers of women do not feel obliged to provide childcare facilities because women are 'lucky' to be in paid employment at all. It should also be remembered in connection with ideologies about women, that just as policy has to be interpreted by local authorities and individual schools, so ideologies still have to be translated into specific policies and practices, and this may lead to inconsistencies. Hence, for example, in the case of the educational system, we should not assume that dominant ideologies about women necessarily give rise to uniform practices in schools and amongst teachers.

THE 1944 EDUCATION ACT AND AFTER

The 1944 Education Act, in theory, was supposed to widen the educational chances of the working classes through the provision of free secondary education for all. In practice, as Halsey, Heath and Ridge (1980) have shown, this has not been the case even for working-class boys. For working and middle-class girls, the benefits have been even smaller. This is not surprising, as the Norwood Report in 1943 stressed the importance of relating boys' education to the labour market, but emphasized that girls' schooling must relate to their eventual place in the family. Despite the demonstration, for instance, by conservative researchers like Douglas (1967) that after 1944 girls in primary schools consistently demonstrated their academic superiority over boys, there is little evidence that this superiority followed girls into their secondary school. There are a number of possible explanations for girls' superior primary school performance. First, the kinds of academic skills important in primary schools—especially reading and writing—are those for which girls' earlier family socialization may have prepared them better. As the Newson's researches on child-rearing demonstrate (Newson and Newson, 1968; 1976) young female children are more likely to be encouraged by their parents to remain indoors, to talk to adults (especially their mothers), to be unadventurous. Secondly, primary schools have a much more 'familial' atmosphere than secondary schools; there is a predominance of female teachers, an emphasis on pastoral care, 'family-group' learning, and less emphasis on cognitive development and formal academic skills. Thirdly, primary schools tend to have little formal curricular differentiation between the sexes, except in physical education (Plowden Report, 1967). Furthermore, in the period after 1944 when selection for secondary schools through the eleven plus examination predominated, girls' 11+ performances were weighted differently from boys' performances so that girls achieved fewer places than their examination results indicated, and boys achieved more places than their results merited. So girls in many areas had less chance of a grammar or technical school place than boys. And even where girls were successful in obtaining grammar school places, they were much more likely as the 1959 Report on Early Leaving (Gurney-Dixon Report) showed, to leave at age 15, before any public examinations had been taken, thus losing one of the 'benefits' of a grammar school education. Further, as Byrne (1975) has shown, the allocation of resources in secondary schools quickly took on a pattern which favoured boys rather than girls, with limited provision of science and technical subject facilities in mixed schools, and minimal provision of these in girls' schools.

Although there was a great deal of debate about education after 1944, much of it up to 1951 focused on the eradication of class differences, not gender differences, in an endeavour to build a more buoyant economy and develop a substantial welfare state. Similarly, social policy continued to emphasize the importance of motherhood and the family, even though women had begun to enter production industry in large numbers during the war, and despite a postwar increase in the numbers of married women doing paid work. So, for example, many of the nurseries opened during the Second World War were closed down after the war. Hence women's domestic role continued to be stressed both ideologically and in state policies, so that where women did engage in waged labour, they did so primarily in low-paid, unskilled jobs.

UPSKILLING AND DUAL ROLES FOR WOMEN, 1951–1963

By the early 1950s, the period of postwar reconstruction was coming to an end, rationing had ceased, wages were beginning to rise, and people were being encouraged to spend more money. Increased numbers of women were already working in manufacturing industry, and by the mid 1950s the process of 'upskilling' had begun in other sectors of the labour market. This process meant that more and more of available jobs were said to require higher technical skills or educational qualifications, and it also altered the context in which debates about education were taking place, because the economy increasingly demanded labour power in the secondary and tertiary sectors. Other debates and ideologies, originating both from state apparatuses and from capital, talked of affluence and a consumer-spending boom, and more education was seen as part of the route to yet greater affluence. Hence the participation of women in the labour market was both 'allowed' by the concerns with economic growth and made more possible by the improved educational opportunities offered to women. Changes in family size with the increased availability of contraception also enabled greater numbers of married women to enter or re-enter paid work. At the same time, the welfare state and associated social services continued to grow, and relieved women of some of their former domestic responsibilities.

But despite greater participation by women in the workforce, ideological emphases on women's place in the home remained strong, albeit tinged with some acceptance of women's secondary place in the labour market. The Birmingham Feminist History Group (1979) have argued that although notions of women's equality were important in the 1950s, nevertheless: 'Ideologies about women in the fifties are underpinned by the notion of equal but different—men and women have their special spheres; and women bring different qualities' (p. 150). And the notion of women's dual-roles (paid work and the family) was overwhelmingly applied only to middle-class women. So, for instance, the Crowther Report of 1959 on the education of 15–18-year-olds talked about the likelihood that middle-class girls would combine a career with motherhood and marriage and the necessity for them to receive an education which prepared them for this future dual-role. A similar argument was presented in the 1963 Robbins Report on higher education although it was couched in terms which spoke of untapped pools of ability (women and the working class) who could be drawn into higher education if more places were available. Robbins also related to the upskilling debate—the expansion of education and the high birth-rate of the immediate postwar period for example, had given rise to a shortage of qualified teachers especially in primary schools, and changes in the numbers of white collar jobs available to women had also given rise to a demand for better qualified and certificated female labour.

However, for working-class girls the emphasis within education remained largely on the preparation for marriage and a family, with little account being taken of their equally likely long-term participation in the labour market. Certainly a slight shift of emphasis was taking place during this time—so that for instance it was recognized in the Crowther Report that girls might need to be aware of scientific and technological developments, but, it was assumed, in different ways and for different reasons from boys. The 1963 Newsom Report on 'average' and 'below average' children says this in a most emphatic way:

> A boy is usually excited by the prospect of a science course ... he experiences a sense of wonder and power. The growth of wheat, the birth of a lamb, the movement of clouds, put him in awe of nature; the locomotive he sees as man's reponse: the switch and throttle are his magic wands ... the girl may come to the science lesson with a less eager curiosity than the boy, but she too will need to feel at home with machinery.
>
> (Newsom Report, 1963, p. 142)

SOCIAL DEMOCRACY AND THE COMPREHENSIVE SCHOOL, 1964–1970

This period, under the banner of a social democratic ideology, having its roots in the increased economic growth and general affluence of Harold Macmillan's 'never had it so good' ethos in the previous period, but also in the contradictions this brought about, saw a massive extension of the social services, intended to attack the structural roots of inequality and poverty, which had interestingly been 'rediscovered' despite the country's apparent wealth. However, this extension of the welfare state was double-edged, because as well as offering services it also involved a measure of control over those who were the recipients of those services. The state reforms of the 1960s arose both from working-class and union pressures but also from capital itself, anxious to restructure Britain's economy in the face of greater overseas competition, industrial disputes and falling profits (Gough, 1980). Partly because of the pressures from capital, there were, as Jessop (1980) notes, no moves to redistribute income, which might have effectively attacked class inequalities; instead welfare services were used as palliatives. Consequently, Jessop argues, the extension of the welfare state had no effects on deprivation but rather encouraged the politicization of various groups in urban areas, for example squatters, tenants' rights and welfare rights groups. It should also be recognized that the emerging women's movement of the late 1960s was part of this politicization process.

In education there was during the 1960s a gradual shift towards comprehensive secondary schooling partly prompted by a (false) belief that such schooling would help eradicate the worst inequalities (class, not gender) of the tripartite system, as shown by researchers in the sociology of education (see Finn, Grant and Johnson, 1978). But this shift was also brought about by an apparent consensus about education in the country as a whole. The growth of the comprehensives brought with it a significant expansion in the curriculum content of secondary schooling, which should have been helpful to girls, except that in many schools expansion meant typing or shorthand or child-care for girls, and quite different subjects for boys. For working-class girls (unlike middle-class girls, for whom comprehensives potentially offered them the academic education denied to many under the systems of 11+ weighting) comprehensives probably made little difference. The Labour government's priority from 1964 onwards was the servicing of the economy in response to demands made on them by capital; in so far as working-class girls could have contributed to this, it would have been only in those unskilled jobs for which greater or better education was not required. Hence, one of the potentially most damaging consequences of the shift to comprehensives—the closing or amalgamating of many single-sex schools—passed almost unnoticed. Yet as Shaw (1980) has argued, the assumption that mixed schooling is preferable on academic grounds is not well supported by educational research. R.R. Dale's (1969; 1971; 1974) three-volume study focuses mainly on the social advantages, and it is possible in any case to challenge the nature of the superior social development of girls which is argued to accompany mixed rather than single sex schooling, since one of the things it may involve is breaking down girls' resistance to the imposition of various stereotypes of femininity to a greater extent than is found in single-sex schools.

Recent research (DES, 1975; Fairhall, 1979) suggests that girls' academic achievements are higher and that they are more likely to make untypical choices of subjects (physics, chemistry, etc.) in single- than in mixed-sex schools. Furthermore, as Shaw (1980) suggests, in a mixed school, boys may use girls as a negative reference group for their own academic performance, with consequent effects on girls' own performance.

In primary schooling the Plowden Report of 1967 found little existence of overt sex discrimination or differentiation in the curriculum except in games. But it is clear that Plowden relied heavily on examining the form rather than the content of schooling (and even then, missed many of the subtler forms of discrimination). Otherwise it might have paid attention to the representations of girls and women found in many primary school texts. In any case the apparent absence of discrimination in primary schooling seemed, on the evidence of Benn and Simon (1970), not to follow through into the secondary school. Those writers found that over half the comprehensive schools studied by them restricted some subjects to one sex only. In the absence of any DES or local state guidance to the contrary on this, such restriction is unsurprising, because of limited resource provision in many schools for craft and science subjects (Byrne, 1975). This period did, however, see some improvements in the educational opportunities available to women who had already left school. For example, the establishment of The Open University (Griffiths, 1980), and the provision of special training or refresher courses for married women taking up or returning to teaching. Nevertheless, the intentions behind these policies almost certainly owed more to the demands of the labour market than to any notion of women's rights.

Nevertheless, the 1960s represented a continuation of the shift begun in the 1950s towards ideologies about women and related state policies which recognized the increasing role being played by women in the sphere of wage labour. And as the Birmingham Feminist History Group (1979) recognize, the tensions of women's dual roles which were accepted in the 1950s, were increasingly being challenged in the early 1960s as more and more women experienced the difficulties and problems of being both wage workers and wives/mothers, and as the development of the contraceptive pill started to decrease the possibility of unwanted pregnancies. By the late 1960s those challenges to the predominance of women's role in the family over her role in the labour market were being made more strongly by a new feminist movement in Britain, and the ground well prepared for the passage in 1970 of the Equal Pay Act (even though this was to take six years to implement).

THE BREAKDOWN OF CONSENSUS ABOUT EDUCATION AND THE DECLINE OF SOCIAL DEMOCRACY, 1970–1974

Even before the election of a Conservative government to power in 1970, an attack had begun to be mounted by the Right against many of the educational policies of the Labour Party. As Finn, Grant and Johnson (1978) say 'during the late 1960s, the Right came to identify education as an important causal factor in the "moral crisis" of the period' (p. 188), and so began to attack comprehensive schools for failing to maintain standards of literacy and numeracy. This was only part of a more general move to cut welfare expenditure and restructure social relations. From 1970 onwards the new Conservative administration concentrated its efforts on undoing much of what Labour had done in the field of social policy, but also focused much of its educational policy on returning 'freedom of choice' to that small minority of parents whose children might go to a grammar school. Signs of an economic crisis were increasingly present, and the previous open encouragement of married women to leave the home for the labour market rapidly disappeared. The Equal Pay Act was also encouraging employers not to employ women or to regrade their work, so that it was no longer comparable to men's work. This gave an indication of the kinds of policies that might be adopted with regard to the education (or non-education) of women. No overt moves were made either to increase or decrease the amount of discrimination faced by women in schooling, but David (1980) argues that the James Report (1972) on Teacher Training suggested changes which in practice would disadvantage women student teachers and women teachers. For example, the Report recommended that the first cycle of teacher training might take place in polytechnics (already heavily male-dominated institutions) and in universities and further education colleges where there were still far fewer females than in the traditional colleges for training teachers (which were a female stronghold in higher education). Also David continues, although the Report made provision for the retraining of married women returners, it did so in a context which assumed that child rearing was of no relevance to a career in teaching, and that years so spent were wasted. This view presents an interesting contrast to the then prevalent assumption that (primary) school teaching was an extension of women's role in the home.

Similarly, the 1973 Russell Report on Adult Education noted that women were prominent students in adult education institutions, but neither adequately considered why this was so nor made special recommendations about how adult education provision for women might be improved and made more accessible to them.

If the previous Labour administration had only been dimly aware of the importance of redressing women's inequalities, the Conservative administration of 1970–74 was even less aware of the problem. It was preoccupied with the problems of capital accumulation and deteriorating relationships between capital and the working class, and state intervention in the economy increased. But women were seen to play only a minor role in that economy; even though this misrepresented their actual participation and despite the existence of an increasingly powerful feminist movement and greater general discussion of women's oppression in society. And women's education gained only a low priority. Hence when in 1973 the Conservatives grudgingly introduced a Green Paper on sex discrimination in public life (pressurized by the House of Lords and a private member's bill) the proposed legislation did not even cover education.

DISCRIMINATION LEGISLATION WITHOUT ACTION, AND THE COLLAPSE OF SOCIAL DEMOCRACY, 1974–79

This period presented the Labour Government of 1974–79 with quite serious problems in respect of its educational policies, not only in terms of the mounting attack on educational standards by the Tories but also because of the deepening economic crisis, which meant that education could not continue to be expanded but indeed had to be cut back, as had many other parts of the welfare state. Yet at the same time it was responsible for the passage of a Sex Discrimination Act (at the end of 1975) which was to be applicable to education. However, no resources were to be made available to remedy existing discrimination. The Sex Discrimination Act did not in any case promise to be very useful in relation to education. As well as a cumbersome procedure for complaints involving the County Courts rather than tribunals, it focused mainly on ending discrimination in entry to mixed schools and on direct discrimination in the kinds of courses offered to pupils, without considering other elements of the form of schooling or, for example, the whole issue of how gender and gender relations are represented in the curriculum. The record of the EOC in education has also been a poor one showing reluctance to tackle the major areas of discrimination which might involve real political confrontation, rather than the contained disputes of the courts which have the advantage of a patriarchal hierarchy. The Great Debate of 1976/77, which may be seen as a response to what Finn, Grant and Johnson (1978) call the breakdown of educational consensus, did certainly consider the issue of women's education, and discuss the importance of preparing both boys and girls for roles in both the home and the labour market, but in the absence of any positive follow-up to this in terms of actual educational policy changes, the Debate remained a not very effective exercise in democratic participation to which few people were actually invited. And it is certainly apparent that the Great Debate was primarily concerned with questions of educational standards and the relation between schools and working life rather than with gender and gender relations within schools or outside them. And even in relation to the discussion about preparing children for 'life' there was no adequate consideration of the failure of many schools to prepare *girls* for wider forms of social, economic and political participation. Since the period from 1976 marked also an ideological shift towards emphasis on the importance of family, the general reluctance to implement non-discriminatory policies in schools is not surprising. The strengthening of the family was seen as a way of re-establishing and re-structuring social relationships in a period of economic and social as well as political uncertainty. And women's position as domestic labourers and rearers of children within a restrengthened family was seen as of crucial importance.

Hence even in the attempts to deal with the increasingly serious problems of youth unemployment, the schemes offered both in the Job Creation Programme and in the Youth Opportunities Programme which superseded it, made no recognition of the fact that the often inferior schooling of girls rendered them as much in need of help in entering the labour market as boys, if for different reasons. The EOC report on the Job Creation Programme in 1978 showed that on all schemes girls formed a minority. And the failure to recognize the entry of girls into the labour market as a problem for education as much as for other agencies was made apparent in the consultative paper on *Education and Training for 18 Year Olds* (DES, 1979) published early in 1979, which made no mention of the special needs for girls.

Reductions in public expenditure during Labour's period of office hit women's education particularly hard, as if to futher underline the inconsistencies between the existence of legislation against sex discrimination and specific policies of different state apparatuses upholding that discrimination. Teacher training received one of the largest cuts at a time when it was still one of the major avenues for women's higher education, especially in certain geographical regions (many women are not as mobile as men and cannot travel as far for their post-school education). Reductions in adult education provision (in some cases complete closure) also affected women more than men, for women are the largest consumers of adult education. And the virtual ending in many areas of discretionary grants for post-compulsory education also reduced the opportunities and financial independence which might otherwise have been afforded to some women. The break-up of the social democratic settlement adversely affected the working classes as a whole, but women in particular. But at the end of this period attempts to eradicate gains already made by women were still being heavily resisted, particularly by the feminist movement.

THE DAWN OF THATCHERISM, 1979–1980

The election of a Tory government in 1979 brought many changes in both policies and ideology, since Thatcherism combines an authoritarian populism appealing to national rather than class interests with a return to nineteenth-century liberalism and an emphasis on the responsibility of individuals. As Gough (1980) notes, a central feature of Thatcherist policy has been an attack on the Welfare State and an attempt to return to the private sector many aspects of education, housing, health care and other social services. The alarming rise in unemployment figures as firms feel the effects of high interest rates and an artificially high pound as well as Britain's failure to compete in world markets (Frayman, 1980; Forester, 1980) has gone side by side with the attempt to make individuals less dependent on state services. In education, policy has concentrated on selective and private schooling, the curriculum, parental choices and school meals. Moves to project or increase women's educational opportunities are unlikely; the Tory party sees itself as a staunch defender of the family unit (Mrs Thatcher said at the Tory Party Conference in 1977, 'We are the party of the family', *The Guardian*, 21/3/80, p. 12) and various Tory spokespersons have made clear the view that women's real place is in the home, not in paid employment or public life. For example, Patrick Jenkins—Social Services Secretary—said in a BBC Radio 4 discussion early in 1980: 'The balance between the national needs for women's directly productive work and the need for them to look after their family is now shifting' (quoted in Barker and Downing, 1980, p. 97).

It is also clear that the existence of 'token women' in the Conservative Party administration offers no encouragement to other women to follow in their footsteps. So for instance Jill Knight, Conservative MP for Edgbaston, argues that a strong country is based on the cohesion of the family unit and that women should see staying at home to maintain that cohesion as their primary occupation (Knight, 1980) and sees no contradiction between this advice and her own very different political career.

So we may expect a gradual return to the education of women for domestic labour, emphasis on the importance of motherhood to the economy and the reproduction of 'suitable' labour power (i.e. that which is prepared to accept low wages and discipline) as the need for women's paid work outside the family evaporates. In many areas, girls leaving school will have little possibility of entering employment at all; if they do find jobs, especially in manufacturing, clerical or secretarial work, it is likely that the microchip will soon begin to eat away at that employment. But the state's apparatuses attempt to hide the gravity of the economic situation from women by ideological emphases on motherhood, women's place in the home, and the family, which mask the real problems facing women (an increasing burden of care of the sick, children and the elderly as welfare services contract, few adult education chances remaining, high male and female unemployment rates, competition between women and men for jobs, the attacks on women's control of their own fertility). Most of the advances achieved by women since 1944, both inside and outside education, have occurred in periods of full employment and in the context of social democratic policies and ideology; the treatment of women in education has been closely linked to other social policies and to prevalent ideologies about women's roles. We are already witnessing a return to the ideologies of motherhood which Davin (1978) noted were so prevalent at the turn of the century when the value of a numerically strong and healthy population to British imperialism was heavily emphasized.

The present situation, in which welfare provisions and expenditure on social policies are being drastically cut back at the same time as the central importance of women's domestic and child-caring role in the family is being re-emphasized, is one in which women can clearly no longer rely on the apparatuses of the state to make moves directed at securing their equality and alleviating aspects of their oppression. The present political and economic situation seems to necessitate the organization of women on a broader political front (with the whole labour movement for instance) than is possible solely through the feminist movement. This might enable women to tackle not only questions about the centrality of the family to society and the kinds of roles which women should play outside and inside the home, and about motherhood versus parenthood, but also to raise equally fundamental questions about the social and economic threats posed by mass labour-market unemployment and the implications for divisions of labour in the home, the defects of monetarism as a viable economic policy, ways in which the economy might be restructured, questions about law and order and about the quality of education in a period of drastic expenditure reductions. Such strategies might enable patriarchal ideologies and practices to be challenged and considered at the same time and in the same way as the ideologies and practices of state apparatuses. If such strategies are not adopted, then women are likely to bear more than their share of burdens imposed by authoritarian populism and monetarist economic policy because on them fall the care of the sick, the disabled, the old, the problems of replacing school meals, and the disappearance of part-time and full-time work for women. Unless women are concerned to work towards the preparation of alternative non-capitalist and non-patriarchal economic and social policies (and this may mean under certain conditions working with men) at the same time as resisting the present direction of state policies and ideologies, then there is no possibility that the conditions for the emergence of a new political ideology, or new economic and social policies will begin to be shaped in anything other than a patriarchal way.

The important message which women both inside and outside formal education must grasp is that if they are both to safeguard existing gains for women in education and seek further change, they cannot confine their protests and political strategies solely to that sector of state affairs but must give their attention to many other aspects and concerns of state apparatuses, as well as to challenging the many capitalist and patriarchal structures which exist both inside and outside the spheres of state influence. Current ideologies and policies are such that challenging them is insufficient; women must also work towards alternative policies, not only for education, but for the whole of society and its economy.

References

Barker, J. and Downing, H. (1980) Word processing and the transformation of the patriarchal relations of control in the office. *Capital and Class* 10 (Spring), 64–99.

Beechey, V. (1979) On patriarchy. *Feminist Review* 3, 66–82.

Benn, C. and Simon, B. (1970) *Half Way There*. Maidenhead: McGraw-Hill.

Birmingham Feminist History Group (1979) Feminism as femininity in the nineteen fifties? *Feminist Review* 3, 148–64.

Byrne, E.M. (1975) Inequality in education—discriminal resource allocation in schools? *Educational Review* 27, 179–91.

Corrigan, D. (1977) The Welfare State as an arena of class struggle. *Marxism Today* March, 87–93.

Crowther Report (1959) *15–18*, a report of the Central Advisory Council for Education. London: HMSO.

Dale, R.R. (1969) *Mixed or Single-Sex School*, Vol. 1. London: Routledge and Kegan Paul.

—(1971) *Mixed or Single-Sex School: Some Social Aspects*, Vol. 2. London: Routledge and Kegan Paul.

—(1974) *Mixed or Single-Sex School: Attainment Attitudes, and Over-view*, Vol. 3. London: Routledge and Kegan Paul.

David, M. (1980) *The State, the Family and Education*. London: Routledge and Kegan Paul.

Davin, A. (1978) Imperialism and motherhood. *History Workshop* 5 (Spring), 9–65.

Deem, R. (1978) *Women and Schooling*. London: Routledge and Kegan Paul.

DES (Department of Education and Science) (1975) *Curricular Differences for Girls and Boys*. Education Survey 21. London: HMSO.

—(1979) *Education and Training for 18-year olds: A Consultative Paper*. London: HMSO.

Douglas, J.W.B. (1967) *The Home and the School*. London: Panther.

Fairhall, J. (1979) Shining bright at all—in schools. *The Guardian* 27 April (University of Lancaster research project report).

Finn, D., Grant, N. and Johnson, R. (1978) Social democracy, education and the crisis. In Centre for Contemporary Cultural Studies *On Ideology*. London: Hutchinson.

Forester, T. (1980) De-industrialisation. *Labour Weekly* 29 August, 9.

Frayman, H. (1980) What about those Korean T-shirts? *Labour Weekly* 29 August, 9.

Gough, I. (1980) Thatcherism and the welfare state. *Marxism Today* July, 7–12.

Griffiths, M. (1980) Women in higher education—a case study of The Open University. In R. Deem (ed.) *Schooling for Women's Work*, pp. 126–41. London: Routledge and Kegan Paul.

Gurney-Dixon Report (1954) *Early Leaving*. London: HMSO.

Halsey, A.H., Heath, A.F. and Ridge, J.M. (1980) *Origins and Destinations Family: Class and Education in Modern Britain*. Oxford: Clarendon Press.

James Report (1972) *Teacher Education and Training*, report of DES Committee of Enquiry. London: HMSO.

Jessop, B. (1980) The state in post-war Britain. In R. Scase (ed.) *The State in Western Europe*, pp. 27–93. London: Croom-Helm.

Knight, J. (1980) Interviewed by A. Hamilton. *The Guardian* 27 August, 9.

Land, H. (1978) Who cares for the family. *Journal of Social Policy* July, 257–84.

Larrain, J. (1979) *The Concept of Ideology*. London: Hutchinson.

Newson, J. and E. (1968) *Four Years Old in an Urban Community*. London: Allen and Unwin.

—(1976) *Seven Years Old in the Home Environment*. London: Allen and Unwin.

Newsom Report (1963) *Half Our Future*, a report of the Central Advisory Council for Education. London: HMSO.

Norwood Report (1943) *Curriculum and Examinations in Secondary Schools*, a report of the Secondary Schools Examinations Council. London: HMSO.

O'Connor, J. (1973) *The Fiscal Crisis of the State*. London: St James Press.

Plowden Report (1967) *Children and their Primary Schools*, a report of the Central Advisory Council for Education. London: HMSO.

Robbins Report (1963) *Higher Education*, a report of the Committee on Higher Education. London: HMSO.

Russell Report (1973) *Adult Education: A Plan for Development*, report of a Committee of Enquiry. London: HMSO.

Scase, R. (ed.) (1980) *The State in Western Europe*. London: Croom-Helm.

Shaw, J. (1980) Education and the individual; schooling for girls, or mixed schooling—a mixed blessing? In R. Deem (ed.) *Schooling for Women's Work*, pp. 66–75. London: Routledge and Kegan Paul.

4   MAKERS OF MEN

MARGARET LITTLEWOOD

Men's banding together in trade unions is often explained (if not forgiven) by a need to prevent their employers using cheap unskilled female labour to undercut their wages. Margaret Littlewood has been studying the National Association of Schoolmasters in the 1920s and 1930s and found instead a situation where men, in a minority, struggled against militant, unionized women, many of whom were better educated than the men themselves. Why and how were the men so successful in asserting themselves that the NAS has come to be the second largest union in the profession?

'Let me wish every one of you the happiest of times, wherever you spend them, so that you will return with renewed vigour and enthusiasm for the greatest job in the world—the making of men.' With these words the President of the National Association of Schoolmasters (NAS) wished his members a good summer holiday in 1935.

The President had some cause for satisfaction. In the twelve years of the men's union's separate existence, he had seen its membership double, from 5,000 in 1923 to a claimed 10,000 in the mid thirties. This was a small proportion of the total number of elementary teachers, three-quarters of whom were women and thus ineligible to join, but it did represent a quarter of the men in elementary teaching.

The reason why the NAS felt that men teachers needed a separate union to represent their interests was simple: they felt their position in teaching was being threatened by an upsurge of 'militant feminism' within the occupation.

The largest teaching union, the National Union of Teachers (NUT), whose membership was open to teachers of both sexes, had come out in favour of equal pay for men and women in 1919, as the result of a prolonged campaign by women teachers within the union. Women teachers saw their struggle within the NUT as an intrinsic part of the wider women's movement's concern for full political, social and economic parity with men, symbolized at the time by gaining the vote. But some of its feminist members, faced with consistent male hostility to their demands (most of the union's conference delegates and executive committee were men), decided to form their own separate union, the National Union of Women Teachers (NUWT), whose members were to be exclusively women. The NUWT published its own journal (*The Woman Teacher*), organized petitions and mass meetings, communicated its

Source: Abridged from *Trouble and Strife* (1985), Vol. 5 (Spring), pp. 23–9.

ideas through a column in a general educational journal *The Schoolmistress*, which claimed to have the largest circulation of all educational magazines among women teachers, and even managed to persuade some local authorities to pay men and women the same on the lower end of the salary scale.

Faced with feminist pressure from outside and inside teaching, men teachers started to meet in small groups in the cities as early as 1913 to see how they could counteract this threat to their privileged status. By 1919, alarmed by the success of those they called 'the worst group of profiteers that took advantage of the war to extort money', they had formed their own separate organization within the NUT, and in 1922 they voted to leave to form their own separate union to defend their gender-based interests.

On the surface it seemed they could not have picked a worse time to leave the shelter of the main union, the NUT. The optimism which led to hopes of an expansion of education at the end of the First World War, had given way to recession. Teachers of both sexes were faced with a proposed contraction of educational provision, especially in elementary education, and a threatened cut of their salaries. As local authorities desperately tried to cut their educational budgets, there was a danger that the increased employment of women teachers at their lower salary levels might prove more attractive than the employment of more expensive men.

In these circumstances it would seem logical that men and women teachers should stand together to argue for a common salary scale and to oppose cuts in expenditure. Women teachers, after all, had proved themselves active unionists, militant in support of their claims. But instead of uniting with their women colleagues, the NAS chose this time to split the ranks of elementary teachers even further, and to argue their case for keeping and extending the privileged position of the male.

THE NEED TO ATTRACT AMBITIOUS MEN

The NAS argued that men needed higher wages to ensure an adequate supply of men into elementary teaching. They argued that 'with the rapid development of all kinds of new industries demanding intellectual attainment of no mean order and offering substantial financial rewards, the possibilities before the ambitious man are endless' (*Equal Pay and the Teaching Profession*, 1921). Many of these 'highly paid callings' deliberately excluded women, leaving educated women of the working and lower middle classes with far fewer employment opportunities. Men in these occupations supported equal pay for men and women workers; but this, according to the NAS, was not through any support of feminist principles, but was rather an attempt to exclude women further from well-paid craft and industrial jobs. Because women were substantially in the minority in such work, equal pay meant that the female rate of pay was increased to that of the male. Employers, themselves men, were reluctant to employ women workers at these increased wages. Thus women were forced out of industry and into the major occupation open to talented girls of the working class—elementary teaching. Since women teachers were essential for the education of girls, men teachers could not use the same exclusionary tactics as their industrial brothers. Instead they sought the integration of women into teaching on radically different terms from men.

Teaching thus attracted adequate numbers of women, many of whom were better educated and came from a slightly higher class background than the available men, who were mainly recruited from the artisan working class. According to Sir Robert Blair, Education Officer for the London County Council, 'the character and ability of the women obtained for the women's salaries is in advance of those of the men attained on the men's scale'. The NAS argued that relatively low rates of pay in teaching would attract only 'the unambitious man of low mental power and low attainment ... content with the narrow limits of his chosen trade' (*Equal Pay*, 1921). This meant that the education of boys would be of a lesser quality than that of girls, as they 'have not only an inferior type of teacher but [these] teachers [have] to work under greater mental stress and consequently lessened resiliency of mind' (*New Schoolmaster* [*NS*], 1922). This argument reverses the normal economic reasoning, where workers argue their superiority over others to justify higher differentials in pay. Instead the schoolmasters were using arguments about their own *inferiority* to justify larger salaries for themselves, and to widen the gap even further between male and female rates of pay.

A MARRIED WAGE FOR MARRIED MEN

Men centred their arguments not on their competence as teachers, but on the distinct roles men and women had within the family. Men needed more money in order to keep a wife and children at home. All men were potential husbands and fathers, so even a bachelor needed more money than his single sister. 'Upon him still rests the initiative in marriage and ... the responsibility for preparing the home and subsequently maintaining it' (*NS*, Nov. 1922).

But marriage, actual or presumptive, did not only justify a higher male wage, it also defined married men as better teachers. 'There are few men and few women so gifted as teachers that they would not be improved through marriage and parenthood' (*NS*, Nov. 1922). As well as throwing doubt on the competence of women teachers, as marriage was increasingly becoming a bar on their employment as teachers, this claim also placed all men firmly in a particular relation of heterosexuality. There was no place for the heterosexual man who wished not to marry, and more importantly there was no room for the homosexual. The recognized existence of such men would have badly undermined the schoolmasters' case for a family wage payable to all men, irrespective of their actual marital status.

What this presumption of heterosexuality did was enable men teachers to present themselves as the champion of true womanhood against the desexed, celibate advocates of female equality. For the NAS, 'a woman's vital force can, and generally does, pour itself into motherhood ... the *best women* find motherhood and prefer to find in it their chief work and their most absorbing interest' (*Equal Pay*, 1921, emphasis in the original).

WOMEN'S TRUE SPHERE IS AS WIVES

Equally women needed to give unstinting support to their husbands. Women were not excluded from the pages of the union journal; instead they were ever present, praised for their supporting role. Men's lives they were told, revolved around three categories: 'earning a living, home life, and associate life, by which we mean that co-operative activity, which makes for evolutionary progress in society' (*NS*, Jan. 1922). The latter meant the schoolmaster's union activity, which necessitated long absences from home. In case wives became dissatisfied with this state of affairs, they were assured that home and family came first and 'the very existence of the Association was largely bound up with the recognition of this hallowed claim' (*NS*, Jan. 1922).

The schoolmasters vehemently defended themselves against charges of sex-hatred. No one, they claimed, was second to them in their respect for the female sex.

> For women men have fought and died, in women poets and writers have found inspiration, without women there can be neither home nor family, in and through women lies the Nation's hope and future moral and spiritual ascendency ... Men cannot withhold from her anything that is good for her or give her anything that is bad for her without injuring themselves and their children.
>
> (*Equal Pay*, 1921)

But, as the second part of this quote assumes, the relationship between men and women was essentially hierarchical. A man's job was 'to train a wife and children in the way they are to go'.

Woman's true sphere was therefore a man's home. Her interests were best represented by a wage paid to her husband so she could devote herself to her family's welfare. But it was important to the men that their wives had a standard of living equal, if not superior, to that of single, women teachers. If single blessedness was as lucrative as married bliss, then women might refuse to enter these relations of subordination and either refuse marriage, or, if married, refuse to give up their occupation. [...]

FIT EDUCATION FOR BOYS AND GIRLS

The presence in teaching of large numbers of women actively pursuing their careers and fighting for equality with men therefore undermined the relation of patriarchal domination on which the men's economic arguments were based. These women, the schoolmasters argued, were a product of the education system. It was not so much that the men felt girls should not be educated, but that the process was fraught with danger. For men, education was 'a mere extension of character ... Education will not change him as a man'; but educational systems 'changed the natures of many of the women subjected to them. They produce a type, a physical and mental type which is distinct from womanhood as a whole. The modern educated woman is ... an artificial product' (*NS*, Jan. 1922). In other words, education produced women who claimed equality with men.

But if girls were threatened by the very processes of education, boys were equally at risk if they came under the influence of women teachers after the age of seven. The union maintained that although

> in the matter of managing and instructing young children the sex of a person may matter but little ... in the great task of educating children the sex of the teacher is of paramount importance. The character of children is the essential consideration, and the essentials of character lie in the sex of the person.   (*NS*, Nov. 1936)

This assertion was linked to theories of natural development.

> All through winter nature is quietly, secretly preparing the blossom that bursts forth with almost startling suddenness in the spring. So in the immature human being we can discern a rhythmic development years before adolescence comes upon them. During these years preceding adolescence, so vitally important in character forming, so impressionable, so open to suggestion, irreparable harm may be done by the wrong influence, the wrong environment, the wrong viewpoint. In the case of young boys, well meaning and conscientious women teachers may do endless harm.
> (*NS*, May 1935)

To understand the nature of the harm that women teachers did to young boys we must understand the nature of the masculinity put forward by men teachers.

Protecting boys' masculinity

The first, but subsidiary point was that masculinity was essentially physical and located in the body. There was a great emphasis on sport and physical exercise in the development of healthy boyhood, but this physical exercise had to take place in an exclusively male environment. The presence of women and girls hindered the development of a boy's masculine pride in his superior strength and agility. Women teachers could and did coach successful football teams, but the good that they did was overshadowed by the embarrassment caused by the supervision of women in this, 'one of the most vital and intimate parts of school life' (*NS*, Nov. 1936). Instead of developing a healthy pride in his body, the presence of women and girls made the young boy feel awkward and ashamed.

[...] Mixed education in any subject was to be avoided.

> From the age of six or seven until the later teens boys tend to avoid girls. They have little in common and no amount of experimenting will alter facts. Most of us have seen the sturdy youngster standing red faced and awkward with his unwilling partner at a school carnival. Those who have taught in a school know that when there is an association of the sexes, it is frequently of a sly and furtive nature of which the youth and girls are later heartily ashamed. Those of us who have had much experience of Evening Institute are aware of the difficulties arising when there are mixed classes of fourteen and fifteen year olds.
>
> (*NS*, May 1936)

But if the mere presence of women and girls so crucially affected male sexual development, the most devastating effect on the emergence of a healthy male sexuality was created by having a woman in authority, a woman teaching in class where boys were present. In these circumstances, the schoolmasters argued, 'Boy nature will out. If it does not, the man will never grow to full stature.' The picture that emerges of 'boy nature' is an attractive one: a generous and warm child motivated by a sense of adventure and fun, in marked contrast to girls, 'the sensible sex' (*NS*, 1937). Boys were essentially anarchic and anti-authoritarian. They pitted themselves against the petty restrictions and rules of society, not because of innate viciousness but because of high spirits and a lively sense of mischief. They were true innocents, to be understood and guided rather than restricted and controlled.

The young boy's first rebellion was essentially against the authority of his mother, at about seven years old. But at this age he was also placed under the control of celibate women in the elementary school, where he naturally rebelled. No self-respecting boy, the schoolmasters argued, would willingly submit to this 'spinster authority', and the scene was set for a bitter classroom battle leading to the breakdown of good classroom relations and law and order in the school.

TOO STRICT AND TOO LAX

Celibate women, the men argued, were by nature unable to understand the masculine need for constructive freedom. This lack of understanding and acceptance of the boy's anarchic lawlessness created the super-masculine figures of juvenile delinquency, the 'gangster and the hooligan', whose existence was a 'message'. 'They give evidence of a lack of understanding in the past; they show us traits that have been neglected and so have found morbid expression' (*NS*, May 1936).

The 'gangster and the hooligan' however, were, at least recognizably masculine, even though their maleness was expressed in violent and anti-social ways. What to the schoolmasters was worse, was the castrating effects of 'spinster authority'. As one delegate to the 1936 NAS conference put it: 'I have witnessed the process of nipping out by Miss Teacher of the budding shoots of young manhood' (*NS*, May 1936). Interpreting high spirits as an evil nature, the woman teacher tended to exercise her authority in an inflexible manner. Rigid, petty and restrictive, she effectively dammed the course of healthy male development. A boy taught by a woman, it was argued, had the manliness knocked out of him because of the harshness of female treatment. This led to his becoming 'unnaturally subdued'. [...]

A woman teacher could also metaphorically castrate the young boys in her care in other ways too. Women were attacked by their men colleagues for being too soft as well as too harsh. Women teachers were among the pioneers of progressive education, with its emphasis on the free development of every child. Such methods of education were all right in the infant school, but the NAS opposed their application for boys over seven. Junior school teaching, they argued, called for a more formal approach with a greater emphasis on concentration and a higher level of self-control. In *this* context, women teachers were seen as too lax, not demanding high enough levels of achievement. They thus infantilized and effeminized the growing boy.

> The plain truth is that boys of normal make-up will inevitably associate instruction by women with their experiences as infants. There is a type of man, well known to the medical psychologist, and marked by a long dependence on maternal care. This type assumes a wholly wrong attitude towards women, but some women like it. One of the biggest dangers of having women as teachers of boys is that the mother-dependant type will become more common.
>
> (*NS*, July 1935)

THE SUPERIORITY OF MEN TEACHERS FOR BOYS

Men teachers offered neither the petty restriction of female authority nor the undemanding routine of the feminine infant school, but the 'free atmosphere' of a classroom controlled by a man. A boy past the infant stage 'no longer looks towards his mother ... for help and guidance, he wants to associate exclusively with boys, he looks forward to entering a class taught by a man' (*NS*, May 1936). Boys thus 'invite the leadership of a man' (*NS*, April 1937). The boy 'needs as a guide and a friend, one who can put himself in the same position; one who has passed through the same experiences and understands his peculiar problems' (*NS*, May 1936). [...] The relationship between master and boy was characterized by the union as a 'friendly intimacy', possible only with a man teacher. 'It is not possible with a woman teacher, and it would be highly undesirable if it were possible' (*NS*, Dec. 1936).

Despite the use of the words 'love' and more especially 'intimacy' to describe the feelings between schoolmaster and pupil, it would be difficult to characterize this relationship as homoerotic, however, for sexuality and the awareness of sexuality were consistently only associated with the presence of women and girls. The all-male school environment was seen instead as essentially an asexual Garden of Eden, where the relation between man and boy was formed around a 'spiritual' bond based on mutual identification.

THE QUEST FOR PROMOTION—THE CONSTRUCTION OF PATRIARCHAL RELATIONS BETWEEN MEN AND WOMEN TEACHERS

But in this paradise lurked a serpent. Not just the spinster teacher—but the spinster teacher who sought authority over the man.

If the authority of women over boys threatened the development of masculinity in the school, how much greater was the threat of the appointment of a woman head over men teachers! The raising of the spinster teacher over the married man was denounced as an 'anti-social absurdity' by the union (*NS*, March 1935). 'The relationship between master and boy is so intimate that the man, especially the young man, cannot get spiritual support if the leadership of a school is entrusted to a woman head' (*NS*, Nov. 1936).

The problem for the NAS was that there was a considerable temptation for local authorities to do precisely this. Single-sex schools, especially junior schools, were being combined to form mixed-sex schools and experienced and qualified women were available for promotion at a lower salary than the equivalent men.

Local authorities were reminded, therefore, that 'sex was a dynamic force in the expression of personality', and of 'the immense importance of the separate but complementary parts men and women must play in the world of teaching' (*NS*, Nov. 1936). This complementarity was not, however, one between equals. Instead, it was argued, 'Few men would willingly serve under a headmistress, and if such schools are to be staffed with the right kind of schoolmasters, a man head is essential' (*NS*, May 1936). 'What right has any administration to rob boys up to eleven of men teachers even if women can take corner kicks or illustrate a tackle. Under male heads, staffing problems in mixed schools largely disappear, school atmosphere develops as it should' (*NS*, Nov. 1936). As the union pointed out, 'there never has been any unwillingness on the part of a woman teacher to serve under a headmaster' (*NS*, May 1936).

What this amounted to was a deliberate policy of non co-operation with any woman appointed to the headship of a mixed-sex school. Although this attitude was denounced as extreme and a form of sex-hatred by some local authorities, who pointed out that if trained and competent women were available at a lower price than men, they owed a duty to their rate payers to appoint them. Such authorities had to count the cost of the disruption caused to schools by the appointment of women over staffs adamantly opposed to women heads.

Women heads and women doctors in the school medical services excited NAS hatred. [. . .] But the most volatile and explosive issue of all was the appointment of women to the inspectorate with special responsibility for handicraft and physical education. That women should invade such traditional male preserves of woodwork and metal work was bad enough, but true venom was kept for the woman PE inspector. 'Professional men carrying on their professional work are "examined" by women even in the most intimate areas of the curriculum' (*NS*, Feb. 1935).

That the authoritative female gaze should examine and evaluate male physical prowess was more than the men of the NAS could stand. A true woman would shrink from such employment through natural delicacy; hence the inspectorate only attracted hybrids of 'muscular femininity' (*NS*, July 1935). In 1935 the proceedings of the NAS conference were halted to show solidarity with a NAS hero, an ex-navy married man and champion boxer, who lost his job rather than submit to such an unnatural inspection.

CONCLUSION: FIFTY YEARS ON

The NAS justified its separate existence because it specifically defended the position of the man in teaching. The largest teaching union, the NUT, merely used

> the married man's financial responsibilities to raise the salaries of unmarried women ... How does the NUT present the man's case. Does it retain the Junior Boys' Schools for him? Does it keep all avenues of promotion open to him? Does it preserve him from the matriarchal headmistress? Does it fight for his retention in the village school? Has it helped him ward off the physical education instructress or female organizer? Does it raise a hand against inspectors of handicrafts—of all subjects in the world—of the opposite sex?   (*NS*, 1937)

This attack on the NUT could hardly be stifled by feminist activity on the part of that union. Although it never changed its policy on equal pay for teachers of the same professional standing, the union did not press women's issues during the depression of the twenties and thirties. Instead it sought to maintain professional unity against threats to teachers' salaries and cuts in educational provision, avoiding any issue which would alienate its male membership.

The fate of the separatist women's union was no more encouraging. Although still arguing the case for the full inclusion of women in all areas of public life and for equality between the sexes, it found difficulty in recruiting new members. Its decline accelerated after the Second World War and it disbanded in 1961 when equal pay was finally implemented in the teaching profession.

The subsequent history of the NAS is in sharp contrast. From a membership of 5,000 in 1922, it grew consistently. By 1960 it had gained representation on the Burnham Committee, which negotiates teachers' salaries, and it is now the second largest teaching union.

The existence of the NAS cannot be argued away as the attempt of men to protect themselves from an influx of cheap female labour which threatened to undercut the male rates of pay. It was true that the government and local authorities did use women, both qualified and unqualified, as a source of cheap labour in the schools, particularly in the early twenties; but it was women teachers who militantly organized to prevent this. It was the militance of these women, directly challenging the subordination of women, which caused the formation of the men's union to defend masculine interests.

The 1920s and 1930s thus saw the emergence in teaching of a group of men organized around the principles of male domination both in the schools and family life, whose ideology and teaching practices were even more patriarchal than that of the State. The male backlash was institutionalized and has remained both in the schools and in the union structure of teaching.

Note

Quotations are taken from *Equal Pay and the Teaching Profession*, 1921, the first of a series of booklets on equal pay, published by the NAS, and from their journal, *New Schoolmaster*, published monthly in the 1920s and 1930s.

5 THE EDUCATION POLICY CONTEXT: THE IDEA OF 'PARENTOCRACY', 1976–1992

MIRIAM E. DAVID

In this article I look at how the relationships between parents and education were altered through changes in the policy context from a social-democratic to a right-wing political position. The focus is on the 'education reforms' which were set in train by the New Right as a reaction to the developments that had occurred during the previous period of 'liberal-democratic' reforms. The political reactions to the previous policies of trying to achieve equality of educational opportunity through attempts either to reduce differences between children on the basis of their *parental* circumstances of privilege or poverty were not, however, based upon any serious social scientific review of the evidence. Indeed, despite the deep involvement of social scientists in both the policy prescriptions and policy evaluations, little evidence had yet been adduced to 'prove' the effectiveness of strategies oriented towards equal opportunities.

The political movement to the right has occurred not only in Britain but also in the US and other advanced industrial nations. Silver comments that:

> As the 1970s moved on, however, attention in both countries was directed by economic and social events to other educational objectives. The 'civic' missions of concern with poverty and disadvantage were increasingly replaced in the late 1970s especially by the 'economic' or 'business' missions of successful international competition, and the training of appropriately skilled manpower for new technologies and a changing world of work. The policy priority, in both Britain and the US, turned to 'standards', 'excellence', and accompanying moves towards more vocational curricula and increased testing . . .

> In terms of research, it is interesting that in the 1980s new directions not only bypassed the focus on disadvantage, but explicitly appeared to eclipse it . . . (Silver, 1990, p. 199)

A number of other writers, but especially Guthrie and Pierce (1990), have

Source: Abridged from David, M.E. (1993) *Parents, Gender and Education Reform* (pp. 53–74). Cambridge: Polity Press.

also investigated the comparisons and contrasts between education reform in Britain and the US, focusing on the implications of economic developments. They have pointed out the extent to which the right-wing movements for education reform have been developing in all advanced industrial societies:

> ... changes in technology, international competition, and markets are forcing industrialized nations to adopt new policies to remain competitive ... in the United States and Europe ... concern about Asian economic competition is creating a major review of public and private economic strategy.
>
> Much of the blame for both America's and the British deteriorating economic position had been placed on each nation's respective education system .... (Guthrie and Pierce, 1990)

Guthrie and Pierce go on to argue that:

> The education reform movements in the United States, Britain and many other industrialized nations ... have accepted the challenging goal of elevating national education performance; even if they do not always have complete agreement regarding means for doing so. (1990, pp. 184–5).

However, Clark and Astuto (1989, p. 3) point out the extent to which the 'language' of education reform is similar, even if the methods of application vary because of differing political and economic contexts. In particular, the right-wing movements emphasize *parental choice*, as a basis for pursuing academic excellence, standards of performance, ability, institutional competition and deregulation over equity, needs, access, social and welfare concerns, regulations and enforcement. Boyd (1991) has also talked of 'a new lexicon' which consists of the five Ds—disestablishment, deregulation, decentralization, de-emphasis and diminution—and the three Cs—core content, moral character and choice of school. This represents a shift from social equality to quality and excellence in education, based upon a different view of the role of parents.

Brown (1990) has also observed that these shifts have been occurring in an international context, but he confines much of his analysis to the socio-historical developments in British education. He states:

> We are entering a 'third wave' ... which is neither part of a final drive towards the 'meritocracy', nor the result of a socialist victory for educational reform. To date, the 'third wave' has been characterized by the rise of the educational parentocracy, where a child's education is increasingly dependent upon the wealth and wishes of parents, rather than the ability and efforts of pupils ... the ideology of parentocracy ... involves a major programme of educational privatization under the slogans of 'parental choice', 'educational standards' and the 'free market'.
>
> (Brown, 1990, pp. 66–7)

In this article, I shall briefly review the origins of the movement to the right, especially for its influence on parents and educational policy, then consider the detailed policy developments in Britain and contrast them with the ways in which such developments have been occurring in the US.

What is important to note is that social scientists were involved to a much lesser extent in the development of policy proposals and prescriptions under the New Right than they had been during the era of social democracy. The kinds of social scientists who were involved in the processes of developing policy tended to be economists and political scientists rather than social policy analysts and sociologists. Nevertheless, social scientists continued to provide policy evaluations and analysis, and have become critical observers rather than being involved in policy creation. There has been an even greater accumulation of social scientific research and evidence about the emergence of the New Right and its 'education reforms' than about the previous period. That may, however, merely bear witness to the spread and significance of social scientific approaches and political endeavours. What remains lacking in this area are any sustained feminist critiques, that focus specifically on education reform. There has, of course, been a proliferation of feminist perspectives on other areas of social life and state policies.

ORIGINS OF THE EDUCATIONAL RIGHT

The origins of the movement to the right in both Britain and the US are to be found in the politics and policies of the 1960s and 1970s. There was a 'liberal-democratic' political consensus on the need for some measure of social and educational provision and support to both families and industry to sustain economic growth after the Second World War (Mishra, 1984). There were political disagreements between the major political parties about the means of ensuring a healthy mixed economy, but left and right alike agreed that at least minimal state intervention was necessary to ensure the smooth running of the economy, and that there should also be educational provision to support economic growth, through an emphasis on ability and merit, regardless of parental circumstance. This social-democratic political consensus reached its apogee in the 1960s, first in the US, later in Great Britain.

However, the expansion of educational and economic opportunities aimed at reducing differences in socio-economic and family circumstances began to come under criticism from right-wing political pressure groups in the late 1960s and early 1970s. There had always been a strand of right-wing or conservative thinking that had been committed to both 'excellence in education' and the promotion of academic standards, rather than to equality of opportunity regardless of home background. The policies of the social-democratic administrations was therefore criticized for being too rapid and too extensive in terms of social class equality. It was argued by the right that they would lead to a reduction in educational standards and create educational mediocrity.

SHIFTS RIGHTWARD IN BRITAIN

In Britain, a group of right-wing academics and political commentators began to give voice to these concerns in a series of what were intially somewhat recherché pamphlets. The pamphlets were given the ambiguous name of the Black Papers. Five different pamphlets were published between 1969 and 1977, all dedicated to the same themes of 'more means worse' and 'the egalitarian threat'. In the 1975 pamphlet, a ten-point set of Black Paper Basics was produced which included these four points:

> If the non-competitive ethos of progressive education is allowed to dominate our schools, we shall produce a generation unable to maintain our standards of living when opposed by fierce rivalry from overseas competitors.
>
> It is the quality of teachers which matters, rather than their numbers or their equipment. We have sacrificed quality for numbers, and the result has been a lowering of standards. We need high-quality, higher-paid teachers in the classroom, not as counsellors or administrators.
>
> Schools are for schooling, not social engineering . . .
>
> You can have equality or equality of opportunity; you cannot have both. Equality will mean the holding back (or the new deprivation) of the brighter children. (Cox and Boyson, 1975, p. 1)

However, these criticisms remained very much fringe or marginal right-wing political concerns in the 1970s. In Britain, they had relatively little influence on the development of social and educational policies, despite the fact that between 1970 and 1974 there was a Conservative government in power (Dale, 1989, p. 106). It remained committed to some equal measures of social and educational provision to maintain economic growth. Mrs Thatcher was the author of the official White Paper, in late 1972, entitled *Education: A Framework for Expansion*. It included attempts to expand nursery education and to achieve some limited kinds of socio-economic equality, by aiming at a social mix of family backgrounds (David, 1980).

However, the international oil crisis of 1974 put paid to many of these plans. In the first place, the Tory government fell as a result of serious economic mismanagement and was replaced by a Labour government with a slender majority. Although the Labour party remained committed to the principle of equality of opportunity and the expansion of equal opportunities in education on the basis of social class or home backgrounds, this became more difficult to achieve given the recurring economic crises. [. . .]

'The Great Debate on Education' was launched by James Callaghan in 1977 specifically to consider how to restructure the educational process so that it tied education and training more clearly to the needs of industry and economy.

Expanding educational opportunities was no longer seen as simply consonant with economic growth. Nevertheless, the Labour government was concerned to ensure that parents played a role in this process of restructuring on the grounds that there was a clear parallel between parental and state needs.

This policy debate was narrowly conceived and did not range over all aspects of education. Despite the Labour government's commitment to equal opportunities through other social or public policies such as those on race relations and sex discrimination, these were ignored in the debate. [...] The outcome of the debate was an official government Green Paper, a discussion document as a prelude to legislation. [...] The paper focused on how children should be prepared for work through schools and other forms of training, in further education or 'on the job'. To the extent that equal opportunities could be said to entail the same education for all, the proposal of a core or a common core curriculum for all schools could be seen to be a continuation of this process. The 'core' was to consist of three basic subjects to be taught, throughout schooling, to all children; namely English, maths, and science with technology. These proposals, however, remained but proposals and were not translated into policy. Yet, they have provided the starting-point for subsequent and more explicitly right-wing debates.

By the end of the 1970s British educational policy was no longer officially debated in terms of its ability to aid in the process of, and achieve, equal opportunities on the basis of reducing differences in socio-economic family backgrounds. This was despite the creation of two quasi-non-governmental bodies (quangos) charged with monitoring those processes for minority ethnic groups and on the grounds of sex. These two bodies were the Commission for Racial Equality (CRE) created in 1976 and the Equal Opportunities Commission (EOC) created in 1975. These two bodies did include equal educational opportunities as part of their brief. Moreover, education required special quasi-judicial processes in both cases (Gregory, 1987). Yet these never influenced the educational debate, except to the extent that a special governmental inquiry was set up to investigate the education of West Indian children in the late 1970s, largely as a result of pressure-group activities. The scene was set for a rightward move as education was increasingly blamed for the economic ills of the nation. The increasingly influential right-wing arguments were that children were not educated with the skills and habits necessary for the 'world of work' and that the educational system was too distant from the needs of the economy.

PARALLEL MOVES IN THE US

A similar process had occurred in the US over a similar period of time. When Richard Nixon became President in 1968, it had been assumed that this signalled a move to the right. However, during Nixon's period of office, social programmes, including education, continued to enjoy some expansion. As in Britain, there were plans further to extend early childhood education through the Comprehensive Child Development Act. However, Nixon vetoed this plan, seeing it as committing the vast moral authority of the nation to socialistic measures. He favoured instead a Family Assistance Plan aimed at giving a basic minimum income to families. Although his measure was never fully implemented, it was seen as 'Nixon's Good Deed' (Burke and Burke, 1974).

Under President Carter, spending on social reforms still continued to rise and plans to expand both education and training continued apace. The Comprehensive Employment and Training Act of 1976, for example, opened up a range of new training initiatives, designed to extend educational opportunities, as did the Education of All Handicapped Children Act of 1975, which attempted to ensure equal protection under the law for all citizens. There were also measures to reduce inequalities in educational opportunities for racial minorities and women.

Nevertheless, in the 1970s the right, in the form of 'single issue' political pressure groups, was also becoming vocal in the US. Their arguments took three forms—one was critical of increased social spending and its impact on the fiscal behaviour of the states and another was critical of the kinds of educational expenditure which were still designed to achieve some measure of educational equity. A third argument raised the question of the content of schooling in terms of the kinds of subjects taught and books used, from moral and religious standpoints. These ideas were expressed both by individuals and by groups on the right. There was, however, no one coherent set of right-wing educational critiques. [. . .]

RETHINKING EDUCATION REFORMS

In Britain, too, the various right-wing critiques initially were not coherently articulated. Dale has argued that, in Britain, the Labour government's policies in the 1970s were:

> . . . a watershed in the post-War history of education . . . because the settlement enshrined in the 1944 Act was showing increasing signs of strain and breakdown . . . the nature of the problems facing the education system have (*sic*) changed so much that only the construction of a new settlement has been adequate to enable an effective response. (Dale, 1989, p. 105)

He goes on to argue that the response of the right was disjointed and complex, not straightforward and coherent. It involved a process of recasting the ideologies underpinning education and then restructuring the system, all taking place over a lengthy period of time from the mid 1970s to the late 1980s (Dale, 1989, pp. 105–21).

Dale identifies five different strands of Conservative thought that could be teased out of this attempt to revise and develop a New Right ideology, with various impacts upon educational policies and developments. He refers to them as 'the industrial trainers', 'the old Tories', 'the populists', 'the moral entrepreneurs' and the 'privatizers' (1989, pp. 80–9). He then asks 'what distillate of these five ingredients constitutes Thatcherism in education?' His argument is that the crucial factor that eventually, in the 1980s, created a coherent philosophy and policy was 'Mrs Thatcher's own personal political stand' (p. 89). [. . .] It remains to be seen quite what influence Thatcherism, as analytically distinct from the other notions of the New Right, had on the development of education reform.

By the end of the 1970s, the New Right or neo-conservatives were in the ascendance in both the US and Britain. In both, they blamed the political parties who had agreed to the 'bipartisan political consensus' on state intervention in social and educational policies for causing their country's serious economic decline and lack of international competitiveness (Guthrie and Pierce, 1990, p. 179). Both Thatcher (in May 1979) and Reagan (in November 1980) gained political office, in part, because of this critique of the failure of social-democratic policies, targeting education among other issues. [. . .] Nevertheless, by the end of the decade, both administrations had come to similar points in the transformation of their education systems from a commitment to equal opportunities to an emphasis on consumer or parental choice, seen as a way of raising academic standards.

THATCHERISM AND EDUCATION REFORM IN BRITAIN

In Britain, Thatcher came to power in May 1979 with a new right-wing platform, blaming social-democratic ideologies for Britain's economic failings. The aim of the New Right government was to reverse Britain's economic decline with new monetarist economic policies and reduced social intervention. Educational policies which aimed at equal opportunties were seen as part of the problem, too. However, the first Thatcher administration did not focus its energies on education reform directly; rather it dealt with it, according to Bull and Glendenning (1983, pp. 53–8), by stealth. It aimed to reduce spending on education, through various local fiscal controls and the reform of local government expenditure.

The three major pieces of educational legislation were all fairly limited in their scope. The first, passed in 1979, reversed the central government requirement that local education authorities (LEAs) reorganize their secondary schools on comprehensive lines. However, in the 14-year period of this policy, the majority of LEAs had already reorganized most of their secondary schools and were loath to undo what had been a costly and difficult process of educational change. However, the effects of the new Education Act were to produce some selective education in a few areas.

The second piece of legislation, the 1980 Education Act, borrowed extensively from the Labour government's draft legislation and a committee of inquiry into how schools should be governed especially in terms of the role of parents. The major aim of the legislation, therefore, was to make schools more open and accountable to the public and particularly parents. In this sense, the Labour government had anticipated the new right-wing mood, by its focus on the questions of accountability to parents.

The legislation, therefore, required schools and LEAs to make public both their 'planned admission levels' or entry numbers and their educational strategies and results. In other words, all schools had to produce both a prospectus and annual report on their achievements, especially in the area of examination results. It was argued that this would lead to parental pressure for improvement in educational standards. Indeed, parents apparently were given more rights, in three separate regards, through this legislation; first to choose schools, called parental preference; second to *complain* about procedures on an individual basis and third to be involved, through parental representation, on school governing bodies. [. . .] Parent governors came to be one of four types of governor in the first level of school management. However, the role of school governing bodies remained quite limited, and they were not a strong influence in the process of educational decision-making.

This piece of educational legislation, like its successors in 1981 for Scotland and for special education in England and Wales, was short on specification of curricular issues and more concerned with parental choice, rights and relationships in education. The third piece of legislation, the 1981 Education Act, was concerned to implement a report on children with special educational needs. It required all LEAs to produce a statement of need for each child's parents and to attempt to integrate all such children into mainstream educational provision. Here it was essentially concerned with the dual issues of parental rights and limited educational expenditures.

One of the main measures implemented from the 1980 Education Act signalled the shape of things to come (Dale, 1989). It concerned the redirection of educational expenditure across different types of schools. In the Education Act 1980, the government announced a modest diversion in public expenditure from state schools to individual children of academic ability who passed a selective test to an independent secondary school: if the child's parents were of low income, the state would pay the cost of the fees to the school. [. . .] This assisted places scheme widened the range and number of private independent schools which were eligible to participate. [. . .]

The second part of the Conservative policy, launched after Thatcher's re-election in May 1983, was the definite attempt to transform the welfare state by putting in place the idea of a market for social and educational provision, with parental/consumer choice its chief selling-point. Stuart Hall argued in 1983 that this process began to happen in the early 1980s:

> The right have temporarily defined the terms and won the struggle because they are willing to engage. For a brief period in the 1960s and 1970s the involvement of parents with the school was the left's most democratic trump card. The dismantling of this into 'parental choice' and its expropriation by the right is one of their most significant victories. They stole an idea designed to increase popular power in education and transformed it into the idea of an education supermarket.
>
> (Hall, 1983, p. 1)

By this stage it was no longer simply consumerism, but enabling parents as consumers to demand higher educational or academic standards. These ideas were presaged in the Conservative manifesto for the election in which the then Secretary of State for Education, Sir Keith Joseph, argued for 'the pusuit of excellence'. This theme took the direction of developing quality, rather than equality, in schools through schemes which attempted to differentiate both between teachers and between pupils. For instance, proposals for merit pay for teachers were mooted and new forms of assessment, through pupil profiles and records of achievement, were initiated. These, and changes in the system of examination to a composite examination at age 16, were intended to placate not only parents as consumers but also industrialists and employers, as were the introduction of new technical and vocational courses and qualifications.

However, although attempts were made to transform school curricula, these were not easily implemented because of the financial stringencies applied to schools at the same time. Thus teachers were continuously involved in action over their pay and conditions for a two-year period. [. . .] In this respect, the 1986 Education Act signalled the beginnings of the new, more coherent approach. It set limits to the kinds of subjects taught in schools, such as political and peace studies, aspects of multiculturalism and sex education. In other words, attempts were made to distinguish between education and indoctrination, on lines similar to those set out by a new group of right-wing pamphleteers (Scruton, Ellis Jones and O'Keefe, 1987). [. . .]

Parents were also afforded a more significant role in the running of schools, through revision to the system of governing bodies. Following the publication in 1984 of the Green Paper, *Parental Influence at School*, a lively debate ensued about the balance between parental and professional influences in the management of schools (Cullingford, 1985, p ix). [. . .]

The Green Paper differed from the kinds of proposals developed by the Taylor Committee in the central focus on parents, rather than a balance between parents, community and professionals. It greatly influenced the development of the legislation which gave parents a majority vote, and required the publication of annual reports from schools, and the holding of a school annual parents' meeting on business lines. This signalled the shifting lines in the reconstruction of an ideology.

A NEW ERA: EDUCATION REFORM BY THE RIGHT?

It was another year and another general election before 'the Thatcherite project' (to borrow Dale's phrase) in education came to full fruition in the form of one comprehensive piece of right-wing legislation (Young, 1991). It has been asked whether it required eight years to change the public ideological commitment from equality to quality in education. Did it also require eight years to transform the political and economic infra-structure to such an extent as to ensure the success of the educational legislation? Given the government's thorough-going commitment to a right-wing ideology, it is likely that this was the case. The then Secretary of State of Education, Kenneth Baker, introducing the new proposed legislation, stated how the bill was informed by the central tenets of Conservative education policy: 'I would sum up the bill's 169 pages in three words: standards, freedom and choice' (quoted in Hansard, 1987, December, column 780). [. . .]

The bill eventually became the Education Reform Act, known as ERA. It was heralded by Baker as creating a 'new era'. Indeed, the Act was unique in the history of British educational legislation in many senses: it covered both schools and higher education; it created parental choices; it allowed educational institutions to be removed from state financial control with impunity (David, 1989).

The key issue claimed by the government in the ERA was that of '*choice*': choice for parents over a range of different types of school and the creation of new ones (Johnson, 1990; Walford, 1990). The right's overt aim with these changes was to produce better educational standards, based upon individual parents' demands. First, parents could choose schools in the LEA based upon information supplied about courses, curricula and examination results. Schools would no longer be able artificially to limit the number of children admitted (as previously specified by the Education Act of 1980), but were to provide open enrolment. Secondly, parents of children currently in a school were offered a chance, through the school governing body, on which there was to be a majority of parent governors, to vote through a secret ballot to take the school out of local authority control. The school would then become a 'grant-maintained' school, supported by central rather than local government; but based upon the per capita amount of money the local authority had to spend upon the school. The grant would be taken from the local authority's revenues through the community charge and central government financial support to local authorities (Fitz and Halpin, 1990). Thirdly, parents of children of secondary school age could choose schools financed variously by special business sponsorship and central government, namely the city technology colleges (Walford and Miller, 1991). Fourthly, parents would also be able to choose private schools, entirely independent of the local authority, which could offer places to children whose parents do not have the financial means to afford the fees. The assisted places scheme was, from the 1980 Education Act, considerably widened to cover the majority of traditional independent and public schools (Edwards, Fitz and Whitty, 1989). In other words, the aim of the central government, in this educational policy, was to move the locus of decision-making about schools away from the state, but most especially local government, and back to individual parents, or the private family.

Part of the concern of the Tory government has been with the monopoly power of local authorities over decision-making in education, in particular that of ILEA, the Inner London Education Authority: hence the change to allow parents to get some schools to 'opt out' of local authority control and become grant-maintained schools. Even those schools which remained within the ambit of local authorities were to be less circumscribed by local government controls than hitherto. First they were given more powers to determine how to finance the schools, through the scheme of local financial delegation now known as local management of schools (LMS). Local authorities are required to determine, through a centrally prescribed formula, the average per capita spending on education in their area and to delegate to individual schools such finances as necessary to spend on their own complement of teachers and educational resources.

Thus local authorities were reduced to being more of a financial conduit than a decision-maker over the determination of educational resources. [...] However, for a time they also retained modest powers of inspection or advice. By the summer of 1992 the Education (Schools) Act 1992 had removed these powers. In other words, the key feature of the legislation was the financial autonomy of each educational institution. Moreover, each LEA was itself to be more controlled by external forces, through parallel moves to alter the funding of local government and central government's control of that. Thus it was intended that each educational institution become subject to the vagaries of the market and parental consumer choice.

Educational institutions were afforded the freedom to raise funds and control their expenditures within clear financial parameters, the explicit aim being to ensure that consumer demand by parents would determine the schools' styles of spending and power. [...]

A second key issue in the legislation was the designation of 'standards' through the specification, for schools, of a national curriculum and related specific assessment tasks or targets, as well as forms of age-related testing. Since the Second World War, there had been no agreed set of subjects to be taught to school-children, except those enjoined by external examinations.

Yet there was a consensus on what that core knowledge would entail, already clearly articulated by the Labour government in the mid 1970s. [...]

The subjects specified in the National Curriculum represented a very traditional view of education. This could be imputed even by the concept of 'national', with standards related to a traditional academic curriculum. This was clearly stated in the Hillgate Group's commentary:

> They can succeed ... only if the curriculum introduced by them is truly national. The attainment targets for history should ensure a solid foundation in British and European history, and should involve no concessions to the philosophy of the 'global' curriculum currently advocated by the multi-culturalists. Teachers of English must be obliged to impart a proper understanding of English grammar and of the written word together with some knowledge of the true monuments of our literature. (Hillgate Group, 1987, p. 9)

The traditional approach was further elaborated through specification of the kinds of modern languages considered appropriate, namely French, German, Spanish and Italian rather than either European or non-European languages related to minority ethnic groups in Britain, such as the Greek, Turkish or various Asian groups. Indeed, minority languages were specifically excluded. Bilingual education was encouraged only for Welsh speakers. In a previous government-sponsored inquiry into multicultural education, eventually published in 1985 after lengthy controversy, bilingual education in the languages of minority Asian groups especially had been rejected even in early childhood education as 'linguistically impoverishing' (Swann, 1985). [...]

The intention of the government, in the National Curriculum, was to inculcate a specifically British set of standards, related to an academic curriculum judged relevant to the more able children. The clear implication was that difference and diversity would be extolled rather than diminished. But no concessions were to be made to children from family circumstances where such quintessentially British experiences had been unknown before the experience of schooling. Rather they were expected to adapt to a specifically British form of education, valuing only traditional English subjects and knowledge, rather than appreciating the diversity and richness of the varied cultures from which British citizens are now drawn. The 'British' approach was further implied by changes in the legislation to ensure that religious education, and daily religious assembly, including the daily act of worship, were specifically Christian, because this was seen as the main religion of the country.

By the end of the 1980s, the educational system of England and Wales had been reformed so that it bore only a little resemblance to that created after the Second World War through the 1944 Education Act. The reforms had set in place educational institutions competing with each other for finances and for consumers or customers as parents and/or students, similar only in the requirement that the subjects taught within the institutions conform to the National Curriculum with its nationalistic emphasis. [...] Some LEAs had already begun to develop magnet schools, focusing on particular subjects within the required National Curriculum, in order to build up particular competencies, such as skills in science and technology. Many schools had begun the process of balloting parents on whether to become grant-maintained schools (Fitz and Halpin, 1991). Indeed by 1991 over 50 such schools had already begun (Fitz, 1991, personal communication). A number of city technology colleges had been established (the establishment of the first has been carefully documented by Walford and Miller, 1991). Local management of the schools that remained within the LEA ambit had also begun with a vengeance (Ball, 1990).

[...] By September 1991, a special Parent's Charter for Education had also been published. In that respect, parental rights to information about schools and their own children's progress and results in the context of wider performance would be mandatory. Moreover, parental governors would be given an even wider role in school decision-making through budgetary control and choice of inspection. On the other hand, testing would be simplified in order to produce national league tables of educational achievements, regardless of the school's socio-economic context, especially through national examination results. These notions were translated into an Education (Schools) Act which received royal assent in the spring of 1992. In essence, this afforded even more powers to parents and individual educational institutions, at the expense of nationwide educational standards, which had been achieved through the inspections of Her Majesty's Inspectorate. The aim has been further to extend parental choice of schools by creating a 'market' in educational provision. In the summer of 1992, a White Paper was published, proposing yet further schemes of parental choice and the abolition of local control of schools through LEAs.

[...] By the beginning of the 1990s, the whole approach to parent–school relations had shifted from one about how to ensure some measures of equity to how to ensure parental rights and responsibilities in order for individual parents to be able to influence each child's educational success in formal examination situations.

EDUCATION REFORM IN THE US

In the US, the same objectives of education reform have been pursued as in Britain. Indeed, it could be argued that Britain followed rather than led the US. Historically speaking, however, some of the actual US policy reforms occurred at a slightly later stage. Indeed, the complexities of the American political system, interwoven with the legal system, meant that national educational reforms were achieved by different means. Until the 1960s, the federal government had played a very limited part in educational provision, responsibility being largely at the state and school-district levels. However, a federal involvement in educational provision became part of the liberal agenda of the 1960s, particularly giving power to the federal Department of Health, Education and Welfare, to achieve some measures of fiscal or financial equity in educational provision by the individual states, and school districts. Reagan's ascendance to power, like Thatcher's, involved a critique of educational policies aimed at achieving equity and equality. One of Reagan's first aims was to reduce that federal role and to abolish the relatively new federal Department of Education. These goals were not easily achieved and the federal role continued, albeit in a different mode from that initially aimed at. It shifted to a concern to deal with public disquiet about the future of the nation's schools, especially the secondary schools and their curricula. [. . .]

In the 1980s, there were also several 'waves' of educational reform to deal with the perceived problems of schools failing to maintain US competitiveness. Guthrie and Pierce identified at least two waves but state that:

> The United States altered its education system in a far less comprehensive manner than the United Kingdom ... even though many national influences came to bear upon US education reform, actual statutory and regulatory changes had to proceed on a state-by-state basis.
>
> (Guthrie and Pierce, 1990, p. 191)

However, to the extent that is is possible to generalize, the first major wave focused on curriculum, the second on raising standards through parental choice and the third, in the Bush administration, on national goals (Boyd, 1991).

In the first place, the Reagan administration, like that of Thatcher, used massive cuts in public expenditure to try to reorient the school system. As Altbach (1985, p. 17) also notes, 'these cuts were particularly difficult, since many programs mandated by the federal government had to be maintained regardless of federal funding'. Federal legislation also continued to require many recent developments similar to those in Britain, such as 'the mainstreaming of handicapped students' by integrating them into regular classrooms with other students.

Secondly, Reagan's Secretary of Education appointed a national commission made up of America's corporate as well as educational elite to inquire into the question of 'Excellence in Education'. Its report, entitled *A Nation At Risk* and published in 1983, had a dramatic impact. It was followed by a spate of other reports from different agencies, a few research-based studies and wide public debate and discussion:

> President Reagan, accurately sensing public sentiment about education, rapidly associated his administration with the report and its recommendations. A wave of reform interest spread rapidly ... Public officials and political aspirants were quick to board the education reform band wagon.
>
> (Guthrie and Pierce, 1990, p. 196)

Altogether about a dozen major reports were produced, all with different approaches but essentially arguing for changes in schools and, given the notion that 'the nation [was] at risk', for a back-to-basics approach (Kelly, 1985, p. 31). [...] In addition, there were recommendations, as in Britain, for foreign-language instruction, relating the school curriculum to the perceived needs of industry and the improvement of the quality of teachers through merit pay. Such was the range of recommendations from these diverse but primarily business sources that it too was named a 'great education debate'. [...] However, the role of government and the courts in ensuring some measure of social justice and equality of educational opportunity for minorities, women and handicapped people had been reduced and reoriented.

The reports themselves produced a spate of responses. One conservative writer argued, in support of the first report's recommendations:

> In our time the public interest groups connected with education are so powerful that they can stop real reform ... Let us hope this will not be so, let us hope that the fifty state legislatures will take an easier path to reform. Let them ignore grandiose schemes to rebuild our public school system. Ask them for no new programs. Merely urge them to unleash the resources and power of citizens, teachers and principals, to rebuild a diverse and locally rooted set of public schools. Then, and only then, will Americans have educational institutions that can do what must be done: provide quality education to our children, who will carry on our glorious experience in self governance.
>
> (Hawkins, 1985, p. 45)

Indeed, these 'conservative' arguments about a reduced federal role—despite the counter-arguments also raised by the right, for a curriculum to reflect the needs of modern industry and technology to improve America's competitive edge—won out by the mid 1980s. Margaret Goertz, summarizing the education politics of the 1980s, has argued that:

> During the Reagan years, the federal government sought to influence

education policy with moral suasion rather than federal aid; to emphasize demonstration over intervention; and to decentralize the administration of federal programs. As the 1980s unfolded, abandonment of education by the federal government created a leadership as well as a financial vacuum ... the 1980s reform was dominated by business leaders and elected public officials. (Goertz, 1989, p. 5)

She goes on to note that:

... the absence of a broad consensus about the purpose of education led to a patchwork of state education programs to meet the demands of different and competing interests. (Goertz, 1989, p. 5)

She also notes that it was 'unique' in the politics of state education that education interest groups played a 'relatively unimportant role ... in the formulation of new state policies'. [...]

In 1986, the Carnegie Corporation issued another important report, entitled *A Nation Prepared*, focusing more on efforts to increase teacher professionalism, restructure schools and develop forms of school site management (Boyd, 1991).

President Reagan and his Secretary of Education, Terrance Bell, also began, in the second administration in 1985, to argue 'strongly in favour of business support of education to compensate for federal spending cuts particularly in the areas of vocational and adult education' (Useem, 1988, p. 21). Ray and Mickelson have commented that:

By 1987, more than 300 business-initiated studies about the quality and content of education, and suggestions for reform had been completed (Business Roundtable, 1988) ... Drawing on the corporate model in its recommendations for school reform, Kearns and Doyle's (1988) book *Winning the Brain Race: A Bold Plan To Make Our Schools Competitive* captured the strong socialization and restructuring themes of business leaders' current attempts.

Ray and Mickelson, 1989, p. 122)

The process was one of government reducing its role to be replaced by business leaders. But as Ray and Mickelson go on to suggest:

Towards the end of the 1980s, corporate leaders still directed their attention at the 'restructuring' of the educational system (Perry, 1988; Kearns and Doyle, 1988) but placed increasingly heavy emphasis on low-income and minority students. At the national level it is clear that the concerns of business leaders about education are directly linked with the productivity crisis, the growing inability of US business to maintain global market leadership, and, most recently, a domestic labour shortage which is

forcing businesses to hire workers previously labelled unemployable.
(Ray and Mickelson, 1989, p.122)

However, the process of educational reform in the US was very different from that in Britain. Given the evidence and ideas underpinning the voluminous national reports in the early to mid 1980s, the approach was one of continuing to reduce the federal and state role in educational provision, rather than of using central government, as in Britain, to insist on reduced spending. So very little legislation, compared to Britain, was attendant upon the spate of recommendations.

Indeed, the approach of the moral right in the US in the early 1980s may have been an object lesson for the neo-conservatives and the corporate and business elites (David, 1986). There were two relatively unsuccessful attempts to reorient aspects of the school curriculum through the Family Protection Act in the early 1980s, which was described by the *Congressional Quarterly* as a 'tidy wish list for the New Right' (David, 1986). The two key issues here were to control the content of school textbooks in terms of their delineation of sex roles and the nature of sex education. At the same time, the right also attempted to introduce school prayer and religious education into hitherto secular schools. However, all these issues were dealt with only cursorily by the federal government. The proposed legislation included the possibility of tuition tax credits for private schools, which was subsequently taken up in a number of states. Nevertheless, the legislation did not provide the new framework initially hoped for it.

So the dominant approach in the US in the 1980s under Reagan became that of fiscal restraint and moral persuasion rather than federal legal edict. [...] President Bush's policies could be considered as the 'third wave of education reform'. As Guthrie and Pierce note:

> Models for a national curriculum have been proposed, but adoption of such an idea has never previously been given serious consideration. However, in a virtually unprecedented Governors' 'Summit' meeting in September of 1989, President Bush first raised the idea of 'national standards' or 'national goals' for American schools. In his January 1990 State of the Union address, Bush proceeded further by specifying seven national goals.   (Guthrie and Pierce, 1990, p. 187)

Boyd also noted how these goals were not dissimilar to those specified in Britain, for a national curriculum, at the same time as implementing devolution in administration. By the end of the 1980s, decentralization and the reduction in the federal role appeared to have been relatively well achieved. On the other hand, the process of setting national standards had also begun.

CONCLUSIONS

In both Britain and the US, by the beginning of the 1990s, the right-wing goal of educational reform seems to have been accomplished, although by very different means. In Britain, the central government has played a key role in attempts to diversify the school system through parental-choice schemes to the extent that there no longer appears to be anything that could be graced with the term 'system'. In the US, it is the reduction in the federal role that has occasioned such decentralization to states and school districts, or schools themselves. Both countries have, in effect, created a range of types of school not wholly reliant on public funds and support. Moreover, in the US, the recommendations for a more defined school curriculum have not been implemented by legislation; rather, individual schools—private or public, parent-run or religious—have been encouraged to foster their own initiatives and developments. Most recently, however, Bush has set out a national framework. Originally the American approach was in marked contrast with Britain, where the main emphasis has been on the detailed specification of a national curriculum not only for state schools, but also for those which choose to opt out of the LEA system. The National Curriculum was also seen as a recommendation for the private, independent schools.

In Britain in the 1980s and early 1990s, the shift to the right has meant an emphasis in policy on diversity and difference, rather than the raising of educational standards. As the 1980s wore on and, especially as the ERA has been developed, school diversification to grant-maintained schools, city technology colleges and magnet schools has been pursued in preference to the National Curriculum. In other words, the aims of the right in their educational reforms have been to widen social differences between schools and therefore social inequalities. They may recreate major disparities between children on the basis of their parental socio-economic circumstances. Although there were major attempts from the 1950s to the 1970s to reduce socio-economic disparities between families through educational policies, all the social research has indicated the difficulties of so doing. Indeed, even British state schools or public education in the US continued to reproduce social inequalities despite differential resources. Policies aimed at diversity rather than equality are likely to build upon these socio-economic differences rather than reduce them.

In the US, the term 'risk' was used originally to illustrate the problems of American international competitiveness. But as Clark and Astuto have pointed out:

> The space between concern and risk is broad . . . The risk lies with poor children who may have meagre home support structures, are lagging far behind in school achievements, may be homeless, are often hungry, ill and can see little chance for a decent job . . . if you are a young Black parent-to-be in our nation's Capital, you can anticipate that your child will have one chance in forty of dying before or within one year after its

scheduled birth date (US Conference of Mayors, 1988, p. 53). That is 2½ times the national average. If the child survives, chances are one to three that s/he will live its childhood in poverty (*ibid*, p. 23). The chances are 50/50 that the child will not finish high school (State Education Performance, 1989) and nearly 50/50 that, if this is the case, the youngsters will be unemployed (Council of the Great City Schools, p. 22) ...

(Clark and Astuto, 1989, p. 16)

The risks of poverty, especially for minority children, increased at alarming rates in the US in the 1980s and, without federal intervention to reverse the trends, may be poised to continue. The Commission on Minority Participation in Education and American Life noted that by the year 2,000, 16% (21.8 million persons) of the US labour force will be non-white and one-third of all school-age children will be minorities. Yet right-wing politicians and their policy analysts have not attended to the potential consequences of these demographic shifts. Rather they have continued to try to develop diversity, ostensibly to raise standards. Indeed, most recently two such policy analysts, Chubb and Moe (1990) have argued that the waves of education reform have not gone far enough in creating markets in education. They advocate more such markets.

Education reforms as currently specified by the right in Britain and the US will contribute to trends towards diversity and difference, rather than equal educational opportunities. Such right-wing education reforms have already begun to produce a new era, which is far from committed to equal rights and opportunities. The polices of the 1990s, are predicated on individual competition, consumerism and educational inequalities. The new era may result in greater bifurcation of society into rich and poor. The Conservative policies of individuality, competitiveness and consumerism have already begun to create a patchwork of educational institutions in Britain. Chances for a good education will depend on parental socio-economic circumstances, area of residence, ability to make demands upon individual schools, as well as intellectual ability and the desire to be educated (Adler, Petch and Tweedie, 1989).

References

Adler, M., Petch, A. and Tweedie, J. (1989) *Parental Choice and Educational Policy.* Edinburgh: Edinburgh University Press.

Altbach, P. (1985) The great education 'crisis'. In P. Altbach, G. Kelly and L. Weis (eds) *Excellence in Education: Perspectives on Political Practice.* Buffalo, NY: Prometheus Books.

Ball, S. (1990) *Education, Inequality and School Reform: Values in Crisis.* Inaugural Lecture. London: King's College, 15 October.

Boyd, W. (1991) Some parallels between British and US education reforms. SIPS Seminar, Centre for Educational Studies, King's College, London University, 1 February.

Brown, P. (1990) The 'third wave': education and the ideology of parentocracy. *British Journal of the Sociology of Education* 11 (1), 65–85.

Bull, D. and Glendenning, C. (1983) Access to 'free' education: erosion by statute and stealth. In D. Bull and P. Wilding (eds) *Thatcherism and the Poor*. London: CPAG.

Burke, V. and Burke, V. (1974) *Nixon's Good Deed*. New York: Columbia University Press.

Chubb, J. and Moe, T. (1990) *Politics, Markets and America's Schools*. Washington, DC: Brookings Institution.

Clark, P. and Astuto, T. A. (1989) The disjunction of federal education policy and educational needs in the 1990s. In D. Mitchell and M. Goertz (eds) *Education Politics for a New Century: The 20th Anniversary Politics of Education Year Book*. Special issue of *Journal of Education Policy* 4 (5).

Cox, C.B. and Boyson, R. (eds) (1975) *Black Paper 1975: The Fight for Education*. London: J.M. Dent.

Cullingford, C. (ed.) (1985) *Parents, Teachers and Schools*. London: Royce.

Dale, R. (1989) *The State and Educational Policy*. Milton Keynes: Open University Press.

David, M.E. (1980) *The State, The Family and Education*. London: Routledge and Kegan Paul.

—(1986) Moral and maternal: the family in the right. In R. Levitas (ed.) *The Ideology of the New Right*. Cambridge: Polity Press.

—(1989) Education. In M. McCarthy (ed.) *The New Politics of Welfare: An Agenda for the 1990s*. London: Macmillan.

Edwards, T., Fitz, J. and Whitty, G. (1989) *The State and Private Education: An Evaluation of the Assisted Places Scheme*. Basingstoke: Falmer Press.

Fitz, J. and Halpin, D. (1990) Researching grant-maintained schools. *Journal of Education Policy* 5, (2), 167–80.

— (1991) From policy to workable scheme: grant-maintained schools and the DES. *International Studies in the Sociology of Education* 1, 129–53.

Goertz, M. (1989) Education politics for a new century: introduction and overview. In D. Mitchell and M. Goertz (eds) *Education Politics for a New Century: The 20th Anniversary Politics of Education Yearbook*. Special issue of *Journal of Education Policy* 4 (5).

Gregory, J. (1987) *Sex, Race and the Law: Legislating for Equality*. London: Sage.

Guthrie, J. W. and Pierce, L.C. (1990) The international economy and national education reform: a comparison of education reforms in the US and GB. *Oxford Review of Education* 16, 179–204.

Hall, S. (1983) 'Education in crisis'. In J. Donald and A. M. Wolpe (eds) *Is There Anyone Here From Education?* London: Pluto Press.

Hawkins, R.B. (1985) Strategy for revitalising public education. In J. Bunzel (ed.) *Challenges to America's Schools*. Oxford: Oxford University Press.

Hillgate Group (1987) *Reform of British Education: From Principles to Practice*. London: Claridge Press.

Johnson, D. (1990) *Parental Choice in Education*. London: Unwin Hyman.

Kelly, G. (1985) Setting the boundaries of debate about education. In P. Altbach, G. Kelly and L. Weiss (eds) *Excellence in Education: Perspectives on Political Practice*. Buffalo, NY: Prometheus Books.

Mishra, R. (1984) *The Welfare State in Crisis*. Brighton: Wheatsheaf.

Ray, F. and Mickelson, R. (1989) Business leaders and the politics of school reform. In D. Mitchell and M. Goertz (eds) *Education Politics for a New Century: The 20th Anniversary Politics of Education Yearbook*. Special issue of *Journal of Education Policy* 4 (5).

Scruton, R., Ellis Jones, A. and O'Keefe, D. (eds) (1987) *Education and Indoctrination*. Harrow: Education Research Centre.

Silver, H. (1990) *Education, Change and the Policy Process*. London: Falmer Press.

Swann, Lord (1985) *Education for All: The Report of the Committee of Inquiry into the Education of Children from Ethnic Minority Groups*. London: HMSO.

Useem, M. (1988) *Liberal Education and the Corporation*. New York: de Gruyter.

Walford, G. (1990) *Privatisation and Privilege in Education*. London: Routledge.

Walford, G. and Miller, H. (1991) *City Technology College*. Buckingham: Open University Press.

Young, H. (1991) *One of Us: A Biography of Margaret Thatcher*. London: Macmillan.

6 SOCIAL ORIGINS OF UNDER-ACHIEVEMENT AMONG SCHOOL-LEAVERS

LINDSAY PATERSON

Class differences in the proportions of school leavers who enter higher education hardly changed during the 1980s. In 1988, the proportion was 36% in the Registrar General's classes I and II, but only 6% in classes IV and V; the corresponding figures for 1978 were 30% and 3%.

This article investigates the source of the class gap. Class differences build up over successive selection points in the educational system—staying on beyond the minimum leaving age, achieving higher-education entry qualifications having stayed on, and deciding to apply to higher education having achieved these qualifications.

The Scottish education system has had the reputation of being open to children of any social background. If this reputation is to offer more than a vague hope to the majority of working-class young people, then access to higher education will have to be widened. The prospects of doing so depend both on broad social change and on action by higher education institutions.

Slow social change is causing the working class to contract; thus the proportion of the whole population affected adversely by social-class inequality is getting smaller. Similarly, a long-term consequence of social-democratic educational reforms in the 1960s and 1970s is that the average level of parental education is rising; parental education has an influence on young people's attainment and aspirations over and above any class influences.

Action by higher-education institutions can have most effect on the final stages of the selection process, by encouraging qualified school leavers to apply. Colleges and polytechnics are better at attracting working-class school-leavers than universities, and so the new Scottish Higher Education Funding Council might help the universities to learn from the colleges about how to expand the social base of their students. Unfortunately, however, the scope for action at this level can have at most only a small effect on the overall class inequalities, the most important sources of which remain staying on and attainment.

Investigating the reason why class is associated with attainment is not the purpose of this article. However, it is as well to have in mind during a

Source: Maguiness, H. (ed.) (1992) *Educational Opportunity: The Challenge of Under-achievement and Social Deprivation*. Local Government Centre, Paisley College.

description of class differences the two main types of explanation which have been given of how social disadvantage impinges on education.

The first is sheer lack of material resources (Mortimore and Blackstone, 1982)—pre-eminently inadequate facilities for study at home, and the expense of staying on in full-time education after age 16.

The second is more problematic. Bernstein (1962) has argued that people can lack cultural as well as material resources, and that the two tend to go together. Rosen (1972) has pointed out, however, that Bernstein does not show that working-class people are culturally deprived. Nevertheless, if success in the educational system depends as much on agility in gaining credentials as on cognitive ability (Collins, 1979), then children of parents who themselves lack educational qualifications might lack access to important relevant experience.

A more subtle version of both these explanations is that teachers might have low expectations of children from materially or culturally deprived homes, and thus induce them to perform less well than they are able to.

DATA AND MEASURES

The data comes from the Scottish School Leavers Surveys, which have been conducted every two years since 1979 by the Centre for Educational Sociology and the Scottish Education Department (Tomes, 1988). For investigating pupils who have passed at least one Higher, surveys exist also from 1977, 1973, 1971 and 1963. Questionnaires were sent by post to random samples of leavers from all Scottish schools (both public and private) in the spring after they left; questions were asked about the experience of school, about transitions to post-school destinations, and about family background. The sampling fraction was mostly 10%, but in 1981 and 1977 it was 37%, in 1973 and 1971 it was 20%, and in 1963 it was 65%. Response rates are high—around 80%—and weighting is used to compensate for the remaining non-response. Therefore, within the limits of random-sampling error, the surveys give an accurate picture of the Scottish education system at the transition from school.

Social class is measured in this article mainly by the Registrar General's class of the father's occupation (OPCS, 1970; 1980). This is not fully satisfactory. It suffers from a lack of a theoretical sociological basis (Marsh, 1986), but the surveys have not collected enough information to enable us to use a more sociologically coherent classification. An advantage of the Registrar General's scheme is, however, that it is familiar: in particular, because it is an official classification, descriptions in terms of it might be more persuasive to government and official bodies than would other measures. Moreover, any class differences which show up on this scale would probably be even larger on a more satisfactory one.

A summary of the class categories is as follows; their distribution among fathers of the respondents in the surveys over the decade 1978–88 is shown in Figure 6.1.

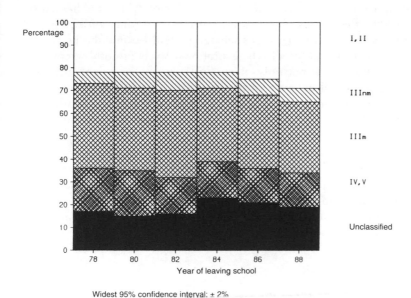

FIGURE 6.1 Composition of school leaving population, by Registrar General's class of father's occupation

I and II   Professional and managerial (for example, doctors, lawyers, teachers, managers)
IIInm   Skilled non-manual (for example, clerks, shop assistants)
IIIm   Skilled manual (for example, bricklayers, coal-miners)
IV, V   Semi-skilled and unskilled manual (for example, bus-conductors, postmen, porters, labourers)
Unclassified   No information (mostly fathers who have been unemployed for a lengthly period of time).

The '95% confidence interval' gives a rough idea of how sampling error might have affected the proportions and shows that the proportions in the diagram are accurate to within plus or minus 2%. For example, the proportion in classes I and II in 1988 is estimated to be 29%, and so we can say with a fair degree of certainty that the true proportion in these classes among the population of all school leavers is between 27% and 31%. (Similar indications of sampling variability are given with each figure throughout this article.)

Father's occupation is used, rather than a combination of mother's and father's, because a high proportion (up to 30%) of the respondents did not report a paid occupation for their mother. A better way of investigating the influence of the mother is to use other measures (Paterson, 1990), which are in any case important in their own right. Three will be mentioned—the effect of belonging to a one-parent family (the majority of which are headed by a woman), the effect of the father being unemployed (one consequence of which often is that the mother earns whatever small income the household has), and—most important of all—the educational levels of both parents.

Class is a characteristic not only of families, but also of neighbourhoods. A brief description will be given of the effect of living in a deprived neighbourhood, over and above the effect of belonging to a deprived family.

The gender of the young people themselves will also be mentioned, but mainly to point out that class differences are very similar for males and females.

Information on small ethnic groups is not reliably available from national surveys such as the School Leavers' Survey, and so unfortunately nothing can be said here about ethnic differences.

Higher education is defined by the Scottish Education Department (SED, 1990). Broadly, it can be thought of as a course at HNC level or above.

CLASS DIFFERENCES

Primary and early secondary

Class differences start at a very early age, and have a cumulative effect throughout primary and secondary school (Mortimore and Blackstone, 1982; Bondi, 1991). Even for pupils of similar academic attainment on entry to secondary school, there is a class gap in attainment in public examinations at age 16 (Willms, 1986; Paterson, 1990). This is one reason why schemes for encouraging more working-class pupils into higher education have to intervene at least as early as second year in secondary school.

In this article, however, only the class differences which have their effect from fourth year onwards are described in detail.

Staying on in school

The first hurdle to be overcome is to stay on at school beyond the minimum age; those who leave miss the main opportunity to sit Higher grade examinations, and so miss also the main opportunity to enter higher education. Figure 6.2 shows the proportion in each class who stayed on voluntarily beyond the minimum leaving age, over the decade 1978–1988. 'Staying on' is defined in Figure 6.2 as being still in school by Easter of fifth year: this definition excludes the large group who are forced to stay on to Christmas of fifth year because they are not yet aged 16 at the beginning of the fifth year (Robertson, 1990a). In each survey year, staying-on rates are highest in classes I and II, intermediate in class III (non-manual), and lowest for the manual and unclassified groups.

These differences in staying-on are partly attributable to class differences in attainment in Ordinary (O) grade or Standard (S) grade examinations. But, even among people with similar attainment in fourth year, there are class differences in staying-on rates. Thus, in 1988, among pupils with three or more awards at levels 1–3 in O or S grade, the proportion staying on was 90% in classes I and II, but only 75% averaged across the other classes; among pupils with two or fewer such awards, the staying-on proportions were 40% for classes I and II, but only 19% on average for the rest.

McPherson, Raffe and Robertson (1990) have argued that pupils are encouraged to stay on at school by the Highers examination, because it does not require such a commitment of time as does, for instance, the two-year A levels which are used in England and Wales. It is possible that a modified form of this argument applies especially to working-class students. If they are inclined to doubt their own abilities (and we will see below that there is evidence from applications to higher education that they do), then committing themselves to the lesser hurdle represented by Highers—particularly spread over both fifth and sixth years—might be less deterring than would the more formidable A level. A committee of the Scottish Office Education Department, under Professor John Howie, is currently reviewing the Higher. Any reform which removed the psychological advantage of stepped progression after fourth year might tend to depress working-class staying-on more than that of the middle-class.

Influences on staying on are investigated thoroughly by Robertson (1990a).

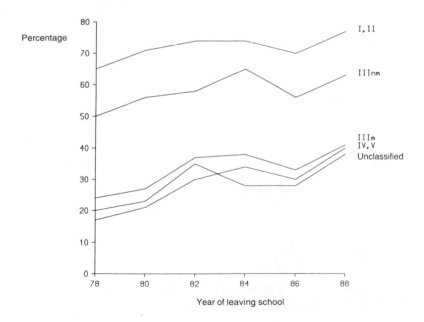

Widest 95% confidence interval: ± 2%

FIGURE 6.2 Proportion staying on to end of fifth year or after, by Registrar General's class of father's occupation.

Qualifying for higher education

The next hurdle is to pass enough Highers to have a reasonable chance of entering higher education. Figure 6.3 shows the proportion who passed three or more Highers, among those who stayed on. Possessing three Highers is officially regarded as the minimum required for entering higher education (SED, 1990). Although it is possible to enter with fewer, the class patterns are no different if the cut-off is taken as two Highers (or, for that matter, four Highers). Again, the classes I and II come out best, followed by III (non-manual), and then the rest. Combining Figures 6.2 and 6.3, we find that the net proportion qualifying has been increasing, but that there is no sign of the class gap diminishing. In 1978, the proportion of all leavers (whether from fifth year or earlier) gaining three or more Highers was 41% for classes I and II, and 8% for classes IV and V; in 1988, the proportions were 46% for I and II, and 10% for IV and V.

Qualifying for higher education is investigated thoroughly by Burnhill, Garner and McPherson (1988).

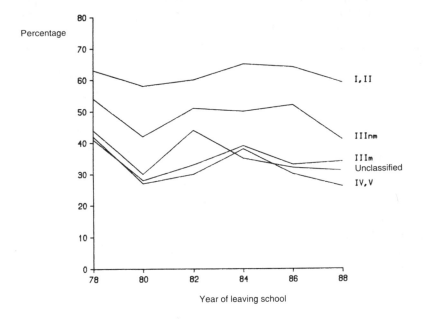

FIGURE 6.3 Proportion passing three or more Highers among those who stay on, by Registrar General's class of father's occupation

Applying to higher education

It might be thought that the achievement of three or more Highers would finally be enough to overcome any remaining social-class differences, but unfortunately not. Figure 6.4 shows the proportions applying for higher education courses, among those who have passed three or more Highers. Once again, although the gap is now narrower, we see classes I and II at the top and usually IV and V at the bottom. (The apparent widening of the gap in the late 1980s is due to a widening of the class gap in attainment at school: see Paterson (1992).) A similar gap appears even if highly qualified pupils are investigated—for example, those with five or more Highers.

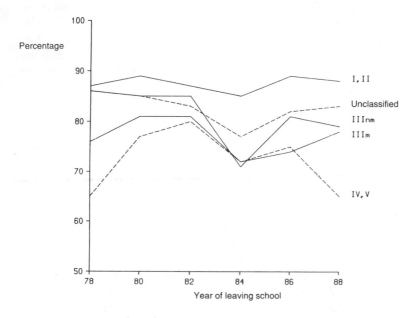

Widest 95% confidence interval: ± 8%

FIGURE 6.4 Proportion applying for any higher education course amongst those with three or more Highers, by Registrar General's class of father's occupation

Probable reasons for the reluctance even of qualified working-class pupils to apply include doubts about their own abilities, lack of encouragement by their family and school, financial pressures to start earning as soon as possible, and being deterred by an image of higher education as being socially remote. Evidence for social remoteness is seen if we compare applying to university with applying to higher-education courses at colleges or polytechnics: the class gap in applications among qualified school leavers is smaller for colleges and polytechnics, which have recently drawn a much higher proportion of their students from local, often working-class, areas than have the universities. This difference between universities and colleges is greater for pupils with three or four Highers than for those with five or more, and so the social group that seems to be most deterred from applying to university is that consisting of working-class pupils with moderate qualifications. Decisions about applying are investigated further by Paterson (1992).

Entering

The one selection point at which there are no class effects is entry by people who do apply. Thus, for example, people with four Highers who apply are equally likely to be accepted whatever class group they come from. This shows that there is no overt discrimination by higher-education institutions. The class differences arise because of the earlier selections that we have been looking at. But higher-education institutions cannot be absolved from responsibility, because they can influence pupils' decisions to apply, and possibly also earlier decisions such as to stay on at school.

Net class differences

Putting together the class differences at all these hurdles, we get Figure 6.5, which shows the proportion entering higher education among all leavers from each class. The familiar pattern dominates: I and II have the highest proportions, the small group III (non-manual) is next highest, and the rest are lowest.

The relative importance of the successive selections can be assessed by graphing the proportion who survive each hurdle: for 1988, this is shown in Figure 6.6. Thus, among all leavers in classes I and II, the proportion who stay on is 77%, the proportion who pass three or more Highers is 46%, the proportion who apply is 40%, and the proportion who enter is 36%. The vertical gap between the lines at the right-hand end is the same as the vertical gap for 1988 in Figure 6.5. We can see from Figure 6.6 that the first two selection points—staying-on and then qualifying—account for the biggest portion of the eventual class gap.

OTHER SOCIAL INEQUALITIES

Unemployment

There is an effect of unemployment, over and above the effect of class. For example, in 1988, the proportion gaining three or more Highers in classes I and II was 46% where the father was employed, but only 39% where he was not; the proportions for classes IV and V were 11% and 7%.

One-parent families

Likewise, there is an effect of being from a one-parent family, over and above the effect of class. In 1988, the proportion gaining three or more Highers in classes I and II was 46% for families with two parents, but only 35% for

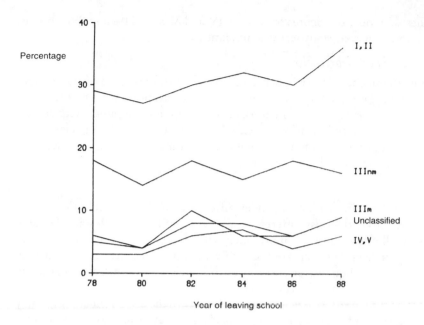

Widest 95% confidence interval: ± 2%

FIGURE 6.5 Proportion entering only higher education by Registrar General's class of father's occupation

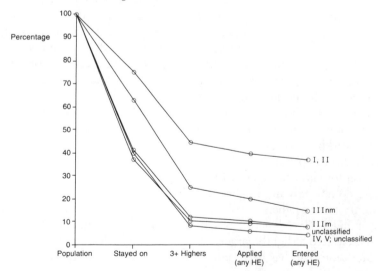

Widest 95% confidence interval: ± 4%

FIGURE 6.6 Proportion surviving beyond various levels, by Registrar General's class of father's occupation for 1988 school leavers

families with one; the figures for classes IV and V were 11% and 9% (this last being not, however, statistically significant).

Neighbourhood deprivation

School attainment is lower in deprived areas, not only because of the poverty of individual families, but also because of the deprivation of the whole neighbourhood. For example, in Fife in the early 1980s, among pupils with similar attainment at the end of primary school, and from similar family-class backgrounds, the gap in O-grade attainment between the most and the least deprived neighbourhoods was about two passes.

Gender

Although there are significant gender differences at all of the selection points discussed above, the class differences are very similar for males and females. Thus, in all classes, girls are more likely than boys to stay on and pass three or more Highers, but then are less likely to apply. The net result is that, in all social class, school-leaver entry rates to higher education are now roughly the same for males and females.

There is, however, a relevant gender difference in the classes concerning entry to non-advanced further education, which might have some consequences for higher education (SED, 1991). We saw earlier that there were class differences in staying-on rates in school at each level of fourth-year attainment. Around an extra 5% of the age group enter full-time further education immediately after the minimum leaving age (Raffle and Courteney, 1988). When we include this—so that we are looking at staying on in any full-time education—the class differences for boys remain much the same: at each level of fourth-year attainment, staying on in full-time education in social classes I, II and III (non-manual) is about 5–10% higher than in the other groups. But the class gap for girls is much greater at low levels of attainment than at high levels: it is about 15–20% for those who do not subsequently pass any Highers at school, but only 5–10% for those who do. Thus entering non-advanced further education seems to be notably more attractive to low-attaining middle-class girls than to low-attaining working-class girls.

It is unlikely that this pattern for low-attaining girls has a large effect on female class differences for entry to higher education, precisely because it is restricted to those who do not pass any Highers at school. Nevertheless, they do have the opportunity to sit Highers at college, and so it is possible that the greater propensity of middle-class than of working-class girls to enter futher education at age 16 could lead to a slightly larger class gap among girls in eventual entry to higher education than has been described for direct school-leaver entry.

PROSPECTS FOR NARROWING THE CLASS DIFFERENCES

Although the class gap remained almost unchanged in the 1980s, there are reasons for cautious optimism that it might narrow in the 1990s.

The first three reasons have to do with slow social change, broadly stemming from the success in Scotland of the educational reforms of the 1960s and 1970s. The main features of these reforms were the comprehensive reorganization of secondary education, the consequent reforms in courses for the age-group 14–16, and the expansion of higher education. A result of these reforms is that, among school-leavers in the 1990s, the proportion of parents who have more than the minimum amount of education is growing for successive school-year cohorts; this has especially benefited parents—that is, school-leavers in the 1970s—who themselves came from working-class origins (McPherson and Willms, 1987). The three reasons for optimism stem from this.

First, the middle class is getting larger as a proportion of the whole population (see Figure 6.1). The most basic explanation of this is that working-class fertility has been falling faster than middle-class fertility, partly because of rising levels of education among working-class parents. For example, the average family size of school leavers in classes IV and V was 3.9 in 1978 and 3.3 in 1988, a drop of 0.6; the corresponding drop for classes I and II was only 0.4, from 3.3 to 2.9. Between generations, this class difference in changes in fertility tends to reduce the proportion of the working class in the whole population, because there is not enough downward social mobility among middle-class children to cancel out the falling working-class birth-rate.

There is another explanation of why the middle class is growing, and this is the second reason for optimism. Even within social classes, the parents' educational levels have an effect on the attainment of young people, and therefore on their chances of moving into the middle class. The effect of having a parent who stayed on beyond the minimum age of 15 is illustrated in Figure 6.7, for class groups I and II and IV and V. (The pattern for other classes is similar.) For each of these groups, there was an advantage associated with having a parent educated beyond the minimum. Some of the working-class children who benefited from this advantage in the 1960s and 1970s will have been able to use their greater education to move into middle-class jobs, and so will appear among the middle-class parents of the late 1980s and 1990s.

This contraction of the working class implies that, although the gap in attainment between the class groups has not narrowed, the proportion of the population which is adversely affected by social-class effects is falling. This point is ignored by several English writers on the ultimate effects of the comprehensive reforms (for example, Heath, 1990). If one of the main effects of a social reform is to reduce the size of the previously disadvantaged group—whether by causing its birth-rate to fall, or by allowing its children to move out of the group—then not to take account of that, and to look only at the remaining members of the group, is to have only a partial view of how political action can bring about social change.

The third reason for optimism is that the effects of the rise in parental edu-

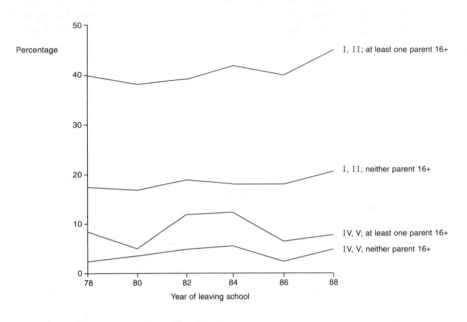

FIGURE 6.7 Proportion entering any higher education, by Registrar General's class of father's occupation and parental education (classes I, II and IV, V only)

cation are already apparent at the first hurdle mentioned in the section on class differences—namely, staying on beyond the minimum leaving age. The class gap in Figure 6.2 is less in 1988 than in 1978 (even though still large): the staying-on rate rose from 65% to 77% for classes I and II, but much more strongly for IV and V, from 17% to 40%.

All political parties now want to encourage the overall staying-on rate to rise further. This is almost certain to lead to a further narrowing of the class gap, because the middle-class rate is already so high that most of any overall increase is likely to be taken up by the working class.

These first three reasons for optimism affect the most important segment of Figure 6.6—the first, and possibly the second, hurdles. By contrast, the action open in the short term to individual higher-education institutions can affect mainly the less important last two hurdles, and we have already seen that the last hurdle (being admitted having applied) is not a source of social-class differences. Therefore, institutions have only one short-term influence open to them—encouraging qualified pupils to apply. The new Scottish Higher Education Funding Council is expected to increase competition among institutions for qualified students (DES, 1991); hence it is in each institution's interest to target those qualified working-class students who do not currently apply, because the shortfall among them is greater than for the qualified middle class (Figure 6.4). The most cost-effective way of doing this is probably by targeting schools in deprived areas, and by persuading pupils there that higher education is not beyond their abilities and is not necessarily socially remote; however, this strategy would miss working-class pupils in non-deprived schools, a group that is probably growing because of the parental-choice legislation of 1981. The likelihood that institutional self-interest (if nothing else) will lead to this targeting of qualified working-class pupils is a fourth reason for optimism.

Beyond that, higher-education institutions have to look further back in the schools, to encourage working-class pupils to stay on and to pass the necessary Highers. The colleges are already better at attracting working-class students than the universities, as Figure 6.8 shows. (Because we are now looking only at students who enter higher education, we can take the picture back to 1962.) Although there is a lot of sampling fluctuation, we can see that the universities broadly have a lower proportion from groups IV, V and unclassified

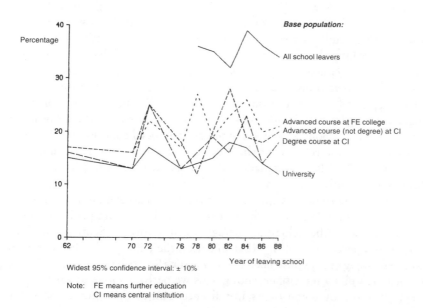

FIGURE 6.8 Proportion with fathers in Registrar General's groups IV, V or unclassified (FE means further education; CI means central institution)

than the colleges. The new unified framework for Scottish higher education might allow the universities to learn from the experience of the colleges. It is possible, for example, that the colleges encourage working-class entry by admitting students to HNCs and HNDs with a mixture of Highers and other qualifications (recently National Certificate modules); evidence for this is that the differences among the sectors in the proportion of working-class students is greater for students with four or fewer Highers than for those with five or more. The prospect of this transfer of experience from colleges to universities is the fifth reason for optimism.

However, all sectors still have a long way to go, as the line at the top of Figure 6.8 shows (from 1979 onwards): the proportion of working-class students even in the colleges falls far short of the proportion among school-leavers as a whole.

The final reason for some optimism has to do with entry by people aged under 21 who do not come directly from school; such entry perhaps shares some of the characteristics of older-ages entry. Robertson (1990b) has shown that, in session 1988–89, around 7% of entrants to higher education who had been in fifth year two years previously had acquired their entrance qualifications in further education, not school. He showed, moreover, that this route was more common among working-class than among middle-class students: for example, of direct entrants from school, over 56% were from classes I and II, and under 17% from IV and V; but, of indirect entrants via further education, only 35% were from classes I and II, and as many as 37% from IV and V. Those higher-education courses which look to local non-advanced courses for their students are likely, therefore, to attract a relatively high proportion of working-class students. They are perhaps most likely to do so if the non-advanced courses are in the same institution as the higher-education course itself, so that transfer does not entail a change of institution.

There are, therefore, some reasons for optimism. But the slowness of social change stemming from earlier decades is a reminder that we should not be hasty in our evaluation of policies which try to equalize social changes. The fruits of the social-democratic reforms of the 1960s and 1970s did not ripen until the Thatcherite 1980s. The maintenance of a broad social-democratic consensus in Scotland probably helped, and probably will for the time being prevent any reversal of the trend toward equalization, but to accelerate the trend will require more than a defence of the status quo, and therefore probably more than can ever again be achieved through an un-reformed Scottish administration. It is a perception of this that underlies the educational agenda which various reforming groups have been preparing for a Scottish parliament (STUC, 1991). It is as well to remember, though—as we perhaps move towards a parliament—that the outcome of its initial enthusiasm might not be seen for another 20 years.

Acknowledgements

The work for this article was supported by the UK Economic and Social Research Council (ESRC) through its funding of the Centre for Educational Sociology (CES) as a Designated Research Centre (ESRC grant number C00280004). The surveys from which the data have been supported by the Scottish Education Department (SED), the ESRC (formerly the Social Science Research Council), the Training Agency (formerly the Manpower Services Commission), the Industry Department for Scotland, and the Department of Employment. Additional support has been received from Fife, Grampian, and Tayside Regional Councils, and from the Western Isles Council. The surveys were conducted either by the CES or jointly by the CES and the SED.

References

Bernstein, B. (1962) Social class, linguistic codes, and grammatical elements. *Language and Speech* 5, 221–40.

Bondi, E. (1991) Attainment at primary school: an analysis of variation among schools. *British Educational Research Journal* 17 (3), 203–17.

Burnhill, P., Garner, C. and McPherson, A. (1988) Social change, school attainment, and entry to higher education, 1976–1986. In D. Raffe (ed.) *Education and the Youth Labour Market* pp. 66–99. Basingstoke: Falmer Press.

Collins, R. (1979) *The Credential Society*. New York: Academic Press.

DES (Department of Education and Science) (1991) *Higher Education: A New Framework*. London: HMSO.

Heath, A. F. (1990) Educational reform and changes in the stratification process in Great Britain. In A. Leschinsky and K. U. Mayer (eds) *The Comprehensive School Revisited: Evidence from Western Europe*, pp. 92–110. Frankfurt: Peter Lang.

McPherson, A., Raffe, D. and Robertson, C. (1990) *Highers and Higher Education*. Edinburgh: Centre for Educational Sociology.

McPherson, A. and Willms, J. D. (1987) Equalisation and improvement: some effects of comprehensive reorganisation in Scotland. *Sociology* 21, 509–39.

Marsh, C. (1986) Occupationally-based measures of social class. In A. Jacoby (ed.) *The Measurement of Social Class*. Proceedings of a Social Research Association Conference.

Mortimore, J. and Blackstone, T. (1982) *Disadvantage and Education*. London: Heinemann.

OPCS (Office of Population Censuses and Surveys) (1970) *Classification of Occupations, 1970*. London: HMSO.

—(1980) *Classification of Occupations, 1980*. London: HMSO.

Paterson, L. (1990) *Socio-economic Status and Educational Attainment: A Multidimensional and Multi-level Study*. Edinburgh: Centre for Educational Sociology.

—(1992) The influence of opportunity on aspirations among prospective university entrants from Scottish schools, 1970–1988. *Journal of the Royal Statistical Society, Series A* 155 (1), 37–60.

Raffe, D. and Courteney, G. (1988) 16–18 on both sides of the border. In D. Raffe (ed.) *Education and the Youth Labour Market*, pp. 12–39. London: Falmer.

Robertson, C. (1990a) *Participation in Post-compulsory Schooling in Scotland*. Edinburgh: Centre for Educational Sociology.

—(1990b) *Routes to Higher Education in Scotland.* Edinburgh: Centre for Educational Sociology.

Rosen, H. (1972) *Language and Class.* Bristol: Falling Wall Press.

SED (Scottish Education Department) (1990) *Higher-education Projections for Scotland.* Statistical Bulletin no. 8/J1/1990. Edinburgh: HMSO.

—(1991). *School Leavers' Destinations.* Statistical Bulletin Edn/E1/1991/8. Edinburgh: HMSO.

STUC (Scottish Trades Union Congress) (1991) *A Power for Change: An Agenda for a Scottish Parliament.* Glasgow: STUC.

Tomes, N. (1988) Scottish surveys since 1977. In D. Raffe (ed.) *Education and the Youth Labour Market,* pp. 266–73. Basingstoke: Falmer Press.

Willms, J. D. (1986) Social class segregation and its relationship to pupils' examination results in Scotland. *American Sociological Review* 51, 224–41.

7 EDUCATIONAL INSTITUTIONS OR EXTENDED FAMILIES? WOMEN'S COLLEGES IN THE LATE NINETEENTH AND EARLY TWENTIETH CENTURIES

ELIZABETH EDWARDS

This article is set in the context of recent scholarship concerning the development of higher education for women in nineteenth-century England. More particularly, I am concerned to build on the insights of Purvis, Dyhouse and Vicinus to show first how the domestic ideology of the Victorian home was recreated in the new institutional setting of women's colleges, and second the difficulties that the principals of these colleges faced in reconciling their public 'masculine' authority with the private needs of their own femininity. Further, I shall use the insights of feminist post-structuralism to illuminate this 'new history' of gender, since feminist post-structuralism enables us to re-examine the existing historical record and to interrogate texts in a totally new way. For instance, I shall show not only how gender discourses can be translated from one context and transformed into another, but also how the meaning of these discourses is altered by relabelling existing practice to conform with new ideas. Informal and unpublished records, like personal reminiscences and oral testimony, gain a new significance in enabling us to tease out, by analysis of the detail of personal experience, the processes of gender formation. (See Pedersen, 1987; Fletcher, 1980; Purvis, 1981; Dyhouse, 1987; Vicinus, 1986, Chapters 4 and 5. For a fuller account of recent developments in the theorization of gender and feminist post-structuralism, see Weedon, 1987; Connell, 1987. For discussion on the 'new history' of gender, see Scott, 1986.)

I shall first discuss how the discourses of social practice and family organization in the Victorian middle-class home were translated from their domestic setting and transformed to provide new meanings in the institutional context of women's colleges. The translation and transformation of these domestic and familial discourses were relatively straightforward; but the construction of the new role of woman principal from the discourses of Victorian middle-class femininity was always highly problematic. In the second part of the article I shall examine the difficulties that women principals faced in constructing their dual

Source: Abridged from 'Educational institutions or extended families? The reconstruction of gender in women's colleges in the late nineteenth and early twentieth centuries', *Gender and Education* (1990) Vol. 2, No. 1, pp. 17–35.

gender role as both father and mother of the institutional families that they served. Finally, I shall attempt to decode the homoerotic friendships that some principals formed in order to express the emotional and sexual needs of their own femininity.

Whilst feminist ideas, such as the right to privacy, personal development and a room of one's own, were by no means absent from women's colleges, many of the prevailing discourses evolved out of the conventions and practices of the Victorian middle-class home. At Homerton College, for instance, students were actually organized into families. Each first-year student was allotted her own 'mother' from among the second-year students. Mothers supervized their daughters' socialization into college life, and acted generally as their mentors and friends. Similarly, when daughters entered their second year, they in turn became mothers to the next generation of students. This replication of domestic family relationships in an institutional setting was an effective method of helping students, many of whom had never been away from home before, to settle into the new environment of college life. A student in 1915, for example, welcomed the system enthusiastically, and interestingly recognized that this re-creation of a mother/daughter relationship in the institutional setting of a women's college involved mothers in paternal as well as maternal duties:

> The family system goes a great way here. To feel that there is one in the college to whom you belong, one who is to be your 'mother' as a helper and guide makes you feel that Homerton is just a huge home and you yourself are one of the big family . . . Just as you would go to the head of your family for advice, so here you go to the 'mother' for information.
> (*Homertonian*, May 1915, p. 6)

This mother/daughter relationship created a discourse that permeated all levels of social organization in the college. At the individual level, mothers would take their daughters to church[1] and 'to see all the picturesque sights of the town' (*Homertonian*, December 1904, p. 1128). The familial bond was further cemented by the performance of the small domestic services that were customary between mother and daughter in the middle-class home. One student, writing in the college magazine, declared that when she was a daughter 'all my spare moments were devoted to the service of my "mamma" in tidying her room, getting her tea, etc.'. Similarly, now she herself was a mother 'we make the tea for our children and take them for a constitutional afterwards' (*Homertonian*, September/October 1905, pp. 1266–7).

Mother/daughter pairs frequently joined together to form larger family groups. These extended families would organize cycling trips[2] and birthday parties for their members.[3] Friendships forged within Homerton families could last a lifetime[4]; moreover, the fact that these relationships were formed within a context that was both familial and institutional gave additional legitimacy to friendships between girls from different social backgrounds, which might not have been possible within the confines of the middle-class home.

At an institutional level, the relationship between the two generations at Homerton was inscribed in the routines of the college's social calendar. Mothers and daughters took it in turns to host social events. In January 1904, for example, it was the college mothers who arranged a dance for their daughters, and 'our mothers presented us with flowers and programmes and at the appointed time piloted us to the dining hall' (*Homertonian*, January 1904, p. 993). Next term it was the daughters' turn to host an entertainment for the mothers; this included a performance of Tennyson's *Foresters* followed by dancing (*Homertonian*, May 1904, p. 1034).

The family ideology of the college was further enhanced by the invention of tradition in the form of the annual Ceremony of Carols at Christmas time, and the festivities of May Day. Although both these ceremonies had a symbolism that went beyond a domestic context, they can be read as surprise and ritualized 'treat' which college mothers provided for their daughters to celebrate special occasions. Such was the Ceremony of Carols when, on the last night of the Christmas term, second year students (mothers), clad in dressing gowns and carrying candles, sang their way round all the rooms and corridors of the college between the hours of midnight and one o'clock.[5] Informal carol singing on Christmas Eve around the Christmas tree in the middle-class home had thus been transformed by its institutional setting into a ceremony that not only underlined the intimacy of college family life but also bore witness to the seriousness and spiritual purpose of the college community. [...]

The May Day ceremony, which was a re-creation of the ancient festivities of May Day, owed its revival in the context of women's colleges to John Ruskin: for Ruskin had created a May Day ceremony for Whitelands Training College back in the 1840s, when the college began its tradition of electing a May Queen annually from among the student body (Grier, 1937; see also Dixon, 1989). At Homerton the May Day ceremony was constructed as a gift by college seniors (mothers) to the juniors (daughters), and it made an indelible impression on many students:

> May morning is unforgettable. The college hall was gay with bunches of cowslips, one by each plate. At prayers Miss Allan read, as only she could, from the *Song of Solomon* the passage that begins: 'Rise up my love, my fair one, and come away'. Then after breakfast the finest singer went with her accompanist to the piano, and sang the May morning song: 'Come out, come out my dearest dear, Come out and greet the May'. How surprised and delighted were the juniors, from whom the secret had been kept. The privilege of going out early to pick the cowslips was handed down from generation to generation of seniors. Later in the day the flowers were sent to a London hospital.
>
> *Homerton Roll News* (1987–8, p. 32; student, 1906–8, recalling her memories in 1957)

This ritual functioned at several levels. The choice by the principal, Mary Allan, of the *Song of Solomon*, and the performance of the May morning song reflected May Day's origins as a spring fertility rite, as did the 'virgin' white dresses that students wore.[6] This coded expression of eroticism was particularly interesting in an institution that otherwise frowned on any overt expression of sexuality. I read it as a Bacchanalian discourse where, in the context of this annual holiday/ holyday, emotions which were suppressed for the rest of the year were allowed a licensed expression. The ceremony was also a celebration of youth and its aspirations, and all the ideals of professionalism and service for which the college stood. It was also an opportunity for the principal to express, in more lyrical and festive terms than usual, her role as the guardian and director of these ideals.

At Westfield College the annual ceremony of 'Marmalade Cutting' was, as with Homerton's Ceremony of Carols, a college tradition that had evolved out of the domestic customs of the middle-class family:

> Volunteers gathered in the dining room after dinner and thinly sliced hundreds of oranges while lustily singing all the college songs. The staff went about sharpening our knives and the maids removed the cut oranges in huge bowls and brought fresh ones.   (Sondheimer, 1983, p. 52)

The participation in this domestic ritual of all members of the college family—principal, academic staff, students and, interestingly, even the servants—underlined the college's familial ideology. But the ritual also functioned as an expression of corporate loyalty, which was signalled in the singing by the family's daughters/students of 'all the college songs' while they carried out their domestic task.

At Homerton College, with each succeeding cohort of students, daughters became mothers, and mothers became grandmothers, and through the medium of the Old Students' Association the metaphor of the extended family became a powerful discourse for promoting the corporate identity of the college. The potential power of this discourse was recognized by the college's first woman principal, Mary Allan, when she took office in 1903. Before that date, small groups of former students had been meeting informally in London. Allan not only transformed these informal gatherings into a formal Homerton Association, but by creating the annual Whitsun Reunion she gave the newly formed Association both a focus and a corporate tradition. The holding of the Reunion at the college and in term-time made it possible for all members of the college's extended family to gather together: not only were current students able to 'tender a hearty welcome to mothers and grandmothers' (*Homertonian*, June 1906, p. 1423), but 'large numbers of past students' could 'partake of college hospitality and renew their youth' (*Homerton Association News*, 1950, p. 6). Allan herself constantly underlined the importance that she attached to the Association's function in promoting her political strategy for the college:

> She often spoke of her pleasure in, and the value of the Homerton Association, for members had in their hands the status and the reputation of the college.[7]

Constance Maynard, Westfield College's first principal, adopted a traditional strategy of middle-class mothers in order to keep her extended college family together. This was the system of communal letter-writing known as the Budget which circulated round from principal to students with each in turn contributing their news. By the time Maynard retired in 1913, eight of these 'budget rings' were 'whirling round'. Moreover, as the centre of each of these rings, Maynard was inscribing her maternal role as the pivot of the college's family life (Sondheimer, 1983, p. 49).

Royal Holloway College was also embued with the ethos of the extended family, but its families were elective families of sisters rather than, as at Homerton, prescribed mother/daughter pairs. It was the custom at Holloway for small groups of first-year students to 'coalesce into a family' which formed a mutual support group for its members (Bingham, 1986, pp. 101–2). The family discourse at Holloway was, however, much weaker than that which pertained at Homerton. For Holloway's families of sisters/friends had none of the prescribed duties and structural importance of Homerton's mothers/daughters. In fact, students at Holloway, unlike those at Homerton, were not required to become members of college families: the distinguished novelist Ivy Compton-Burnett, for example, remained outside the system altogether (Spurling, 1974, p. 152).

The ritual of meal times was an essential component of the social practice of the Victorian middle-class home, and [. . .] the discourse of meal times was universally adopted by women's colleges and adapted to serve their institutional ends. As in the middle-class home, this discourse functioned not only as an essential part of the socialization of individual students into college life, but also as an important instrument of social/family control.

Meal times had their own status hierarchy. Breakfast, like dinner, was a formal meal at which all students had to be present, but, unlike dinner, there was no socializing between staff and students. At Newnham College, for instance, the vice-principal and the dons sat alone at high table for breakfast, while students sat together at their own tables. Social control was enforced and punctuality encouraged by the requirement that any student who arrived after prayers had to go up to the high table and shake hands with the vice-principal (Phillips, 1979, p. 54).

Lunch was usually an informal meal. At Westfield College, lunch was 'spread on the dining table and could be taken at any time between twelve and two-thirty' (Sondheimer, 1983, p. 34). There were, however, interesting class differences in the lunch ritual. Homerton College's lack of social status was signalled by its custom of treating the midday meal, which it called 'dinner', as the most formal of the day, while the evening meal, which Homerton called 'supper', was comparatively informal. This was in sharp contrast to the practice in the women's university colleges, where evening dinner, as in the upper-middle-class home, was the most formal of the day. At Homerton it was at the midday meal that students were obliged to take it in turns to become 'the victims' who sat next to the principal at high table and made polite conversation with her and members of the academic staff.[8] In the evenings, by contrast, the principal and the academic staff took their supper apart from the students, in the privacy of the principal's dining room.[9]

The requirement that students take their turn in conversing with the principal at high table ensured that students, like daughters in the upper-middle-class home were equipped to make polite dinner party conversation with their parents' guests. At dinner they were also required to emphasize their femininity by the elaboration of their dress. The dinner ritual at Royal Holloway College, for instance, was unusually elaborate, in keeping with the college's massive financial endowment. Prompted by a dressing bell, the whole community changed into evening dress for dinner, and dinner partners were selected in advance in strict conformation with the social hierarchy of the college. The assembled party, led by the principal and her partner, proceeded into the dining hall where they were served a four-course meal by the college's butler and a full complement of maids (Bingham, 1986, pp. 80–1, 139).

Similarly, at Westfield College the ritual for college dinner bore a striking resemblance to a formal dinner party in an upper-middle-class home. Maids brought round hot water for all staff and students before dinner, and the principal sat at high table with students who had been selected beforehand (Firth, 1949, pp. 124–6). The somewhat guilty pleasure that the college's principal, Constance Maynard, took in her own toilette, and the delight she took in her students' attire, reflected both the difficulties she faced in constructing her own femininity, and her maternal pride in her student daughters. Thus Maynard recorded in her diary how, when looking at herself in the mirror 'dressed for dinner in black lace over red silk with a lace ruffle, diamonds and silver buckles', she felt that her own mother would not have approved: 'Sweet mother am I too well dressed for a pilgrim?' However, her confidence in her feminine role as mother of the college was restored when a student 'dressed for dinner and looking lovely' interrupted her musing with a request that she comfort a student who was 'miserable' (Firth, 1949, pp. 251–2). [. . .]

The principal's role in women's colleges was always problematic, and her subjectivity was the site of conflicting and competing subject positions. If the college was organized as a family, the principal, as its head, must of necessity take on the role of father; but as a woman, she also felt the need to perform a mother's role. Principals tried to solve this problem by dividing their lives into public and private spheres. On all public occasions they would adopt the role of the powerful authoritative father; privately and in their relations with students on an individual basis they could show a softer maternal side. This doctrine of separate spheres was always difficult to maintain, and each principal had to make her own resolution of the conflict between the discourses of gender and power, and of masculinity and femininity, when constructing her principal's role.

Even when giving play to her private feminine side she could never forget (and nor could anyone else) that in spite of her sex she was the head of the college family, the fount of all power, as in the conventional Victorian family.

The problematics of the construction of women principals' subjectivity are amply demonstrated in the career of Homerton College's first woman principal, Mary Allan, who was principal from 1903 to 1935. There was never any doubt that Allan's public persona was that of father of the college. Former students are unanimous in employing masculine adjectives to describe her public behaviour—strict, fair, formidable, austere, unapproachable, aloof and strong[10]—and comments that 'she was entirely in command'[11] and 'held Homerton in her hand'[12] bear witness to the strict control that she exercised over the college's affairs. Equally masculine was Allan's political strategy, which never lost sight of her aim to establish the college as a respected academic institution for the training of women teachers.[13] She realized, for instance, that for her to achieve this aim, no breath of scandal must touch the college. This was particularly crucial in view of the college's marginal position in Cambridge society, Cambridge being a town dominated by the male values of its university, which barely tolerated its own women students, let alone those in an obscure teacher-training institution. [...]

The overwhelming need to maintain the college's respectable image lay behind Allan's annual homily to students that it was her proud boast that for years she had had 200 women students among 5,000 men (university) and had never had any trouble.[14] Students were expected to behave 'with dignity and a sense of vocation',[15] and they were constantly made aware of the necessity to 'uphold the reputation of the college'[16] at all times. But the contrast between Allan's masculine political strategy and the feminine tactics she sometimes employed to carry out this strategy showed clearly the conflicting discourses of her dual gender role. It is difficult to imagine that a male principal would have thought that if students were seen carrying bags of sweets back to college 'local residents would think Homerton girls were not getting enough to eat'[17], or that he would have instituted an *in camera* enquiry as to whether a student had been wearing stockings or not.[18]

This intrusion into Allan's masculine persona of a feminine concern with domestic trivia was an example of how social practices are actively transformed 'to construct gender relations in a continuing historical process' (Connell, 1987, p. 79). For Allan was constructing the new role of woman principal out of the prevailing discourses and practices of middle-class femininity. Even though she was sure of her paternal role as head of the college, she was nevertheless unable to transform all her social practices to conform with this masculine image. It is interesting that the interruption of her strong masculine discourse by a weaker feminine one was at the most vulnerable point of Allan's political strategy—the public behaviour of her students. She never had trouble in maintaining strong paternal authority in her dealings with the college's trustees,[19] the Board of Education,[20] or even with difficult parents.[21] [...]

Allan's feminine sympathy was most readily extended to her poorer students. From humble origins herself (Sallie Purkis, personal communication),
she was always concerned lest poverty should prevent students from participating fully in college life. One student who had been ill and had no father
was allowed to stay on in college for an extra term, free of charge.[22] A sympathy that was strategic rather than sentimental was entirely in keeping with
the principal's masculine role. For Allan saw students' problems in the context
of what was best for the college as a whole, rather than in terms of individual
students' needs. Her general lack of sympathy with illness, for instance was
attributed to her concern that it 'could hold up students' progress'.[23]

Allan signalled her dual gender role in her dress. Her daytime clothes were
chosen to enhance her dignity and status as head of the college, and were a
feminine equivalent of the masculine suit. She wore dark, well-cut tailor-made
dresses and jackets, of good material[24], 'without much attention to current
fashion'.[25] She never went out of the college grounds without a hat.[26] 'Off-
duty', however, Allan signalled she was entering the private sphere by more
feminine attire: for informal evening supper with her staff she was reported
as wearing 'a deep blue mandarin robe'.[27] [. . .]

The clothes worn by Ellen Higgins, Mary Allan's contemporary as principal of Royal Holloway College, were also emblematic of the principal's
masculine authority and power. Higgins asked the famous dress-designer
Worth for advice and he created 'a suit with a jacket of masculine cut
with a long skirt' (Bingham, 1986, p. 114). For evening wear, in keeping
with the splendours of Royal Holloway's domestic arrangements, Higgins
wore 'a magnificent evening dress, of sombre colour and rich material with
a splendid necklace of cornelians and diamonds' (Bingham, 1986, p. 115).

The novelty of the position of woman principal and the lack of exemplars
for her guidance meant that each principal made her own interpretation of
her dual gender role. In Elizabeth Wordsworth—the first principal of Lady
Margaret Hall at Oxford—the intersection of class and gender discourses was
critical. Unlike Allan, Wordsworth was born into the heart of the clerical
middle-class elite (Battiscombe, 1978, p. 19) and she was specifically chosen in
1878 to be principal of Lady Margaret Hall because her social connections made
her acceptable to Oxford society (p. 66), although significantly Lady Margaret
Hall was founded ostensibly for academic purposes (pp. 65–6) the prospectus
emphasized the domestic side of college life in its declared aim to provide 'a
common life with the ways and tone of a Christian family' (p. 68).

Wordsworth was conscious at all times of her power and status as head of
her college family and of her duty as principal to direct the college's political
strategy. Nevertheless she constructed her role as principal out of the maternal
rather than the paternal discourses of the upper-middle-class home. For it was
as mother rather than father that she sought to make the experience of college
life 'an excellent training for future wives and mothers' (p. 102) by taking students with her when she paid social calls in Oxford, and expecting students to

help her in college with her own entertaining (p. 69). Wordsworth delegated her other public masculine duties as principal to others. The college's academic arrangements, for instance, were the responsibility of the Oxford Association for the Higher Education of Women (p. 65), and this umbrella organization also provided her with volunteers to run the domestic and administrative side of college life (p. 67).

In spite of her acknowledged public success in giving Lady Margaret Hall 'its command over public confidence' (p. 180), and the recognition, even by her critics, that she was the college's 'unique, original and much-respected mother' (p. 80, quoted by Vera Brittain), Wordsworth was less successful in the private/pastoral side of her maternal role. She had not had a good relationship with her own mother and she replicated her mother's lack of 'demonstrative affection' (p. 265) towards her, in her own dealings, as mother, with the students who were her daughters. [. . .] Wordsworth's difficulties with her maternal role were not confined to her insensitivity and lack of sympathy, but more crucially her erratic and indiscreet behaviour at the personal level, earned her the disrespect of her more critical students—'She said the first thing that came into her head' (p. 158) and employed 'blazing indiscretion not without intention to her confidantes' (p. 89). [. . .]

Constance Maynard, who founded Westfield College in 1882 was, like Elizabeth Wordsworth, profoundly influenced in the construction of her principal's role by the effects of her early upbringing. The repressive and rigid religious atmosphere of her home was always at odds with her strong and passionate nature (Firth, 1949, pp. 124–6), and the ensuing tensions remained embedded in her personality throughout her life. Maynard's political aim was to re-create at Westfield the educational environment that she had enjoyed as a student at Girton College—but to enhance it by making Westfield a specifically Christian foundation (Firth, 1949, p. 133).

Maynard's charismatic personality inspired great loyalty and affection in her staff and students—but the strong leadership she exercised as head/father of the college was constantly intersected by the complex demands of her own femininity. Like Wordsworth, she delegated the administrative side of the principal's public role to two colleagues—but her relationship with these colleagues was always problematic. Tensions arose, not only because of the sexual and emotional relationships between the three women (Vicinus, 1986, pp. 159–61) but also because Maynard was unable to resolve the conflicts between masculine and feminine discourses and the public and private spheres in her construction of the principal's role. Her use of masculine power as head of the college was often autocratic and unreasonable, with little feminine concern for her colleague's interests. Nevertheless, she was unable to exercise this power with full confidence unless her two colleagues gave her not only their unquestioning obedience but their love and approval as well (p. 159). Vicinus uses specifically familial language to describe this dilemma—'They were expected alternately to behave like dutiful daughters under her leadership and to be her equal who would support her in troubled times' (p. 158).[...]

Outside commentators were also aware of the duality of women principals' gender role. But the awkwardness and imprecision of their language showed how difficult it was to express this duality in terms of the gender discourses of the time. For example, the obituary of Emily Penrose, Principal of Royal Holloway College from 1898 to 1907, described the woman principal's role as ultimately supra-gender: 'For all her masculine powers and feminine accomplishments her great qualities were neither masculine nor feminine' (Bingham, 1986, pp. 93–4). The dual gender role of Winifred Mercer, principal of Whitelands Training College from 1918 to 1934, was articulated more precisely, but the text revealed the author's masculine belief in the essential inferiority of women:

> She possessed a man's mind and something of a man's way of looking at problems—so much so that, once they knew her, men never found any difficulty in discussing ideas with her, a thing rare in their experience of women. But with this went all, and more than all, a woman's tenderness and compassion.   (Grier, 1937, p. xiii)

On the other hand, the memorialist of Ellen Higgins, principal of Royal Holloway College from 1907 to 1935, found it easier to articulate the masculinity of her interpretation of the principal's role because Higgins herself accentuated this masculinity in both her dress (Bingham, 1986, p. 114) and her sexual behaviour (pp. 132–5):

> Her struggle for the rights of women perhaps made her accentuate the masculine, as though she would fight the battle on equal and level grounds.
> (Bingham, 1986, p. 114)

The difficulties that women principals faced in constructing their dual gender role as both father and mother of the institutions they served were compounded by the difficulties they faced in finding suitable expression for their own emotional and sexual needs.

As respectable, unmarried middle-class women, principals had to express their sexuality, if they expressed it overtly at all, in relationships with their own sex. Vicinus (1986, p. 158) has shown that, in fact, most women's colleges 'nourished and (were) nourished by the homoerotic friendships of women'. These friendships were always problematic—not only because of the difficulties women faced in constructing emotional/sexual relationships that lay outside the prevailing heterosexual discourse of sexuality, but also because, as women in positions of power, they needed to reconcile their emotional and sexual needs with the realities of this power.

During the course of the nineteenth century, historical shifts in the construction of sexuality had caused the meaning of sexual/emotional relationships between women to change. In the earlier part of the century, the labelling of relationships between women as 'romantic friendships' signalled their acceptance as appropriate feminine behaviour under certain circumstances—either as an 'apprenticeship to heterosexual love' or as a consolation for women who could not find husbands (Faderman, 1981, p. 17). Romantic friendship, however was only acceptable because it did not challenge hegemonic discourses of gender and power. For not only did women at this period lack the economic resources to lead independent lives outside marriage, but they were also encouraged to believe that, unlike men, they had no innate sexuality which needed physical expression (pp. 17–19). Romantic friendship could not, therefore, threaten the subordination of women within the sexual and power dynamics of heterosexual marriage.

From the 1870s onwards, however, changes in the social and economic position of women, coupled with developments in medical opinion, led to relationships between women being reconstructed as potentially threatening to the hegemonic heterosexual discourse. For the increase in employment opportunities for middle-class women now allowed some women to lead economically independent lives, and so to be in a position to reject marriage altogether (p. 178). Furthermore, medical theorists like Kraft-Ebing and Freud had now problematized the whole area of sexuality and, as part of this radical new sexual discourse, were declaring that women, as well as men, needed to express their sexuality by physical means (p. 241). Under the challenge of these new discourses of gender and power, romantic friendship as it had previously been construed could not survive, and its reconstruction was signalled by an increasingly ambivalent attitude towards close friendships between women.

Women principals were therefore, constructing their own relationships in a climate where close friendships between women were being increasingly challenged—although they had not yet been openly outlawed. Indeed, the label 'homo-erotic', which Vicinus gives to them, signals an intermediary phase in the construction of those relationships between the socially acceptable 'romantic', and the unequivocally condemnatory 'lesbian'—a label that was to follow in the third decade of the twentieth century (Faderman, 1981, p. 311; Vicinus, 1986, p. 158). Nevertheless, homoerotic friendship was always a marginal sexual discourse which was only tolerated provided that it remained invisible to the outside world.

The decoding of homoerotic friendship is difficult. The evidence we have is shadowy and opaque, not least in the most 'hidden' area of all—the physical expression of sexuality. In my judgement, the prevailing discourses of middle-class femininity, and particularly that of feminine respectability, would have precluded women principals from engaging in relationships with their own sex, in which physical sexual satisfaction rather than emotional intimacy was the primary goal. By this I mean that although homoerotic friendship was frequently physically expressed with gestures like hand-holding and kissing, such gestures—even if they were sexually inspired—were unlikely to lead to explicit genital stimulation with the purpose of sexual release. For, as we have seen, women principals constructed their roles out of the conventions and practices of the middle-class home. In such homes, sexual expression was confined to the marriage bed; sexual relationships were not a subject for family discussion; and most middle-class girls had only a shadowy knowledge of the facts of hetero-sexuality, let alone the possibility of homosexuality. Interestingly, Constance Maynard, Westfield College's first principal, assumed that sexual feeling could only be heterosexual: 'It is all very well to call my loneliness "sex feeling" but I can honestly say my thoughts never strayed to a man (Vicinus, 1986, p. 160, quoting C. Maynard's unpublished autobiography). I read women principals' homoerotic friendships as primarily a strategy for emotional support. Prin-cipals needed emotional support in the public sphere to help them bear the burden of their role as father of the college. More crucially, as individuals within the private sphere, they needed to express their femininity as ordinary women, and to be loved and to love for themselves within the intimacy of a close personal relationship.

The dynamics of homoerotic friendship can be followed in the career of Mary Allan, Homerton College's first woman principal. In 1903, immediately after her own appointment, Allan appointed Margaret Glennie to her academic staff. Two years later she gave a temporary contract for one year to Edith Waterhouse, to cover another lecturer's leave of absence.[28] Both these women enjoyed from the first an intimate personal companionship with Allan—but ultimately Waterhouse became Allan's 'closest friend' although Allan always retained 'a great affection' for Glennie.[29] That Glennie was in the end 'pushed out'[30] by Waterhouse was due both to differences in the two women's per-sonalities and also to Allan's ultimate preference for the person who could best serve both her public and private needs. [. . .]

Allan was quick to recognize her need to retain Waterhouse's services on a permanent basis. Long before Waterhouse's temporary contract had expired, Allan wrote to the Chairman of the Congregational Board of her desire 'to secure her [Waterhouse's] services' which were of a 'thoroughly satisfactory kind'. Allan also pointed out that Waterhouse was 'applying for another job'. So keen was Allan to keep Waterhouse, that she went so far as to write to sev-eral members of the board privately to secure their support.[31]

Nevertheless, although Waterhouse's appointment was made permanent,[32] her ambition led her the following year to accept the post of vice-principal at Avery Hill College. Allan signalled the closeness of their relationship in words which expressed in coded official language the loss that she, as well as the College, had sustained: 'I cannot adequately state my appreciation of Miss Waterhouse's work. Her post will be very hard to fill'.[33] Waterhouse's defection now left the field clear for Glennie—but Allan did not lose touch with Waterhouse, and five years later she reported to the college's Governors that she was retaining Waterhouse's services on a part-time basis as a super-visor for School Practice.[34] This proved to be the thin end of the wedge, and by the end of the year, Waterhouse was back at Homerton with a full-time lectureship in education.[35]

It is difficult to believe that Waterhouse would have taken such a seemingly backward step in her career unless she had a compelling personal reason to do so. Certainly, the rivalry between her and Glennie now became visible[36] and a year later Glennie was given leave of absence for unstated reasons.[37] The power struggle between the two women was finally resolved eight years later when, on the retirement of the college's vice-principal, Allan appointed Waterhouse to take her place; Glennie was given the consolation prize of Resident Tutor.[38] [. . .] Allan chose Waterhouse rather than Glennie as her vice-principal because she judged that Waterhouse's ability and previous experience as a vice-principal[39] made her better fitted to support her public role as father/head of the college. But a close working relationship in the public sphere need not of itself have led to a similar intimacy in the private sphere. However, because the college was organized as a family it was not inappropriate that the woman who was the principal's consort/wife in the public sphere should also play that role in private.

Vicinus has drawn attention to the structural problems that women principals faced in entering into homoerotic 'marriage'. The intersection of the discourses of gender and power, for instance, 'when distance was lost but inequality remained' (Vicinus, 1986, p. 201) was always problematic. Furthermore, emotional overloading was a constant danger in a relationship 'where "work, friends, pleasure, everything shared" gave no room for disagreement' (Vicinus, 1986, p. 201, quoting Constance Maynard).

Allan and Waterhouse were able to overcome these problems by a combination of personal compatibility and flexible role reversal. In the public sphere, Waterhouse accepted that as vice-principal she was the principal's consort and necessarily subordinate to her power as father and head of the college. Allan rewarded Waterhouse's devotion by frequent public tributes to 'her work as vice-principal which I particularly prize'.[40] Yet in the intimacy of their private relationship, both women were able to put aside the power inequality of their professional life, and to express their mutual femininity in a flexible, equal partnership in which 'it was uncertain as to who dominated whom.'[41] This private equality was made possible because both women had equally 'formidable' characters[42]; it is difficult to believe that the domineering Allan would have been able to establish such mutuality with the self-effacing and humble Glennie (*Homertonian*, 1950, p. 7). [. . .]

Waterhouse's warmth[43] and her sense of humour[44] made possible her intimacy with the dour and aloof Allan. These qualities, in alliance with the mutual respect that both women had for each other, also allowed Waterhouse to take the initiative in the private sphere, and to encourage Allan, for example to relax with her in their shared enjoyment of Gilbert and Sullivan opera.[45]

Compatibility of personality, shared ideals and mutual respect allowed Allan and Waterhouse to forge a partnership in which the inequality of their power in the public sphere was balanced by an equal relationship in their private intimacy. Other principals, however, were less successful in harmonizing inequality of power and emotional needs within homoerotic friendship.

Constance Maynard, first principal of Westfield College, was never able to reconcile the discourses of gender and power in her triangular relationship with two members of her staff—Anne Richardson and Ralph Gray. For Maynard expected as head and father of the college to be obeyed and supported by her 'dutiful daughters' at all times in both public and private. But she also expected them in the private sphere to subvert their professional public role and to form an intense emotional relationship with her, in which Maynard could express the conflicting needs of her own femininity. For, in private, Maynard wanted to be both wife and mother and to express her strong emotions and suppressed sexual needs in a relationship of physical intimacy. But this intimacy was necessarily subversive of the discourses of both gender and power. Maynard could not, for instance, seek emotional reassurance in the private sphere by courting Gray with overt sexual play, 'biting her finger and snarling and growling like a jaguar', if she also wished to be accepted in the public sphere as the authoritarian head and father of the college; nor could she behave like a mother 'rocking (Gray) in her arms and calling her baby' if she also expected Gray to behave like a professional colleague and equal (Vicinus, 1986, p. 160). Maynard's excessive emotional demands also put a strain on Gray's long-standing intimacy with Richardson—an intimacy that had pre-dated their triangular relationship with Maynard. Eventually, Gray solved the problem for all three women by leaving to take up an independent command (Sondheimer, 1983, p. 54).

Winifred Mercer, principal of Whitelands Training College from 1918 to 1934 (Grier, 1937, pp. 93, 156), was another woman principal who formed a triangular homoerotic friendship. But, unlike Maynard, Mercer's two partners, Jean Borland and Kate Scott Moncrieff, were never members of her own staff (p. 27). This lack of a power dimension to their relationship was critical in enabling the three women to maintain a long-term friendship without emotional discord. Moreover, Mercer realized that an emotional intimacy shared between three people was more supportive of her professional life than a single partnership, the private demands of which might have interfered with her public role: 'Love for an individual would have had to be quite overwhelming to take her from the life to which she had given herself' (Grier, 1937, p. 18). [. . .] Mercer's letters used language that betrayed the suppressed sexuality which underlay the relationship. In 1902, for instance, she wrote to Borland, whom her friends always revealingly called 'Donald', with a concern for her friend's body and its attractiveness, which was overtly sexual:

> 1. Do you sleep well? 2. Do you feel hungry? 3. Has anyone remarked on your looks, if so, what did they say? 4. Are you any fatter? 5. Have you any black rings (under your eyes)?   (Grier, 1937, p. 32)

In my article I have shown how gender relations were constructed in the early women's colleges by translating the social practices of the Victorian middle-class home, the metaphor of the Victorian family and the ideology of Victorian femininity, into a new institutional setting. The transformation of social practices, like meal times, and the adaptation of a family metaphor for the organization of college life provided few problems. But the construction of the principal's role from these discourses was always highly problematic. For it was always difficult for women principals to reconcile the conflicting discourses of their dual gender role as both father and mother of the institutions they served. It was also difficult for them to harmonize their own private gender needs with the power discourse of their public role. I am conscious also that the homoerotic friendships of women principals need further discussion within the wider debate on the nature of women's sexuality at the time. What effects, for example, did the denial of the sexual needs of the body have on the whole construction of femininity? Did such a denial lead to the development of sado-masochistic relationships between women with power and their subordinates? Was a full discourse of sexuality ultimately incompatible with the responsibilities of power for single women, because such a confluence of discourses would conflict with the hegomonic discourse of respectability for middle-class women?

Notes

1. Homerton College Archive (hereafter HCA), acc. no. 807: reminiscences of a former student 1922–5.
2. HCA, acc. no. 417: annotated photograph belonging to a former student 1925–7.
3. HCA, acc. no. 807: reminiscences of a former student 1922–5.
4. HCA, acc. no. 1026: reminiscences of a former student 1920–2.
5. HCA, acc. no. 1189, no. 7: reply to questionnaire on Miss Allan, Principal 1903–35, from a student 1918–20. My colleague, Sallie Purkis, who is researching for a biography of Miss Allan, sent a questionnaire on Miss Allan in 1988 to some 120 of her surviving students. The 80 replies have been deposited in the College Archive (acc. nos. 1189–91).
6. HCA, acc. no. 1191, no. 23: reply to questionnaire on Miss Allan from a student 1931–3.
7. *Fifty Years of the Homerton Association.* HCA. acc. no. 630, p. 11.
8. HCA, acc no. 1190, no. 25: reply to questionnaire on Miss Allan from a student 1929–31.
9. HCA, acc. no. 1189, no. 8: reply to questionnaire on Miss Allan from a student 1916–18.
10. HCA, acc. nos. 1189–1191 *passim*; replies to questionnaire on Miss Allan.
11. HCA, acc. no. 1189, no. 9: reply to questionnaire on Miss Allan from a student 1917–19.
12. HCA, acc. no. 1189, no. 7: reply to questionnaire on Miss Allan from a student 1918–20.
13. See, e.g., *Principal's Reports 1903–1933.* HCA, acc. no. ACa 58. March 1922.
14. HCA, acc. no. 1190, no. 39: reply to questionnaire on Miss Allan from a former student 1925–7.
15. HCA, acc. no. 1189, no. 7: reply to questionnaire on Miss Allan from a former student 1918–20.

16. HCA, acc. no. 1190, no. 44: reply to questionnaire on Miss Allan from a former student 1927–9.

17. HCA, acc. no. 1190, no. 44: reply to questionnaire on Miss Allan from a former student 1927–9.

18. HCA, acc. no. 1191, no. 14: reply to questionnaire on Miss Allan from a former student 1932–4.

19. *Principal's Reports 1903–33*, HCA, acc. no. ACa 58, *passim.*

20. See, e.g. *Principal's Reports 1903–33*, HCA, acc. no. ACa 58, December 1924.

21. See, e.g. *Principal's Reports 1903–33*, HCA, acc. no. ACa 58, letters to parent 11 and 14 March 1905.

22. HCA, acc. no. 1191, no. 12: reply to questionnaire on Miss Allan from a former student 1932–4.

23. HCA, acc. no. 1189, no. 5: reply to questionnaire on Miss Allan from a former student 1904–6.

24. HCA, acc. no. 1190, nos. 3 and 13: replies to questionnaire on Miss Allan from a student 1927–9 and a student 1929–31.

25. HCA, acc. no. 1190, no. 10: reply to questionnaire on Miss Allan from a student 1926–8.

26. HCA, acc. no. 1191, no. 5: reply to questionnaire on Miss Allan from a student 1932–4.

27. HCA, acc. no. 1190, no. 28: reply to questionnaire on Miss Allan from a student 1923–5.

28. *Principal's Reports 1903–33*, HCA, acc. no. ACa 58, July 3, 1905.

29. HCA, acc. no. 1190, no. 42: reply to questionnaire on Miss Allan from a former student 1922–5.

30. HCA, acc. no. 1192: reminiscences of a former student 1915–17.

31. *Principal's Reports 1903–33*, HCA, acc. no. ACa 58, 21 February 1906.

32. *Principal's Reports 1903–33*, HCA, acc. no. ACa 58, 26 November 1906.

33. *Principal's Reports 1903–33*, HCA, acc. no. ACa 58, 25 February 1907.

34. *Principal's Reports 1903–33*, HCA, acc. no. ACa 58, 29 February 1912.

35. *Principal's Reports 1903–33*, HCA, acc. no. ACa 58, 9 December 1912.

36. HCA, acc. no. 1192: reminiscences of a former student 1915–17.

37. *Principal's Reports 1903–33*, HCA, acc. no. ACa 58, 9 February 1914.

38 *Principal's Reports 1903–33*, HCA, acc. no. ACa 58, March and June 1922.

39. *Principal's Reports 1903–33*, HCA, acc. no. ACa 58, 25 February 1907. See also A. Davies (1989) *Prin.* Play premiered at Lyric Theatre Hammersmith, August 1989, for a portrayal of a homoerotic friendship between the principal and vice-principal in a women's teacher-training college.

40. *Principal's Reports 1903–33*, HCA, acc. no. ACa 58, June 1929: *see also* March 1922.

41. HCA, acc. no. 1028: reminiscences of a former student 1932–4.

42. HCA, acc. no. 1028: reminiscences of a former student 1932–4.

43. HCA, acc. no. 1191, no. 24: reply to questionnaire on Miss Allan from a former student 1921–3.

44. HCA, acc. no. 1191, no. 15: reply to questionnaire on Miss Allan from a former student 1933–5.

45. HCA, acc. no. 1190, no. 16: reply to questionnaire on Miss Allan from a student 1929–31.

References

Battiscombe, G. (1978) *Reluctant Pioneer: The Life of Elizabeth Wordsworth*. London: Constable.

Bingham, C. (1986) *The History of Royal Holloway College 1886–1986*. London: Constable.

Connell, R.W. (1987) *Gender and Power*. Cambridge: Polity Press.

Dixon, A.C. (1989) Ruskin's romantic fancies. *Country Life* 183, 130–3.

Dyhouse, C. (1987) Miss Buss and Miss Beale. In F. Hunt (ed.) *Lessons for Life,* pp. 22–38. Oxford: Blackwell.

Faderman, L. (1981) *Surpassing the Love of Men*. London: Junction Books.

Firth, C. B. (1949) *Constance Louisa Maynard: Mistress of Westfield College*. London: Allen and Unwin.

Fletcher, S. (1980) *Feminists and Bureaucrats*. Cambridge: Cambridge University Press.

Grier, L. (1937) *The Life of Winifred Mercer*. London: Oxford University Press.

Pedersen, J.S. (1987) *The Reform of Girls' Secondary and Higher Education in Victorian England*. New York: Garland.

Phillips, A. (ed.) (1979) *A Newnham Anthology*. Cambridge: Cambridge University Press.

Purvis, J. (1981) Towards a history of women's education in nineteenth century Britain. *Westminster Studies in Education* 4, 45–79.

Scott, J.W. (1986) *Gender and the Politics of History*. New York: Columbia University Press.

Sondheimer, J. (1983) *Castle Adamant in Hampstead: A History of Westfield College 1882–1982*. London: Westfield College.

Spurling, H. (1974) *Ivy When Young: The Early Life of I. Compton-Burnett 1884–1919*. London: Gollancz.

Vicinus, M. (1986) *Independent Women*. London: Virago.

Weedon, C. (1987) *Feminist Practice and Poststructuralist Theory*. Oxford: Blackwell.

Part 2 Equal Opportunity Policies

8 EQUAL OPPORTUNITIES IN EDUCATION IN THE NETHERLANDS AND THE POLICY OF THE ILEA

JENNY ARENDS AND MONIQUE VOLMAN

In Anglo-Saxon literature a number of attempts have been made to classify different perspectives on the issue of gender and education. Acker (1987) identifies three major approaches—those of socialist feminism, radical feminism, and liberal feminism. Weiner (1986) suggests a polarization between equal opportunities and anti-sexist approaches: the former seeks to redistribute the rewards of education, and the latter wants a transformation of the educational system. Although this is a theoretical typology, in practice different conceptualizations of gender and different goals and implementation strategies might be identified as typical of these perspectives.

[...] This article is based on a research project that sought insight into the policies developed by other authorities and governments, and the implementation of such policies in the schools.[1] Our main concern was the extent to which the methods used by the Inner London Education Authority (ILEA) and the Dutch Government reflected differing perspectives on the problem of gender and education and also differing implementation policies. Although the administrative and regional levels through which the Dutch Government and the ILEA operated differed, we hoped that the approach used by the ILEA might provide us with ideas for improving equal opportunities policy in education in The Netherlands. We were fortunate to have the opportunity to talk to ILEA employees and teachers a few months before the abolition of the ILEA.

Government policies on gender and education are usually inspired by a liberal feminist or egalitarian—equal opportunities—perspective (Wilson, 1989). Acker (1987) considered this to be the only perspective acceptable to the general public. At the local level, however, there have been a number of initiatives designed to develop more-radical, anti-sexist educational policies. The anti-sexist policy of the ILEA, the local authority that, until April 1990, was responsible for education in the 12 inner London boroughs, is a case in point. [...]

Source: Abridged from 'A comparison of different policies: equal opportunities in education in the Netherlands and the policy of the Inner London Education Authority', *Gender and Education* (1992) Vol. 4, No. 1/2, pp. 57–66.

THE DUTCH POLICY ON EQUAL OPPORTUNITIES IN EDUCATION

From the age of 5, Dutch children are required to attend school full-time, and education is compulsory until the age of 16. At the moment there is no comprehensive secondary education in Holland, although it is the subject of serious discussion. After pupils leave primary education (aged 12 years), they are directed *either* into one of the three different levels within general advanced education *or* into vocational education. This selection is based on the intellectual level of the pupil, as measured by a test, and is also based on the advice of the headteacher. [...] Although the differences between girls and boys are decreasing, more girls than boys follow general advanced education: in 1987/88, 75% of the girls and 63% of the boys who left primary education entered general advanced (academic) education, whereas 17% of the girls and 23% of the boys entered vocational education. Within vocational education a choice has to be made between several courses of study: few girls (6.4% of the girls in vocational education in 1988/89) are directed into technical education, and few boys into home economics education (2.8% in 1988/1989). In general, advanced education students have to choose different subjects, and at this stage relatively few girls choose science and mathematics, whereas boys seem to prefer these subjects to languages and humanities. For instance, in 1988/89, at the middle level of general advanced education, 51% of the girls and 80% of the boys chose mathematics; only 12% of the girls chose physics, whereas 51% of the boys chose this subject. In higher education also, students are distributed along lines of gender. Altogether, the educational careers of girls lead to less favourable positions in the labour market. Moreover, on average girls leave education at an earlier age than boys (see Dam *et al.*, 1992).

Another important phenomenon in the Dutch educational system is so-called 'pillarization'. The educational system is segregated ('pillarized') on ideological-religious grounds. Every school belongs to one of the four 'pillars': state education, Roman Catholic education, Protestant education, or non-denominational private education. State schools are run by central or local government, while private schools (Roman Catholic, Protestant and non-denominational private) are funded and administered by private bodies—Roman Catholic and Protestant schools on a religious basis, and non-denominational private schools (for example, Montessori and Jena plan schools) on a pedagogical basis. Since 1917 the Dutch constitution has provided for a complete financial equalization of state education and private education: this means that the state gives financial support to schools of all 'pillars'. Still, all schools, whether state, Protestant, Roman Catholic or non-denominational (and recently also Islamic), remain free to arrange their curricula, as long as they meet certain basic requirements. This 'freedom of education' means that central government is able to impose policy measures on state schools alone, an important factor where the implementation of equal opportunities policy in education is concerned.

To understand the Dutch policy on equal opportunities in education it is useful to consider the position of women in education against the background of their position in the labour market. Participation of women in paid employment in The Netherlands is among the lowest in Europe. In 1986, only 41% of women were in paid employment, whereas in Sweden the figure was 78% and in Britain it was 61%. Only Ireland and Spain have lower participation of women in the labour market than The Netherlands. Moreover, in Holland, women comprise over 75% of part-time workers. In common with other European countries, the majority of women are concentrated in areas of work that are characterized by low levels of pay, low skills and low status (see Brouns and Schokker, 1990).

In 1975, the position of women became the official concern of the Dutch Government. In 1979, the Dutch Ministry of Education and Science initiated a policy on equal opportunities for boys and girls. A first policy document was published, called 'Outline of a policy for emancipation in education and academics', and 92 policy measures were announced, ranging from developing curriculum materials and financing school projects to promoting research and organizing conferences and information campaigns. The motive for an active policy was that girls did not benefit optimally from their formal educational opportunities, and it was claimed that this affected their later position in society, particularly in the labour market. The aims of this policy were: (i) a reduction of factors that hamper freedom of choice, including breaking with traditional sex-stereotyped roles; (ii) a revaluation of feminine qualities; and (iii) an increase in educational opportunities for women to enable them to 'catch up'.[2] As we have seen earlier, central government in Holland has only limited influence in education, and measures for equal opportunities can therefore only be imposed on state schools. Other schools can be encouraged to make use of the 'offer' from central government concerning equal opportunities: for example, they can use non-stereotyped curriculum materials developed on the initiative of central government, or they can participate in equal opportunities projects, with teachers making use of in-service training.

In 1980, the next steps were taken when a second Ministry document appeared (Ministry of Education and Sciences, 1980). The document stressed that emancipation in education implies the preparation of both girls and boys for domestic as well as societal tasks. Even so, feminist criticisms were voiced (see Arends, 1988). It was said that, in spite of the wider intentions, the emphasis of the policy had been on the stimulation of educational opportunities for women—the third policy aim, (iii) listed above. The educational revaluing of supposed 'feminine' qualities such as domestic, social and emotional skills (the second policy aim) had hardly been elaborated into policy measures. Moreover, the measures were aimed mainly at influencing the educational choices of individual pupils and students. The educational system itself had remained out of the picture. Another problem of the policy was, in fact, pointed out by the Government, namely that this was a 'specific policy', i.e. it did not necessarily relate to mainstream policy on education. Educational materials on sex-role stereotyping were developed, experiments with emancipatory projects in schools were carried out, in-service training on equal opportunities for interested teachers was offered, and an advisory board on the issue of girls' subject choices was established. Many of these measures, however, remained marginal.

It took several years and a good deal more criticism from feminist educationalists before a third document, called 'A little wiser', appeared in 1985 (Ministry of Education and Sciences, 1985). In this document the emphasis shifted from a specific policy to a so-called 'facet policy', indicating a policy on equal opportunities which—instead of setting up special emancipatory projects, as had previously been done—integrated equal opportunities as an aspect (i.e. facet) into the general policy on education. Facet policy implied that all newly developed general policy would be examined for its quality in terms of equal opportunities. The specific policy approach developed earlier was continued alongside the new facet policy, although the former received less emphasis. The document of 1985 also stated that attention should be shifted from individual pupils and students towards the organization of education. A third shift concerned the sectors at which the policy was aimed. Initially, the focus was on secondary education because it was in this sector that sex differences in school careers first became apparent. The focus now shifted to primary education, since it was recognized that, in this phase, processes contributing to undesirable sex-specific differences in secondary education were already evident.

In the last two or three years, however, the concept of facet policy has served as a cloak for abandoning an active policy. The Government has increasingly shifted its attention away from the school level, concentrating again on the subject choices of girls. The policy developed to change these choices has been limited to providing information. In practice, this has meant a campaign to convince girls that they should choose science and mathematics. Again, the measures are aimed mainly at individual pupils and students; girls are seen as 'the problem' because they make the 'wrong' choices. [. . .]

THE DUTCH CONCEPTUALIZATION OF THE PROBLEM: LIBERAL FEMINIST OR RADICAL FEMINIST INFLUENCES?

The aims of the Dutch policy on equal opportunities in education represent a more complex conceptualization of the problem of sex inequality than the measures taken would suggest. Unlike many other central governments, the Dutch Government has played an active part in initiating an equal opportunities policy in education. Moreover, it has been an exception to the rule that government policies favour egalitarian strategies for change. Although Dutch feminists have always felt that too much emphasis was placed on the third policy aim, i.e. combating the fact that girls lag behind, the policy as a whole has never been considered exclusively liberal feminist and egalitarian. On the contrary, the second policy aim, the revaluation of feminine qualities, can be seen as the opposite of an egalitarian approach.

It is striking that in discussion of gender and education in England, the notion of revaluing the feminine is almost entirely absent. [...] However, there has recently been a great deal of discussion about the two apparently opposing feminist strategies that have characterized feminism from its beginning: the elimination of gender roles on the one hand, and the valuing of the female being on the other hand (Cott, 1984); in other words, equality versus difference (Scott, 1988).

The Dutch educational policy on gender can be analyzed in terms of these two strategies. The second policy aim emphasizes difference between and equivalence of the sexes, pointing to the value of feminine qualities and their undervaluation in society and education. The third aim emphasizes equality and focuses on the elimination of differences (and especially of 'feminine' choices) that currently cause women to lag behind in education. The first aim can be considered from one of two perspectives: either boys should develop feminine qualities, like domestic, social or emotional skills, or girls should become more like boys and choose mathematics, science and careers. Although the emphasis of the policy measures has been on the egalitarian approach, the aims of the Dutch policy combine these contradictory strategies of equality and equivalence, demonstrating a dilemma that is inherent in many feminist strategies.

[...] According to Weiner and Arnot (1987), egalitarians no longer reject notions of equivalence in favour of equality. The principal aim of egalitarians is to equip girls and women, through improved schooling and counselling, to move into more highly paid jobs, but egalitarians also address the issue of sex roles and socialization: girls are encouraged to make non-stereotyped choices, i.e. to move into male-dominated areas of the curriculum, while boys are encouraged to take up traditionally female subjects. Moreover, the strategy of making schools more responsive to the needs of their female pupils, 'girl-friendly schooling' (Whyte *et al.*, 1985), is increasingly being advocated from a liberal feminist standpoint (Arnot, 1987). The second Dutch policy aim, focusing on the qualities and needs of girls, appears to correspond to this strategy. It may be regarded as an egalitarian strategy because, although the method is one of recognizing difference, the ultimate aim is equality, in the sense of girls making more appropriate (masculine) educational choices. Thus, the Dutch aims of revaluation of the feminine and combating the fact that girls lag behind appear as different aspects of one and the same approach—the liberal feminist or equal opportunities approach. Still, in this analysis one aspect of the Dutch policy remains unexplained—the radical potential of its equivalence aim.

We suggest that an equivalence strategy can be either radical or moderate. 'Revaluation of the feminine' can be explained as 'being responsive to the needs of girls' (as in girl-friendly education), but it also implies the more-radical possibility of a criticism of the undervaluation of the feminine in society. It is the way in which the 'equivalence aim' is actualized in the Dutch policy that makes it moderate. It is translated into the elusive aim of a change of mentality on the one hand, and of responsiveness to the needs of girls (e.g. recognizing their learning styles) on the other hand.

Indeed, anti-sexist or radical feminist concepts such as 'female oppression', 'empowering girls and women', or even 'anti-sexism' are lacking in the Dutch policy. The absence of radical notions is especially obvious in the main policy objectives of the Government. Increasingly, it is again defining girls and women as 'the problem', either as a group or as individuals, instead of concentrating on the roles played by the educational system and educational processes in sex inequality.

Thus, the feminist criticism that too much emphasis is being laid on the fact that women lag behind can have two different meanings: it can be interpreted as a radical feminist critique of the individualism of the equal opportunities approach which blames girls and women for their educational positions, or it can be a difference-feminist criticism of the male standard which is used to measure the position of girls and women. Both kinds of criticism are useful in assessing today's equal opportunities policy, which tends to be discussed only in economic and individual terms with participation in the labour market as the main aim.

THE DUTCH IMPLEMENTATION STRATEGY

[...] In The Netherlands the implementation of the policy has not been without problems. In analyzing these problems we consider implementation at three levels: the level of individual teachers, parents and pupils; the level of the schools; and the level of governmental policy. At the level of individuals we conclude that equal opportunities in education is an accepted topic of discussion, although this is not necessarily reflected in the ways people act. Ten years ago equal opportunities initiatives would have been considered as a kind of 'missionary' work, whereas these days almost every teacher and parent would agree with the statement that it is as important for girls as for boys to reach the highest educational level within their reach. At the level of the school as an institution, we can see that equal opportunities for boys and girls is on the agenda; indeed, in primary schools it is a compulsory part of the school curriculum. Yet it remains unclear exactly what measures schools are taking, and much still depends on individuals (for example, many school counsellors continue to advise girls in traditional ways). At the national policy level, central government is increasingly inclined to abandon an active policy, and the policy has now been reduced to campaigns advising girls to choose science.

In Holland, there has never been a planned implementation strategy for equal opportunities. Because of the 'freedom of education' resulting from 'pillarization', the aims of equal opportunities were global, and few guidelines were provided at the practical level. Furthermore, the measures that were taken were not compulsory and were, in fact, individual measures; the aims and procedures of a project on equality were to be defined by the schools themselves, so projects were fulfilled in different ways in different schools. The Government assumed that each project would have its own cascade effect, but this proved unrealistic. Moreover, the projects were carried out by individual teachers in isolation.

In short, the approach was directed at individuals and not at whole schools; *ad hoc* initiatives were not translated into a structural policy, and in the background the problem of pillarization always remained. There also remained the problem of transforming an unsystematic, project-like approach into a structural basis for equal opportunities.

[...] We now turn to the strategy of the ILEA, which made implementation an explicit part of its educational policy agenda.

THE ANTI-SEXIST POLICY OF THE ILEA

In 1985 the ILEA published an 'anti-sexist statement' on the extent of sex inequality in education. The statement was intended to set up a framework for developing equal opportunities policies within the ILEA.[3] [...]

The ILEA was quite clear about the premise of its policy: girls and women are not 'a problem'. The statement identified both institutional sexism and unconscious sexist attitudes as barriers to genuine equal opportunities between the sexes. The aim of the ILEA policy was, therefore, not only to make girls achieve to the same extent as boys, but also to 'free both sexes of the restrictive stereotypes which undervalue and undermine girls and women, and which convince boys and men that their superiority is "natural"' (ILEA, 1985, p. 3). The ILEA not only focused on the visible aspects of the problem, such as sex differences in participation and achievement, but also on the processes that lead to those differences, for example the ways in which boys, girls and teachers interact.

The anti-sexist statement was sent to all ILEA schools, and the schools were required to develop their own equal opportunities policy on the basis of this statement. But the ILEA did not only ask the schools to play an active part in the creation of anti-sexist education; it created a structure for facilitating the development of equal opportunities policies at school level. From 1982 onwards, support, advice and inspection were all part of that policy.

At the administrative level an Equal Opportunities Sub-Committee was set up; while at the executive level the Equal Opportunities Unit was established, charged with stimulating and monitoring equal opportunities in other departments of the ILEA. A special inspector for equal opportunities was appointed to monitor the situation in schools and to give advice when necessary. As the inspector was not able to visit all the schools herself, the monitoring task was delegated to the subject inspectors. An *aide-memoire* was provided to help them to ask relevant questions and to look at the appropriate things. The inspector was assisted by a team of advisory teachers, who could support schools on the basis of their special expertise. Alongside general advisory activities, these teachers were responsible for special projects, such as anti-sexist work with boys, initiatives in schools with a gender imbalance, and the tackling of sexual harassment.

In addition to the organization and support structure, resources were also available for sex equality activities; for example, schools could apply for a grant from the Sex Equality in Education Fund (SEEF). During the academic year 1988–9, 46 projects were supported financially, the subjects ranging from curriculum design to the purchase of construction materials for girls. The most important requirement for obtaining a grant from the SEEF was that the proposal should be part of a wider school policy on equal opportunities. Another facility was the resources centre where teachers could borrow materials from a special gender collection. Moreover, the librarian provided in-service education and training (INSET) courses on sex equality in education, though INSET generally was organized by local teacher centres which could also offer courses on equal opportunities. Finally, the ILEA had its own research branch which reported regularly on the participation and achievement of pupils according to sex. Additionally, a number of special research projects on gender issues were co-ordinated and evaluated by the same department.

[. . .] It was believed that each school is unique, and that attitudes, awareness and priorities vary from one school to another and are subject to different forms of change. For this reason, schools were encouraged not just to copy the ILEA statement, but to formulate a policy appropriate to the school. Accordingly, an equal opportunities policy could only be successful if it were linked to current priorities within the school. To assist in the difficult task of turning policy statements into practice, guidelines were developed which offered practical help and support to teachers. The guidelines distinguished three aspects of implementation: identifying sexism in the school, bringing about change in the school, and planning a programme of action.

Despite the favourable conditions that the ILEA offered, like the Dutch policy the ILEA equal opportunities policy was not without problems. Within the ILEA, as elsewhere, the success of the policy depended on the commitment of individuals. Like the Dutch Government, ILEA had few sanctions when schools would not co-operate. Also, ILEA policies, including those on race and gender, drew many criticisms from the educational press, and ILEA was finally disbanded by the Conservative Government in 1989.

A COMPARISON OF DIFFERENT POLICIES

[. . .] We have examined the manner in which the Dutch policy has regressed to the level of the individual pupil. It is not exclusively egalitarian, but combines an equal opportunities approach with a difference/equivalence approach. This policy cannot have radical outcomes, because of the way it has been developed with the aims of a change of mentality and of meeting girls' 'needs' in education. In any case, it fails to address necessary changes to the educational system and educational processes as producers of inequality. The ILEA combined egalitarian and radical terminologies, but the implementation of its policy was radical. It focused not on individual girls but on the structures that produce difference. It considered schools as both instruments of change and producers of inequality. This focus on the schools also brought with it another task at the policy level: the development of strategies to involve schools actively in formulating their own policy-making.

Notes

1. This article is based on a research project, which was funded by the Stimuleringsgroep Emancipatieonderzoek (STEO), a Dutch fund for women's studies. The first phase of the project consisted of a literature study and interviews with Dutch specialists in the field of gender and education. In the second phase, a questionnaire was sent to ILEA employees, and a number of them were interviewed. In the third phase, ILEA teachers and 'advisory teachers' were interviewed.
2. In Holland the concept of *achterstand* (lagging behind in educational career and position in the labour market) is at the centre of the debate. This concept points to the disadvantaged position of women and the necessity to 'catch up' mainly in science, mathematics and technology), but it also suggests that women and girls are to be blamed for their educational position. The fact that this concept is unknown in English might reflect different approaches. The question remains whether it also has consequences for the strategies used.
3. In this article we use 'equal opportunities' to indicate a liberal feminist approach toward sex inequality. The ILEA, however, used this term for its policy, which was anti-sexist.

References

Acker, S. (1987) Feminist theory and the study of education. *International Review of Education* 33 (4), 419–37.

Arends, J. (1988) *Sociale Atlas van Meisjes [Social Atlas of Girls]*. Den Haag: DOP.

Arnot, M. (1987) Political lip-service or radical reform? Central government response to sex equality as a policy issue. In M. Arnot and G. Weiner (eds) *Gender and the Politics of Schooling*, pp. 309–32. London: Hutchinson/Open University.

Brouns, M. and Schokker, A. (1990) *Arbeidsvraagstukken en sekse [Issues of Work and Gender]*. Den Haag: STEO.

Cott, N. (1984) Feminist theory and feminist movements: the past before us. In J. Mitchell and A. Oakley (eds) *What is Feminism?* Oxford: Basil Blackwell.

Dam, G. ten, Eck, E. van and Volman, M. (1992) *Onderwijs en sekse: een verkenning van researchprogramma's [Education and Gender: An Exploration of Research Programmes]*. Den Haag: STEO.

ILEA (Inner London Education Authority) (1985) *Race, Sex and Class. 6 A Policy for Equality: Sex.* London: ILEA.

— (1986) *Implementing ILEA's Anti-Sexist Policy.* Individual guides for schools, colleges, youth clubs, etc. London: ILEA.

Ministry of Education and Sciences (1979) *Schets van een beleid voor emancipatie in onderwijs en wetenschappelijk onderzoek [Outlines of a Policy for Emancipation in Education and Academics]*. Den Haag.

— (1980) *Voortgangsnota onderwijsemancipatie [Second Policy Document on Emancipation in Education]*. Den Haag.

— (1985) *Een stukje wijzer. Derde nota onderwijsemancipatie [A Little Wiser. Third Policy Document on Emancipation in Education]*. Den Haag.

Scott, J.W. (1988) Deconstructing equality-versus-difference: or, the uses of poststructuralist theory for feminism. *Feminist Studies* 14 (1), 33–50.

Weiner, G. (1986) Feminist education and equal opportunities: unity or discord? *British Journal of Sociology of Education* 7 (3), 265–74.

Weiner, G. and Arnot, M. (1987) Teachers and gender politics. In M. Arnot and G. Weiner (eds) *Gender and the Politics of Schooling*, pp. 354–70. London: Hutchinson/Open Univesity.

Whyte, J., Deem, R., Kant, L. and Cruickshank, M. (eds) (1985) *Girl Friendly Schooling.* London: Methuen.

Wilson, M. (ed.) (1989) *Girls and Young Women in Education: A European Perspective.* Oxford: Pergamon Press.

9 GIRLS' EDUCATION IN THE BALANCE: THE ERA AND INEQUALITY

SHEILA MILES AND CHRIS MIDDLETON

The opening section of the 1988 Education Reform Act (ERA) asserts that 'a balanced and broadly based curriculum' is one which prepares pupils 'for the opportunities, responsibilities and experiences of adult life' (ERA, 1.2). This key statement, however, is open to alternative interpretations. For some (but not all) liberal-feminists the National Curriculum can be seen as a welcome opportunity for promoting girls' education, though even within this perspective there are grounds for caution about some of the Act's implications. But from a more sceptical standpoint it might well be observed that the opportunities, responsibilities and experiences facing most girls in adult life are severely constrained, especially if they come from black or working-class backgrounds. An educational reform that disregards this reality, and actually marginalizes those parts of the curriculum that aim to develop a critical social awareness in children, will merely help to reproduce existing inequalities.

This article will explore such issues in the context of the underlying economic rationale of the Act and the present underachievement of girls in key areas of education. It will examine the argument that the National Curriculum could promote equal opportunities by giving girls access to traditionally masculinized subject areas and occupations, and will suggest grounds for scepticism that the principle of increasing access will be sufficient for meeting even these limited objectives. Some of the factors that might inhibit the implementation of equal opportunities (such as classroom processes, teacher recruitment and training, and pupil attitudes to subject content and testing) will be considered, and it will be argued that in some respects, at least, the Act will prove deleterious in its effects. Differing strands of Conservative ideology represented in the Act may also have contradictory implications for girls' education. The National Curriculum is the DES's response to employers' demands for an educated workforce that would draw on a wider pool of ability regardless of gender, but the preference for traditional, subject-based forms of education may, in fact, prove damaging both to training efficiency and equal opportunities. Moreover, the Conservative commitment to 'traditional' family life

Source: Abridged from Flude, M. and Hammer, M. (eds) (1990) *The Education Reform Act 1988: Its Origins and Implications* (pp. 187–206). Basingstoke: Falmer Press.

(Hiskett, 1988), as reflected in the Act by the call for greater parental 'choice', may conflict with moves that could improve career prospects for girls. Finally, it will be suggested that the liberal-feminist conception of equal opportunities which has informed much of the discussion around the National Curriculum is too limited. There is a need to question the social relationships of adult life into which girls and boys are being inducted, and within this framework to consider afresh what a balanced and broadly based curriculum would entail.

THE EDUCATION REFORM ACT, EQUAL OPPORTUNITIES AND THE ECONOMY

The ERA is not about equal opportunities. It is about raising educational standards to meet the needs of the economy and of industry—an objective which, according to social market theory, is best realized by making education more reponsive to consumer demand. The Act seeks to reflect this imperative in two ways: by centralizing the curriculum (with the Government effectively acting on behalf of employers), and by removing education from the control of teachers and local education authorities (LEAs). [. . .]

The clear inference from the legislation is that the Government perceives teachers and LEAs as the inhibiting forces from which schools must be freed if they are to be responsive to consumer demand. [. . .] Centralization of the curriculum would not be inconsistent with the decentralization of control if, as the Government expects, the demands of parents (consumers) were to converge with their own view of what employers need. The education of girls may turn out to be one area where the choices of consumers are not always congruent with the needs of the market economy.

It should be noted that not all industrialists agree with the Government's prescription for meeting their training needs. Many believe that the enterprise culture, with its demand for transferable skills, is best fostered through an interdisciplinary curriculum 'focused on *doing* rather than simply on *knowing*', and they have been critical of the National Curriculum's return to traditional subject-based learning (as advocated by the right-wing Hillgate Group). These divisions are reflected in the divergent strategies advocated by different government departments, particularly by the Department of Trade and Industry (DTI) and the Department of Education and Science (DES), and it appears that the 'traditionalists' have been notably successful in influencing the direction that the ERA has taken (Jamieson and Watts, 1987). [. . .]

There is a broad political consensus in the UK that future national prosperity depends on increasing the supply of highly qualified recruits to the labour force, especially in the fields of science and technology (Hough, 1987). The educational system has long been criticized for failing to meet this demand and thus of wasting the abilities of many young people. Leading industrialists have accused it of failing to 'provide a general training which adequately prepares young people for work' and for training teachers in a way that is 'remote from industry' (NEDC, 1982). The National Curriculum's provision of a core education emphasizing maths, science and technology is seen by the Government as a vital move in securing the future of the British economy.

The recurring theme of wasted talent has served as a link between the needs of the capitalist economy and for the provision of wider educational opportunities. [...] In the 1970s, equal educational opportunities for girls were to become a prominent public issue. [...] The intellectual and political framework for the growing concern with equal opportunities is usually described as liberal-feminist, which we may define as an attempt to remove or compensate for the ascriptive and social impediments that prevent women from competing on equal terms with men, without otherwise challenging the hierarchical structures within which both sexes operate. However, this term does tend to obscure the presence of two rather different perspectives within the equal opportunities tradition. First, there are those who, in keeping with the liberal and individualistic traditions of Western culture, wish to ensure that pupils' ascribed characteristics do not serve as the basis for discriminatory and exclusionary practices against them. In this context the National Curriculum can be defended as offering considerable leverage for implementing equal opportunities as an entitlement curriculum, prioritizing those very areas where girls are known to be underrepresented and to underachieve, and making them compulsory for all pupils. But, secondly, there are those who, in accordance with social democratic traditions of thought, lay more emphasis on the complex *social* bases of disadvantage and the necessity of overcoming them if equal opportunities are to be effectively implemented. From this point of view the formal structural reforms instituted by the National Curriculum seem unlikely to herald any drastic changes. The liberal-feminist arguments for and against the ERA are set out in the remainder of this section.

The National Curriculum: Girls into science and technology?

In 1986–7 there were almost 25,000 full-time undergraduates in the UK studying engineering and technology, of whom only 2,741 were women (Association for Science Education, 1988). In view of the falling birth rate there are likely to be fewer entrants to these subject areas during the next decade and this is causing concern among scientific and engineering employers. Women are an obvious source of recruitment for making good the shortfall. According to the 1988 *Statistical Bulletin* from the DES, twice as many boys as girls gain an A-level pass in mathematics, and three times as many do so in physics (DES, 1988a). Among those leaving school at 16, twice as many boys as girls have a higher grade O-level/CSE qualification in physics, and the proportion of boys with higher grade passes is also greater in mathematics, chemistry and, particularly, CDT subjects. Unfortunately, we have no indication of how ethnic minority or working-class girls fare in these subjects, as the *Bulletin* does not provide the relevant statistical breakdowns. This is an important omission to which we shall return later.

TABLE 9.1   School leavers in England: Leavers with higher[1] grade passes at O level or CSE in selected subjects — percentage of all leavers

	1976–7			1986–7			Percentage change 1976–7 to 1986–7		
	Boys	*Girls*	*Total*	*Boys*	*Girls*	*Total*	*Boys*	*Girls*	*Total*
Any subject	49.5	53.3	51.4	51.3	57.9	54.5	+ 4	+ 9	+ 6
English	31.9	42.0	36.9	34.3	45.5	39.7	+ 8	+ 8	+ 8
Mathematics	28.0	20.5	24.3	32.6	27.7	30.2	+ 16	+ 35	+ 24
Physics	18.1	5.0	11.7	21.9	9.2	15.7	+ 21	+ 84	+ 34
Chemistry	12.7	6.1	9.5	15.8	11.5	13.7	+ 24	+ 89	+ 44
Biological sciences	11.9	17.7	14.8	12.3	18.6	15.4	+ 3	+ 5	+ 4
Craft design, technology and other sciences	17.5	2.5	10.1	17.1	4.5	10.9	– 2	+ 80	+ 8
French	10.8	16.6	13.6	10.9	18.2	14.5	+ 1	+ 10	+ 7
History	13.7	15.3	14.5	13.3	14.9	14.1	– 3	– 3	– 3
Geography	17.7	13.7	15.7	18.1	14.2	16.2	+ 2	+ 4	+ 3
Creative arts	10.8	15.1	12.9	11.0	18.1	14.5	+ 2	+ 20	+ 12
Commercial and domestic studies	1.8	17.1	9.3	4.1	17.4	10.6	+ 128	+ 2	+ 14
General studies	2.2	1.9	2.1	2.6	2.6	2.6	+ 18	+ 37	+ 24

1. O-level grades A–C, CSE grade 1.
Source: *Statistical Bulletin*, Table 8 (DES, 1988).

Table 9.1 shows that in the decade to 1987 there were substantial rises in the proportion of girls achieving higher grade O-level/CSE passes in physics, chemistry, and craft, design and technology (84, 89 and 80% respectively), but it must be borne in mind that, given the minute number of girls studying these subjects in the late 1970s, small gains make a falsely dramatic impact. Despite the improvement, fewer than one in ten girls are now achieving higher grades in physics (compared with more than one in five boys), and fewer than one in twenty girls gain these grades in CDT (compared with more than one in six boys).

Under the National Curriculum, it could be argued, girls will no longer be able to opt out of traditionally male areas of the curriculum and will therefore have the chance to gain qualifications equipping them for a much wider range of prestigious and highly paid jobs. Boudon argues that the provision of unlimited subject-choice and 'branching off' points in the school system can foster inequality by allowing differential cultural expectations to structure achievement along lines of class, gender and race, so that paradoxically a reduction in choice may enhance equal opportunities (Green, 1988). Moreover, it is not only pupils' expectations that may be neutralized by this means. The specification of a core curriculum and content for each subject, the setting of attainment targets, and a national system of testing with published results might also conceivably help to overcome the effects of low teacher expectations as an important factor in working-class, black and female underachievement. [. . .]

THE LIMITATIONS OF 'COMPULSORY ACCESS'

The argument in favour of the National Curriculum concentrates on the *formal* provision of equal access, but takes insufficient account of the kinds of issue that have been raised within the social democratic tradition of liberal-feminism. In a society permeated by gender divisions and inequalities, it is implausible to suppose that the treatment of girls and boys as though they were already equal will result in the creation of genuine equality of opportunity. Gender is well established as an organizing principle of the practices and power structures embedded within educational institutions and these will need to be fully addressed if access is to be made meaningful. Management hierarchies within most schools are dominated by male teachers especially in most of the subject areas given prominence by the National Curriculum. Within the classroom there is evidence that both male and female teachers give more of their time and attention to boys, ask them more questions, give them more praise and generally find them more interesting. Boys monopolize formal interaction, classroom workspace and resources especially in lessons on science and technology (Licht and Dweck, 1987; Buswell, 1981; Stanworth, 1983; Mahoney, 1985; Kelly, 1987; Arnot and Weiner, 1987; Wolpe, 1988).

Pupil attitudes are also important. Research by the Assessment of Performance Unit has shown that 15-year-old boys enjoy maths and science subjects (with the exception of biology) more than their female peers, find these subjects less difficult and achieve better results. But it stresses that these findings must be interpreted with care. Boys fare better in applying concepts in physics and chemistry and in tests of physics *knowledge*, but do less well than girls in observational tests. Competence in the use of measuring instruments seems to be influenced by out-of-school familiarity with their use, girls and boys performing equally well on instruments used for measuring time, temperature, volume, mass and weight. The differences observed at age 15 do not appear to reflect *natural* aptitudes. Boys and girls have similar attitudes towards maths at age 11—both sexes recognize its usefulness, find it equally difficult, and girls actually enjoy it slightly more than boys. Variations in attitudes towards maths emerge at a later stage. Performance and attitude differences in physics, however, are established at a much earlier age and may plausibly be interpreted as 'arising from differences in the science relevant out-of-school activities and interests of boys and girls as young children' (APU, 1988; see also Johnson and Murphy, 1986; Joffe and Foxman, 1988).

In part, girls' disaffection from science appears to be a response to science's masculine and impersonal image. Whereas boys are interested in controlling the material world, girls consistently show greater interest in subjects they regard as having more to do with 'people' than 'things' (Gilligan, 1982). There is a danger, then, that in forcing girls to study, for such a substantial part of their school lives, subject areas to which they have a real aversion, the National Curriculum could end up by transforming disaffection from certain subjects into a rejection of schooling itself. [. . .]

Low achievement on the assessment tests (see below) may aggravate this problem. A recent investigation into truancy among girls found that, apart from problems at home or with health, fear of failure was the main reason given by interviewees for absenting themselves from school. Girls 'bunked' individual lessons because they disliked the subject or the teacher (Le Riche, 1988).

The possibility of an increased number of disaffected girl pupils should not lead us to abandon the 'science for all' policy. Rather, attention should be paid to the structure and content of the science curriculum and to the way in which it is taught. Many science educators have proposed the development of a 'girl-friendly' science which would aim to teach traditional scientific principles, but would do so initially through topics that are likely to interest girls (Kelly, 1988; Harding, 1983; Smail, 1984). It would also work towards a more contextualized approach that would include a consideration of 'the implications and applications of the subject as a fundamental part of the syllabus' (Kelly, 1988, p. 169). Other approaches emphasize the importance of encouraging co-operation rather than competition within the classroom and developing a concern for social, moral and ethical issues (Bentley and Watts, 1986), or of challenging the nature of science itself by questioning its claims to objectivity and disinterestedness.

[. . .]

Equal opportunities initiatives under threat?

The story of the ERA is not simply one of missed opportunities. [. . .] However, certain aspects of the ERA seem destined to place in jeopardy the small number of positive equal opportunity initiatives that have been undertaken in recent years.

The main institutional base for systematic equal opportunities work (and for more radical anti-sexist and anti-racist interventions) has been located in a minority of committed LEAs and groups of progressive teachers. Several LEAs have produced equal opportunities policy statements, while some have appointed Equal Opportunities Advisers or advisory teachers and have organized In-Service Training (INSET), including the use of Baker Days, to raise these issues. Schools within these authorities have also been encouraged to produce their own 'whole school' policies in which every aspect of the curriculum and school organization is subjected to scrutiny. At least two projects have been jointly funded by the School Curriculum Development Committee

(SCDC), the Equal Opportunities Commission (EOC) and participating LEAs to produce materials for teachers and develop equal opportunities work in primary and secondary schools. (Genderwatch, and the Greater London Consortium on Gender in which eight boroughs were involved.) The continuation of this kind of work must now be seen as under threat as control of educational policy-making is shifted away from the LEAs and teachers. The SCDC has been closed down, while the abolition of the Inner London Educational Authority (ERA, Part III) may be seen as an additional blow since ILEA had an outstanding record of equal opportunities work on gender, class and race and, through its Research and Statistics Branch, was responsible for generating an impressive body of relevant research. In fact, Government hostility to these 'producers' of education has been due, in no small measure, to the widely publicized endeavours of those tackling sexist and racist attitudes and discriminatory practices. Right-wing lobbies such as the Adam Smith Institute and the Hillgate Group argue that education has suffered the hallmarks of 'producer capture' and that it has come to serve the interests of teachers and administrators, leading to the study of subjects which promote egalitarian principles and thus 'distract the child's attention away from serious forms of learning' (Omega Report, quoted in Demaine, 1988; Hillgate Group, 1986).

In reducing the power of LEAs and teachers, the Government claims it will make education more responsive to consumer demand. 'Parents' are to be given more choice and influence through open enrolment, participation as governors, opting out and Local Management of Schools (LMS). But the formally neutral categories conceal a sharply inegalitarian reality. As Rosemary Deem has observed, 'parent power may turn out merely to add to the power of those parents who already have access to mechanisms of power rather than those who have little or no access at present' (Deem, 1988, p. 186).

A 'balanced and broadly-based' board of governors (if we may borrow the phrase) depends on the willingness and confidence of parents to put themselves forward, but a recent NFER survey commissioned by the DES reveals concern among LEAs that not enough governors come from underprivileged backgrounds or from black or Asian communities (Jefferies and Streatfield, 1989). Yet, as governing bodies take up their new responsibilities under the Act, pressures will arise that could make them even less representative of their communities than they are now. Their enhanced role means that they will need to recruit individuals with particular administrative and financial skills, and members will also be required to devote much more of their time to governing activities. Lack of relevant expertise and domestic commitments may discourage many women from coming forward, especially if they are from working-class or some ethnic backgrounds, while those members (mostly professional males?) who possess the relevant skills may acquire a disproportionate influence in the government of schools.

Under local management of schools the extension of governors' powers in relation to staffing will be considerable, including the selection of head-teacher. In this connection, the EOC's education officer fears a serious deterioration in career development for women teachers through 'a re-intro-duction of traditional employment practices with reduced opportunities for part-time work and job sharing' unless information on sex discrimination is included in governors' training (Lynda Carr, quoted in Pandya, 1989). [...] The Government has rejected the EOC's recommendation that training should be compulsory. Governors will not be required to adhere to equal opportunities in terms of employment or the curriculum beyond the requirements of the Sex Discrimination Act, and even then it will be the LEA rather than the governors themselves who will be legally liable for any discrimination that takes place (Pandya, 1989).

In-Service Training (INSET) on equal opportunities is another key area of work which must be considered under threat from the new legislation. A National Curriculum briefing document, *From Policy to Practice*, distri-buted to all teachers, states that there should be 'coverage across the cur-riculum of gender and multi-cultural issues' (DES, 1989), whilst also acknow-ledging that the commitment of individual teachers will be crucial in making the National Curriculum work. Yet research into teachers' attitudes suggests that, in the absence of appropriate INSET, many remain far from convinced of the need for or even the desirability of equal opportunities. A study undertaken by the EOC found that nearly half the secondary school teachers surveyed were 'overall, unsympathetic to equal opportunities in school'. Among male teachers 50% expressed opposition, and more than half of these fell into the most hostile category. When classified by subject area, teachers in maths, physical sciences, technical crafts and languages were found to predominate among those least in favour (Pratt, 1985; Pratt, Bloomfield and Seale, 1984). Secondary school teachers also seem to rate technical education as more important for boys than for girls, and it is among science teachers themselves that this opinion is held most strongly (Spear, 1987). Moreover, with moves towards school-based teacher training the danger arises that existing inegalitarian practices will simply be reproduced (Miles and Furlong, 1988). [...]

A testing time for girls

Finally, there must be concern that the National Curriculum will exacerbate existing inequalities of gender by giving a more prominent role to assessment procedures. According to the teachers' briefing document, assessment is held to lie 'at the heart of the process of promoting children's learning' (TGAT quoted in *From Policy to Practice*). An unprecedented decision has been made to test the performance of seven-year-old children against centrally determined

Attainment Targets, as well as to introduce additional stages of testing in later years. The target-related assessments are intended to be formative, summative, evaluative and informative; that is, they are supposed not only to evaluate the child's development to date, but to influence decisions affecting her or his subsequent educational experience.

Assessment will be by a combination of national external tests and assessment by teachers. The kind of external testing envisaged for the National Curriculum entails a departure from the principle (established by GCSE) that assessment procedures should be designed to examine what the pupil knows rather than what she or he does not know. Since evidence suggests that girls tend to be more frightened of making mistakes and hence more cautious about attempting answers, particularly in areas already known to provoke anxiety, they may be less likely than boys to function to the best of their ability in such a formal testing situation.

Research by Goldstein and others has shown that there are important gender differences in the test performances of boys and girls which stem as much from the design of the tests as from the characteristics of individual children (Goldstein, 1987). Several of these findings were noted in a document submitted by the EOC to the Task Group on Assessment and Testing (TGAT), but were only included as an appendix to their report (DES, 1988b). It appears, in particular, that the format of a test is of crucial significance. There is evidence, for instance, that although girls perform better on more open-ended tasks requiring extended writing, they fare worse than boys on multiple choice questions and (from age 13) non-verbal tests. Gender differences in skill and conceptual ability may well be open to social modification and we are certainly not suggesting that they are 'natural' in any deterministic sense. But, for so long as they do persist, test performances of girls and boys will vary according to the relative proportions of different kinds of item included in the assessment. [. . .]

The part to be played by teachers may be a further area for concern. Caroline Gipps believes that this could potentially be the most discriminatory area of national assessment: 'We have plenty of evidence to show that teachers' judgements of children are deeply affected by stereotypes. There will be plenty of scope for the score of boys and girls who perform marginally at a particular level of maths and science to be edged up and down' (*Times Educational Supplement*, 24 March 1989). Gipps emphasizes the importance of addressing the problem of gender stereotyping in in-service training on teacher assessment. [. . .]

There is clearly a need for stringent monitoring of gender differences in relation to assessment and testing. Tests and assessment procedures which avoid gender-bias need to be carefully designed and sensitively administered. Yet, as the DES admit, the TGAT's suggestions on moderation 'appear complicated and costly' (DES, 1988c). If past experience of public testing can be taken as a guide, the proposals on assessment will introduce new rigidities

into the educational careers of children, and these rigidities will tend to dis-
criminate against girls.

Of words and deeds

The impression that the Government's commitment to equal opportunities
is less than wholehearted is reinforced by its use of sexist language in
the wording of the Act. The world encompassed by the legislation is
consistently masculine: pupils, parents, teachers and governors (not to
mention the Secretary of State!) all being referred to as if they were invariably
male.

Even more crucially, perhaps, the process of implementation has shown
that this language is not some legal anachronism, irrelevant to the world
we live in, but continues to reflect political and administrative relations to
a significant degree. The number of women appointed to the National
Curriculum Council's Working Groups has been disgracefully small—
roughly three women to every thirteen men according to the EOC's Education Officer, Lynda Carr. The working groups provided a rare opportunity
for a systematic review of teaching content and the creation of curricula
that were free from gender bias and appealing to girls. Yet the Secretary of
State failed to ensure the widespread involvement of those equal opportunities
researchers responsible for devising programmes of intervention in schools,
and the documentation so far produced has done little more than pay lip-
service to these ideals.

The NCC has established several task groups to explore cross-curricular
links including personal and social education, Special Educational Needs and
multicultural issues. A further task group on gender had originally been proposed, but this plan was abandoned. [...]

BEYOND EQUAL OPPORTUNITIES

We have devoted most of this article to a consideration of the ERA's implications for equal opportunities as these might be debated by different strands
within the liberal-feminist tradition. They are important debates, but their
horizons are strictly limited. We could, of course, have adopted a different
approach. We could, with some justification, have set out to demonstrate the
irrelevance of the ERA to most of the issues that have concerned socialist-
feminists over the past two decades, but this would have been to eliminate
nearly all substantive comment on the Act itself. On this occasion, the limits
of the analysis must be set by the boundaries of our terms of reference. The
ERA offers no radical departure for girls' education. If its strategies are often
unfamiliar within the context of British educational policy, its central objective—the gearing of education more closely towards the perceived needs of

industry—is remarkably traditional. Its rhetoric is that of creating a balanced and broad curriculum to prepare pupils for adult life, yet it fails to acknowledge that in reality adult life varies for different groups in the population. [. . .]

The limits of equal opportunities

We do not wish to underestimate the value of equal opportunities work. If a group is denied full rights of social citizenship, remedial action should not be postponed until a more profound transformation of social relations can be accomplished. (Nor would many progressive teachers find such a stance helpful.) In Juliet Mitchell's words, 'a new society that is built on an old society that, within its limits, has reached a certain level of equality clearly is a better starting point than one that must build on a society predicated on privilege and unchallenged oppression' (Mitchell, 1976). Nevertheless, it is important to recognize what those limits are.

We have described the liberal-feminist project, and the equal opportunities work that reflects its concerns, as an attempt to remove or compensate for the ascriptive and social impediments that prevent women from competing on equal terms with men. But the language of equal opportunities is deceptively neutral. While it appears to embrace all women within its objectives, it does so only by overlooking the social realities of class and ethnic division. It is significant, in this context, that nearly all the research on equal opportunities treats girls as a homogenous category, failing to acknowledge the variety of their other social characteristics. [. . .] In all the material on girls and science, for example, we could find no figures analyzing the class and ethnic origins of girls who go on to do sixth-form science, though it would indeed be surprising if these were not significant variables.

But a girl's experience of gender cannot be abstracted so neatly from any other aspects of her life. Girls from different social backgrounds will not experience patriarchal culture in identical ways, and the adult lives they anticipate will promise different kinds of opportunity, responsibility and experience. Their priorities as girls will reflect those disparities. [. . .] The ERA will not be neutral in its effects on different classes and ethnic groups, and these consequences may prove more significant for many girls than some of those we have been discussing. To take one example, how will increasing access via the National Curriculum improve the life-chances of girls trapped in under resourced, struggling inner city schools? The implications of the clauses on opting out, open enrolment and devolved management will have significant and divisive effects on large numbers of pupils, both girls and boys, and will cause increasing polarization.

Even if we could somehow set aside issues of class and ethnic *origins*, a liberal-feminist reform of education would benefit only a minority of girls. Equal opportunities perspectives are circumscribed by the fact that they offer only the prospect that some individuals will advance in an unequal world. The framework within which men and women, as social equals, are intended to pursue success remains a meritocratic and competitive one. We have seen, indeed, that this openly inegalitarian government is not averse to equal opportunities measures in so far as these may enlarge the pool of talent from which employers may draw. But highly paid and prestigious jobs are, by definition within such an order, relatively scarce, so that the achievement of parity between the sexes will still leave the inequalities *between* women (as well as those between men) unimpaired. It is always important to ask what happens, under such circumstances, to the majority population that inevitably falls behind. [. . .]

The reinforcement of gender hierarchies

If we ignore the rhetoric and consider the substance of the National Curriculum proposals, including the guidelines that Kenneth Baker issued to the subject working groups, we can see that they are informed by a set of linked assumptions and priorities concerning the economy, technology and education. It is assumed, in the first instance, that the British economy can prosper in the world markets only by pursuing a vigorous policy of *growth* based on investment in high-technology industries; secondly, that the market is the only mechanism for efficient economic expansion, and that business must therefore be set free from all forms of collective constraint; and, thirdly, that the main function of education is to serve the needs of the 'enterprise culture', even if this can only be achieved at the expense of other educational objectives.

The pedagogic implications are captured by the word 'training' rather than education. The issue involved is not whether scientific and technological subjects should have a place within the core curriculum, but how these and other subjects should be taught and in what context. The Government's commitment to a regime of high-tech economic growth is not to be deflected by encouraging debate about the social context and limits of technology, or centering issues of social control and responsibility in science. The kind of education apparently favoured by the Secretary of State (Kenneth Baker) is non-reflexive in character, essentially encouraging the learning of 'facts' rather than skills of interpretation, critical enquiry or aesthetic appreciation. (His guidelines to the History Working Group, stressing pupils' acquisition of their national culture, are another example of this outlook.) Values are not excluded from the educational process, but they enter as the inculcation of a *particular* set of viewpoints rather than in a spirit of open enquiry and with a due sense of relativity. [. . .]

The ERA's privileging of maths, science and technology incorporates a hidden curriculum on gender. It has been widely observed that the values and procedures of Western science tend to be gender-specific, reflecting distinctly masculine modes of thought and understanding (for example, Easlea, 1981;

Keller, 1982). These differences, we would contend, are social and historical in origin, not innate, but their effective presence in contemporary culture is hardly in dispute. Under the Act, male-dominated areas of achievement and masculine styles of learning will be accorded even higher status than before, while feminine intellectual qualities and those subjects which girls currently find most attractive and accessible will be correspondingly devalued. We would not suggest that the gender contouring of this hierarchy of knowledge is intended, but the message that it will convey to girls and boys will be none the less powerful for that. (It is an ironic feature of equal opportunities perspectives that, far from challenging this principle of 'male-as-norm', they tend to endorse it by focusing so heavily on gaining entry for women into masculinized areas of life.)

The reverse side of this coin is the marginalization of that special curriculum for girls, organized around preparation for family life and motherhood, which has informed British education since Victorian times (Wolpe, 1974; Purvis, 1984). Although Home Economics may still be taken as an option, it will have to compete in a restricted timetable with other subjects outside the core curriculum. From an equal opportunities perspective this could be interpreted favourably as representing a defeat for those conservative policy groups advocating separate adult roles for men and women and an appropriately differentiated curriculum for boys and girls (Anderson, 1988). But this would be to take a restricted view of the possibilities. The most likely outcome of excluding the personal and caring components of the curriculum from the core will be to preserve them as girls-only enclaves taken mainly by pupils with low career prospects (which means, of course, that the tension between 'industry-led' conservatives and 'family traditionalists' will be substantially reconciled). If the government were concerned to foster sexual equality in adult life, it would accord these subject areas high status and, following the example of some LEAs, would seek to make them relevant for both sexes. [...] Equal opportunities policies pursued in isolation tend to lead only to the phenomenon of the 'double working day' for women, or else to an increase in personal and domestic service as professional couples employ young or working-class women to look after their children or do the housework. Persuading men to take on the routine responsibilities of caring, whether inside or outside the home, is quite as important for sexual equality as the conventional concerns of liberal-feminism. A curriculum that fails to acknowledge this can be considered neither balanced nor broad.

Finally, however, a vision of girls' education that goes beyond equal opportunities cannot be satisfied with adjustments in the sexual division of labour. 'Who does what?' is an important issue, but one that has to be transcended (not displaced) by questions concerning the social organization of caring, reproduction, production and welfare. The preparation of children for adult life cannot be indifferent to the nature of a society in which women are systematically subordinated to men, yet divided in their experiences of inequality by dint of class and race. In some ways, women's appreciation of the world is distinct from that of men. Perhaps it is by virtue of the fact that they 'straddle public and private worlds in different ways from men [that] they cannot so readily conceive of themselves in public terms alone' (Phillips, 1987), and so, as girls, are more interested in subjects having to do with 'people' rather than 'things'. But if all this is true, education to make children aware of their social and political environment, including anti-sexist and anti-racist work, has to be built into the foundations of the curriculum, not added on as an after-thought. The greatest threat to girls' education posed by the ERA may have nothing to do with its immediate implications for equal opportunities. The threat will come from its contribution to Government efforts to stifle dissent and to exert control over the way we think.

*   *   *   *   *

POSTSCRIPT, APRIL 1994

In our article we stressed the importance of looking beyond the limited horizons of liberal-feminist agendas for equal opportunities if the educational needs of *all* girls, and not just those of the brightest, were to be addressed. In particular, we took this to require a commitment to a funding policy that would seek to redress social inequalities as well as a commitment to anti-sexist and anti-racist work. The Conservative Party's 1992 election victory ensured the extension of market principles (where oversubscribed schools 'choose' parents) that reinforce rather than mitigate inequalities and lead to increasing social polarization. We reiterate the point that this may have as many, if not more, damaging effects on the quality of education provision for many working-class and minority ethnic girls as more obvious issues of gender differentiation.

The continuation of Conservative rule also meant that the influence of LEAs, the institutions best placed for developing equal opportunities initia-tives among teachers, continued to decline. Many LEAs have been forced to cut their services, and there are fewer equal opportunities advisory teachers in post to ensure that policies are transformed into practice. The Greater London Consortium on Gender no longer exists due to LEA cuts. Equal opportunities have, as predicted, been marginalized. They are included as a cross-curricular dimension, but this is vaguely defined and is non-mandatory. As such, along with cross-curricular themes such as Citizenship and Economic and Indus-trial Awareness, they have so far had little space for development (though the Dearing review could change this) (Whitty, Rowe and Aggleton, 1994). Given this marginalization, schools that opt out are unlikely to prioritize equal opportunities work—though the research on this still needs to be done. According to the Annual Report of HM Senior Chief Inspector of Schools for 1992, 'Progress on *equal opportunities* is best described as patchy. In some schools and colleges, awareness of the take-up of educational opportunities as between the sexes and among ethnic minority groups is high; in others, it is totally inadequate. Most institutions have policies for promoting equality of opportunity but too often the gap between policy and practice is unacceptably wide' (DES, 1992, para. 28).

The picture on the 'entitlement' curriculum is somewhat brighter, though this cannot be attributed to the ERA. Between 1987 and 1992 there was a marked improvement in the proportion of girls achieving O-level/GCSE grades A–C or equivalent in science, both absolutely and relative to boys (from 26% to 37% for girls; from 34% to 37% for boys.) In mathematics, achievements of grades A–C were also equal for girls and boys, but the massive gap in the numbers of boys and girls attempting technology persists (DFE, 1993, para. 6, Table 4). But fewer girls continue to science A level except in biology. Science at this level is still a predominantly male domain (DFE, 1993, para. 15), and the 'modernizers' in the government are still concerned to encourage more girls to take science. The Committee on Women in Science, Engineering and Technology, set up by the Science Minister, William Waldegrave, in 1993, saw women as 'the country's biggest single most undervalued and therefore under-used resource' (HMSO, 1994). Yet the conflicts between Conservative 'modernizers' and 'traditionalists', far from abating, seem to have sharpened, and such comments must be seen against the background of a concerted, if accident-prone, 'Back to Basics' campaign stressing traditional family values, parental responsibilities and the supposedly damaging consequences of single motherhood. Such conflicts indicate how precarious are the advances towards a more equitable education for girls. The future direction of that education remains very much 'in the balance'.

References

Anderson, D. (ed.) (1988) *Full Circle.* London: Social Affairs Unit.

Arnot, M. and Weiner, G. (eds) (1987) *Gender and the Politics of Schooling.* London: Hutchinson.

APU (Assessment and Performance Unit) (1988) *Science at Age 15.* London: HMSO.

Association for Science Education (1988) *Gender Issues in Science Education.* Working Party Draft Statement of Policy. Hatfield: ASE.

Bentley, D. and Watts, M. (1986) Courting the positive virtues: a case for feminist science. *European Journal of Science Education* 8, 121–34. Reprinted in Kelly, A. (1987) *Science for Girls?,* pp. 89–99. Milton Keynes: Open University Press.

Buswell, C. (1981) Sexism in school routines and classroom practices. *Durham and Newcastle Research Review* IX, 195–200.

Deem, R. (1988) The great Education Reform Bill 1988—some issues and implications. *Journal of Education Policy* 3 (2), 181–9.

Demaine, J. (1988) Teachers' work, curriculum and the New Right. *British Journal of Sociology of Education* 3, 247–64.

DES (1988a) *Statistical Bulletin,* December.

— (1988b) *National Curriculum Task Group on Assessment and Testing: A Report.*

— (1988c) *DES News,* No. 175/88, 7 June.

— (1989) *National Curriculum: From Policy to Practice.*

— (1992) *Education in England 1990–91.*

DFE (1993) *Statistical Bulletin.* Issue No. 15/93.

Easlea, B. (1981) *Science and Sexual Oppression.* London: Weidenfeld and Nicolson.

Gilligan, C. (1982) *In a Different Voice.* Boston: Harvard University Press.

Goldstein, H. (1987) Gender bias and test norms in educational selection. In M. Arnot and G. Weiner (eds) *Gender and the Politics of Schooling,* pp. 122–6. London: Hutchinson.

Green, A. (1988) Lessons in standards. *Marxism Today,* January, 24–31.

Harding, J. (1983) *Switched Off: The Science Education of Girls.* Longman for the Schools Council.

— (ed.) (1986) *Perspectives on Gender and Science.* Lewes: Falmer Press.

Hillgate Group (1986) *Whose Schools? A Radical Manifesto.* London: Hillgate Group.

Hiskett, M. (1988) Should sons and daughters be brought up differently? Radical feminism in schools. In D. Anderson (ed.) *Full Circle,* pp. 153–68. London: Social Affairs Unit.

HMSO (1994) *The Rising Tide: Report on Women in Science, Engineering and Technology.* London: HMSO.

Hough, J.R. (1987) *Education and the National Economy.* London: Croom Helm.

Jamieson, I. and Watts, T. (1987) Squeezing out enterprise. *The Times Educational Supplement,* 18 December.

Jefferies, G. and Streatfield, D. (1989) *Reconstitution of School Governors.* Slough: NFER.

Joffe, L. and Foxman, D. (1988) *Attitudes and Gender Differences: Mathematics at Age 11 and 15.* Windsor: NFER-Nelson.

Johnson, S. and Murphy, P. (1986) *Girls and Physics.* APU Occasional Paper 4. DES.

Keller, E.F. (1982) Feminism and science. In N.O. Keohane *et al.* (eds) *Feminist Theory: A Critique of Ideology,* pp. 113–26. Brighton: Harvester Press.

Kelly, A. (1987) Why girls don't do science. In A. Kelly (ed.) *Science For Girls.* Milton Keynes: Open University Press.

— (1988) Towards a democratic science education. In H. Lauder and P. Brown (eds) *Education in Search of a Future,* pp. 150–73. Basingstoke: Falmer Press.

Le Riche, E. (1988) *Why Do Teenage Girls Truant?* London: Roehampton Institute of Higher Education, Department of Sociology and Social Administration.

Licht, B.G. and Dweck, C.S. (1987) Sex differences in achievement orientations. In M. Arnot and G. Weiner (eds) *Gender and the Politics of Schooling,* pp. 95–107. London: Hutchinson.

Mahoney, P. (1985) *Schools for the Boys? Co-education Re-assessed.* London: Hutchinson in association with the Explorations in Feminism Collective.

Miles, S. and Furlong, J. (1988) Teachers training teachers: an opportunity for a sociological break in education transmission? In P. Woods and A. Pollard (eds) *Sociology and Teaching,* pp. 76–91. London: Croom Helm.

Mitchell, J. (1976) Women and equality. In J. Mitchell and A. Oakley (eds) *The Rights and Wrongs of Women,* pp. 379–99. London: Penguin. Reprinted in Phillips, A. (ed.) (1978) *Feminism and Equality,* pp. 24–43. Oxford: Blackwell.

NEDC (National Economic Development Council) (1982) *Education and Industry.* Memorandum by the Director General, ref. NEDC (82) 85.

Pandya, A. (1989) Equal but different. *Education,* 24 March.

Phillips, A. (ed.) (1987) *Feminism and Equality.* Oxford: Blackwell.

Pratt, J. (1985) The attitudes of teachers. In J. Whyte *et al.* (eds) *Girl Friendly Schooling.* London: Methuen.

Pratt, J., Bloomfield, J. and Seale, C. (1984) *Option Choice: A Question of Equal Opportunity.* Windsor: NFER-Nelson.

Purvis, J. (1984) *Women's Education*, Open University Course E205, Block 6, Unit 25. Milton Keynes: Open University Press.

Smail, B. (1984) *Girl Friendly Science: Avoiding Sex-Bias in the Classroom.* London: Longman.

Spear, M. (1978) Teachers' views about the importance of science for boys and girls. In A. Kelly (ed.) *Science for Girls*, pp. 52–7. Milton Keynes: Open University Press.

Stanworth, M. (1983) *Gender and Schooling: A Study of Sexual Divisions in the Classroom.* London: Hutchinson in association with the Explorations in Feminism Collective.

Whitty, G., Rowe, G. and Aggleton, P. (1994) Paper delivered to International Sociology of Education Conference, Sheffield.

Wolpe, A.M. (1974) The official ideology of education for girls. In M. Flude and J. Ahier (eds) *Educability, Schools and Ideology*, pp. 139–59. London: Croom Helm.

— (1988) *Within School Walls.* London: Routledge.

10 WOMEN, EQUALITY, AND EQUITY IN LIBERAL EDUCATIONAL POLICIES, 1945–1988: A FEMINIST CRITIQUE

SUE MIDDLETON

The shift to the right in social policy in capitalist states during the past decade has been subjected to a considerable amount of feminist analysis. The restructuring policies of New Zealand's fourth Labour government (1984–90) are generating similar critiques. As in Britain, Australia and North America, (for example, Britain — David, 1986; Australia — Yates, 1986; North America — Eisenstein, 1982) such feminist critiques have been particularly strong with respect to education. While feminist theories, political strategies, and agendas differ widely (for a detailed account of the different feminist positions on women's education, see Middleton, 1988), the major themes of the policy critiques these have generated can readily be reduced to one key question: what are the implications of these policies for women's lives and, more generally, for relations between the sexes in both public and private life?

This article offers a feminist analysis of two versions of liberal theory which have influenced New Zealand's educational policies since the Second World War. Drawing on key educational policy documents, it compares and contrasts the liberal-left, social-democratic ideals of the first labour government (1935–49) with the liberal-right (or market-liberal) assumptions which are strongly shaping those of the fourth. In particular, it focuses on similarities and differences between the earlier ideal of equality of opportunity and contemporary notions of equity with respect to the education of women and girls. It is argued that *both* versions of liberalism—and the educational policies in which they are embodied—rest on *contradictions* between individualism (or personal autonomy) and the imperatives of government for planning, monitoring and regulating the population (social control). A feminist reading of policy statements shows that their assumptions about individuals and about controlling the population are androcentric (male-centred): they are derived from the experiences and perspectives of (Pakeha, middle-class) men, and render women invisible or marginal. [. . .] I shall argue that educational practices based on analyses that marginalize women cannot bring about equality.

Source: Abridged from Codd, J. and Jones, A. (eds) (1990) *New Zealand Education Policy Today* (pp. 68–93; 218–20). Wellington, New Zealand: Bridget Williams.

WOMEN, INDIVIDUALISM, AND THE CONTROL OF POPULATIONS

The tension between liberal notions of the primacy of individual liberty and the practical problems of how to manage and control large populations has permeated modern social policy. Classical liberal theories of the individual have been traced to their origins in the demise of feudalism, the growth of industrial capitalism, and the rise of the *bourgeoisie.* Particularly influential were the French Enlightenment philosophers, who argued that rationality, not inherited privilege, should be the basis of citizenship. As Poster (1984, p. 11) has summarized it, classical liberal thought was centred on 'the notion that freedom depends on the reason of the individual and the individual can exercise freedom best in a condition of autonomy'.

However, classical liberal theories were androcentric: the rationally autonomous individual was a white, property-owning *male.* Together with savages (non-Europeans), the indigent (unpropertied classes), and the insane, women were perceived as irrational creatures of passion, who could therefore justifiably be denied the rights of citizenship (such as the right to own property or to vote). In the eighteenth and nineteenth centuries, middle-class Western feminists like Mary Wollstonecraft (1972, first published 1792) accepted the liberal notion of the supremacy of reason over passion—an essential dualism and conflict in human nature. Women, she argued, were capable of rational thought, but were denied the opportunity to develop their capacity to the full because of their inferior education. At the same time, she esteemed motherhood and women's 'domestic virtues'. The suffrage, she believed, would enable women's moral superiority to influence public life. Nineteenth-century British liberal reformers such as John Stuart Mill (1983, first published 1869) made similar arguments. Women must have equal rights with men to be educated, to vote, to own property, and to accumulate wealth within the existing hierarchies of capitalism. But Mill believed that if men made marriage and motherhood sufficiently attractive, most women would, of their own free will, rationally choose to devote their energies to domestic duties. Only a few exceptionally talented women would choose to enter public life in the same way as middle-class men. Writing in times before contraceptive technology made 'careers and sex' possible for women, classical liberal feminists accepted domesticity as the destiny of most women.

Liberal feminism, like the classical liberal theories from which it derived, was a perspective mainly of the middle class. Liberal feminists fought, not only for rights such as access to the type of education that would develop rational autonomy, but also for property rights such as the right to own and manage personal property and wealth after marriage. However, at the time these arguments and political strategies were being developed in the nineteenth century, more-radical thinkers argued that capitalism and private property were the basis of women's oppression. Concepts originating in Marxist thought have provided contemporary sociologists with useful theoretical tools to use in analyzing modern liberal educational policy.

According to Marxists, women were particularly oppressed under capitalism. Within the family, women's unpaid labour served the capitalists through the processes of biological and social/cultural reproduction. Biologically, women gave birth to successive generations of workers and capitalists. Socially, through their domestic labour, they ensured their husbands and children were fit to work. Culturally, through child-rearing, they taught skills, attitudes and values needed in the capitalist workplace. As paid workers, women and children were paid lower wages on the whole than their male counterparts and functioned as a reserve army of labour. [...] While liberal feminists regarded women as disadvantaged individuals who could be emancipated by legislative means, Marxists saw them as an oppressed class whose subordination was grounded in the economic imperatives of industrial capitalism. (For a useful summary of Marxist-feminist positions, see Barrett, 1980.)

[...] Although liberal reforms in the twentieth century have gone a long way towards achieving equal opportunities for men and *single* (or child-free[1]) women, social policies have, in the main, remained premised on the assumption that domestic work, including child-rearing, will be carried out unpaid by women within the patriarchal nuclear family. While liberal policy rhetoric has increasingly offered women equal opportunities (in the sense of the same options) at a formal, or legal, level, state apparatuses such as the tax structure, the organization of work, the lack of good quality, affordable childcare, and the social welfare benefits system have ensured continuing domesticity as the major role of the majority of women with young children.[2] [...] Thus liberalism constitutes a contradiction between women's intellectuality/professionality and the full expression of their reproductive sexuality.

Sexuality is rarely visible within liberal social theory; in placing primacy on rationality, liberal thought consigns sexuality to the realm of irrationality, or passion. However, because women's capacity for biological reproduction is so central in their lives, any theory that excludes it cannot take women sufficiently into account. In understanding this, Foucault's writing is useful. Foucault studied the development of modern technologies of government—the practices through which governments regulated, monitored and controlled whole populations. He identified powerful disciplines ('discourses'), such as demography, which had become incorporated into the various apparatuses of the state as 'manpower planning'. Many practices of modern government rested, not on a view of society as composed of rational individuals, but on powerful 'knowledges' about 'masses' or 'populations'. Social policies required analysis of:

... population as an economic and political problem: population as wealth, population as manpower and labour capacity, population balanced between its own growth and the resources it commanded.

(Foucault, 1980, p. 25)

Foucault's framework has proved useful to feminists because it places sexuality at the centre of its analysis of governments' monitoring and regulation of populations:

At the heart of this economic and political problem of population was sex: it was necessary to analyze the birth-rate, the age of marriage, the legitimate and illegitimate births, the precocity and frequency of sexual relations, the ways of making them fertile or sterile, the effects of married life, or of the prohibitions, the impact of contraceptive practice.

(Foucault, 1980, p. 26)

For example, governments regulate reproductive sexuality through controlling women's access to contraception and abortion, through prescribing which types of family can receive financial support from the state, and through regulation of the labour force (such as the encouragement or discouragement of married women's engagement in paid work).

This analysis is useful in developing a feminist perspective on the rhetoric of manpower planning, which has substantially informed New Zealand's educational policies since the Second World War. [. . .] Functionalists analyze the social functions of institutions, such as education, in maintaining social cohesion and stability. Policy-makers have found this perspective useful because it offers a way of relating education to other objects of government planning such as the economy. Within functionalist perspectives, education can be studied as an instrument of government. [. . .] Functionalists see education not as the initiator of change, but as the obedient servant of the economy. Acting as a sorting mechanism, it selects the fittest for leadership positions and allocates workers to positions in the economy. [. . .] Within this discourse, people are reduced to 'manpower units', 'human resources', or 'personnel'. Education is seen as a technical problem for government—the problem of education and the economy is constituted as scientific/technological in nature, as a problem of bringing about social efficiency.

Functionalist discourse has been much criticized by feminist sociologists because, like classical liberal theories, it renders women invisible or marginal. For example, functionalist research on New Zealand women teachers in the 1950s and 1960s presented women as a problem for planners. Married women were a problem if they could not be lured back into teaching during the teacher shortage. At the same time, working mothers were a problem because, according to the Maternal deprivation rhetoric of the 1950s, they were likely to produce delinquent children. (Maternal deprivation theories in New Zealand have been discussed by May, 1988; for a functionalist study of women teachers, see Watson, 1966, discussed in Middleton, 1986.) While the manpower planners could see women as a disposable reserve army of labour, to be shunted in and out of paid work with the vicissitudes of the capitalist economy, for women so affected the experience of being simultaneously a needed worker and a bad mother was confusing and stressful. The androcentricity of functionalist theory had real repercussions on women's everyday lives. These androcentric theories have remained in liberal educational (and other social) policy.

WOMEN, SOCIAL DEMOCRACY, AND MARKET LIBERALISM: CASE STUDIES OF EDUCATIONAL POLICY TEXTS

It has become common for left-wing Labour activists to look back with nostalgia to the good old days of the first Labour Government. Recoiling in horror from what they see as a Treasury-led market-liberal takeover, they extol the virtues of post-war social-democratic values. This section compares and contrasts a key educational policy document of 1945 with an influential education report of 1987—respectively a case study of a social democratic perspective and an example of market-liberal educational analysis. With regard to their assumptions about women there is surprisingly little difference between the two perspectives. [. . .]

Two liberal positions in educational policy: An introduction

The first report to be discussed, commonly known as the Thomas Report, was the product of the Beeby administration's inquiry into the post-primary school curriculum. Entitled *Report on the Post-Primary School Curriculum*, this document sketched the blueprint for New Zealand's state secondary schools—prescribing what was to be taught and why it was to be taught. It remains the most comprehensive statement we have of the first Labour Government's educational philosophy and its vision of the role of education in a capitalist social democracy. The second document is the New Zealand Treasury's 1987 analysis of New Zealand education, *Government Management: Vol. II, Education*. It is not, in the sense of the Thomas Report, a government policy statement; rather, it is one government department's briefing paper to an incoming government after a general election. However, there are good reasons for comparing it with the Thomas Report. First, it provides a very comprehensive statement of a market-liberal position on education. Second, Treasury officials have been involved in the production and implementation of the fourth Labour Government's policies on educational restructuring: their input is evident, for example in the rhetoric of the Picot Report, and the Hawke Report. [. . .]

The adoption of a market-liberal position as a basis for educational (and other social) policy has been seen as marking a dramatic shift in liberal ideology. Recently, one of the architects of postwar Labour educational policy,

Dr C.E. Beeby, reflected on his own, and his contemporaries', youthful visions for New Zealand's educational future:

> Most teachers of my generation ... were not very interested in politics. At training college in the early 1920s, our most heated discussions were on religion and ethics, not on politics.... Other people with more taste for politics would look after the economic and political sectors of the front; our best contribution was to create an education system that could serve the more equitable kind of democracy we hoped, rather vaguely, to see emerge. We were encouraged in this attitude by an exaggerated idea of the effect an improved form of education could have on social change. Our overriding interest in educational equality for the individual would, we thought, itself contribute, through the next generation, to the growth of a more equitable society; the liberal education we were planning was calculated to help produce citizens who would be likely to appreciate and foster such a society.   (Beeby, 1956, p. xxxii)

Beeby described the intellectual base of his contemporaries as shaped by the dominant theories of the day in the disciplines of psychology, history and philosophy. Sociology and economics, he noted, did not at that time shape the key educational decisions. In contrast, it is these disciplines (or, rather, specific and narrowly technocratic theoretical tendencies within them) which have informed much of the rationale and rhetoric of educational policies during the term of the fourth Labour Government of the late 1980s. [...]

The appointment of management experts, whose experience and perspectives have been determined by the imperatives of the commercial world, ensures the continued influence of economics as a dominant force in educational policy. Such perspectives can reduce education to a commodity. As one top public servant expressed it, in a speech to a group of school principals:

> There is always some kind of education market in which people are trading goods and services. You are traders with an important position in that market ... you are managing on behalf of someone who must be the owner ... Your market will be contestable and changeable, it will be efficient and have equity in it.   (*Dominion*, 4 July 1988)

In its pure form, a market-liberal analysis sees a centralized state apparatus as inhibiting individuals' abilities and rights to engage in free competition. It favours increased privatization of education on the grounds that this would enhance individuals' freedom of choice. It recommends the dismantling of large state bureaucracies, regarding the role of the state as minimal and serving mainly to guarantee and protect the (person and property) rights of competitive individuals. [...]

In contrast, the dominant ideology of postwar social-democratic liberalism was more collectivist or socialist in emphasis. Education was, above all, to promote the common good and was seen as an instrument to help achieve social progress. The Thomas Report emphasized progressivist ideals in its view that education could help prevent the resurgence of fascism and would work for the reconstruction of social democracy and equality (Department of Education, 1944, p. 2). [...] In this report, the 'social' was given primacy over the 'economic'. Fearing the threat of totalitarianism, the designers of post-war education saw it 'less as a means of individual advancement and more as a means of creating an educated community' (Department of Education, 1944, p. 2). The generation that had experienced the Second World War was only too aware that fascism, rather than liberalism, could become the dominant ideology of a capitalist state.

Despite these major philosophical differences and the contrasts in the relative emphasis given to different disciplines (political theory, economics etc.), neither of the two liberal positions is likely to bring about gender equality. For deeply embedded in both are the androcentric perspectives of liberal individualism and of technocratic functionalism.

The Thomas Report and equality of opportunity

The overarching educational aims of the first Labour Government were outlined in 1939 by Peter Fraser, Minister of Education at the time:

> The government's objective, broadly expressed, is that every person, whatever his level of academic ability, whether he be rich or poor, whether he live in town or country, has a right, as a citizen, to a free education of the kind for which he is best fitted and to the fullest extent of his powers.   (Fraser, cited in Beeby, 1986, p. xxxii)

At this time, equality of opportunity meant providing all students with formal rights of access to the same sorts of education. The only limits to such opportunities were to be those of merit (thus it was what later writers have termed a 'meritocratic' vision of society). [...]

The flaws in this vision of educational equality became evident as statistics showed a concentration of Maori children and children from low socio-economic status families in the lower, non-academic streams of secondary schools. Sociologists of the time explained this by means of the 'deficit' model, which had developed in Britain and the United States of America within functionalist sociology of education. Such researchers argued that the school failure of working-class children and Black children could be explained by their home backgrounds in that they were culturally deprived or disadvantaged. (A more detailed review of such research is in Ramsay, 1985; for a critique of 'deficit' theories, see Keddie, 1973.) [...]

However, by the early 1970s, educators and researchers were developing more radical explanations. It was not the *children* or their families who were to blame for failure, but the school itself. What counted as school knowledge and school success was drawn from the cultural values of the dominant class in society—the (mainly white) middle class. The nature of schooling itself—both overt and hidden dimensions of the curriculum—must change to come into line with the cultural backgrounds, experiences and concerns of the pupils and their families. White middle-class pupils had what schools recognized as 'cultural capital'—the kinds of language, tastes, manners, and modes of inquiry and expression that teachers identified as 'academic'.[3] The concept of intelligence as measured in IQ tests came under attack as being a measure of a particular culture rather than a sign of innate academic potential (Olssen, 1988). Western education systems were challenged by activists from minority ethnic groups, and demands for alternatives increased. Such challenges—from Maori people—face New Zealand educators today. The demand is for a pluralist approach—the right to be treated differently rather than to be equal in the sense of becoming 'brown Pakeha'. Bill Renwick, Director-General of Education 1975–87, referred to the shift in those years from 'equality as sameness' to 'equity as diversity' (Renwick, 1986, p. 111). [. . .]

Postwar secondary schools were usually organized on the basis of streaming. The streams were commonly decided by the optional subjects pupils took in addition to those of the compulsory core curriculum. These streaming practices had the effect of stratifying knowledge into high- and low-status subjects and, within the pupil culture, produced high- and low-status pupils. The following example, taken from a wider study, depicts one Maori girl's experience of the way streaming and the stratification of knowledge served to reproduce the class and ethnic power relations of a rural district in the 1960s. Hine came from a family with negative experiences of school (her parents had been punished for speaking Maori). However, one teacher in her primary school had picked her out as 'bright' and encouraged her *whanau* to help her to aim for a career in teaching:

> I remember before I went from primary school to secondary school, the test we had to sit there—the OTIS . . . and I failed that miserably. They all had high expectations of me passing through that with flying colours and I didn't, and I remember having to sit it again. They just couldn't understand why I failed that test. When I first went to high school, there was streaming at the time—I was streamed into the academic level even though I failed the OTIS test. They just put me into that one and I refused to go there, because all my cousins who were my mates, were put into the commercial stream or even lower—which I guess was the home science course. So I went into that for the first day and then they came and got me out of there and I remember crying the next day because I didn't want to be in there and I was the only Maori in the class . . . For several years I was the only Maori, so it was a very lonely existence. I could see the gradual drifting with my cousins at this stage.
>
> (Middleton, 1985, p. 221)

While working-class boys and Maori boys often experienced similar alienation from what counted as high-status school knowledge, there were many differences between the sexes in schools. Such differences can be explained by the androcentricity in the liberal notions of equality and its contradictory images of women. For example, the core curriculum as laid down in the Thomas Report took for granted the sexual division of labour within the home and in paid work. It rested on firm assumptions about 'women's work.' Schools were to educate each student to be a good 'worker, neighbour, homemaker and citizen' (Department of Education, 1944, p. 5). Yet, homemaking skills were to be taught only (and compulsorily) to girls:

> An intelligent parent would wish a daughter to have . . . the knowledge, skill and taste required to manage a home well and make it a pleasant place to live in.   (Department of Education, 1944, p. 17)

This, and later reports such as that of the Currie Commission in 1962, also constituted certain school subjects and jobs as men's and women's work. Schooling was to reproduce the sexual division of labour. However, while the liberal rhetoric of the Thomas Report exalted motherhood and domesticity, in practice it simultaneously (as Hine's experience illustrates) degraded women's domestic work as being of low status, for the 'dumb' or the unskilled. (This analysis of the Thomas Report is developed more fully in Middleton, 1986.)

As part of its concern with constructing and reproducing an orderly democracy, the Thomas Committee had emphasized the importance of the monitoring and regulation of adolescent sexuality in schools. The committee regarded it as important to give secondary school pupils the 'biological facts' about sex. Consistent with the liberal emphasis on rationality, this belief was based on the idea that factual information would facilitate individuals' rational choice with respect to sexual conduct. Such concerns stemmed from the widespread moral panics during the 1950s over what was then termed 'juvenile delinquency', which, for girls at least, meant 'having sex'. Since the monitoring and regulation of sexuality was construed as largely a *medical* matter, sex became a topic in the general science curriculum [. . .]: sex would thus be set within the domain of controllable reason rather than the anarchy of feelings and passion.

For girls, the regulation and monitoring of their sexuality created contradictions. For example, the dominant ideology of equality of opportunity was premised on assumptions that intelligence and ability were innate and normally distributed and that, to promote equal opportunities, schools must select the able. For many girls, the resulting streaming practices served to reproduce contradictions between the sexual and the intellectual, as well as the sexual double standard. This double standard divided girls, constituting them as good or bad, as rational or passionate. Being an intellectual was socially constructed as contradictory to being overtly sexual, which was culturally appropriate only in the lower streams. 'Academic' girls were expected to delay sexual activity until they had completed their training for suitably feminine professions such as teaching, nursing, or secretarial work. Schooling, then, reproduced a gendered intellectuality. [...]

The school system that resulted from the Thomas Report's recommendations, then, reproduced the fundamental contradiction between rationality and sexuality that is inherent in Western liberal thought. 'Intellectual' women were faced with a choice: to follow male careers, to have a family, or to have a career only as 'a short adventure between school and marriage' (Watson, 1966, p. 159). However, the reality of labour shortages, particularly in teaching, drew many married women back into paid work. As Zillah Eisenstein observed, such women's experiences helped create the preconditions for feminist protest as the contradictions within the liberal ideology of equality of opportunity became evident:

> Advanced capitalism ... has required married women to enter the labour force. Although the structure of the capitalist market is patriarchal, its ideology is definitely liberal ... Therein lies the crisis for liberalism: an ideology of (liberal) equality and a contradictory reality of patriarchal inequality.   (Eisenstein, 1982, p. 38)

Education and the second wave of feminism

The second wave of feminism crashed across the Western world in the late 1960s and early 1970s. [...] Here was the first generation of women to be *promised equality*, [...] yet many were to experience marginality or alienation from the culture of the academic. As rural, as Maori, as working-class, as female—as combinations of some or all of these—many experienced a distancing, an exclusion from what counted as advanced educational knowledge. They lacked the academic cultural capital of the educated urban *bourgeoisie*. They sensed 'something wrong', something unfair, about the education they were receiving.[4] In the late 1960s, some gained access to radical ideas—about race, about class—through some academic subjects and through social movements such as protests against the Vietnam War or against sporting contacts with South Africa. Personal experiences of discrimination or oppression were translated by these theories from mere personal problems to broader public or political issues. The sense of discomfort that they felt made change seem desirable. The social theories to which they gained access and the prevailing security of economic prosperity and full employment helped to make change also seem possible.

Many such educated and politicized young women began to sense 'something wrong' in their experiences as *female* in education. Their marginalization in academic discourse made it difficult to articulate these feelings, as first-wave feminist theories were not made available in the curriculum. At first it was the sharing of personal experiences in consciousness-raising groups that helped some educated women of the time to begin to develop collective analyses of, and strategies to address, their marginality and oppression as women in education. Education was central in second-wave feminism: as an object of demand, as a means of employment, as a source of ideas, and as a site of struggle for broader social change. Feminists sought equal access for women and girls to the various curriculum subjects and to non-traditional occupations; they also sought equal representation in senior positions in educational hierarchies, and increased visibility of women in curriculum content. Feminists developed new theories to explain past and present patterns of gender relations. Academic feminists began to include these theories in university courses in the traditional disciplines, as well as developing the transdisciplinary field of women's studies.

[...] Freed by contraceptive technology from continual child-bearing, feminists argued that legal equality, or equal rights of access, were not enough. Instead, they sought ways of bringing about an equal numerical distribution of the sexes in positions of power and across the full spectrum of paid occupations; their version of liberalism, then, was more *interventionist* than previous feminist movements. The social theory available to them at the time was functionalism. Women and girls were disadvantaged in relation to men, and measures of compensation were needed to remedy this. Legislative changes (such as the Equal Pay Act of 1972 and the Human Rights Commission Act of 1975) aimed to prevent discrimination against women in the public sphere. Measures of affirmative action were sought in the workplace. In schools, efforts were made to remove sex-stereotyping from subject choice and from texts and to encourage women teachers to apply for senior positions.

Other feminists (known as radical feminists) argued tht emulating men would not liberate women. Rather, women should reclaim their history and culture. [...] Radical feminist political agendas focused on *sexuality*. They argued that the so-called sexual revolution, which had followed the invention and availability of the contraceptive pill and other improved contraceptive technologies, had not liberated women but had compounded their oppression. Through the mass media, and especially in pornography and images of women as 'playmates' or 'pets', women's sexuality became a commodity—women were alienated from their own sexuality. Radical feminists advocated educating girls separately and celebrating women's past and present achievements instead of emulating men. Nevertheless, it is *liberal*, not radical, feminist rhetoric that has, at least partly, been incorporated into the policy statements of the 1980s; this is because it speaks the language of the policy-makers. The more radical feminist positions on sexuality and power remain invisible in the rhetoric of educational policy.

While liberal feminism was initially a powerful force within both the Labour and National Parties, the past two elections (1984, 1987) have seen an increasing polarization between the two parties on issues pertaining to gender and sexuality. The economic recession which began in the mid-1970s saw a backlash against working mothers who were accused of stealing jobs from men and school leavers: there was pressure on the reserve army to return to the home. American-inspired fundamentalist Christianity offered many a sense of security and a reaffirmation of traditional roles. Seen as denigrating 'the family', feminists were portrayed as evil, even as part of an international communist conspiracy (Ryan, 1988). In 1984, conservative women—many inspired by the teachings of fundamentalist churches—mobilized against two liberal reforms initiated by the newly elected Labour government: the setting up of the Ministry of Women's Affairs and the Homosexual Law Reform Bill. Largely because of these measures, fundamentalists and other conservatives campaigned against Labour in the 1987 general election. Gender and sexuality had once more become a hot political issue. This was the state of the debate at the time the Treasury briefing papers were written.

The Treasury papers, women and equity

The Treasury analysis of education is, at root, a market-liberal position. It sees the ideal role of government as limited to providing information to enable individuals to maximize their freedom of choice in the educational/vocational marketplace. However, political imperatives require a modification of such a position. First, New Zealanders demand that their governments attempt to reduce social inequality—unfettered free competition is not acceptable. Second, the government has made a commitment to honouring the Treaty of Waitangi as a constitutional foundation of the country. Treasury's individualist philosophy, then, is modified by the imperatives of governing, regulating and monitoring the population.

In this, it draws on functionalist rhetoric. Education is to prepare the population to meet contemporary social needs—described as the need to adapt to 'rapid technological change', 'exposure to the competitive realities of the international market', and 'rising unemployment' (New Zealand Treasury, 1987b, p. 5). Its vision of people's working lives is austere:

> Formal education ... necessarily reflect[s] the values of a capitalist society and as indicating acceptance of the social and economic imperatives in the young ...   (New Zealand Treasury, 1987b, p. 95)

> [The *Curriculum Review* places] emphasis on learning as an end in itself and as needing to be fun. These are not values that will assist most pupils in the marketplace.
> (New Zealand Treasury, 1987b, p. 115, no. 6)

A particularly narrow view is taken of education—it is primarily an instrument of servicing what policy-makers and business leaders perceive as the needs of the economy.

The political imperatives of egalitarianism and honouring the Treaty of Waitangi are dealt with within the functionalist framework of equity, which is to be addressed through targeting additional resources to disadvantaged groups. The first few pages of the 195-page Treasury report mention the broad social objectives to which New Zealand education must contribute.

The foundational ideology of New Zealand education is defined as equality of opportunity. To illustrate this, Peter Fraser's 1939 statement (as cited above) is quoted. Without mentioning its flaws (such as its assumptions about innate ability), this is left standing as Treasury's statement of educational aims. But the ideology of equality is explicitly rejected as outdated—as appropriate only for the postwar era in which it was created. The major function of education is to be economic. In addition, training for citizenship is mentioned, though this is seen solely in terms of learning how to live in a culturally pluralist society. It is difficult to ascertain what Treasury's vision of such a society would look like, since, by using the deficit model, Treasury reduces the disadvantaged to failed white male *bourgeoisie.*

Although the report devotes considerable attention to Maori pupils and those from low socio-economic groups, there is no chapter, or even section, specifically devoted to women and girls. [. . .] The chapters on Maori education contain no references to Maori women and girls—the group with the highest rate of unemployment in the country. There are brief references to girls' unequal participation rates in certain academic subjects and their resulting disadvantage in vocational choice. State intervention in such processes, however, is to be limited to providing information to parents and students. Such information is seen as facilitating informed (and therefore rational) freedom of choice. Stronger measures of affirmative action for women—such as subsidized childcare—are seen as unnecessary. [. . .]

Market-liberal discourse constitutes motherhood as a contradiction. The rational individual competes in the marketplace. Having children is an irrational decision because it prevents this. At the same time, women's unpaid work in the family is viewed as an essential part of their children's education. Women with children who also wish to work outside the home are seen as endangering their children's well-being. As individuals competing in self-interest, mothers and children are locked in conflict: 'the trade-off between benefit to the child and benefit to the parents is natural and inevitable' (New Zealand Treasury, 1987b, p. 57). Day-care, it is argued, is potentially harmful to some children. Echoing postwar maternal deprivation theory, the report views the role of the state in childcare as limited to providing care for the severely disadvantaged ('welfare') and to the provision of ('scientific/objective') information to parents 'about the long-term effects of different forms and sources of education'. Functionalist assumptions of working mothers as deviant permeate this discussion.

For Treasury, as Rosemary Novitz has pointed out, '"the family" has a *natural* cohesiveness and unity' [my emphasis], 'which cannot be changed or changed easily by policy-makers' (New Zealand Treasury, 1987a, p. 7; discussed by Novitz, 1987). Even so, numerous examples are given of ways in which governments do, in fact, regulate and monitor the family and sex-roles within it. For example:

Because the state does not tax the internal provision of household services, but does tax the external provision of the equivalent of such services, the state is effectively encouraging the family to provide its own early childhood services rather than to utilise external providers.

(New Zealand Treasury, 1987b, p. 275)

Not only does the state regulate family roles—it also regulates women's fertility:

... the provision of state subsidised education will reduce the costs to parents of child-rearing, hence encouraging child-bearing and affecting the birth-rate. (New Zealand Treasury, 1987b, p. 40)

In Treasury's discussion of education and paid work, women and girls are barely visible—relegated to those sections of the report that deal with early childhood and the family. Sexism is viewed as a purely *personal* matter. For example, some parents:

... may not ... appreciate the advantages, in the contemporary labour market and with advances in female emancipation of their daughter undertaking further education. (New Zealand Treasury, 1987b, p. 167)

In summary, then, Treasury's position on women's education is contradictory. On the one hand, it embodies liberal feminist rhetoric (albeit in its most minimal, non-interventionist sense—the provision of formal equal rights to freedom of choice in a marketplace of atomized, competitive individuals, with the role of the state in gender equity limited to providing students and their parents with information about the options open to them. (The different degrees of 'interventionism' within liberal feminism are all discussed by Eisenstein, 1981.] On the other hand, Treasury's functionalist analysis rests on tacit support for a patriarchal nuclear family shored up by the tax system and by the dissemination of information that points out potential hazards of day-care for young children. Such a family form is seen by the manpower planners as necessary for economic (and social) efficiency. In this, the report embodies the contradictions in liberal ideology between a woman's intellectuality/professionality (as a rationally autonomous individual) and her reproductive sexuality (as a domestically feminine woman).

EDUCATIONAL RESTRUCTURING: SOME FEMINIST QUESTIONS

Labour's current [from 1988 on] restructuring of New Zealand education shares the tensions of previous liberal reforms between an individualist philosophy and a functionalist view of education as a means of social control. This concluding section reviews some of the concerns and questions that feminists have raised about the recommendations put forward in *Administering for Excellence* (the Picot Report, 1988) by the Taskforce to Review Education

Administration and in the ensuing policy blueprint, *Tomorrow's Schools*. Such concerns can be traced to the androcentricity of liberal/functionalist social thought. The notion of equity implicit in these documents goes no further than an untheorized deficit model of women in relation to men. In this, as Mary O'Brien has expressed it, the policy-makers are guilty of 'commatization',

> ... in which social activities related to race comma ... gender comma are simply added to class, with no attempt to analyse the actual relations and differentiation of cross-class movement of a progressive kind.
>
> (O'Brien, 1987, p. 42)

While postwar liberal reforms were implemented in a period of economic boom which made freedom of choice for many women seem a real possibility, the Picot restructuring is taking place during a recession when there is pressure on many women to take pressure off the job market by making domestic life their priority. While postwar educational rhetoric placed top priority on education as a means of achieving an egalitarian social democracy, current political priorities are those of managing the economy, with education as a tool to achieve this end. While the dominant educational issues of the postwar years were curricular (what should be taught and why), those of the 1980s have been defined as economic—how to curb public expenditure and get value for money.

The present government has separated curriculum from administration, thus making the content and form of education separate issues. Content was the concern of the *Curriculum Review* produced during Russell Marshall's term as Minister of Education. The review was hailed by liberal-left educators as a progressive document. However, it was attacked by Treasury for its priority in 'meeting Maori aspirations, countering racism and sexism, and creating an enabling and challenging curriculum' (Codd, Gordon and Harker, 1988) —an approach, it was argued, that was an inadequate blueprint for the development of school education because, among other things, it overlooked 'the relationship between education and the economy'. It appears that political pressure from the liberal-right as well as from conservative groups has led to the shelving of the *Curriculum Review*.

This makes the present restructuring particularly worrying for liberal-left and more radical educators. Such concerns have centred on the policy-makers' assumptions that centralization of state power is 'bad' and that small communities are 'good'. The Picot taskforce argued that, with centralized decision-making, 'the pattern of educational decision-making becomes that of pressure group politics at the centre rather than mutual co-operation of professionals and consumers locally' (Picot Report, 1988, p. 23). Feminists, and other critics, have viewed this as a false dichotomy. Rather than being mutually co-operative, many school communities are torn apart by conflict. Events surrounding the Springbok tours, homosexual law reform, and the regional forums associated with the setting up of the Ministry of Women's

Affairs are examples of bitter tensions between those members of communities who fight against sexism and racism and those who believe that their personal religious beliefs should be the underpinnings of law. In fact, anti-sexist and anti-racist initiatives in education, as in other social policy, have come in the main from the centre.

The new policies embody a curious tension between devolution and centralization. The hiring and firing of teachers, the choice and purchase of textbooks and other teaching resources, the purchasing of advisory services, and in-service teacher education (redefined as 'staff development') are to be largely devolved to school boards of trustees. Feminists and others have argued that locating such decisions in the community merely allows the already-powerful to dominate the directions and provision of education. For example, they argue, middle-class communities with professional know-how and other forms of cultural capital will be advantaged in the purchasing of goods and services, and Maori (and other ethnic) minorities in predominantly Pakeha communities will see their concerns and cultural identity further marginalized. Conservative take-overs of boards are possible—requirements that women and Maori be represented are insufficient guarantees that anti-sexist and anti-racist education will take place. It seems unlikely that conservative boards would appoint, for example, feminist women or anti-racist Maori activists to senior positions. A narrow view of the world could be promoted in schools where such boards select the staff, the texts, the professional advisers, and the staff training programmes.

With its expressed commitment to equity, the Picot taskforce attempted to confront such possibilities by means of legal contracts—the charters in which each school is to state its educational aims and objectives. By law, these will have to include certain requirements with respect to equity, such as equal opportunities provisions. To make boards accountable to the state, schools are to be audited and monitored every two years by an Education Review Office which is to replace the present school inspectorate.

With regard to gender equity, we do not yet know what criteria the review teams will use. While numerical distribution of the sexes in teaching hierarchies is easy to measure, the study of other concerns such as the gender inclusiveness of the total curriculum requires sophisticated understanding of, for example, androcentricity within the various school subjects and the academic disciplines that influence them. The knowledge-base of the members of the review teams, then, is all-important. Questions of how such teams are to be selected and trained (and by whom) remain unresolved. Many feminists believe that women's interests will be even less central in the teams' concerns than they have been under a more centralized administration. These beliefs have been further reinforced by the apparent shelving of the *Curriculum Review* with its strong commitment to the eradication of sexism and racism. [...]

Another feminist concern with respect to educational restructuring is the hidden curriculum—those features of a school's pattern of social relations that send (often unintended) messages about, among other things, the sexual division of labour, power relations between men and women, and 'proper' sex-roles. [...] The division of labour *between* board members, and other volunteers, is an issue that may need to be researched. For, while the new provisions offer financial reimbursement to compensate for lost earnings and/or to cover costs of transport or childcare for board members on days when meetings are held, their duties are likely to involve many hours of unpaid labour on tasks that presently are done by trained professionals. While some tasks, such as the budgeting, may tend to be carried out by (professional) men, other school voluntary work is more likely to fall on the shoulders of women, particularly housewives, thus reinforcing the sexual division of labour and prejudices against mothers who go out to work.

CONCLUSION

The liberal educational policy rhetoric of the postwar years and of the late 1980s rests on contradictions between liberal notions of the rationally autonomous individual and centralist political imperatives of manpower planning—monitoring and regulating the population in response to economic requirements. While postwar policy-makers saw the individual as subsumed to collectivist notions of progress, democracy and the public good, those of the 1980s see individuals as basically competitive and self-interested. Concepts of equality and equity have also differed. The postwar policy-makers saw equality of opportunity as an outcome of access for all to the same sorts of education, while—at least with respect to Maori pupils—contemporary policies rest on notions of equity in the sense of parity between groups in a pluralist society. This article has argued that both versions of liberalism embody contradictions with respect to girls and women. While girls are seen as potentially the same as boys in their capacities and in the opportunities offered them for rational choice of life style and career, liberal social thought leaves largely unquestioned the assumption that the stability, cohesion and well-being of society rest on essential differences between the sexes. For both versions of liberal theory—sometimes explicitly, sometimes implicitly—rest on the expectations that the patriarchal nuclear family will be the very foundation of society.

In the postwar years, the contradiction experienced by educated women between the liberal ideal of equality (as sameness) and domestic femininity (as difference) helped generate the second wave of feminism. These women's education and the opportunities they had in times of full employment helped change—on both personal and broader social levels—to seem *possible*. Ironically, a sexually conservative curriculum contributed to such women's radicalization. However, in the late 1980s such challenges to tradition—even the chance for economic independence—may not seem possible to many young women. Growing up during an economic recession, many girls see choice as being between going on the dole or becoming economically dependent on a husband, boyfriend or the Domestic Purposes Benefit. It is crucial, then, that their schooling offers them visions of the full spectrum of women's past and present lives—their history, achievements, political struggles. Such a gender-inclusive curriculum must not denigrate women's traditional achievements or see a male life style as the ideal. Rather, it must portray honestly and critically, to children of both sexes, the problems that currently face New Zealanders—in race relations, gender relations, and economic self-sufficiency. The true meaning of untheorized contemporary notions of equity will have to be worked out within every aspect of the education system. These are some of the challenges that those working within the new structures will have to address.

Notes

1. The term 'child-free' here refers to both childless women and those who are wealthy enough to afford alternative childcare. For example, well-off British women have traditionally employed nannies and/or sent children to boarding school, thus making it possible to pursue careers similarly to men.
2. Although many married women now work outside the home, much of this is part-time or casual work and does not constitute a continuous 'career'. See Department of Statistics (1986); also Ministry of Women's Affairs (1988). Studies of women, the family and social policy in New Zealand are in Brooks *et al.* (1986).
3. The term 'cultural capital' was developed by the French sociologist, Pierre Bourdieu. For New Zealand studies that use this perspective, see the chapters in Part 1 of Codd, Harker and Nash (1985).
4. The phrase 'something wrong' used in this sense comes from Mitchell (1973), p. 28). This analysis of the relationship between postwar education and feminism comes from Middleton (1987).

References

Barrett. M. (1980) *Woman's Oppression Today.* London.

Beeby, C.E. (1986) Introduction. In W.L. Renwick *Moving Targets.* Wellington.

Brooks, B. *et al.* (1986) *Women in History.* Wellington.

Codd, J., Gordon, L. and Harker, R. (1988) Educational administration and the role of the state: devolution and control post-Picot. Paper presented to the first Research into Educational Policy Conference, Wellington, August.

Codd, J., Harker, R. and Nash, R. (eds) (1985) *Political Issues in New Zealand Education.* Palmerston North.

David, M. (1986) Teaching family matters. *British Journal of Sociology of Education* 7 (1), 35–57.

Department of Education (1944) *Report on the Post-primary School Curriculum.* Wellington.

Department of Statistics (1986) *Profiles of Women.* Wellington.

Eisenstein, Z. (1981) *The Radical Future of Liberal Feminism.* New York.

— (1982) The sexual politics of the new right: understanding the 'crisis of liberalism' for the 1980s. In N. Keohane *et al.* (eds) *Feminist Theory: A Critique of Ideology.* Chicago.

Foucault, M. (1980) *A History of Sexuality, Volume 1.* New York.

Keddie, N. (1973) *Tinker, Tailor: The Myth of Cultural Deprivation.* Harmondsworth.

May, H. (1988) Post-war women 1945–1970 and their daughters 1970–1985. PhD thesis, Victoria University of Wellington.

Middleton, S. (1985) Feminism and education in post-war New Zealand: a sociological analysis. DPhil. thesis, University of Waikato.

— (1986) Workers and homemakers: contradictions in the education of the New Zealand 'post-war woman'. *NZJES* 21 (1), 13–28. (Reprinted in Middleton, 1988, Ch. 6.)

— (1987) Schooling and radicalisation: life histories of New Zealand feminist teachers. *British Journal of Sociology of Education* 8 (2), 169–89.

— (1988) Towards a sociology of women's education in Aotearoa. In S. Middleton (ed.) *Women and Education in Aotearoa*. Wellington.

Mill, J.S. (1983) *The Subjection of Women*. London. (First published 1869.)

Ministry of Women's Affairs (1988) *Women in the Economy*. Wellington.

Mitchell, J. (1973) *Woman's Estate*. Harmondsworth.

New Zealand Treasury (1987a) *Government Management: Volume I*. Wellington.

— (1987b) *Government Management: Volume II, Education*. Wellington.

Novitz. R. (1987) Treasury: a sociological analysis. Paper presented at the annual conference of the Sociological Association of Aotearoa/New Zealand, Massey University, Palmerston North.

O'Brien, M. (1987) Education and patriarchy. In D. Livingstone (ed.) *Critical Pedagogy and Cultural Power*. Massachusetts.

Olssen, M. (ed.) (1988) *Mental Testing in New Zealand*. Dunedin.

Picot Report (1988) *Administering for Excellence*. Report of the taskforce to review education administration. Wellington.

Poster, M. (1984) *Foucault, Marxism and History: Mode of Production Versus Mode of Information*. London.

Ramsay, P.D.K. (ed.) (1985) Editorial introduction to *Family, School and Community*. Sydney.

Renwick, W.L. (1986) *Moving Targets*. Wellington.

Ryan, A. (1988) The 'Moral Right', sex education and populist moralism. In S. Middleton (ed.) *Women and Education in Aotearoa*. Wellington.

Watson, J. (1966) Marriages of women teachers. *NZJES* 1 (1), 149–61.

Wollstonecraft, M. (1972) *Vindication of the Rights of Women*. Harmondsworth. (First published 1792.)

Yates, L. (1986) Theorising inequality. *British Journal of Sociology of Education* 7 (2), 119–34.

11 FEMINISM, EDUCATION AND THE NEW RIGHT

MADELEINE ARNOT

Recent socialist feminist writings suggest that existing understandings of the New Right have paid inadequate attention to 'the patriarchal basis of the state and society' (Eisenstein, 1987). Gender relations have, yet again, been marginalized in the conceptualizations of contemporary politics. According to ten Tusscher,

> ... the debate around the New Right has become moribund—stuck in a treadmill of male-defined analyses offering male answers to male questions on what has become the dominant force in contemporary western politics. This gender bias has led to a partial explanation of the New Right—on the left, one couched in economic and class terms—which fails to explain (and indeed lacks the analytical tools to be able to explain) the moral/traditional/familial aspects of the present administration's ideology and politics.   (ten Tusscher, 1986, p. 67)

[. . .] The starting point for my analysis will be a broadly defined 'sociology of women's education' (MacDonald, 1980). Although some feminist research fits easily within the conventional boundaries of 'sociology', other feminist analyses or projects have contributed to sociological debates from outside the academic discipline. Patriarchal relations within higher education have positioned women as a minority of the academic profession and a majority of those in lower-status academic-related posts. So feminist educational research has been generated in the various niches that women academics have managed to find for themselves not just in sociology or education departments but also in, for example, curriculum studies, adult education, and extra mural studies. Black female sociologists, with a few exceptions, have been excluded from the academic profession and can be found working as education advisers, local authority personnel, and in black feminist collectives. It is essential, therefore, that such feminist authors are not further excluded from the academic arena.

Research on women's educational experiences began to emerge in the United Kingdom in the early 1970s in the context of growing disillusion with the social

Source: Abridged from Arnot, M. and Barton, L. (eds) (1992) *Voicing Concerns, Sociological Perspectives on Contemporary Education Reforms* (pp. 41–65). Wallingford, Oxfordshire: Triangle Books.

democratic principles underlying education and social policy. The principles of universalism and collectivism had not, it seemed, delivered the promised equality of opportunity to women.

After a slow start at the margins of the sociological world where issues of social class dominated, British sociological research projects and texts on female educational experiences grew in number, and the majority, ironically, were published well after the 1979 election when Mrs Thatcher led the Conservative Party to victory. The next ten years were to witness a phenomenal growth of interest in feminist educational analyses at a time when, paradoxically, the 'pursuit of equality' was increasingly challenged by central government initiatives.

Yet the shift in political discourse and the reality of the new educational era promoted by the Conservative government rarely attracted the attention of feminist academics and teachers. Sometimes it appeared as if the educational processes that feminist researchers identified, and indeed the research agenda itself, existed within a political vacuum, so devoid was gender research of any mention of the political and economic climate of the period. On the whole, the foci of feminist research were the discourses and internal structures of a liberal democratic state shaped by the ideologies of welfarism. Consequently, there seemed to be little preparation for the attack on 'egalitarianism', allegedly brought to an abrupt end (or so claimed the then Secretary of State for Education, Kenneth Baker) by the successful passage of the 1988 Education Reform Act. It is only in the last year (1991/2) that we can see the emergence of a more sustained feminist response to the educational programme of the New Right.

One way to explain this delay in analyzing the significance of the New Right's education policy for women is to consider the relationship that feminist education theory has had to educational policy-making. The relationship between theory and practice is different in the context of gender and education to that in sociological analyses of class or 'race'. Like those committed to 'race' and, to some extent, class equality, feminist academics and sociologists have attempted to engage with broader political liberation movements. However, the issue of gender in education differs in that women are the majority of the teaching profession. Many of the reference points for feminist educationalists, therefore, are to be found not just in the sociological domain but in female teachers' campaigns and initiatives. Thus feminists may have waited to see the impact of the latest round of contemporary reforms on women teachers before responding publicly to these reforms.

[...]

MODERN FEMINISM AND THE CRITIQUE OF SOCIAL DEMOCRATIC EDUCATION POLICY

Feminist analyses of education, in much the same way as the sociology of family and school, can only be understood as an integral part of the political constellations of the postwar period. The coincidence of social democratic reforms and the women's liberation movement of the 1960s generated major contractions and a new agenda for women. The results of such conflict were the development of a sustained critique of the purposes and shape of social policy and practice, as well as an ambivalence towards the role of the state in promoting female rights. Such feminist criticism was further strengthened by its interaction with anti-racist and socialist analyses of state action in this period.

The aims of the postwar settlement were to promote not merely economic growth and, ideally, full employment, but also to try to ensure that all benefited in some way from that prosperity. Promises were made to use schooling to encourage the full development of an individual's abilities and talents and to ensure genuine equality of opportunity (Finch, 1984). Thus the education system was to be used as a major vehicle for social engineering. On the one hand, the welfare state could try to meet individual needs, especially those of the socially disadvantaged, and on the other, it could try to alleviate various social problems within the existing social and economic framework. The main objective was not the transformation of social inequalities or power relations within society, it was essentially the redistribution of resources within it.

With such an agenda, it was not surprising that doubts were consistently and frequently expressed about the strength of the political commitment of politicians, and particularly of educational policy-makers, to the promotion of social equality. The version of social equality being used emphasized equality of access rather than equality of outcome—a much weaker version, therefore, than some would have wished. In the liberal democratic state, open access would ensure that those with merit would succeed in a competitive environment, whilst compensatory programmes might help others to overcome the effects of their disadvantaged social origins (Arnot, 1991).

Contained within the 1944 Education Act, with its promise of education for all, were the possibilities of women's liberation from their domestic destinies, even if little was done actively to ensure that this goal was fulfilled (Burton and Weiner, 1990). Ironically, it was precisely the ensuing expansion of education that 'hurtled a generation (of women) beyond the confines of their mothers' world into the male sphere of public affairs and work', only to discover that no provision had been made to care for their children (Rowbotham, 1986, p. 85). The liberalism which framed social policy remained firmly committed to the division between the public sphere and the private domestic sphere. Also, traditional and unequal gender relations within the family were to be supported rather than challenged by the provisions of the welfare state (Pascall, 1986; Williams, 1989).

As might be expected, current re-evaluations of social democracy in the postwar period are highly critical of the stance adopted by central government on women's issues. In her wonderfully entitled book, *Only Halfway to Paradise*, Elizabeth Wilson (1980), a leading socialist feminist, argues that between 1945 and the late 1960s, women's oppression was not only invisible but women had been silenced by the ideology of equality of opportunity. [. . .]

By the late 1960s the tensions between women's position in the home and in the labour force were to surface and explode in the second wave of the women's liberation movement. This found expression in a variety of spheres: as Rowbotham (1986) comments, the project became one of extending the definitions of political or economic democracy

> . . . to include domestic inequality, identity, control over sexuality, challenge to cultural representation, community control over state welfare and more equal access to public resources.   (Rowbotham, 1986, p. 86)

Rowbotham's retrospective analysis of the 1960s shows how the women's movement drew upon the insights of the American new left and the civil rights, black power and student movements. The idea that the 'personal is political' drove the concept of democracy deep into the personal relations of everyday life, particularly in the areas of sexuality and morality, and the concept of equal rights was exchanged for a demand for 'equality of power'.

Feminist struggles within education were part of this movement, and the range of perspectives found within feminist educational thinking and practice has much in common with the political philosophies that have shaped the women's movement since the 1960s (Eisenstein, 1984). Indeed, in recent years it has become common practice to identify the various tendencies of liberal feminism—radical, socialist and black feminism—in educational analysis (Middleton, 1987; Acker, 1987; Arnot and Weiner, 1987). Lesbian feminism, more developed in the United States, has had a twilight existence in the context of British educational work (see recent contributions in Jones and Mahony, 1989), especially since sexuality has been such a studiously avoided aspect of school life.

Yet despite such similarities, there are also key differences between feminist educational analysis and the work related to mainstream feminist political or sociological theory. The material location of academics and teachers as employees of the state education system has had an impact on the evolution of feminist educational thought. Teachers and academics were partly responsible for the framing of the postwar settlement and for its maintenance. The selection and organization of school curricula were a case in point, left as they were predominantly in the hands of a relatively autonomous education profession rather than under the control of central government.

It is not surprising, therefore, that the principles of social democracy, not merely those of the women's movement, informed feminist educational theory and practice. Even when, by the 1980s, feminist and sociological analyses became more sophisticated and attempted to identify diverse female needs within education and to remove the more subtle obstacles to individual advancement, one can still find a strong commitment to the tenets of individualism, teacher autonomy, and the use of education as the means of social reform (see, for example, Acker and Warren Piper, 1984; Thompson, 1983; Whyte, 1986).

But the support that educational policy-makers in the postwar period gave to the division between public and private spheres, between employment and family, was always likely to cause major difficulties for feminist educational research. Early analyses of the official ideology for girls' education, contained within, for example, the Crowther (1959), Newsom (1963) and Plowden (1967) Reports, often assumed a homogeneity of female interests, notably with regard to domesticity (Wolpe, 1976); moreover, such analyses revealed an androcentric bias in their concepts of vocationalism, meritocracy and access to higher education. The Centre for Contemporary Cultural Studies (CCCS) (1981) confirmed that not only was there no evidence of 'discomfort' about gender issues in these reports, but that the 'political arithmetic' of social democracy had failed even to 'count in' women. Similarly, Wickham (1987) showed how state training policy, particularly in relation to skilled occupations, had been designed by men and for men.

Such government approaches to women's education and training set an agenda for the development of female educational studies. The initial concerns, quite naturally, were to make women's education visible to policy-makers and to analyse the ways in which female pupils and students might be prevented from developing their full potential and from participating in the whole range of educational and training opportunities (see, for example, Byrne, 1978; Delamont, 1980).

Increasingly, however, feminist critiques of social democracy bit deeper and deeper, challenging the liberal philosophy at the heart of educational policy and the specific sets of relations constructed within the liberal democratic state and its institutional arrangements. This more-radical thrust to analyses of gender and education in the late 1970s and early 1980s can be summarized in terms of four themes, as detailed below.

The reproduction of public and private spheres

As Pascall (1986, p. 103) notes,

> Educational institutions stand at the junction of private and public worlds, mediating between the family and paid employment ... There is thus an ambiguity at the heart of girls' education.

Evidence for the continued existence of the low status of female occupations, the ghettoization of female workers into a narrow range of jobs and training routes, the persistence of women's low-paid part-time employment and lack of promotion prospects (Holland, 1981) provided an implicit, if not explicit, starting point for those concerned with contemporary forms of gender differentiation in education. Research focused, therefore, on discrimination in curriculum provision, option choice mechanisms, the ideological content of school tests, and the channelling of female and male pupils into certain curricular and, hence, occupational routes (see, among others, Deem, 1980; Whyld, 1983).

The fact that 'schooling faces two ways' (CCCS, 1981) was also of key importance to feminists, particularly after the so-called domestic labour debate of the 1960s and 1970s highlighted the relationship between capitalism and the family. That women's political and economic destinies were so closely tied in with their position in the domestic sphere and its patriarchal relations was evident from the historical shaping of the schoolgirls' curriculum (see, for example, Dyhouse, 1978; Purvis, 1987). Feminist sociologists revealed the continuity of that tradition and identified the ways in which the contemporary school curriculum continued to reproduce 'female domestic ideology' within and across class boundaries.

Patterns of gender differentiation and hierarchy found in school provision were interpreted as key to the continuing 'reproduction' of patriarchal relations in the family and in employment (see, for example, Wolpe, 1977; MacDonald, 1980). Women were being prepared, albeit often indirectly, for a range of low-status economic positions within the dual labour market, for unpaid domestic labour, and for membership of a reserve army of labour. Ideologically, girls of different social classes were being subjected (often in different and somewhat contradictory ways) to an education that was as oppressive as it was exploitative.

By the 1980s, this analysis was both criticized and developed by black feminist researchers. Carby (1982), Bryan, Dadzie and Scafe (1985), Phoenix (1987) and Amos and Parmar (1987), among others, focused attention on the ideological impact of imperialism and of institutional racism—most evident in the racial segregation of the labour market and the historical shaping of the structure and culture of black families. They drew attention to the need to integrate into the analysis of private and public spheres the impact of racial as well as class and gendered discourses and divisions.

The illusions of both the neutrality of school knowledge and schools' ability to deliver equality of opportunity to different groups of girls through a liberal education were seriously challenged by such research. Female education was repeatedly shown to lend support, in a different way from that of male education, to a patriarchal, racially and class-divided society. According to Whitty (1985), such research succeeded in contesting the view that class relations were of primary and, indeed, sole importance in shaping educational provision. Further, it 'helped to make the cruder forms of neo-Marxist theory inadequate to an understanding of contemporary social relations' (Whitty, 1985, p. 55).

Gender relations and the organization of schooling

Whilst the official ideology of female education and curriculum policy was challenged by such research, feminist sociological analyses of the organizational features of schooling raised serious doubts about the co-educational and comprehensive principles that had shaped educational planning since the 1960s. Feminists had been alerted to the dangers of co-education by R.R. Dale's (1969; 1971; 1974) assessment of the value of single-sex and mixed schools. His findings focused on the academic advantages for boys of co-education and identified only social advantages for girls in the creation of a 'healthy' heterosexual environment in which both sexes played different but complementary roles. Further, the HMI report (DES, 1975) on curriculum differentiation in primary education and in the tripartite system of secondary schools suggested that gender differences were being promoted, if not as a positive goal, then as a matter of convention. Research evidence on the curriculum and organization of the newly introduced mixed comprehensive schools also revealed that such gender patterning was being reinforced rather than challenged (Arnot, 1983).

In the late 1970s and early 1980s, numerous small-scale research projects on girls' experiences, taken together, constituted a substantial critique of school organization within comprehensive secondary schools. Although research on gender interaction in classrooms, teaching styles, modes of assessment and teachers' expectations rarely referred to educational policy as such, the research could be said to represent a form of policy evaluation (for overviews of this work, see Deem, 1980; Weiner and Arnot, 1987). It challenged the principle of universalism and asked if girls really were receiving the same education as boys. Moreover, in documenting the continued inequalities between male and female education, it challenged the principle of comprehensivization.

Increasingly, gender relations in education were also being subjected to more sustained and detailed inquiry. The diversity of gender cultures found in schools was demonstrated in studies of, for example, different types of primary schools (Clarricoates, 1978), private and state secondary schools (Connell *et al.*, 1982), and the experiences of different ethnic groups (see, among others, Brah and Minhas, 1985). Sociological and feminist research on gender in schools offered fascinating insights into the hidden organization of educational experiences: for instance, at the age of four, male pupils were locked in sexual power struggles with female teachers, having already learned to use the language of sexual abuse (Walkerdine, 1987); within secondary classrooms, male and female pupils of different ethnic groups were united in experiencing hostile racist confrontations with teachers (Wright, 1987); in different subjects, male and female students were active participants in the 'feminization' or 'masculinization' of both their own identities and educational knowledge (Kelly, 1985).

In light of such evidence, Middleton (1990) argues that liberal education, with its stress on the rationally autonomous individual, appears to have benefited male pupils more than female pupils, despite the successful performance of some girls in formal school-leaving certificates at 16. It was precisely in the spaces created by concepts such as freedom of choice, teacher autonomy and child-centred education that sexism was repeatedly found unchallenged and often thought 'natural' (Arnot, 1991). Feminist research had begun to challenge many dearly held assumptions. For example, it challenged the view that progressive child-centred education would extend girls' development in their early years and that coeducation would make comprehensive secondary schools beneficial to girls. Similarly, teachers' policy of 'non-intervention' in gendered practices and relations (documented in classrooms in infant schools, and in secondary and further education by, among others, Walkerdine, 1987, and Stanworth, 1983) were also being held in question by such feminist analyses.

The effect of social democratic reforms on girls' education had been shown to be uneven. On the one hand, many girls—particularly those from the middle classes—had benefited academically from the opportunities provided by the introduction of comprehensive schools, the raising of the school-leaving age and the expansion of tertiary education. On the other hand, traditional female course choices and the low proportion of working-class and black female students achieving the necessary qualifications for entry to further and higher education raised serious doubts about the long-term effects of girls' school experiences on their self-esteem, their ambitions and their prospects. The whole organization of schooling (from staffing patterns to classroom interaction) had been rendered deeply problematic.

Gender and the concept of power

Theories of power in the sociology of education are located at the centre of critiques of social democratic education policy. The relation between capital and labour provided the guiding theme for radical critiques of liberal education in the late 1970s (Bowles and Gintis, 1978; Bourdieu and Passeron, 1977; Apple, 1982; Giroux, 1983). [. . .]

Socialist feminist research contributed to the theoretical debates and policy analyses, notably by offering ethnographic studies of working-class and black girls' responses to schooling (see, among others, Anyon, 1983; Griffin, 1985). This research challenged Willis' (1977) analysis—his celebration and romanticization of white working-class male culture despite its explicit racism and sexism (McRobbie, 1978, 1980). The social relations of schooling, and in particular the 'correspondence principle', have now been shown to be gendered relations (Valli, 1986).

Perhaps the most critical analyses of power relations in schooling have concerned sexual relations. Here, the dominance of heterosexuality has been found, for example, in the school curriculum (most markedly in topics dealing directly with personal relations) and in the treatment of lesbian and gay pupils and staff. Research on gender dynamics in schools suggests that male dominance has a considerable impact on girls. The language of sexual abuse, physical harrassment and the male colonization of the space of the school (Mahony, 1985; Jones and Mahony, 1989) shape girls' negotiation of the academic ethos of the school as well as their confidence in their own abilities. Their experiences at school affect their entry not just into the labour market but also into the marriage and sexual markets (Griffin, 1985).

The identification of these sets of social relations and of female pupils' and teachers' struggles within education reveal the hegemonic role of state schools in sustaining patriarchal as well as race and class structures. By the 1980s such research, although diverse and even at times contradictory, had demonstrated that at the very least no simple concept of equality of opportunity, especially one based upon freedom of choice, could be effective as a means of transforming this web of power relations within schooling.

Gender politics and the 'partnership'

Feminist studies of educational policy-making have drawn on the direct experience of teachers and academics working within a range of contexts (Whyte *et al.*, 1985). Teachers, advisers, researchers and lecturers have written about their experiences of setting up equal opportunities/sex equality policies and initiatives. Their analyses have focused on, among other things, the strengths and weaknesses of 'bottom up' or 'top down' approaches to promoting educational reform, the difficulties of deciding between strategies of coercion versus consent, and the marginalization of women's concerns. Other collective projects such as those of action research and teacher research have attempted to break down the hierarchies between academics and researchers and between teachers and taught, in the name of social justice (cf. Weiner, 1989; Weiner and Arnot, 1987). The lessons learnt through such projects have revealed the possibilities and limits of democratic educational reform within the existing social structure.

Pluralism, a guiding thread within liberal democracy, has also been challenged by feminist research and practice. From a feminist perspective the process involved in educational policy-making is seen less as the result of democratic and consensual politics and more as the result of the exercise of male power. [. . .] Increasingly, feminist researchers have revealed the ways in which knowledge, whether contained in educational policy documents or in the school curriculum, has been shaped by (white) men, and often in male interests.

[. . .] Moreover, the relations between teachers and the state within social democracy have been shown to have been affected by the feminization of the teaching profession. The debate about teacher professionalism and the proletarianization of teachers is now no longer possible without some recognition of the politics of gender (see, for example, Lawn and Grace, 1987; Acker, 1989). Promoting change within the alleged 'partnership' between central and local government and teachers in the postwar period has, therefore, been shown to be circumscribed by patriarchal relations in education.

FEMINIST CRITIQUES OF THE NEW RIGHT AND EDUCATIONAL REFORM

Despite the consistent growth of feminist research throughout the 1980s, any initial unity seemed to have been lost by the end of the decade. [. . .]

The existence of different feminist approaches might appear challenging, suggesting that the time was ripe for a sustained theoretical debate on gender. For feminists, however, the disarray and fragmentation and 'miserable welter of conflict' in the women's movement was deeply depressing, not least in relation to the emergence of Thatcherism (Loach, 1987).

[. . .] Increasingly, radical 'egalitarian' approaches had drawn apart from liberal perspectives, with the former more closely associated with the politics of municipal socialism and women's campaigns for sex equality, rather than with mainstream equal rights initiatives promoted by central government agencies (for example, the Women into Science and Engineering Year organized by the Women's National Commission and the EOC) (see Weiner and Arnot, 1987; Arnot, 1991).

There was also conflict within the 'egalitarian' movement – between radical and socialist feminism on the one hand, and groups of an ever more sectarian character within the Left, on the other hand. This made it difficult, in effect, to identify the communality of women's experiences across the divisions of class, race, sexuality and disability—and even more difficult to frame a unified political constituency. Implicit in many of the discussions on gender was the assumption that there were 'hierarchies of oppression'. 'Identity politics', or what Parmar (1989) called the 'politics of difference', limited the ability of feminists to frame a coherent political strategy. In the educational world, feminist analyses, whether radical or liberal, were more and more often being identified as white, middle-class and heterosexual in orientation (see, for example, Carby, 1982; Brah, 1988; Phoenix, 1987; Connell, 1987).

Ideological disarray in feminist educational thought, therefore, cannot be solely attributed to Conservative government policy, especially since the initial impact of Thatcherism was felt more in the context of economic and family policy, rather than in education policy (Pascall, 1986; Williams, 1989). The recession and cuts in local government budgets had affected women, particularly their post-school opportunities (Deem, 1981; David, 1983a, b). However, schools still retained a reasonable level of autonomy over the curriculum, and local authorities still had sufficient finance to invest in equality initiatives, if the political will was there. If anything, the early 1980s was a time of relative excitement and possibility for those committed to sex equality. Local government (chiefly in Labour-controlled metropolitan authorities) and the teacher unions were being used as a means of fighting sex and race discrimination, but they also served as sites of political opposition to the Conservative government (Arnot, 1991).

Even though such egalitarian approaches and campaigning were unlikely to have any major impact on the state education system as a whole (Dale and Foster, 1986), it would have been naive to have imagined that they would have no political impact. Such developments, along with comparable endeavours in the area of 'race', were regarded as subversive by a central government influenced by the radical right (Klein, 1989; Davies, Holland and Minhas, 1990).

Patriarchal structures, particularly heterosexual monogamous marriage as the stable institutional form, had been threatened by the egalitarianism and the libertarianism in the women's movement. Feminist campaigns for more state intervention in family life and personal liberty had threatened the distinctions between public and private worlds sustained by a liberal democratic state. Patriarchy, not just the capitalist economy, was already in crisis (ten Tusscher, 1986; Eisenstein, 1987).

Not surprisingly, feminist demands for equality were seen by members of the New Right as 'ideological extravagances' and as part of the 'forces in contemporary society which are deeply inimical' to the family (Centre for Policy Studies, quoted in Campbell, 1987, p. 170). Demands for sex equality were especially blamed for the rise in the divorce rate and single parenthood.

In retrospect, it seems extraordinary how little concern was shown in feminist educational writing about the build up of this Conservative opposition. However, two factors might explain the seeming lack of interest. First, the legacy of social democracy as the main target of sociology of education proved hard to break in all aspects of the discipline. Secondly, in contrast to Reagan's government in the United States which supported an aggressive Moral Right political movement (Dworkin, 1983), the first Thatcher government made few explicit 'anti-feminist' statements. It did not directly attack the women's movement, repeal anti-discrimintion legislation or shut down the Equal Opportunities Commission or the Commission for Racial Equality as some expected it would (David, 1983a). Initially, Thatcher's government remained 'officially neutral' on issues such as abortion, divorce and homosexual rights (Segal, 1983).

David (1983a, b; 1985) and Segal (1983) revealed the more subtle forms of anti-feminism used by the Thatcher government in its first period of office. The initial implications of Thatcherism could apparently be found in a family ideology and policy that emphasized 'Victorian values', in particular the bourgeois family form of the male wage earner and the dependent wife and mother. The much-quoted outburst of Patrick Jenkin in 1979 (later to be Social Services Minister), that 'If the Good Lord had intended us to have equal rights to go out to work, he wouldn't have created men and women' (quoted in Gardiner, 1983, p. 195) was put a little more delicately but no less conservatively by a 1986 Institute of Economic Affairs report when it commented: 'Men will expect to specialise in market work and women will expect to specialise in household work' (quoted in Williams, 1989, p. 120).

Underlying the notion that a 'woman's place is in the home' was the assumption that biological and natural instincts determined both the sexual division of labour within the family and the separation between the private and public spheres. For Roger Scruton, a leading neo-conservative educationalist, the family was therefore a 'natural form':

> The family ... is a small social unit which shares with civil society the singular quality of being non-contractual, of arising (both for the children and the parents) not out of choice but out of natural necessity.
>   (Scruton, quoted in Williams, 1989, p. 119)

It is generally recognized that the family occupied a privileged place in New Right ideology. However, the sheer range of functions that the family should perform within contemporary society revealed more about the attempts of the Conservative Party to hold together various tendencies within its own organization, than any deep understanding about the actual shifts in contemporary family life (David, 1983a; Campbell, 1987). On the one hand, the family was responsible for the 'defence of the individual against socialism and excessive state power'; on the other hand, it was the basis of private property and the location of the consumer responsible for the management of his/her financial affairs. Then again, the family was the 'centre of affections', 'the transmitter of traditions' and the necessary condition of authority. Such functions transcended all allegiances of class, indeed of history itself (Campbell, 1987).

In the context of this vision of family life, the concept of parenthood, actively promoted by the Black Papers (quoted in CCCS, 1981) in their discussion of education reform, became the symbol not just of the economic values of consumerism: parenthood represented, for neo-conservatives such as Scruton, the political and moral values of hierarchy, authority and loyalty (Williams, 1989).

Because of this role as guardian of social stability within an aggressively competitive economy, family life, it seemed, had to be supported by the state. Paradoxically, 'the family had to be maximized in order to minimize the state'. By rehabilitating the family, arguably the government could break down the 'scrounger welfare state' and through a 'moral crusade' counter the effects of permissiveness that grew out of the 1960s (Campbell, 1987, p. 166).

Such ideology concerning the family, incoherent as it seems, has been interpreted by feminists as a significant attack on women's position in the employment sector and in the family. This was hardly surprising, given that cuts in state welfare provision made it more likely that women would be left to cater for young children, the aged, the mentally ill and the unemployed members of the household. If this dismantling of the welfare state assumed rather than asserted the need for women to remain at home, educational policies emphasizing the values of a patriarchal family life were given the responsibility of actively promoting traditional sexual divisions. Early statements by Conservative politicians suggested that all children would be

encouraged to receive an education in moral values and in parental responsibilities (David, 1983a, b)—thus girls would be prepared for the role of wife,
mother and carer, and boys would learn the role of head of household and
main wage earner.

Fears were expressed that this rekindled interest in moral education was the
thin edge of the wedge. It represented the first attempt 'to rescind equal opportunities policies . . . and to replace them with specific policies which promote
sex difference' (David, 1983b). Added to other attacks on women's rights, particularly in terms of sexuality and employment, this educational approach was
interpreted as an effort to restore patriarchal values.

According to ten Tusscher (1986), the New Right's concern to link
monetarism and moralism was an attempt to tackle the dual crises of the
capitalist economy and patriarchy and to reunite their interests. [. . .] Yet
the patriarchal ideology of the New Right, when applied to policy, was not
unproblematic. It generated considerable contradictions, especially in relation
to women (Gardiner, 1983; Segal, 1983; Campbell, 1987; Wilson, 1987), and
was also not very effective. The impact of the women's movement in the country—even if disorganized—had changed public opinion sufficiently to be able to
curtail the extent to which the New Right could promote traditional values,
particularly those surrounding women's domesticity. Segal (1983) argues that
the Conservative government was held back by the 'continual vigour and
success of feminism in mobilizing support for women's rights and equality'.
Moreover, changes in women's employment since the Second World War
had encouraged middle-class career women—some of whom could be found
as Conservative Party members—to fight against any simple equation
between women and motherhood, excessive moralizing, restrictions on sexual
freedom or even cut backs in child benefits (Campbell, 1987).

In the event, despite harsh social policies, women did not go back *en
masse* to their homes, instead they continued to carry the dual burden
of being wives and workers (Wilson, 1987). The early educational initiatives were also less than successful. Curricular reforms that encouraged
traditional parenting roles were hard to implement within a decentralized
system. Education for parenthood and sex education were unlikely vehicles
for such a 'moral crusade' since these courses were not mandatory. As Wolpe
observed:

> The implications of a third term of Thatcherism in the field of sex edu-
> cation are not straightforward . . . Moral values are seen to have declined
> and there are moves to combat this . . . What is not clear is whether the
> way to combat this will be through the provision of sex education, given
> the opposition to its inclusion in the school curriculum in some quarters.
> (Wolpe, 1987, p. 45)

Ironically, new legislation had made sex education the responsibility
of school governing bodies, and they could choose to remove such a

controversial topic. Courses on family living were also likely to be optional and have the low status ascribed to non-examined subjects. Far more significant to this programme of moral 'clean up' was the legislation against 'promoting homosexuality' through section 28, although here again the impact on schools nationally was not likely to be great since few local authorities had developed policies on sexuality.

RETHINKING WOMEN'S RIGHTS

It has become increasingly clear from recent feminist analyses that the Conservative government, despite its emphasis upon traditional family structures, still wished to be seen as committed, at least in rhetoric, to a version of equality of opportunity and equal rights. Conservative women themselves sustained notions of being equal to men 'in the sight of God' (Campbell, 1987). Neo-liberals, in particular, encouraged the notion of individual liberty, especially economic freedom in the marketplace and political freedom from coercion and excessive state control. Hayek and Friedman, often quoted as leading theorists of monetarism, saw such freedom being provided by an autonomous and private family unit (equated with women's role) and being found within the public sphere (equated with male activity). The assumption of such gender differences led feminist critics to conclude that logically 'the promise of liberty can only apply to men'. Individualism, property ownership and consumerism were men-only concepts (Segal, 1983, p. 119) even if, as Ferdinand Mount, right-wing author of *The Subversive Family* (1982), argued, 'women's rights to equality are unassailable because women are human beings' (quoted in Williams, 1989, p. 119).

The solution to this contradiction could not necessarily be found by expelling women from the marketplace, not least because capital still required female waged labour. Instead, the notion of competitive individualism could be selectively applied to men and women who had no family responsibilities (David, 1983), or alternatively to women who had already fulfilled their role as home maker and could now play the role of paid worker. Indeed, as Mrs Thatcher herself argued in 1982:

> It is of course true that women of our generation are often still comparatively young by the time our children are grown up and therefore we have an opportunity further to develop our own talents ... For many that experience can enhance their lives and enlarge their interests.
>
> (Quoted in Wilson, 1987, p. 295)

Such statements from Mrs Thatcher represent for Wilson (1987) an insight into the ways in which the Conservative Party sought to represent itself as 'the modern party':

> The party that welcomes and harnesses change and is committed to an attack on the 'old fashioned' dogmas of trades unions and an assortment of blinkered ideologues—Fabians, Marxists, feminists and the like—whose

time is past and who have got fatally out of step with the world we live in.   (Wilson, 1987, p. 205)

The 'modernizing tendencies' within Conservative Party policy were also to find somewhat confused expression within the various education reforms of the 1980s. Cuts in state funds (particularly in adult education, in subjects such as the arts and humanities, in discretionary grants for further education) threatened educational and training opportunities for women (Deem, 1981). Also, the failure to fund pre-school education (and even moves to reduce the existing provision of such education in some localities) restricted considerably the chances that married women had to fulfil that 'second role' as paid workers in anything other than part-time and low-paid employment. The DES under Thatcher's government also continued its largely indifferent stance to issues of sex equality, even though the HMI were able to offer explicit but not very strong support to those concerned about female educational experiences and achievement (Acker, 1986; Orr, 1985). Political complacency and inadequate suppport for gender issues in education seemed to be the main criticisms made by feminists when analyzing central government policy in the 1980s (Arnot, 1987).

Strangely enough, the concept of equal rights in Conservative Party thinking emerged most obviously in relation to the so-called 'new vocationalism' which attempted to restructure and 'modernize' the economy through direct state intervention. [. . .] The Manpower Services Commission (now known as the Training Agency), in contrast to the DES, appeared to take more interest in equal opportunities issues. Although it largely ignored the extent of gender differentiation in its youth training schemes and as a result dismally failed to break down sexual divisions (Fawcett Society, 1985; Wickham, 1987), its attempt to ensure that all Technical and Vocational Educational Initiatives (TVEI) in secondary schools tackled equal opportunities between the sexes could be interpreted as a significant attempt to 'reshape' gender relations in education.

The promotion of equal opportunities within such vocational initiatives, according to Weiner (1989a), had economic as well as political benefits, especially with regard to the needs of the capitalist economy for a 'free (that is, unsegmented) labour market' and 'a flexible work force, undif-ferentiated by sex'. In other words,

> Liberal/progressive ideas concerning freedom for girls and women to move upwards in educational and occupational hierarchies have become syn-onymous with 'liberal', 'laissez faire' ideas about labour market freedom.
>   (Weiner, 1989a, p. 121)

Ironically, the funding criteria which made it compulsory that all TVEI projects promote equal opportunities came to represent one of the most progressive aspects of the initiatives, even though help and support from the MSC/Training Agency were thin on the ground. A full evaluation of the strategies adopted by TVEI to promote equal opportunities was even commissioned and published (Bridgwood and Betteridge, 1989). In practice, the experience gained by schools suggested that equal opportunities could not be based on principles of individualism and free choice. Increasingly, schools were developing their own form of a common compulsory curriculum. They were also pushed into challenging (although slowly at first) the gendered nature of school knowledge, the naming of subjects and the occupational associations of particular courses (Millman and Weiner, 1987).

Perhaps this experience, together with a long history of calls from the Left and from feminists such as Byrne (1985) for a common curriculum to tackle social inequality, prepared the ground for a muted response to the introduction of the National Curriculum. But also, ideological disunity, the lack of consistent committed political support (Loach, 1987) and, possibly, an over-emphasis on personal politics (Rowbotham, 1986) might have weakened feminist campaigns. In the event, despite years of academic research and policy development in schools and colleges, feminist opposition to the Education Reform Act was neither public nor organized. When responses to the Education Reform Bill (GERBIL) were collected, the voices of women were not heard (Haviland, 1989). Apart from within those organizations in which women had struggled successfully (for example, NUT, NATE), feminist educational concerns ironically were represented by the Equal Opportunities Commission (already becoming more partisan in its appointments).

The absence of a coherent feminist response either by sociologists or by women's education groups and networks might also be explained by the confusion over the likely effects of the legislation. The impact of a combination of centralized control of the curriculum and a blatant lack of concern with the form of pedagogy (other than formal assessment) was not immediately obvious. Early commentators (Kant, 1987; Myers, 1989; Arnot, 1989b) interpreted the legislation as yet another instance of 'missed opportunities' to tackle sex discrimination in education rather than a case of virulent anti-feminism. But the list of subjects to be included in the National Curriculum, based on a traditionally 'male' grammar school curriculum, provided early evidence of an androcentric structure. Whilst girls could benefit from the compulsory science and technology, many of them were likely to choose the least intensive or more traditionally 'feminine' options within these subjects. Girls' schools were also threatened by lack of sufficient resources, especially for technology.

National Curriculum planning could theoretically challenge male biases in subject content. Yet as evidence emerged of the low level of female representation on subject working groups, the lack of reference to gender research, the absence of consultation with women's groups, and the derisory reporting on the issue by the National Curriculum Council (Arnot, 1989b; Davies, Holland and Minhas, 1990; Weiner, 1990), it became clear that masculinist and racial biases within most subjects were not going to be challenged officially. Indeed, working groups have not, to date, taken a major stand on promoting anti-sexist or anti-racist curricula content—arguably, subject content and pedagogy have regressed to outmoded styles, reasserting male-centred forms of knowledge (Burton and Weiner, 1990).

The ideological significance of the National Curriculum in terms of gender, therefore, is somewhat unclear. If this centralized control of the curriculum represented a victory for the neo-conservatives, then why were precisely those courses closest to parental education (i.e. child care and domestic science) demoted to the margins of the curriculum? The downgrading of these 'female' domestic courses could be seen either as fortuitous for girls, releasing them from domestic ideologies, or alternatively as a signal of the Conservative government's lack of concern for the subjects in which girls achieve. Certainly it is not clear that family values have shaped the selection of subjects nor indeed that subject working groups were actively encouraged to find ways of valuing family life in anything like the same way that they were pressured to celebrate English history and nationhood (Jenkinson, 1990). Apart from failing to refer to anti-sexist or anti-racist education, the National Curriculum supposedly leaves schools with the duty to choose their own pedagogy and to find ways of 'promoting equal opportunities'.

The ideological tensions within the Government concerning equal opportunities can also be glimpsed in the approach adopted by the National Curriculum Council. Equal opportunities, for example, was listed as only one of two cross-curriculum dimensions for schools to develop as part of the whole curriculum. At the same time, the Council's chief executive, Duncan Graham, indicated that because gender was such a 'delicate' issue, no task group would be formed to consider it and hence no specific non-statutory guidance for schools would be produced. This approach, coupled with the fact that there was no official commitment to monitor sex bias in assessment, nor to train governors in sex discrimination legislation, nor to encourage the teaching profession to improve its expectations of female pupils or reassess teaching styles, was unlikely to win support from those committed to sex equality.

In effect, centralized intervention appears to have reinforced male control of education policy-making and to have delegated the issue of sex equality to teachers to implement (Arnot, 1989b). Whilst at first glance this may seem beneficial, the evidence provided by sociological research on teachers' attitudes to gender difference suggests that although there is likely to be considerable rhetoric about the importance of equal opportunities policies, in practice little will happen. In other words, the rump of teacher autonomy still allowed within the new educational system may well serve to marginalize gender issues and to sustain continued discriminatory behaviour.

CONCLUSIONS

The effects of the Education Reform Act on women have yet to be evaluated. Current sociological understandings of the policy intentions and expected outcomes of the Education Reform Act and the National Curriculum have tended to ignore the significance of the gender dimension, preferring to focus predominantly on the relationship between schooling, the state, ideology and the economy (see, for example, Whitty, 1990; Ball, 1990). These accounts sit well within the tradition of the British Left, which has failed to 'understand the nature of the New Right through a gender blind analysis' (ten Tusscher, 1986). There has been a failure to consider whether the New Right in the United Kingdom had any similarity with the emergence of the New Right in the United States. The latter movement, as Andrea Dworkin (1978) found in her influential study, was a 'social and political movement controlled almost totally by men and as such it was fundamentally anti-feminist in stance'.

The gender analysis offered here demonstrates, I hope, that the context for the emergence and success of the new Right was not just a 'crisis in capitalism'. Feminism, along with anti-racism, had thrown liberalism itself into crisis. As Eisenstein (1987) put it in the context of the United States:

> Feminism has uncovered the truth that capitalist patriarchal society cannot deliver on its liberal promises of equality or even equal rights without destabilising itself.   (Eisenstein, 1987, p. 239)

This challenge was particularly true in education, where feminist educationalists and researchers were shattering the illusions of the social democratic project. Many of the fundamental beliefs in equality of opportunity, universalism, co-education, comprehensivization and progessive teaching styles had been challenged by gender research. Further, the more that power relations in education were being exposed, the greater were the demands for gender, class and race equality and the more outspoken were the calls for increased state intervention to limit liberal so-called 'freedoms' and to help restructure domestic relations in the name of social equality (Arnot, 1991).

Thatcherism, if it existed at all as a coherent political philosophy, was not synonymous with the moral right nor, indeed, with pure neo-liberalism. It attempted to respond to the interests of capital and patriarchy and also to the threat to British nationhood. However, as far as women were concerned, since Thatcherism reasserted a form of competitive individualism and attempted to reinforce sexual divisions within and between public/private domains, it did not represent a significant break from social democratic thought.

In the event, the strength of the women's movement in shaping public opinion over the last two decades restricted the options available to the New Right to respond to such crises. Despite the attempt at a 'moral crusade', there has not been a concerted ideological attack on wage-earning women *per se*. Instead, we find an assault on the working classes in an apparent attempt to raise productivity, increase profits and weaken collective organization, especially trades unions. Meanwhile, as Wilson (1987) has shown, the range of strategies adopted by the Conservative government in the 1980s had the effect of incorporating women into the labour force but under the worst possible terms—by reducing their protection, raising unemployment rates and failing to establish childcare provision, thus adding to their domestic burdens.

The new vocationalism and modernizing influences in education arguably promised women more opportunities to extend their occupational horizons. The National Curriculum—at least in its early formulations—would make available to girls traditionally male subjects and professional scientific and technological careers. The effects of such reforms, however, are most likely to be felt by middle-class women whose opportunities could be enhanced through consumer choice in education and increased concern about access and training.

Working-class women and black and ethnic minority women, in contrast, are likely to find their opportunities even further reduced and their rights to choose their own work patterns restricted by Conservative economic and family policies. It is not difficult to predict that there will be a widening class gap between women. Miles and Middleton (1990, p. 201), for example, observe that 'the Education Reform Act will not be neutral in its effects on different classes and ethnic groups . . .'. [. . .]

The key issue for sociologists should, therefore, be an investigation of the processes involved in the attenuation of class relations in the context of gender and race. Such analyses would need to draw upon the insights that gender research brings to bear on social democracy, on the nature of the public—private division, on the impact of school organization and gender dynamics within schools. Research into such themes will also, no doubt, take into account the new era of centralized control which extends male power even further with respect to educational policy-making over a predominantly female teaching force. It should also consider open enrolment and opting out, issues which raise yet again the question of parental choice of single-sex or coeducational schools; particularly in relation to separate schools, and it should look at local management of schools, which will highlight the priorities of educational managers and affect the development of equality policies. Sociological research which takes account of gender, race and class will provide valuable insights into whether full 'entitlement' is either possible or being achieved by such educational reforms.

As far as women's position within the family is concerned, the impact of educational reforms is somewhat different. It is difficult to argue that the attempt to use education to regenerate patriarchal values and thus counter the excesses of the egalitarian movements of the 1970s has been effectively orchestrated. Instead we find an attempt through centralized control of the curriculum to reassert outmoded educational formats against increasing professional resistance. It seems, though, that feminist research (particularly on the effects of school organization and patriarchal relations within the educational system) has had little to no impact on the architects of the new education system. The forms of control over gender relations within schooling have been left largely intact for the 1990s but are embedded in a new more rigidly classified structure of school knowledge. How this new 'gender code' (MacDonald, 1980) will shape the masculinizing and feminizing processes of schooling in the next generation of children is another important topic for sociological investigation.

Let us hope that Segal was right when she argued that:

> Thatcherism ... has not successfully crushed a feminist consciousness which is aware of the oppression of women's lives as vulnerable and exploited workers and as hopelessly overburdened housewives, mothers and daughters.   (Segal, 1983, p. 214)

Feminist research still has a valuable role to play in maintaining that consciousness within the sociology of education, but equally important is the integration of that perspective into mainstream sociological theorizing and evaluation of these educational reforms.

References

Acker, S. (1987) Feminist theory and the study of gender and education. *International Review of Education* 33, 419–35.
— (ed.) (1989) *Teachers, Gender and Careers*. Basingstoke: Falmer Press.
Acker, S. and Warren Piper, D.W. (eds) (1984) *Is Higher Education Fair to Women?* London: SRHE-Nelson.
Amos, V. and Parmar, P. (1987) Resistance and responses to the experiences of black girls in Britain. In M. Arnot and G. Weiner (eds) *Gender and the Politics of Schooling*. London: Hutchinson.
Anyon, J. (1983) Intersections of gender and class: accommodation and resistance by working class and affluent females to contradictory sex-role idologies. In S. Walker and L. Barton (eds) *Gender, Class and Education*. Lewes: Falmer Press.
Apple, M. (1982) *Education and Power*. London: Routledge and Kegan Paul.
Arnot, M. (1983) A cloud over coeducation: an analysis of the forms of transmission of class and gender relations. In S. Walker and L. Barton (eds) *Gender, Class and Education*. Lewes: Falmer Press.
— (1987) Lip service or radical reform? Central government responses to sex equality issues. In M. Arnot and G. Weiner (eds) *Gender and the Politics of Schooling*. London: Hutchinson.
— (1989) Consultation or legitimation? Race and gender politics and the making of the National Curriculum. *Critical Social Policy*, Issue 27, 20–38.
— (1991) Equality and democracy: a decade of struggle over education. *British Journal of Sociology of Education* 12, 447–66.
Arnot, M. and Weiner, G. (eds) (1987) *Gender and the Politics of Schooling*. London: Hutchinson.
Ball, S. (1990) *Politics and Policy Making in Education*. London: Routledge.
Bowles, S. and Gintis, H. (1978) *Schooling in Capitalist America*. London: Routledge and Kegan Paul.
Bourdieu, P. and Passeron, J.C. (1977) *Reproduction in Education, Society and Culture*. London: Sage.
Brah, A. (1988) Extended review. *British Journal of Sociology of Education* 9, 115–20.
Brah, A. and Minhas, R. (1985) Structural racism or cultural difference: schooling for Asian girls. In G. Weiner (ed.) *Just a Bunch of Girls*. Milton Keynes: Open University Press.
Bridgwood, A. and Betteridge, J. (1989) *Equal Opportunities for Boys and Girls with TVEI*. Windsor: NFER Training Agency.

Bryan, B., Dadzie, S. and Scafe, S. (1985) *The Heart of the Race: Black Women's Lives in Britain.* London: Virago.

Burton, L. and Weiner, G. (1990) Social justice and the National Curriculum. *Research Papers in Education* 5, 203–27.

Byrne, E. (1978) *Women in Education.* London: Tavistock.

— (1985) Equality of equity? A European view. In M. Arnot (ed.) *Race and Gender: Equal Opportunities Policies in Education.* Oxford: Pergamon Press.

Campbell, B. (1987) *The Iron Ladies.* London: Virago.

Carby, H. (1982) Schooling in Babylon. In Centre for Contemporary Cultural Studies *The Empire Strikes Back.* London: Hutchinson.

Centre for Contemporary Cultural Studies (CCCS) (1981) *Unpopular Education: Schooling for Social Democracy in England since 1944.* London: Hutchinson.

Clarricoates, K. (1978) Dinosaurs in the classroom: the hidden curriculum in primary schools. *Women's Studies International Quarterly* 1, 353–64.

Connell, R.W. (1987) *Gender and Power.* Sydney: Allen and Unwin.

Connell, R.W., Ashenden, D.J., Kessler, S. and Dowsett, G.W. (1982) *Making the Difference: Schools, Families and Social Division.* London: Allen and Unwin.

Crowther Report (1959) *15–18* (Central Advisory Council for Education). London: HMSO.

Dale, R.R. (1969, 1971 and 1974) *Mixed or Single Sex School, Vols I–III.* London: Routledge and Kegan Paul.

Dale, J. and Foster, P. (1986) *Feminists and State Welfare.* London: Routledge and Kegan Paul.

David, M. (1983a) Teaching and preaching sexual morality: the New Right's anti-feminism in Britain and the USA. *Journal of Education* 166, 63–76.

— (1983b) Sex, education and social policy: new moral economy? In S. Walker and L. Barton (eds) *Gender, Class and Education.* Lewes: Falmer Press.

— (1985) Motherhood and social policy—a matter of education. *Critical Social Policy* 12, Spring, 28–43.

Davies, A.M., Holland, J. and Minhas, R. (1990) *Equal Opportunities in the New ERA.* Hillcole Group, Paper 2.

Deem, R. (ed.) (1980) *Schooling for Women's Work.* London: Routledge and Kegan Paul.

— (1981) State policy and ideology in the education of women 1944–1980. *British Journal of Sociology of Education* 2, 131–44.

Delamont, S. (1980) *Sex Roles and the School.* London: Methuen.

DES (1975) *Curricular Differences for Boys and Girls*, Education Survey 21. London: HMSO.

Dyhouse, C. (1978) Towards a feminine curriculum for English school girls: the demands of ideology 1870–1963. *Women's Studies International Quarterly* 1, 291–311.

Dworkin, A. (1983) *Right Wing Women.* London: Women's Press.

Eisenstein, H. (1984) *Contemporary Feminist Thought.* London: Counterpoint Unwin.

Eisenstein, Z. (1987) Liberalism, feminism and the Reagan state: the neoconservative assault on sexual equality. In R. Miliband, L. Panitch and J. Saville (eds) *Socialist Register.* London: Merlin Press.

Fawcett Society and the National Joint Committee of Working Women's Organisations (1985) *The Class of 84.* London: Fawcett Society.

Finch, J. (1984) *Education and Social Policy.* London: Longman.

Gardiner, J. (1983) Women, recession and the Tories. In S. Hall and M. Jacques (eds) *The Politics of Thatcherism.* London: Lawrence and Wishart.

Giroux, H. (1983) *Theory and Resistance in Education: A Pedagogy of Opposition.* London: Heinemann.

Griffin, C. (1985) *Typical Girls?* London: Routledge and Kegan Paul.

Haviland, J. (1988) *Take Care Mr. Baker!* London: Fourth Estate.

Holland, J. (1981) *Work and Women*, Bedford Way Papers 6. University of London Institute of Education.

Jenkinson, F. (1990) Multicultural education and the National Curriculum. Unpublished MPhil dissertation, University of Cambridge.

Jones, C. and Mahony, P. (eds) (1989) *Learning Our Lines: Sexuality and Social Control in Education.* London: Women's Press.

Kant, L. (1987) National Curriculum: nationally equal. *NUT Education Review* 1 (2), Autumn.

Kelly, A. (1985) The construction of masculine science. *British Journal of Sociology of Education* 6, 133–54.

Klein, G. (1989) New Right—new ERA. *NUT Education Review* 3 (2), 14–18.

Lawn, K. and Grace, G. (eds) (1987) *Teachers: The Culture and Politics of Work.* Basingstoke: Falmer Press.

Loach, L. (1987) Can feminism survive a third term? *Feminist Review* 27, 27–36.

MacDonald, M. (1980) Socio-cultural reproduction and women's education. In R. Deem (ed.) *Schooling for Women's Work.* London: Routledge and Kegan Paul.

McRobbie, A. (1978) Working class girls and the culture of femininity. In Centre for Contemporary Cultural Studies Women's Studies Group *Women Take Issue.* London: Hutchinson.

— (1980) Setting accounts with subculture: a feminist critique. *Screen Education* 34, 37–49.

Mahony, P. (1985) *Schools for the Boys: Coeducation Reassessed.* London: Hutchinson.

Middleton, S. (1987) The sociology of women's education. In M. Arnot and G. Weiner (eds) *Gender and the Politics of Schooling.* London: Hutchinson.

— (1990) Women, equality and equity in liberal educational policies, 1945–1988. In S. Middleton, J. Codd and A. Jones (eds) *New Zealand Education Policy Today.* Wellington, New Zealand: Allen and Unwin.

Miles, S. and Middleton, C. (1990) Girls' education in the balance. In M. Flude and M. Hammer (eds) *The Education Reform Act 1988: Origins and Implications.* London Falmer Press.

Millman, V. and Weiner, G. (1987) Engineering equal opportunities: the case of TVEI. In D. Gleeson (ed.) *A Critical Appraisal of TVEI.* London: Routledge and Kegan Paul.

Myers, K. (1989) High heels in the market place. *Education*, 16 June.

Newsom Report (1963) *Half Our Future.* Central Advisory Council for Education. London: HMSO.

Parmar, P. (1989) Other kinds of dreams. *Feminist Review* 31, 55–65.

Pascall, G. (1986) *Social Policy: A Feminist Analysis.* London: Tavistock.

Phoenix, A. (1987) Theories of gender and black families. In G. Weiner and M. Arnot (eds) *Gender Under Scrutiny.* London: Hutchinson.

Plowden Report (1967) *Children and their Primary Schools.* Central Advisory Council for Education. London: HMSO.

Purvis, J. (1987) Social class, education and the ideals of femininity in the nineteenth century. In M. Arnot and G. Weiner (eds) *Gender and the Politics of Schooling.* London: Hutchinson.

Rowbotham, S. (1986) Feminism and democracy. In D. Held and C. Pollitt (eds) *New Forms of Democracy.* London: Sage.

Segal, L. (1983) The heat in the kitchen. In S. Hall and P. Jacques (eds) *The Politics of Thatcherism.* London: Lawrence and Wishart.

Stanworth, M. (1981) *Gender and Schooling: A Study of Sexual Divisions.* London: Hutchinson.

ten Tusscher, T. (1986) Patriarchy, capitalism and the New Right. In J. Evans *et al.* (eds) *Feminism and Political Theory.* London: Sage.

Thompson, I. (1983) *Learning Liberation: Women's Responses to Men's Education.* London: Croom Helm.

Valli, L. (1986) *Becoming Clerical Workers.* London: Routledge and Kegan Paul.

Walkerdine, V. (1987) Sex, power and pedagogy. In M. Arnot and G. Weiner (eds) *Gender and the Politics of Schooling.* London: Hutchinson.

Weiner, G. (1989) Feminism, equal opportunities and vocationalism: the changing context. In H. Burchell and V. Millman (eds) *Changing Perspectives on Gender.* Milton Keynes: Open University Press.

— (1990) The future for social justice in the 1990s. *NUT Education Review* 4, 56–9.

Weiner, G. and Arnot, M. (eds) (1987) *Gender Under Scrutiny.* London: Hutchinson.

Whitty, G. (1985) *Sociology and School Knowledge.* London: Methuen.

— (1990) The New Right and the National Curriculum: state control or market forces. In M. Flude and M. Hammer (eds) *The Education Reform Act 1988: Its Origins and Implications.* London: Falmer Press.

Whyld, J. (ed.) (1983) *Sexism in the Secondary Curriculum.* London: Harper and Row.

— (1986) *Girls into Science and Technology.* London: Routledge and Kegan Paul.

Whyte, J. *et al.* (eds) (1985) *Girl Friendly Schooling.* London: Methuen.

Wickham, A. (1987) *Women and Training.* Milton Keynes: Open University Press.

Williams, F. (1989) *Social Policy: A Critical Introduction.* Cambridge: Polity Press.

Willis, P. (1977) *Learning to Labour.* Farnborough: Saxon House.

Wilson, E. (1980) *Only Halfway to Paradise.* London: Tavistock.

— (1987) Thatcherism and women: after seven years. In R. Miliband, L. Panitch and J. Saville (eds) *Socialist Register.* London: Merlin Press.

Wolpe, A.M. (1976) The official ideology of education for girls. In M. Flude and J. Ahier (eds) *Educability, Schools and Ideology.* London: Croom Helm.

— (1977) Education and the sexual division of labour. In A. Kuhn and A.M. Wolpe (eds) *Feminism and Materialism: Women and Modes of Production.* London: Routledge and Kegan Paul.

— (1987) Sex in schools: back to the future. *Feminist Review* 27, Autumn, 37–48.

Wright, C. (1987) The relations between teacher and Afro-Caribbean pupils: observing multiracial classrooms. In G. Weiner and M. Arnot (eds) *Gender Under Scrutiny.* London: Hutchinson.

12 THE MYTH OF UNDERACHIEVEMENT

HEIDI MIRZA

Black girls do relatively well at school. But although the scholastic attainment of young black women has been documented, it has rarely been discussed. Research investigating the educational experience of young black *people* persistently fails to integrate satisfactorily into its findings the differential achievement of black girls. [...]

Why has the phenomenon of black female scholastic success been consistently neglected for more than three decades? To answer this question, it is revealing to chart the historical development of the debate on race and educational achievement. From such an exercise it becomes clear that the marginalization of the gender issue is a consequence of the political undercurrents that have shaped research on race and education.

LAYING THE GROUNDWORK FOR NEGLECT: 1958–1970

The current neglect of black girls in educational research had its foundation over thirty years ago—in 1958. The racial unrest of 1958 was a significant watershed, not only in terms of its generally recognized political implications, but also for an influential though much less widely acknowledged reason. The 1958 race riots set in motion the wheels of what Hall (1978) described as the 'new and indigenous racism of the post-war period'. The nature of this new British racism, characterized by white fear and hostility towards the newly arrived Commonwealth immigrants, had the effect of determining the terms of reference that have since shaped the debate on race and education, the key concepts being race and culture (Parekh, 1988). The overwhelming emphasis on race and culture meant that, right from the start, gender was not considered to be a major area of concern. Gender, it was believed, could not lend any valuable or illuminating insights to a debate in which the underlying premise was about racial differences.

From the early to mid-1960s, policy initiatives in the field of race relations were directed towards the goal of assimilation (Mullard, 1982). 'Commonsense' racist assumptions about the inherent inferiority of non-European languages, family structures and life styles determined the content of the educational developments during this period.

Source: Abridged from Mirza, H. (1992) *Young, Female and Black* (pp. 10–31; 197–198; 206–230). London: Routledge.

That little or no academic research had yet been undertaken to qualify or quantify the nature of immigrant educational needs did not inhibit the DES from producing Circular 7/65 in 1965. This controversial directive was guided largely by uninformed opinion as to the nature of the perceived 'immigrant problem': it aimed to 'thin out' the Asian and West Indian presence, and it instructed local authorities to disperse the immigrant pupil population.

This dispersal policy, commonly known as 'bussing', was racist both in philosophy and in consequence. The Circular reinforced the general and pervasive view that all Asians and West Indians, regardless of class and sex, and solely by virtue of their race, presented a problem for the education system. Thus began the exclusive focus on the black child as responsible for his (and not her) educational failure. What mattered was not whether children were male or female, but that they were black and not white.

So, even before any informed academic research had been undertaken, race and culture were already firmly established as the terms of reference and, as such, were responsible for shaping the debate on educational research for the ensuing three decades. Gender became submerged in the highly charged political exchanges that characterized this early period.

In the late 1960s, with the inception of multi-cultural education (later to be called multi-racial education), the fine-tuning of racial and cultural explanations for underachievement commenced. From 1966 onwards there was a further escalation of anti-immigrant hostility, exacerbated by Enoch Powell's speeches on race in 1967 and 1968. In this overall climate of hostility towards black migrants, educational testing was called upon to measure scientifically the relative educational inferiority of the black child. During these early days, crude and simplistic notions of genetic intellectual inferiority were fuelled by Jensen in Britain and by Eysenck in America.

This early tradition in academic research, emphasizing IQ and intellectual ability by race, has been an influential undercurrent in the debate on race and education despite being publicly discredited as repugnant and insulting. Measuring differences *between* groups was clearly the order of the day in academic research on race, and not measuring differences *within* groups.

In 1966, research by Houghton showed for the first time that Jamaican girls were performing slightly better than boys on reasoning tests. Houghton, like others who followed (for example, Little, Mabey and Whitaker, 1968; Payne, 1969) showed that gender differences did exist, but never explored this finding as significant in itself. These studies were concerned with measuring the comparative ability and performance of minority-group children and indigenous children, and little else. Females inevitably found their way into the samples by virtue of their existence in the population. However, the failure to incorporate the gender issue into these analyses cannot be regarded as a calculated omission. It was, rather, the outcome of the intellectual poverty and assumptions inherent in IQ studies. The most recent research in Britain to address the issue of IQ was a study by Mascie-Taylor and Mackintosh (DES, 1985).

Written nearly 20 years after the Houghton study, it still ignored the issue of gender differences in educational attainment. [. . .]

A DECADE OF CONSOLIDATION AND THE INVISIBILITY OF GENDER: 1970–1980

[. . .]Research in the 1970s continued to refine the idea, already established in the 1960s, that poor home background, particularly adverse socio-economic circumstances, contributed greatly to low achievement among West Indian children. But the emphasis now moved away from racial inferiority towards social and cultural inadequacy. Nowhere was this more evident than in government research and policy, which reflected this national trend.

In response to the increasing inner-city unrest during the late 1960s and early 1970s, the Labour government launched a number of projects aimed at tackling the problem of urban deprivation. Both the Urban Aid Programme and the Educational Priority Projects (Halsey, 1972) marked a new era in the discussion of race and underachievement. Influenced by the findings of the Plowden Report (Central Advisory Council for Education, 1967), which highlighted social class deprivation, the government's Community Education Programmes of the early 1970s were not directed at alleviating racial inequality, but focused on the disadvantaged in general. Class now became the central issue on the research agenda, not race, and least of all gender.[1]

In America, the 1966 Coleman Report (Coleman *et al.*, 1969) was influential in bringing about this apparent shift towards social and cultural inadequacy as an explanation for the underachievement of the black child. Furthermore, the report gave impetus to the notions of negative self-esteem and negative ethnic identity that have since dominated educational research on the black child, notions that further established the invisibility of gender.

The idea that black children were failing relative not only to middle-class but also to working-class children for psychological reasons became a popular myth in the 1970s. It was a widely held belief that black children did not merely share the disadvantage of indigenous working-class children but also suffered discrimination, prejudice and rejection by the dominant group (Coard, 1971; Little, 1975; Milner, 1975; 1983). The 'commonsense' argument of what came to be known as the 'self-fulfilling prophecy' was that black children internalize the negative racial values that society ascribes to them, and as a result, regardless of whether they are male or female, they come to see themselves as failures and non-achievers in school.

Thus, by 1970 the terms of reference established in the late 1950s—race and culture—were still dominant in the debate on underachievement; but now the emphasis was less on race and inherent genetic ability, and more on culture and its presumed negative effects. An aspect of the race and education debate that contributed to the general tendency in the 1970s to overlook gender was the 'fashion' for comparing West Indians' academic performance with that of their Asian counterparts. [...] This suggested that there is a hierarchy of 'superior' and 'inferior' cultures. The relative cultural deprivation between ethnic groups, especially Asians and West Indians, became a popular research theme and played an important role in influencing multi-cultural policy initiatives in schools.

The self-concept theorists were influential in shaping the multi-cultural education debate. [...] The prescribed curriculum changes that provided the mainstay of policy initiatives were aimed at enhancing self-esteem, identified as the source of 'the education problem'. For example, a 'special educational' concession to enhance the self-esteem of black girls was to have, in addition to their home economics curriculum, 'Caribbean flavour cooking' and 'hair braiding' (Stone, 1985).

What is fundamentally inaccurate about the self-concept theory is its assumptions about the underachievement of all West Indian pupils. If black female academic success was taken into account, the basic assumption of negative self-esteem upon which the notion rests becomes questionable. It would appear, therefore, that the omission of gender renders unreliable this influential period of research on negative self-esteem.

Young black women were rendered invisible in both theory and policy during this era. Black identity, as the self-concept theorists described it, was clearly black *male* identity. Carby (1982a) explained that in reality generalizations cannot be made about the black experience. Young black women are subject to a very different type of stereotypical image from black men. The specific image of them as unfeminine and sexually overt has consequences for the way in which black females are treated by others and the opportunities available to them.

Just as the previous decade was not completely devoid of educational research acknowledging the presence of black females, so several studies in the late 1970s commented on the differential achievement of black girls (Allen and Smith, 1975; McEwan, Gipps and Sumner, 1975; Yule *et al.*, 1975; Jones, 1977; Phillips, 1979; Bagley and Verma, 1980; Rosen and Burgess, 1980). These studies began to emerge in 1975, after a period of almost six years during which there was a complete absence of gender from educational research—six years that were, in effect, dominated by the work of the self-concept theorists.

However, none of the studies can be said to be particularly significant because, although they did acknowledge gender differences, they failed to use their findings to explore new and enlightened directions in the race and education debate. The reason for this, it seems, was that none of these studies set out to address specifically the issue of black female academic achievement, so references to gender were purely observations of a general kind about variations in the data.

YOUNG BLACK WOMEN IN EDUCATIONAL RESEARCH: A REAPPRAISAL OF CURRENT TRENDS

[. . .] When studies that actually considered the issue of black females in schools began to emerge they were characterized by a distinct underlying ideological premise: the central role of the black mother. Unlike those early, distinctly pathological explanations of black disadvantage that suggested that the matriarchal structure of the black family caused it to be weak and disorganized (Moynihan, 1965, in Rainwater and Yancey, 1967; Gibson, 1986), black achievement was now being seen as the outcome of the strong and central position of the female in the black family (Fuller, 1982; Phizacklea, 1982; Dex, 1983; Sharpe, 1987).

Both theoretical positions, though they appear outwardly to be constructed in opposition to each other, in effect draw on two similar assumptions: the presumed matriarchal structure of the black family, and the marginalization of the black male within that structure. While the early explanations regarded the centrality of the females' role as 'seriously retarding the progress of the group as a whole' (Moynihan, 1965, in Rainwater and Yancey, 1967, p. 76), the later celebratory approach drew on the commonsense myth of the black females' 'tradition of self-reliance' (Phizacklea, 1982).

The trend to pathologize the black female in educational research in Britain was influenced by the 1965 Moynihan Report from America (Rainwater and Yancey, 1967). At the core of Moynihan's thesis on black disadvantage was the alienated and rejected black male and the mother-centred black family. In this and other clearly ethnocentric accounts that victimized the black woman, structural black male unemployment in America was overlooked (Ryan, 1967, 1971; Davis, 1982; Staples, 1985a; b). By failing to acknowledge the true significance of racial discrimination in the American labour market, education took on a special meaning in the Moynihan analysis. [. . .]

Even though Moynihan was prepared to recognize and document the obvious academic success of black women, it is clear why he was prepared to do this. For Moynihan, black academic success was regarded as a negative rather than a positive phenomenon.

Black female achievement, which so often contradicts and upsets the established tradition of overall black underachievement, does not, in this case, detract from the argument. On the contrary, the recognition of black female academic success appears to support Moynihan's thesis. The presence of a dominant female is seen to undermine the social fabric. [. . .]

The recognition of the importance of black female academic success became sacrificed to the wider political debate on the status of the black American family. As an outcome of the Moynihan Report, the Compensatory Eduction Programs established in America, such as Headstart, ignored black female achievement and aimed at redressing black underachievement. In America, as in Britain, policy-makers failed to see black female academic success as offering a new direction in the understanding of black educational issues.

Like Moynihan, the 'progressive' cultural theorists of the 1980s emphasized matriarchy as the key to understanding black female academic success. But, unlike the cultural pathologists, they interpreted this success as a positive outcome of a female-centred society. Whatever the emphasis, the fact remains that the family, and not society, is seen as the dynamic for change in both perspectives.

The strong black female as an explanatory model for the high educational aspirations of young black women, though appearing 'progressive', is at present an ill-conceived and underdeveloped idea. It represents an unsuccessful attempt to transfer the necessary and celebratory tradition of black women's writing[2] into educational and labour-market analysis.

An analysis that on the one hand talks about black women's 'subordinate position in economic, politico-legal and ideological relations' (Phizacklea, 1982, p. 115), but on the other hand suggests that these women resist occupying such a position by 'drawing on their West Indian roots' (Dex, 1983, p. 69) does appear contradictory.

It is naive to suggest that black women possess internal and natural strengths that account for their endurance and ability to overcome the structural racism and sexism they face in the workplace and in the home. Bryan, Dadzie and Scafe (1985) explained the shortcomings of such 'well-intentioned' attempts at analyzing black women:

> They have tended, however, to portray black women in a somewhat romantic light, emphasising our innate capacity to cope with brutality and deprivation, and perpetuating the myth that we are somehow better equipped than others for suffering. While the patient, long-suffering victim of triple oppression may have some heroic appeal, she does not convey our collective experience.
>
> (Bryan, Dadzie and Scafe, 1985, pp. 1–2)

The 'superwoman' image of the black woman (Wallace, 1979), which comes from the 'tradition of self-reliance', reifies the black female experience, suggesting that the black woman is somehow exceptional. Such a perspective implies that the dynamic which structures the black female experience is unlike that experienced by other groups in the labour market, be they black men, white women or white men. While black women do have traditions of work and marriage that are important in shaping their working lives, their situation is essentially determined by the dynamics of an economy with a sexually differentiated labour force, fundamentally distorted by racism.

Nevertheless, research perspectives that stress the centrality of the matriarchal or matrifocal black family characterize many contemporary educational studies in Britain. However subtle, the pathological tradition so well established in British research (see Carby, 1982a; Lawrence, 1982a, b; Phoenix,

1987) remains a feature of the many 'progressive' studies on black girls that have been undertaken in the 1980s: studies such as those undertaken by Driver (1980), Fuller (1982) and Eggleston *et al.* (1986).

DRIVER, RUTTER AND THE LIBERAL TRADITION

The publication in 1980 of a highly controversial report written by Geoffrey Driver, entitled *Beyond Underachievement*, was significant.[3] To explain the apparent academic success of West Indian girls (and the relative failure of white girls), Driver examined the respective positions of women in the West Indian and British social structures. From a brief consideration of the differences he contended that in the West Indies, women have a higher social and economic status than men and, as such, are generally regarded as the 'guardians of their family's good name' and the providers of its stable income.

His thesis appeared deceptively simple. [. . .] He argued that in (white) British culture with its patriarchal structure, women have a lower status than men and are socialized to occupy subordinate social and economic roles. In West Indian culture, Driver claimed that the opposite is true. It is the girls rather than the boys who are socialized to occupy superordinate positions and who are inculcated with values and expectations generally held to be conducive to educational success. In the same way that academic achievement is explained by cultural factors, underachievement is simply explained away in terms of the social structure of the West Indian family, in a manner similar to Moynihan.

In the wake of Driver and his conclusions came another important milestone in the analysis of 'race' and underachievement. In 1982, Rutter and his team in their much publicized DES report (*Times Educational Supplement*, 8 October 1980) found that black pupils, and in particular black girls, were more likely to stay on at school after the fifth year in order to gain qualifications equivalent to those of their white peers.

Rutter *et al.* argued that it was the parents' positive involvement in the education of their children that helped the West Indian pupils to overcome the social deprivation and the negative schooling that they were likely to experience.

Unlike Driver, Rutter *et al.* did not offer any explanation as to why black girls should be more persistent in gaining educational qualifications than any of their peers. For Rutter and his colleagues the gender issue did not appear to merit any separate attention. The girls' persistence is seen only as an extension of the general West Indian commitment to education.

This emphasis on individual initiative and school-based factors overlooks the fact that schools do not operate in isolation from the rest of society. It is hardly surprising, therefore, to find that Rutter and his team, with their school-based explanations, were unable to do any more than acknowledge that gender differences do exist.

The studies by Driver and by Rutter *et al.* had little in common, although they both highlighted the presence of black achievement in schools. What they did have in common was the media interest that greeted the publication of their respective findings. The political implications of West Indian achievement were clear. That blacks were doing well was not only controversial but was also regarded as highly 'suspect' by the differing political camps, both radical and conservative. In fact, this period in educational history was marked by a mixture of hostility and indifference towards the academic performance of young black women.

BLACK FEMALE ACHIEVEMENT: THE OFFICIAL RESPONSE

The 'official' government and local authority responses to gender and race in the 1980s were characterized by both insincerity and neglect. [...]

It was hardly surprising that official government reports, which persisted in defining the problem for West Indians in Britain as 'underachievement', should have continued to identify it as a male problem. These reports, it must be remembered, were written in the wake of the black action in Brixton, Toxteth and Bristol in the early 1980s when both the media and sociologists, black and white alike, were responsible for establishing the marginalization of black women: in the explanations for black 'disaffection' and 'alienation', the image of youth that was presented was invariably black and male (Cashmore and Troyna, 1982; Gilroy, 1981; 1982; Sivanandan, 1982; Benyon and Solomos, 1987).

The Rampton Report, *West Indian Children in our Schools* (DES, 1981), made no secret of the fact that gender was of little significance in its investigation. [...] The message of the Rampton Report was clear: underachievement, not minority scholastic success, was the issue to be explored. Rampton's emphasis was on negative self-esteem and on the notions of the self-fulfilling prophecy, teacher stereotypes and the operation of institutional racism, so the recognition of gender would have clearly upset Rampton's well defined paradigms.

Taking up the recommendations of the Rampton Report, not so much in word as in deed, the ILEA policy statements made in 1983 emphasized the eradication of teacher racism. However, the ILEA's definition of racism precluded the satisfactory incorporation of black girls into its policy initiatives. On political rather than academic grounds, the ILEA suggested that racism and sexism are separate but parallel experiences.

[...] For the ILEA, gender was distinctly a white issue and race clearly a male matter. Because black females transcend all three areas of 'concern'—black, working-class and female—they become invisible by failing to comply with the rigid race, class and sex categorization set up by the ILEA team. As Troyna and Williams (1986, p. 35) suggested, this reactive approach to multi-racial initiatives was not so much inspired by 'pedagogical foresight', as impelled by more immediate political and social considerations.

The Swann Report, entitled *Education for All* (DES, 1985) like its predecessor, the Rampton Report, investigated the problem of West Indian underachievement in British schools. Its authors made clear, right from the start, that an association between gender and achievement was not a link that they wished to pursue: in the entire 806 pages of the report, only 18 pages make any direct reference to girls, let alone to the wider gender issue (Mirza, 1986).

[. . .]

By suggesting that there may be a gender variation in academic performance, while simultaneously casting it aside, both the Rampton and Swann reports are indeed guilty of fulfilling the cliché that sociologists so often use: that theory, methods and ethnographic material 'neglected', 'could not find', 'cannot incorporate' or simply 'forgot' the gender element (Allen, 1982).

FROM SUBCULTURES TO SUBORDINATION: BLACK GIRLS AND THE ANALYSIS OF MARY FULLER

Mary Fuller's study of black girls in a London comprehensive school is one of the few attempts to analyse the bearing that a pupil's sex and race might have on academic aspirations and achievements (Fuller, 1978, 1980, 1982). In her study, Fuller confirmed the finding that differential academic outcomes exist between black boys and girls.[4] To investigate why black girls were orientated toward academic achievement, Fuller looked at the experiences of a small group of black girls in their final year of compulsory schooling. She argued that these girls formed a discernible subculture within the school, and that within the context of the school the black female subculture had peculiar characteristics. She claimed that it was neither one of resistance nor of conformity to the school (see also Wright, 1987). In terms of classroom behaviour, this meant that the black girls gave all the appearance of being disaffected, stating that they saw school as 'trivial', 'boring' and 'childish'. Yet the girls, when interviewed or observed away from the classroom, were seen to be strongly committed to some aspects of schooling.

The situation, as Fuller saw it, was that the girls knew their self-worth but believed this was often denied by parents and their male peers, so the pursuit of educational qualifications took on special meaning. The girls did not need qualifications to prove their own worth to themselves, but rather as a public statement of something that was not otherwise given sufficient recognition.

Fuller argued that the black girls were trying to effect some control over their present and future lives by proving their own worth through their academic success. Thus the structure of the subculture, she argued, emerged from the girls' positive acceptance of being both black and female. She ascertained that the 'particular flavour' of the subculture was the outcome of the girls' critical rejection of the negative connotations that the categorizations of female and black commonly attract.

Although Fuller's study is both a clear and stimulating account of black girls in schools, it is necessary to take issue with some of the fundamental assumptions that she made with regard to the structure and function of the subculture, and in particular with her descriptions of the influence of the black family, male peers and the role of what she calls 'double subordination' for the black girls concerned.

Fuller suggested that major influences on the girls' feelings of isolation and anger, which in turn determined the characteristics of the subculture, were the low value of domestic work in the home and the girls' negative relationships with black male peers. However, Riley (1985) found that African Caribbean girls looked forward to relationships with men, and she reported that the girls in her study felt that parents encouraged boys and girls equally. It was a sense of responsibility, and not the need to establish their self-worth, that Riley suggested gave black girls their stronger commitment to education.

Fuller, in emphasizing the oppressive nature of the black family, supported the belief that cultural obstructions to fuller participation in society are reproduced within black families by black people themselves (see Foner, 1979; Pryce, 1979; Gibson, 1986). Such assumptions are clearly the outcome of 'commonsense' pathological ideas about the black family and inappropriate definitions of sexism which have been imposed on the black experience.

The notion of 'subculture' employed by Fuller implies the central importance of 'cultures of resistance' (Willis, 1977). In Fuller's work, as in so many other studies of black girls (Griffin, 1985; Riley, 1985; Mac an Ghaill, 1988; Wulff, 1988; Coultas, 1989; Reid, 1989), the notion of subculture has been employed because it appears to offer some understanding of creativity, activity and resistance. For example, Wulff (1988), in using the subcultural model, suggested that black girls' active pursuit of 'excitement' on the street, in clubs and in school characterized their micro-culture and structured their experience of 'growing up'.

Hall and Jefferson (1976) argued that to emphasize the subcultural features of youth is to divert attention away from the issues that they saw as determining the quality of the experience of those being studied—issues such as unemployment, compulsory mis-education, low pay and dead-end jobs.

Fuller's use of the concept of 'cultures of resistance' results in an unrealistic, 'romantic' reappraisal of black girls' actions and decisions. Fuller's belief that these girls were highly politicized about unemployment, racism and sexism during their educational career, and planned their actions as a defiant gesture to the world, does not stand up to close scrutiny. Research by Ullah (1985) indicated that, compared with other groups in the study, young black women, at the point of entry into the job market, were the least aware of the racism they would encounter in the workplace.

In relation to black females, it is necessary to incorporate not just an understanding of the girls' 'lived-out experiences' of racism in the classroom, but also an analysis of how the ideology of racism structures opportunity and limits economic horizons. It is not sufficient to demonstrate how the ideology of racism and sexism is constructed in the consciousness of individuals or groups; it must also be shown how the ideology of sexually structured racism, as a dynamic and politically constructed ideology, maintains disadvantage by its effect on economic assumptions and values. Thus it is important to investigate the mechanisms of racial discrimination by going beyond a mere discussion of the dominant ideology and the subsequent creation of 'cultures of resistance', and including an explanation of how such discrimination operates in the various agencies, such as the school, the careers service, youth schemes and other institutions.

In addition to her subcultural analysis, Fuller employed the concept of 'double subordination' to describe what she called the 'unique' social and economic position of black women in the economy. [...] This model, which has its roots in the dual systems or multidimensional approach to social stratification, sees gender, age, race and class as independent dimensions which cut across one another, giving rise to a complex structure of inequality (Crompton and Mann, 1986). In this essentially additive and hierarchical model, inappropriately defined concepts of race, class and sex are often meaninglessly described as either 'intersecting', 'interpenetrating', 'simultaneous' or 'carried out in harness'.[5] The vague and problematic concept of 'double or triple subordination'—sometimes referred to as 'double or triple jeopardy' (King, 1988) or 'whammy'—appears to stem from a simple theoretical confusion. What are essentially *ideological* manifestations of oppresssion are described interchangeably with an *economic* evaluation of labour-market inequality. Those most ideologically oppressed may not always be the most economically disadvantaged. For example, the labour-market position of the black female may not always be as objectively 'disadvantaged' as the black male location.

The concepts of 'double and triple subordination' present other problems in analyses. Societies are not built up of independent dimensions or levels which are universally experienced. Carby (1982b) directed our attention to the fact that existing assumptions made by white feminists, in particular their notions of what constitutes patriarchy, the family, dependency and reproduction, become problematic when applied to the lives of black women. Bhachu (1986) also made an important point with regard to the ethnocentricity inherent in the concepts of 'double and triple subordination'. She argued that by focusing too much on seemingly static and unchanging traditions, the thesis of 'double and triple subordination' fails to recognize the strengths of cultural forms that can be liberating to black women. Though black women writers have been critical of the less than satisfactory theoretical treatment of black women in academic research, the matter still remains unresolved.[6]

[...] It has been over a decade since Fuller first published her findings, yet in those years little *innovative* research has been undertaken to explore further the value of differential gender achievement among West Indian pupils or to investigate the racial dimension of female studies. Much of the work on black girls is still largely influenced by the concept of subculture that was first employed by Fuller. Thus, while academic achievement for girls is explained in terms of subcultural resistance, boys' educational performance is still regarded as the outcome of self-concept and the self-fulfilling prophecy (Wright, 1987).

FROM MATRIARCHY TO MOTHERHOOD: BLACK GIRLS IN THE EGGLESTON REPORT

[. . .] Hirsch (1989) warned of the dangers of idealizing and mystifying a certain biological female experience and, in so doing, reviving an identification between femininity and maternity that in the past has not served the interests of women. Though Fuller herself referred to this image of black women, the use of the strong black female role model in the Eggleston Report (1986)[7] illustrates more aptly how this misrepresentation of black girls, originally instigated by Moynihan, has become integrated into everyday sociological thinking.

The Eggleston Report, entitled *Education for Some*, was an investigation into the vocational and educational experiences of young people from various ethnic minority groups. In the Report's conclusion, Eggleston and his colleagues asserted that social processes in schools and society work against the efforts of young black people in Britain, and they also acknowledged that there is differential achievement among black boys and girls.

The performance of black females in their final examinations was acknowledged to be far higher than that of black males, and equal to, if not as good as, that of white males. Because the authors did not confront the issue of gender in the Report, they in fact presented confused and contradictory statements as to why this difference should occur. The Report claims that obstacles to equitable entry to examinations are an important factor in explaining the maintenance of black underachievement. To have asked why African Caribbean girls should be more likely to be entered for specific examination subjects than boys, or to have investigated the way in which the black male experience of racism differs from that of girls, would surely have been appropriate in an investigation of young *people's* educational and vocational situations. By black underachievement, Eggleston *et al.* must surely, by their own criteria, have meant black *male* underachievement.

The aspirations of the young women studied in the Eggleston Report, unlike their academic attainment, are given some marginal consideration. In a two-page (pp. 93–4) analysis, the concept of motherhood and the strong black female role model are implied when accounting for the incidence of high occupational aspirations among the 38 African Caribbean girls in the study. It was suggested that, like their mothers, black girls wish to 'better themselves'. [. . .] The authors pointed to a link between the mothers' occupational status and their daughters' aspirations. However, in making such a connection they were acknowledging the thesis that black females exhibit a form of cultural strength and resourcefulness that they transmit to their daughters, who wish to emulate the strong role model provided. This analysis not only marginalizes the male, it also fails to investigate the influence of the labour-market structures that determine the job opportunities for migrant women and their children.

A further common misrepresentation made by Eggleston *et al.* in their report concerns the notion of West Indian girls' attitudes toward their own mother-hood and careers. The authors suggested that because African Caribbean girls are more likely than any of their peers to take as little time off work as possible when having a child, they are more 'careerist'. [. . .] This interpretation of the girls' desire to remain at work as 'careerist' implies that Eggleston *et al.* assumed a singular, universal orientation to work is shared by all girls irrespective of their racial and class background. It should be noted that black girls may not regard having children and continuing to work in the same way as their white peers. For many West Indian women, to work and bring up children is not so much a 'careerist' choice as a historical necessity.

In conclusion, the Eggleston Report, while occasionally referring to young women in its statistical data, does not attempt to integrate a gender analysis into the investigation of ethnic differences. Thus, although Eggleston *et al.* claimed to have investigated *black youth*, that claim cannot be supported as the experiences of black females are overlooked.

GENDER AND THE WORK OF THE BLACK 'SELF-CONCEPT' CRITICS

In the late 1970s and early 1980s, another trend emerged in educational research that made black girls more visible. This was exemplified, in particular, by two black sociologists, Delroy Louden (1978; 1981) and Maureen Stone (1985; first edn 1981), who included the experiences of black female pupils in their work. These writers, in their efforts to challenge the 'self-concept' theorists' notion of negative black self-esteem, employed evidence provided by the actions and beliefs of black girls.

However, because Louden and Stone were attempting to refute an estab-lished school of thought they had little choice but to adopt the traditional terms of reference— 'race and culture'— from which to launch their own attack. This fact, more than any other, inhibited the extent to which black females could be incorporated into their studies. Thus both authors, rather than in-tegrating gender into their analyses, used their findings about girls to demon-strate the point that high black self-esteem does exist among all black pupils, particularly the girls. This period of research was important as it demonstrated differences between boys and girls of the same racial origin, which had so often been ignored in the work of the self-concept theorists of the 1970s.

STATISTICAL SURVEYS AND EMPIRICAL EVIDENCE

Although not specifically aimed at West Indian girls, empirical and statisti-cally orientated research has dominated the most recent efforts to investigate the black female situation. National surveys and large-scale empirical studies provide further evidence that young black women have differential experiences in education and the labour market, which contrast with those of both their male peers and their white female peers. The ongoing Labour Force Surveys (Central Statistical Office, 1991; OPCS, 1985, 1987; *Employment Gazette*, 1985, 1987, 1990, 1991) and the Policy Studies Institute (PSI) studies (Brown, 1984; Smith and Tomlinson, 1989), for example, show the educational and occupational characteristics of young black women on a nationwide basis. Reports by the DES, the DoE and the ILEA,[8] which include a breakdown of results by gender, provide detailed studies suggesting that generalizations about the outcomes for all black pupils cannot be made. [. . .] However, the patterns emerging from the figures show black women of all ages to be committed to further and continuing education, to be better qualified than black males and to be more active in the labour market than their white female counterparts.

The findings of the DES School Leavers Survey 1981/82 (DES, 1985, p. 110) with regard to gender are clear. From their statistical presentation the authors concluded:

> West Indian children, more especially the girls, also tend to stay on longer than other children ... they also tend to go more frequently than the average child from school to some form of full-time education course—but not to university or to pursue a degree course—and to have obtained a lower general level of academic achievement at school.
>
> (DES, 1985, p. 116)

Similarly, the ILEA Research and Statistics Report on examination results and ethnic background (ILEA, 1987, pp. 7, 19) observes that in all ethnic groups, girls did better. African Caribbean girls were notably performing much better than African Caribbean boys, and even than white boys.[9]

Although Sillitoe and Meltzer (1985) employed a more interpretative account in their study of West Indian school leavers in London and Birmingham, the statistical information they provided on gender is useful. Their investigation into career aspirations showed the similarities and differences between West Indian males and females, indicating that, while West Indians in general were more ambitious than whites, the girls had a marked preference for non-manual work compared with the boys' desire for skilled manual work (p. 46). Sillitoe and Meltzer also noted that, in conjunction with 'high ambitions', black girls showed a 'striking enthusiasm' for part-time further education, especially in contrast to white females; this was particularly impressive because of the difficulties that black girls encountered in getting time off from work to undertake such studies (p. 98). However, in seeking to explain their observations, Sillitoe and Meltzer made many of the 'commonsense' assumptions that we saw earlier in the Eggleston Report. Links were made between mothers' work and daughters' aspirations purely on the basis of an 'educated' guess rather than considered investigation.

The third PSI Survey, *Black and White in Britain* (Brown, 1984), gives a detailed and informative account of living and working conditions for black people in Britain. In so doing, it is one of the few studies that gives substantial consideration to the characteristics of West Indian female experiences. With regard to education, Brown declared:

> It is notable that West Indian women are involved in part time study to a greater extent than Asian and White women . . . . The spread of quali-fications pursued by West Indian women is very broad: 18 per cent of them are studying for 'O' level, 25 per cent for clerical or commercial qualifications, 10 per cent for a degree, 10 per cent for City and Guilds exams and 6 per cent for nursing exams.   (Brown, 1984, p. 136)

Evidence such as this demonstrates not only the levels of commitment but, more importantly, the results of restricted access to educational opportunity (that is, black women have to return to get basic qualifications, and few actually achieve the privilege of a university education). The PSI evidence also helps dispel many myths, such as the belief that nursing is a preferred profession among skilled and educated black women. As such, it confirms the influence of the labour market in shaping the destinations of many black women in contemporary Britain.

The 1986–8 Labour Force Survey gives a picture of overall statistical trends for black people in general but also provides a useful breakdown according to gender. It shows the extent of disadvantage encountered by West Indian men and women relative to their white counterparts of equivalent qualifications, age and sex. The survey also reveals the reproduction of disadvantage within the second-generation males and females; this it does by examining their high and disproportionate rates of unemployment in the context of their improved levels of education. For example, West Indian females aged 16–24 had an unemployment rate of 21%, and West Indian males aged 16–24 had a rate of 31%; while for their white male peers the rate was only 16%, and for white females, 14%. The employment experience of the parents of these West Indian youths, who, as the Labour Force Survey points out, were less qualified than their children, was clearly determined by different labour-market demands over time: West Indian males 45–64 years old had an unemployment rate of 18%, and West Indian females 45–59 years old had a rate of 10% (OPCS, 1987). This still compared unfavourably with their white counterparts' experiences: white females over 45 had an unemployment rate of 6%, and males of 8%.

The information provided by the Labour Force Survey is useful, as it puts the black female experience into a comparative context. It shows that, regardless of qualifications or aspirations, black women (who often have the higher and more determined record of attaining qualifications) like their male peers suffer substantial disadvantage and discrimination in the job market. At the same time it also shows that the experience of black women differs in kind from that of their black male and white female peers.

Thus it is clear from our discussion of empirical research that, while black females struggle to do well, the constraints of the economic and political environment in which they live severely curtail whatever achievements and aspirations they might have.

CONCLUSION: A HISTORY OF NEGLECT

What has been illustrated in the review of the early literature on race and education in Britain is that the terms of reference that shaped the debate on race and education since its beginnings in the 1950s remained firmly established. These terms of reference, politically defined as 'race and culture', encouraged a perspective that resulted in gender being marginalized in the educational analysis of underachievement. Comment on black female performance was either absent from or, if noted, simply ignored in such diverse research areas as IQ, self-concept, cultural and socio-economic disadvantage. The consequence of this oversight was more far-reaching than is often acknowledged. By failing to recognize the significance of differential achievement, research on racial and educational issues confined itself to specific avenues of investigation—avenues that often perpetuated ill-defined or unsubstantiated theoretical explanations for West Indian underachievement.

Studies of the 1980s that do take account of black females, though they vary in substance and in kind, all agree that black girls not only have high aspirations but also have higher levels of academic attainment than their male peers. However, because underachievement has remained the overriding concern of educational research with regard to the black child, these observations, as indeed the whole matter of gender, have been marginalized in the academic debates.

In studies that do address the issue of black scholastic success, boys are clearly overlooked. For example, Eggleston and Driver associated high aspirations among West Indian girls with the strong role model of the mother. Fuller, on the other hand, suggested that positive orientation to education can be explained by a black female subculture of resistance. Boys, who it is assumed are not affected by their parental orientation, least of all by any maternal influence, are thus not regarded as part of the equation. Unlike the girls, who are seen as part of a privileged and select club, the boys remain subject to the injustices of institutional racism and are victims of the self-fulfilling prophecy of failure and underachievement.

Finally, the question remains as to why the gender issue should be perceived so negatively.[10] The answer appears simply: the spectre of achievement among some blacks would suggest that a radical reappraisal of contemporary thinking on the subject is essential. Rather than focusing on the family, parental social status, economic and social disadvantage, IQ, poor self-concept and ethnic self-esteem, commentators on the issue may have to address the far more controversial matter of the fundamental social inequality in British society.

Notes

1. Even research investigating scholastic success suggested that it was the children of middle-class black parents who would do well at school, unlike their working-class counterparts (Bagley, Bart and Wong, 1979).
2. Unlike white feminist writers who often define themselves in opposition to their mothers, American black women writers since the 1960s have engaged in a celebration of the maternal presence, emphasizing the generational continuity between mothers and daughters (Washington, 1984; Willis, 1987; Carby, 1987; Hirsch, 1989).
3. It has been suggested that Driver sensationalized his findings in a *New Society* article entitled 'How West Indians do better at school (especially the girls)' (17 Jan. 1980), and that the claims he made could not be substantiated in his study (see Carrington, 1981, p. 299).
4. Black girls obtained a mean of 7.6 passes at 'O' level and CSE compared with a mean of only 5.6 for the black boys (Fuller, 1982).
5. See Phizacklea (1983, p. 7); Allen (1987, p. 177); Brittan and Maynard (1984, p. 7); Fuller (1982, p. 88), respectively.
6. In the UK, issues surrounding invisibility and the various cultural interpretations of 'the family', 'motherhood' and 'marriage' have been the subjects of an ongoing black and white socialist feminist debate.

    For black British women writers, see Carby, 1982b; Anthias and Yuval-Davis, 1983; Amos and Parmar, 1984; Bhavnani and Coulson, 1986; Ramazanoglu *et al.*, 1986; Phoenix, 1987; Parmar, 1989.

    For white British women, see Bourne, 1983; Barrett and McIntosh, 1985; Segal, 1987; Ramazanoglu, 1989; Ware 1991.
7. The Report was first submitted to the DES in 1984. Its release two weeks after the Tottenham uprising was met with a substantial amount of publicity. See *Guardian*, 17 Oct. 1985, 'Schools hamper hopes of young blacks'; *Guardian*, 17 Oct. 1985, 'The teachers at the heart of the crisis'; *Guardian*, 31 Oct. 1985, 'Low achievement of the young pupil is often the consequence of the system'.
8. *School Leavers Survey*: see Swann Report (DES, 1985); Sillitoe and Meltzer, 1985; *Ethnic Background and Examination Results*: Research and Statistics Report, 1987 (ILEA/RS/1120/87).
9. The mean performance score for African Caribbean girls was 15.9 compared with 11.2 for the boys, 13.6 for the ESWI boys and 16.9 for the ESWI girls. (ESWI refers to the countries of the British Isles: England, Scotland, Wales and Ireland.)
10. This, however, does not mean that there has not been any 'public' interest in the issue. Recent years have been characterized by a 'sensational' media curiosity with regard to the academic achievement of black girls. For example, a report in the *TES* (3 April 1987), which suggested 'Black girls flying high in reading and writing', was referring to the findings of a recently published report (Tizard *et al.*, 1988), which among its many conclusions makes only mention of the fact that black girls at the end of infants' school were ahead in their reading and writing skills (p. 180).

References

Allen, S. (1982) Confusing categories and neglecting contradictions. In E. Cashmore and B. Troyna (eds) *Black Youth in Crisis.* London: Allen and Unwin.

— (1987) Gender, race, and class in the 1980s. In C. Husband (ed.) *Race in Britain, Continuity and Change: The Second Edition.* London: Hutchinson.

Allen, S. and Smith, C.R. (1975) Minority group experience in the transition from education to work. In P. Branner (ed.) *Entering the World of Work: Some Sociological Perspectives.* Department of Employment. London: HMSO.

Amos, V. and Parmar, P. (1984) Challenging imperial feminism. *Feminist Review. Special issue: Many Voices One Chant, Black Feminist Perspectives*, 17 (Autumn).

Anthias, F. and Yuval-Davis, N. (1983) Contextualizing feminism: gender, ethnic and class divisions. *Feminist Review* 15 (Winter).

Bagley, C. and Verma, G. (1980) Brimer wide-span reading scores in pupils aged 14–16 years in English secondary schools. Unpublished paper, University of Surrey.

Bagley, C., Bart, M. and Wong, J. (1979) Antecedents of scholastic success in West Indian ten year olds in London. In G.K. Verma and C. Bagley (eds) *Race, Education and Identity*. London: Macmillan.

Barrett, M. and McIntosh, M. (1985) Ethnocentrism and socialist-feminist theory. *Feminist Review*, 20 (Summer).

Benyon, J. and Solomos, J. (eds) (1987) *The Roots of Urban Unrest*. Oxford: Pergamon Press.

Bhachu, P. (1986) Work, dowry, and marriage among East African Sikh women in the United Kingdom. In R.J. Simon and C.B. Brettell (eds) *International Migration: The Female Experience*. Totowa, NJ: Rowman and Allenheld.

Bhavnani, K. and Coulson, M. (1986) Transforming socialist feminism: the challenge of racism. *Feminist Review* 23, 81–92.

Bourne, J. (1983) Towards an anti-racist feminism. *Race and Class* 25 (1).

Brittan, A. and Maynard, M. (1984) *Sexism, Racism and Oppression*. Oxford: Basil Blackwell.

Brown, C. (1984) *Black and White in Britain: The Third PSI Survey*. London: Heinemann.

Bryan, B., Dadzie, S. and Scafe, S. (1985) *The Heart of the Race: Black Women's Lives in Britain*. London: Virago.

Carby, H.V. (1982a) Schooling in Babylon. In Centre for Contemporary Cultural Studies *The Empire Strikes Back: Race and Racism in Seventies Britain*. London: Hutchinson.

— (1982b) White woman listen! Black feminism and the boundaries of sisterhood. In Centre for Contemporary Cultural Studies *The Empire Strikes Back: Race and Racism in Seventies Britain*. London: Hutchinson.

— (ed.) (1987) *Reconstructing Womanhood: The Emergence of the Afro-American Woman Novelist*. New York: Oxford University Press.

Carrington, B. (1981) Schooling an underclass: the implications of ethnic differences in attainment. *Durham and Newcastle Research Review* 9 (47) (Autumn).

Cashmore, E. and Troyna, B. (1982) *Black Youth in Crisis*. London: Allen and Unwin.

Central Advisory Council for Education (1967) *Children and their Primary Schools* (The Plowden Report). London: HMSO.

Central Statistical Office (1991) *Social Trends 21*. London: HMSO.

Coard, B. (1971) *How the West Indian Child Is Made ESN in the British School System*. London: New Beacon Books.

Coleman, J.S., Campbell, E., Hobson, C., McPortland, J., Mood, A., Weinfeld, F. and York, R. (1969) *Equality of Educational Opportunity*. Cambridge, MA: Harvard University Press.

Coultas, V. (1989) Black girls and self-esteem. *Gender and Education*. Special issue: Race, Gender and Education. O. Foster-Carter and C. Wright (eds), 1 (3).

Crompton, R. and Mann, M. (eds) (1986) *Gender and Stratification*. Cambridge: Polity Press.

Davis, A. (1982) *Women, Race and Class*. London: The Women's Press.

DES (1981) *West Indian Children in Our Schools: A Report of the Committee of Inquiry into the Education of Children from Ethnic Minority Groups* (The Rampton Report). London: HMSO, Cmnd 8273.

— (1985) *Education for All: The Report of the Committee of Inquiry into the Education of Children from Ethnic Minority Groups* (The Swann Report). London: HMSO, Cmnd 9453.

Dex, S. (1983) The second generation: West Indian female school leavers. In A. Phizacklea (ed.) *One Way Ticket.* London: Routledge and Kegan Paul.

Driver, G. (1980) *Beyond Underachievement: Case Studies of English, West Indian and Asian School Leavers at Sixteen Plus.* London: Commission for Racial Equality.

Eggleston, J., Dunn, D., Anjali, M. and Wright, C. (1986) *Education for Some. The Educational and Vocational Experiences of 15–18 Year Old Members of Minority Ethnic Groups.* Stoke-on-Trent: Trentham Books.

Employment Gazette (1985) Ethnic origin and economic status. Department of Employment (Dec.). London: HMSO.

— (1987) Ethnic origin and economic status. Department of Employment (Jan.). London: HMSO.

— (1990) Ethnic origins and the labour market. Department of Employment (March). London: HMSO.

— (1991) Ethnic origins and the labour market. Department of Employment (Feb.) London: HMSO.

Foner, N. (1979) *Jamaica Farewell: Jamaican Migrants in London.* London: Routledge and Kegan Paul.

Fuller, M. (1978) Dimensions of gender in a school. Unpublished PhD thesis, University of Bristol.

— (1980) Black girls in a London comprehensive school. In R. Deem (ed.) *Schooling for Women's Work.* London: Routledge and Kegan Paul.

— (1982) Young, female and black. In E. Cashmore and B. Troyna (eds) *Black Youth in Crisis.* London: Allen and Unwin.

Gibson, A., with J. Barrow (1986) *The Unequal Struggle: The Findings of a West Indian Research Investigation into the Underachievement of West Indian Children in British Schools.* London: The Centre for Caribbean Studies.

Gilroy, P. (1981) You can't fool the youths: race and class formation in the 1980s. *Race and Class* 23 (2–3).

— (1982) Steppin' out of Babylon—race, class and autonomy. In Centre for Contemporary Cultural Studies *The Empire Strikes Back: Race and Racism in Seventies Britain.* London: Hutchinson.

Griffin, C. (1985) *Typical Girls? Young Women from School to the Job Market.* London: Routledge and Kegan Paul.

Hall, S. (1978) Racism and reaction. In *Five Views of Multi-racial Britain.* London: Commission for Racial Equality.

Hall, S. and Jefferson, T. (eds) (1976) *Resistance through Rituals: Youth Sub-cultures in Post-war Britain.* London: Hutchinson.

Halsey, A.H. (1972) *Educational Priority Problems and Policies, No. 1.* London: HMSO.

Hirsch, M. (1989) *The Mother/Daughter Plot: Narrative, Psychoanalysis, Feminism.* Bloomington, IN: Indiana University Press.

Houghton, V.P. (1966) A report on the scores of West Indian immigrant children and English children on an individually administered test. *Race* 8 (1).

Inner London Education Authority (1987) *Ethnic Background and Examination Results.* London: ILEA Research and Statistics (ILEA/RS/1120/87).

Jones, P. (1977) An evaluation of the effect of sport on the integration of West Indian school children. Unpublished PhD thesis, University of Surrey.

King, B. (1988) Multiple jeopardy, multiple consciousness: the context of a black feminist ideology. *Signs* 14 (1).

Lawrence, E. (1982a) Just plain common sense: The 'roots' of racism. In Centre for Contemporary Cultural Studies *The Empire Strikes Back: Race and Racism in Seventies Britain.* London: Hutchinson.

— (1982b) In the abundance of water the fool is thirsty: sociology and Black 'pathology'. In Centre for Contemporary Cultural Studies *The Empire Strikes Back: Race and Racism in Seventies Britain.* London: Hutchinson.

Little, A. (1975) The background of underachievement in immigrant children in London. In G. Verma and C. Bagley (eds) *Race and Education Across Cultures.* London: Heinemann.

Little, A., Mabey, C. and Whitaker, G. (1968) The education of immigrant pupils in primary schools. *Race* 9 (4).

Lomax, P. (1980) The school career of West Indian immigrant girls. *Journal of Applied Educational Studies* 9 (1), 29–36.

Louden, D. (1978) Self-esteem and the locus of control: some findings on immigrant adolescents in Britain. *New Community* 7 (3), 218–34.

— (1981) A comparative study of self-concepts among minority and majority group adolescents in English multi-racial schools. *Ethnic and Racial Studies* 4 (2).

Mac an Ghaill, M. (1988) *Young, Gifted and Black: Student Teacher Relations in the Schooling of Black Youth.* Milton Keynes: Open University Press.

McEwan, E., Gipps, C.V. and Sumner, R. (1975) *Language Proficiency in the Multi-Racial Junior School.* Slough: NFER.

Milner, D. (1975) *Children and Race.* Harmondsworth: Penguin.

— (1983) *Children and Race: Ten Years On.* London: Ward Lock Educational.

Mirza, H.S. (1986) Absent again? No excuses: Black girls and the Swann Report. *Ethnic and Racial Studies* 9 (2), p. 247–9.

Mullard, C. (1982) Multi-racial education in Britain: from assimilation to cultural pluralism. In J. Tierney (ed.) *Race, Migration and Schooling.* Eastbourne: Holt, Rinehart and Winston.

Office of Population Censuses and Surveys (1985) *The Labour Force Survey 1983 and 1984.* Series LFS No. 4, OPCS. London: HMSO.

— (1987) *The Labour Force Survey 1985.* Series LFS No. 5, OPCS. London: HMSO.

Parekh, B. (1988) The Swann Report and ethnic minority attainment. In G. Verma and P. Pumfrey (eds) *Educational Attainments.* Basingstoke: Falmer Press.

Parmar, P. (1989) Other kinds of dreams. *Feminist Review,* Special issue, 'Twenty Years of Feminism', No. 31.

Payne, J. (1969) A comparative study of the mental ability of 7- and 8-year-old British and West Indian children in a West Midlands town. *British Journal of Educational Psychology* 39.

Phillips, C.J. (1979) Educational under-achievement in different ethnic groups. *Educational Research* 21 (2).

Phizacklea, A. (1982) Migrant women and wage labour: the case of West Indian women in Britain. In J. West (ed.) *Work, Women and the Labour Market.* London: Routledge and Kegan Paul.

— (1983) In the front line. In A. Phizacklea (ed.) *One Way Ticket.* London: Routledge and Kegan Paul.

Phoenix, A. (1987) Theories of gender and black families. In G. Weiner and M. Arnot (eds) *Gender Under Scrutiny.* London: Hutchinson and the Open University Press.

Pryce, K. (1979) *Endless Pressure.* Harmondsworth: Penguin.

Rainwater, L. and Yancey, W.L. (1967) *The Moynihan Report and the Politics of Controversy.* Cambridge, MA: The MIT Press.

Ramazanoglu, C. (1989) *Feminism and the Contradictions of Oppression*. London: Routledge.

Ramazanoglu, C., Kazi, H., Lees, S. and Mirza, H.S. (1986) Feedback: feminism and racism. *Feminist Review* 22 (Spring).

Reid, E. (1989) Black girls talking. *Gender and Education*. Special Issue: Race, Gender and Education. O. Foster-Carter and C. Wright (eds), 1 (3).

Riley, K. (1985) Black girls speak for themselves. In G. Weiner (ed.) *Just a Bunch of Girls*. Milton Keynes: Open University Press.

Rosen, H. and Burgess, T. (1980) *Language and Dialects of London School Children: An Investigation*. London: Ward Lock Educational.

Rutter, M., Gray, G., Maughan, B. and Smith, A. (1982) School experiences and the first year of employment. Unpublished report to the DES.

Ryan, W. (1967) Savage discovery: *The Moynihan Report*. In L. Rainwater and W. Yancey *The Moynihan Report and the Politics of Controversy*. Cambridge, MA.: The MIT Press.

— (1971) *Blaming the Victim*. New York: Random House.

Segal, L. (1987) *Is the Future Female?* London: Virago.

Sharpe, S. (1987) *Just Like a Girl: How Girls Learn to be Women*. Harmondsworth: Penguin. (First edn, 1976.)

Sillitoe, K. and Meltzer, H. (1985) *The West Indian School Leaver: Vol. 1, Starting Work*. OPCS, Social Survey Division. London: HMSO.

Sivanandan, A. (1982) *A Different Hunger*. London: Pluto Press.

Smith, D. and Tomlinson, S. (1989) *The School Effect: A Study of Multi-racial Comprehensives*. London: PSI.

Staples, R. (1985a) Changes in black family structure: the conflict between family ideology and structural conditions. *Journal of Marriage and the Family* 47, 1005–13.

— (1985b) The myth of matriarchy. In F.C. Steady (ed.) *The Black Woman Cross-culturally*. Cambridge, MA: Schenkman Books.

Stone, J. (1985) *Racial Conflict in Contemporary Society*. London: Fontana and William Collins.

Stone, M. (1985) *The Education of the Black Child: The Myth of Multicultural-Education*. London: Fontana Press. (First edn, 1981.)

Tizard, B., Blatchford, P., Burke, J., Farquhar, C. and Plewis, I. (1988) *Young Children at School in the Inner City*. London: Lawrence, Erlbaum Associates.

Troyna, B. and Williams, J. (1986) *Racism, Education and the State*. London: Croom Helm.

Ullah, P. (1985) Disaffected black and white youth: the role of unemployment duration and perceived job discrimination. *Ethnic and Racial Studies* 8 (2) (April).

Wallace, M. (1979) *Black Macho and the Myth of the Superwoman*. London: Calder.

Ware, V. (1991) *Beyond the Pale: White Women, Racism and History*. London: Verso.

Washington, M.H. (1984) I sign my mother's name: Alice Walker, Dorothy West, Paule Marshall. In R. Perry and M. Watson Brownley (eds) *Mothering the Mind*. New York: Holmes and Meier.

Willis, P. (1977) *Learning to Labour: How Working Class Kids Get Working Class Jobs*. Farnborough: Saxon House.

Willis, S. (1987) *Specifying: Black American Women Writing the American Experience*. Madison, WI: University of Wisconsin Press.

Wright, C. (1987) The relations between teachers and Afro-Caribbean pupils: observing multi-racial classrooms. In G. Weiner and M. Arnot (eds) *Gender Under Scrutiny*. London: Hutchinson and the Open University Press.

Wulff, H. (1988) *Twenty Girls: Growing Up, Ethnicity and Excitement in a South London Microculture.* Stockholm Studies in Anthropology, 21. Stockholm: University of Stockholm.

Yule, W., Berger, M., Rutter, M. and Yule, B. (1975) Children of West Indian immigrants, intellectual performance and reading attainment. *Journal of Child Psychology and Psychiatry* 16.

13 GENDERED PRACTICE IN SPECIAL EDUCATIONAL NEEDS

HENRY DANIELS, VAL HEY, DIANA LEONARD and MARJORIE SMITH

Since the early 1980s, the UK has supposedly seen increased integration into mainstream classrooms of children who need special educational provision. Previously a high proportion of children with not only physical and severe learning difficulties, but also moderate and mild learning and behavioural difficulties, were taught separately, in special schools, or in special units attached to mainstream schools (see Swann, 1985). The findings of the Warnock Report of 1978 argued for reducing this separation and for a range of intermediary types of provision. The case was accepted in principle by the government and given some legal support in the Education Act (1981) and again in the Education Reform Act (1988), although the latter is posing problems for integration in practice.

The 'over-representation' of certain ethnic groups and socio-economic groups in special schools and among those excluded (suspended or expelled) from school has been commented on for many years, but only belatedly have feminists paid attention to the continuing 'under-representation' of girls in all provision for special educational needs (SEN)—from schools for the sight and hearing impaired, to language support sessions and support for reading in mainstream classrooms.

The number of black children identified as having special needs and requiring separate provision, particularly the proportion of boys of African Caribbean descent classified as having moderate learning difficulties (MLD) and emotional and behavioural difficulties (EBD), has been a political issue since the mid 1970s. It has been hotly debated to what extent schools themselves create or exacerbate learning and behavioural difficulties in certain children, and how much of an 'advantage' it is to a child to be placed in a special school or unit, or even to be identified as 'special' in a mainstream school. The 'over placement' of African Caribbean children in schools for the moderately educationally subnormal (ESN-M) or MLD,[1] remedial classes and behavioural units, and in particular their disproportionate representation among those excluded from schools, have all been challenged as damaging (See Coard, 1971; Ford, Mongon and Whelan, 1982; Tomlinson, 1981; 1982; ILEA, 1985; Wright, 1986).

However, although gendered processes in education generally have been the

Source: This article has been specially commissioned for this Reader.

focus of an effective and comprehensive feminist critique during the same period (Byrne, 1978; Marks, 1976; Wolfe, 1977; Delamont, 1978 a, b; Deem, 1978, 1980; Spender, 1982; Jones, 1985; Mahony, 1985; Whyte *et al.*, 1985; Cunnison, 1989), and despite the close relations of race and gender issues in Equal Opportunities legislation initiatives, almost no one looked at gender and SEN in the UK until the late 1980s (as Delamont commented in 1989).[2] Yet there has been a marked disparity of provision for boys and girls in access to provision for learning support and in their experience of schooling in special needs situations throughout the postwar period.[3] Girls are relatively rarely identified as having SEN, but in contradistinction to race, this is now being viewed as discrimination against girls. One of the reasons for this shift in emphasis is the recognition that the resources allocated to boys' special educational needs massively outweigh those for meeting the special educational needs of girls.

The disparity of provision by sex in special schools (whether for physical, emotional and behaviour, or learning difficulties) has recently been confirmed by large-scale surveys (ILEA, 1988; Cooper, Upton and Smith, 1991). Boys have been seen to get twice as many places overall in special schools and units, with the disparity especially marked in EBD schools (6–8 times as many boys), language units (4 times) and autistic schools (2.4 times as many).

In such schools the ratio between African Caribbean boys and girls is close to the average. But African Caribbeans of both sexes are over-represented in various sorts of special schools, notably those for EBD, and in school exclusions (see ILEA, 1990; Cooper, Upton and Smith, 1991). Asian pupils are both under-represented generally, and the ratio of Asian boys to girls is frequently markedly different from the average. For example, there are five Asian girls to every four Asian boys in language units (against the average of four boys to each girl), and very few Asian girls at all in autistic schools or EBD schools (against an average of seven boys to three girls and eight boys to one girl, respectively) (ILEA, 1988: Appendix 4). While special schools contain disproportionately high numbers of children whose parents are unemployed or absent, and fewer with parents in non-manual and skilled occupations, it is not possible to say whether boys and girls are differently affected (i.e. there are no available breakdowns of sex by class in the various types of school). The disparity by sex in special schools has been commented upon in official reports (see, for example, ILEA, 1985; DES, 1989), and concern has been expressed about the (bad) effects it has on girls' learning and day-to-day experiences when they are outnumbered by five, ten or even twenty to one (DES, 1989).

Almost nothing has been recorded about the situation in mainstream schools, however, nor about the gendered processes that result in children being placed in different categories of special schools or units (i.e. about differential 'statementing'[4] and exclusions, though see ILEA, 1990). Two of us therefore collected information on the gender ratios in special schools from several local education authorities (LEAs), and also undertook some pilot work in two mainstream primary schools to see how they handled in-school SEN provision.[5] We chose LEAs with established Equal Opportunities (EO), (gender) policies and asked LEA Advisers to indicate 'good' EO schools (i.e. 'best cases', where we thought schools would be least likely to show gender inequalities). In one school, pupils were indicated as having SEN (for reading, language and mathematics) by the use of formal tests, and in the other by teachers' records. All the data we have gathered so far show boys getting substantially more provision than girls. In the mainstream primary schools we visited, three to five times as many boys as girls were being given extra help in school in the later years, i.e. from reading or maths support teachers working with small groups in classrooms, or by being withdrawn from classrooms for language support, and with maths 'high flyers', from the educational guidance and educational psychology services, and through having a statement of SEN. This was despite the fact that both systems of indication (formal testing and referral by teachers) suggested only twice as many boys as girls had special needs.

When we reported back the figures we had collected to the staff in the LEAs and schools concerned, they were concerned, even shocked. Teachers often realized more boys than girls were being given special treatment, but even those sensitive to the issue through involvement in Equal Opportunities work, underestimated the extent to which this was occurring. Teachers might believe that boys show a greater range of ability—that there are more boy 'slow learners' (and more 'high flyers') than girls—and that therefore more boys need, and should get, extra help, especially with reading (the prime concern in most 'remedial' teaching in primary schools). But what they had not realized, and did not consider justified, was that boys should get four to five times the resources given to girls, when tests etc. indicate they need only twice as much. They were thus concerned about the considerable slippage between identification of need and provision of resources.

EXPLAINING THESE DISPARITIES

If we focus not only on *who* gets special educational provision, but also on *how* and *why*, we need to look both at national, local and institutional (school) policies and provision, and at the social processes through which children come to be identified as having special needs, understand themselves to have 'special needs', and receive (or do not receive) available provision—as well as at how all such policies and processes are gendered. However, we are a long way from being able to provide such a full account, largely because explanations in the three areas involved—the nature of special educational provision, the conceptualization of special educational needs, and analyses of gender inequalities—each have their specific foci and are the concern of different academic disciplines (and hence use different language and concepts/discourses);

moreover, these different sorts of explanation have been assiduously kept apart. We will now go on to consider each in turn.

Explanations focused on the nature of provision for special educational needs in the UK

We propose here to describe the changes in provision and policy that have taken place over the past fifty years. Since there has never been any attempt to ensure equitable distribution of resources across the gender or race divides, the changes have represented little more than successive placing of 'new wine in old gendered bottles'.

The 1944 Education Act This act introduced a system that associated categories of disability of mind and body with a need for particular forms of help. Problems were thought to exist within individuals, and it was important to classify children with problems in order to assign them relevant support. Children were therefore diagnosed as having particular disabilities, usually by medical authorities, and the various disabilities were given a particular curriculum and 'special' provision. Needs were thus formulated into recognized categories and often in terms of the provision that was available, and the system allowed for practices which prioritized some needs rather than others. It explicitly encouraged the transposition of complex needs on to a restricted set of categories of provision.[6]

The 1981 Education Act A key aspect of the 1981 Education Act was the introduction of the concept of 'special educational needs' (SEN). Instead of practitioners allocating children to fixed categories of existing 'handicap' and provision, they were to formulate children's needs in terms of the provision required to help a given individual to make progress. School governors were required to ensure their pupils' specific needs were identified and met: 'A child has special educational needs if he has a learning difficulty which calls for special educational provision to be made for him' (Section 2(5)).

Individual needs were thus defined in terms of the action required in particular contexts, and this tacitly involved an imperative to improve the provision required. Critics have commented, however, on the extent to which this new formulation allowed LEAs and educational psychologists to continue to match needs with existing provision (Tomlinson, 1985; Goacher *et al.*, 1988), teachers to express their own needs, and existing practices to remain unchanged or even to expand (Tomlinson, 1985; Swann, 1985).

The period following the introduction of the 1981 Act witnessed the development of the commonly held view that as many as 20% of the school population (2% in special schools or units and 18% in mainstream education) might have special needs at some time during their schooling. It was always assumed that the majority of educational needs would be met by classroom teachers, and the slogan developed that 'every teacher is a special needs teacher'. Intervention by specialist teachers shifted from being exclusively focused on particular children, to their being involved in some combination with a child and its teacher. Previously remedial teachers had withdrawn children from ordinary lessons, but increasingly support teachers work alongside classroom teachers in ordinary classrooms, or offer advice outside of lesson times.

The 1981 Act was concerned not only with the nature of special educational needs, but also with giving parents more say, and with the effectiveness of the means to identify, assess and meet special educational needs (Goacher *et al.*, 1988). However, although these principles may underpin the legislation, they are in themselves open to actions designed to avoid their implementation. Thus, while the legislation stipulates that provision for individuals within a mainstream school is dependent upon: (a) their receiving the special educational provision they require; (b) the provision of efficient education for the other children with whom they will be educated; and (c) the efficient use of resources. These three conditions are often incompatible with integration where resources are concentrated in specialist institutions. LEAs and schools have therefore selected their own priorities and, since 1981, much of the development of SEN provision has taken the form of LEA-provided resources and support services, including support within mainstream classrooms, together with schools' development of their own special needs policies and practices—with considerable variation between LEAs and between schools (Moses, Hegarty and Jowett, 1988; Gipps, Gross and Goldstein, 1987).

LEAs have continued to guarantee support for placements of individual children with formal statements of SEN (Goacher *et al.*, 1988), but many mainstream teachers have felt, and still feel, that they lack sufficient training to meet the challenges presented by having increasing numbers of pupils with other, less formally defined, SEN in their classrooms. Schools have reported a lack of support in dealing with the problems which have inevitably arisen (Daniels and Ware, 1990).

The 1988 Education Act The 1988 Education Act introduced a demand-led, consumer-orientated system with a built-in financial incentives scheme. This has raised many further questions about the future of post-Warnock SEN developments. Ordinary schools are now required to have open enrolment and to publicize their National Curriculum assessment results. They are encouraged to market themselves in order to attract the highest numbers of pupils possible, and thereby to ensure their own economic security. The most powerful indicator of school 'effectiveness' which is likely to be available to those undertaking these marketing exercises will be the eventual pattern of aggregated subject attainment scores (if these survive the ongoing review exercise); and it has been suggested some schools may seek to increase the numbers of children they refer for statutory assessment so as to get formal statements issued on certain pupils in order to be able to exclude them from their annual returns, if not from their school itself (Daniels and Ware, 1990).

In addition, the reduction in LEA support services following the delegation of funds under local management of schools may mean some schools use delegation of funds for other than SEN purposes. So even the past limited support that mainstream classroom teachers were getting with such pupils could be reduced. Further, LEA scope for co-ordinating SEN support in their areas will be progressively limited as the proportion of opted-out schools increases (despite a 1987 report by the House of Commons Select Committee on Education which stressed that special needs provision was too complex to be left to the responsibility of individual schools). Patterns of provision are therefore undergoing a period of forced change.

According to Wedell (1993), there is already cause for concern in many schools. He notes a decrease in SEN staffing and an associated rise in the number of schools reporting concerns about the resource implication of SEN pupils. In addition, an increase in the percentage of pupils with statements has been reported (Evans and Lunt, 1992), and an increase in the numbers of pupils excluded, with 12.5% of the pupils excluded having statements of SEN (DFE, 1992).

In line with changes being introduced in other areas of state services, the Audit Commission and HMI have recently proposed (see Evans and Lunt, 1992) that LEAs should act as clients, purchasing SEN provision on behalf of pupils, from schools and ancillary services. This suggestion is offered as a way of achieving the politically required delegation of resources, and at the same time affording LEAs a new role as the protector of the interests of those with SEN in the context of devolved finances.

The 1993 Education Act The 1993 Act announced a code of practice on special educational needs, which was circulated in draft form by the Department for Education for wide-ranging consultation. At the time of writing in mid 1994, the consultation process is still not complete.

There are three main aspects of the code which are concerned with:

- the ways schools come to meet SEN
- the ways in which decisions come to be made, and
- the ways in which reviews are carried out.

It remains open as to whether the code will maintain the rights of participants, be effective in promoting the meeting of SEN in integrated settings, and/or will promote the efficient use of resources.

The 1993 Act also introduced a new system of SEN tribunals, and set out their composition, duties and procedures. These independent tribunals may serve to correct the imbalances in legal power inherent in the appeals procedures of the 1981 Act, but they may also consume large amounts of time and thus drain the limited resources available to finance SEN arrangements.

The Association of Metropolitan Authorities (AMA) made the following comment in relation to parents' rights:

> One underlying problem which has bedevilled SEN in the decade since implementation of the 1981 Act has been ... the availability of resources. Much of the dissatisfaction with special educational needs provision is caused by the difficult decisions occasioned by finite LEA resources. Improved rights of parental appeal will not, for example, improve provision, although one effect may be to sharpen the quality of decision making about the allocation of available resources.
>
> (AMA, 1993, p. 69)

The changes introduced with the 1981, 1988 and 1993 Acts have made the job of the SEN co-ordinator in a school increasingly that of coping or managing—as in other areas of state provision. This produces considerable tension between individuals' training and philosophy as teachers, concerned to foster the development of each individual child, and what they are required to do when allocating and rationing limited resources. In addition, the demands of the statementing process are now so stringent that it is going to be impossible for many schools to fulfil the law. The new code of practice assumes, first of all, that every school has an SEN co-ordinator, and secondly, that s/he has time to maintain records and arrange and attend reviews. This certainly does not apply to primary schools, where many SEN co-ordinators are full-time classroom teachers. The demands of the code are such that it will be unworkable in schools with high proportions of pupils with special educational needs. The likelihood of limited resources being tied up in purely 'procedural' (rather than 'educational' activities) has to be recognized.

Thus SEN co-ordinators will be managing limited resources in very 'busy' contexts. They will be subject to a wide range of pressures and likely to adopt strategies for coping with an intolerable work-load. The priorities which emerge may well remain outside the immediate gaze of equity monitoring systems, and may involve a degree of stereotyping. These priorities may be to 'cope with' behaviours which schools are unwilling to tolerate in stressful circumstances. These behaviours may be predominantly male.

Explanations focused on practices that 'individualize'

The Warnock Report (DES, 1978) conceptualized SEN in terms of interactions between the strengths and weaknesses of the child, and the positive and negative aspects of the environment, rather than in terms of 'deficiencies' within the child. 'Need' was argued to arise from the interaction between the pupil and the learning environment. When a need arose, the environment for that child should be changed. However, despite this apparently significant change, the effective conceptualization of SEN remains in-person and individualized. The diagnosis of special needs may have moved from medicine to educational psychology in the postwar period, but the construct of SEN continues to be influenced by individual, not social psychology.

It is also notable how 'having special educational needs' is seen as different from 'underachieving' educationally, and how in consequence solutions are sought for 'special needs' with no reference to the social factors now recognized to influence other types of educational success and failure. Finally, probably because of the influence of psychology as a would-be value-free science, some sections of the SEN field are marked by a general lack of political awareness.

The move towards more systems-focused or contextual support proposed by Warnock on the basis of the interactive conceptionalization, struggles to find a place in practice. What undermines it is the way in which funding for special educational needs continues to be allocated. Almost without exception, resources for special needs are targeted on individual pupils, not on the 'environment'; there is also an increasing tendency to demand detailed information about the performance of individual pupils in order to secure continued funding. The focus thus remains on the pupil, not on the school or classroom, and this confirms the idea that the problem is rooted in the child, and that the school's role is to support the individual pupil, not to change itself.

The Warnock Report introduced the concept of 'Warnock's 18%'—the recognition that a significant proportion of non-statemented pupils, already in mainstream schools, are experiencing special educational needs. A statistical expectation was born—but there were, and still are, no objective ways of determining which pupils require extra resources. Whilst it may be possible to identify those pupils most in need in any one school, any attempt to allocate resources fairly across schools is invariably problematic. The '18%' of pupils are not evenly spread across schools, and some schools will have very high proportions of pupils with identifiable and significant needs.

Local management of schools (LMS) and the publication of league tables of 'good schools' are likely to amplify the tying of resources to individual pupils, because it will be in the ultimate interest of a school to exaggerate the problems of certain pupils in order to provide adequately for their educational needs, and it may well be easier to exaggerate the problems of individuals than to argue the needs of a school as a whole.[7] Hence there is likely to be an increase in statementing and in the aggressive pursuit of the need for statements, and the construction of particular pupils as unacceptable 'deviants'.

Explanations focused on gender inequalities
To an extent, the bias of resources towards boys may generally be accepted and justified by educational psychologists and teachers on biological or quasi-medical explanations: there are biological and developmental differences between the sexes which result in larger numbers of boys requiring special schooling or additional support in mainstream school.[8] There are a number of accounts which posit race and gender differences in various cognitive functions, and in some instances recourse to an account of biological determination of (or at least substantial contribution to) a disability may be appropriate, for example, sex-linked genetic factors determine such conditions such as Duchenne muscular dystrophy.

These 'within-person' accounts of causation fail to explain the consistent trend in the extent of patterns of placement (Galloway and Goodwin, 1987). The less severe types of learning difficulty which apply to a shifting population of pupils are certainly affected by a wide range of social factors. The degree of bias, and the apparent acceptance of differential resource allocation within the field of special educational needs cannot go unchallenged. There are clearly processes at work within the system of identifying, assessing and providing for special educational needs which are gendered, and which militate against resources being allocated to girls.

Despite the many changes in procedures and provision described earlier, there are nevertheless many aspects of provision which remain the same and will tend to reiterate the status quo. The support which exists in mainstream schools, for example, has been dominated for decades by provision for pupils with reading difficulties (a massive industry with attendant vested interests). Most pupils with reading difficulties appear to be boys. The fact that so much of what is available is directed towards an area in which girls may (debatably) experience less difficulty, constitutes a gendering effect on the allocation of resources. In contrast, there is no time given to testing, and no support provided, for deficiencies in spatial and mechanical ability, which girls might be thought more likely to show in the later years of primary school (Byrne, 1978).

Reading tests tend to focus on the skills of reading rather than on the uses made of reading, so there may be girls who achieve reasonable scores on reading tests who need help in making effective use of a science textbook, for example. Furthermore, it may be that certain boys are given preferential treatment in the allocation of reading support. (Recall that we found the tests used indicated twice as many boys as girls needed help with reading, but four to five times as many were actually receiving help.)

Another example of the gendered nature of provision is that of segregated special schools or units for pupils considered to have emotional and behavioural difficulties. This type of placement is so heavily loaded in 'favour' of boys that the over-representation of boys in itself renders the provision inappropriate for girls, for whom there is no equivalent.

Other writers have stressed that the concentration on a few 'difficult' pupils (mainly boys) can mean that the possible special educational needs of other pupils (especially of girls but also of some boys) are not being considered at all (Malcolm and Haddock, 1991). Pupils who show distress by withdrawal, shyness or docility, or non-attendance involving staying at home[9] or early leaving, get less attention—because they present less of a problem in the classroom (or are away from it altogether). Their difficulties may instead be stored up for the future, and/or they may present as problems defined as 'medical' not educational, such as anorexia, stomach pains, mental breakdown or attempted suicide.

Under the constraints of bidding for a slice of funding, teachers and schools are going to tend to construct a view of special needs that will be productive of some sort of provision; and if the provision itself is gendered, then it is inevitable that the SEN construct itself will also be gendered and that more resources will go to boys. If there is no provision for certain areas (for example, support in maths, assertion training), this implies that there may be pupils who are not worth referring because there is no appropriate provision for their difficulties.

We are wary, however, of falling into the trap of assuming that needs would be met just by allocating resources more equally between boys and girls. For instance, if more SEN resources were earmarked for girls, spending the money in traditional ways (for example, by giving them more help with reading) might not prove the most effective use. Help aimed at motivating and enabling girls may need to take quite different forms.

It is also important to take account of abilities and qualities which some girls bring with them which permit them to cope more effectively with any learning difficulties they may have. Some girls with difficulties may actually be coping—they may be 'on task', getting help from friends, encouragement from parents, and enjoying a supportive culture in school where they are willing to ask for and receive assistance—so they do not need to be marked out by receiving in-class support or to be segregated.[10]

Finally, it may not be simply a question of teachers not recognizing girls' needs—as some suggest. Teachers may *know* that certain girls have needs, and may be aware of (and unhappy about) any neglect of less demanding pupils. However, in a context where the needs of certain boys dominate, teachers may find themselves unable to change the situation. Any available resources for special educational needs may be allocated to those boys because it is the only response the teacher can make which will render the learning environment more effective and thereby help other pupils in the class.

CONCLUSION

We said at the start of our analysis that an account of gender disparities in SEN needs to include consideration of educational policies and provision, along with the social processes of identification of children as having special needs, and the relevant analyses of gender (and race and class). We also said that we are a long way from being able to provide such a full account, because the research which exists uses different, and often mutually incompatible, sorts of explanations; moreover it rarely covers two, let alone all three, issues.

The definition of what constitutes SEN is largely psychological, and provides individualized accounts, focused on 'the needs of individual children', with little reference to social factors, despite occasional references to 'interactive causation'.

Accounts of changes in education provision, and in particular its 'marketization', have been developed by Marxist sociologists and social administrators as part of their analysis of a supposed general 'crisis' of the state in late capitalist societies, and a decline in the welfare state in particular. Such research privileges class and is more developed in relation to changes in health and social policy than education.[11]

Work concerned with gender has been largely influenced by feminist sociology and has stressed the disadvantaging of girls as a group structurally located within the wider patriarchal system, though there is also an increasing concern with more fluid theorization of gender as 'enacted'.

The incompatibility is shown by the fact that while there has been work on race and SEN, which is rather determinist, there is very little on SEN and gender.[12] There are some arguments about how SEN provision is being influenced by marketization—but not about how this is differentially affecting boys and girls; there is also occasional work on how marketization is affecting the distribution of resources by gender (but this has not included consideration of pupils with SEN).

What we need to work towards, therefore, is empirical work which covers all three areas simultaneously, and a conceptual model which holds onto a material analysis of the macro structures of class and gender which frame educational endeavours[13] but which also includes the fluid processes through which individuals as agents actively and flexibly negotiate and construct their lives in classroom and schools. For instance, we need to develop an account of local marketization which captures the changeability of the economic and ideological forms which both structure and express the gendered nature of special education needs. The intellectual and political challenge will lie in recognizing the valency of agency without endorsing a mindless voluntarism, at the same time as registering the material and ideological logics of the forces and forms of societies, such as ours, which endorse, indeed positively produce, individualism.[14]

Notes

1. The categories of special need were changed as a consequence of the implementation of the 1981 Education Act. Whereas the 1944 Act had defined categories of (within-person) disability of 'mind and body', the 1981 Act employed a relativistic and interactionist concept of 'need': the terms shifted from those such as ESN (M) (educationally subnormal (moderate)) to MLD (moderate learning difficulty) although educational practices were not always affected.

2. The absence of comment in recent comparative studies of policy and practice would point to a similar situation in the rest of Europe and the USA. See, for example, Fulcher (1989).

3. See Burgess (1983), Winter (1983), Woods (1984), Millman (1985), Malcolm and Haddock (1991). The different views of experts on race and gender must, however, make us question what constitutes 'disadvantage' and inequity in the context of special educational needs. Certainly, groups of children and young people who have educational needs which are not met experience disadvantage, but so too do those who are marked out from their peers because of their disabilities or learning difficulties. Also disadvantaged are those pupils who receive additional support of a kind which is ineffective in meeting their needs. In this context, whilst there is massively uneven distribution of resources between the sexes, it would not be reasonable to argue that this simply disadvantages girls and only girls.

4. A legal statement of a child's special educational needs should outline the resources required for that child to make educational progress. The protection of the child by a statement was envisaged as a way of avoiding the practice of categorization which was not seen as necessarily guaranteeing the provision required. The regulations governing the process are being redrawn as a result of the implementation of the 1993 Act and its associated code of practice when they are involved in statutory assessment.

5. The authors constitute the research team in an ESRC funded project which is concerned with gendered processes of assessment, identification and resource allocation in non-statemented SEN support in mainstream junior schools.

6. Once classified, however, children were often only considered in terms of their needs with respect to a particular category of disability. For example, a child with a hearing impairment who was also seen as experiencing learning difficulties, might be categorized as ESN (M); and as a consequence, the official view of his or her needs would be focused on the ESN (M) provision—at the expense of needs arising from the hearing impairment.

7. Temporary allocations of SEN funding based on proxy indicators (ethnicity/free school meals, etc.) practised by some LEAs may provide interesting results, in that this applies, criteria for funding which are free of the construct of individual special educational needs.

8. Presuming (and it is a major presumption) that the processes of identification and resource allocation are objective and unbiased.

9. Those who are out on the street (mainly boys) are likely to get picked up by the police, and so attract EOW and other attention.

10. However, care must be taken not to read the existence of these learning networks in too optimistic a manner, as evidencing girls' more nurturant nature. Counter data from other sources suggest girls' fastidious attention to normalizing discourses within which they seek endlessly to position 'others', be they boys (Walkerdine, 1985) or 'other' girls, as the despised bearers of deviant social mores and behaviours (Lees, 1986; Hey, 1987), whilst other work shows how

working-class maternal practices produce girls' compliance with the social expectation of female docility and 'helpfulness' (Walkerdine and Lucey, 1989). Many commentators propose that girls and boys bring differential emotional and subjective investments to group membership, demonstrating that female behaviour is more restrictively policed and enforced than male behaviour (see Stanworth, 1981; French, 1986).

11. Though see Hargreaves and Reynolds (1989), Davies, Holland and Minhas (1990), Daniels and Ware (1990), Wedell (1993), Daniels and Anghileri (1994).

12. Because the concern used to be almost entirely with integration, and girls were not seen to be at issue because they were already 'integrated'.

13. Hargreaves and Reynolds' (1989) discussion of privatization and centralization is a case in point.

14. For a useful deconstruction of the discursive repertoire of government ideological dualities in the educational context, see Ball (1990, especially p. 45). Note how the respective 'sacred' list produces a differentiated individual reader, in counter-distinction from the collective subjects set down in the 'profane' list. See also Daniels and Anghileri (1994) for a discussion of the individualistic presumptions of the Code of Practice (1993).

References

Association of Metropolitan Authorities (1993) *Education Act 1993: A Critical Guide.* London: AMA.

Ball, S. (1990) *Politics and Policy Making In Education: Explorations In Policy Sociology.* London: Routledge.

Burgess, R.G. (1983) *Experiencing Comprehensive Education.* London: Methuen.

Byrne, E. (1978) *Women and Education.* London: Tavistock.

Clarricoates, K. (1980) The importance of being Ernest, Emma, Tom, Jane. In R. Deem (ed.) *Schooling For Women's Work.* London: Routledge and Kegan Paul.

Coard, B. (1971) *How the West Indian Child is Made Educationally Subnormal in the British School System.* London: New Beacon Books.

Cooper, P., Upton, G. and Smith, C. (1991) Ethnic minority and gender distribution among staff and pupils in facilities for pupils with emotional and behavioural difficulties in England and Wales. *British Journal of Sociology of Education* 12, (1).

Cunnison, S. (1989) Gender joking in the staffroom. In S. Acker (ed.) *Teachers, Gender and Careers.* Basingstoke: Falmer Press.

Daniels, H. and Ware, J. (eds) (1990) *Special Educational Needs and the National Curriculum: The Impact of the Education Reform Act.* London: Bedford Way Series/Kogan Page.

Daniels, H. and Anghileri, J. (1994) *Secondary School Mathematics and Special Educational Needs.* London: Cassell.

Davies, A.M., Holland, J. and Minhas, R. (1990) *Equal Opportunities in the New ERA.* Hillcole Group, Paper 2. London: Tufnell Press.

Deem, R. (1978) *Women and Schooling.* London: Routledge and Kegan Paul.

— (1980) *Schooling for Women's Work.* London: Routledge and Kegan Paul.

Delamont, S. (1978a) The contradictions in ladies' education. In S. Delamont and L. Duffin (eds) *The Nineteenth Century Woman: Her Cultural and Physical World.* London: Croom Helm.

— (1978b) The domestic ideology and women's education. In S. Delamont and L. Duffin (eds) *The Nineteenth Century Woman: Her Cultural and Physical World.* London: Croom Helm.

— (1989) Both sexes lose out: low achievers and gender. In A. Ramasut (ed.) *Whole School Approaches to Special Needs.* Basingstoke: Falmer Press.

DES (1978) *Special Educational Needs* (Warnock Report). Cmnd 7212. London: HMSO.
— (1989) *Discipline in Schools* (Elton Report). London: HMSO.
DFE (1992) *Exclusions: A Discussion Paper*. London: HMSO.
Evans, J. and Lunt, I. (1992) *Developments in Special Education under LMS*. London: Institute of Education, London University.
Ford, J., Mongon, D. and Whelan, M. (1982) *Special Education and Social Control*. London: Routledge and Kegan Paul.
French, J. (1986) Gender and the classroom. *New Society* (7 March).
Fulcher, G. (1989) *Disabling Policies: A Comparative Approach to Education Policy and Disability*. Basingstoke: Falmer Press.
Fuller, M. (1980) Black girls in a London comprehensive school. In R. Deem (ed.) *Schooling for Women's Work*. London: Routledge and Kegan Paul.
Galloway, D. and Goodwin, C. (1987) *The Education of Disturbing Children: Pupils with Learning and Adjustment Difficulties*. London: Longman.
Geertz, C. (1973) *The Interpretation of Cultures*. New York: Basic Books.
Gipps, C., Gross, H. and Goldstein, H. (1987) *Warnock's Eighteen Per Cent*. Basingstoke: Falmer Press.
Goacher, B., Evans, J., Welton, J. and Wedell, K. (1988) *Policy and the Provision for Special Educational Need? Implementing the 1981 Act*. London: Cassell.
Hargreaves, A. and Reynolds, D. (1989) Decomprehensivisation. In A. Hargreaves and D. Reynolds (eds) *Education Policies: Controversies and Critiques*. Basingstoke: Falmer Press.
Hey, V. (1987) The company she keeps: the social and interpersonal construction of girls' same sex friendships. Unpublished PhD thesis, University of Kent.
ILEA (1985) *Educational Opportunities for All? Report of the Committee Reviewing Provision to Meet Special Educational Needs* (Fish Report). London: Inner London Education Authority.
— (1988) Characteristics of pupils in special schools and units. Research and Statistics Branch, RS 1198/88 (mimeo).
— (1990) Suspensions and expulsions from school 1987/88. Research and Statistics Branch, RS 1270/90 (mimeo).
Jones, C. (1985) Sexual tyranny in mixed-sex schools: an in-depth study of male violence. In G. Weiner (ed.) *Just a Bunch of Girls*. Milton Keynes: Open University Press.
Lees, S. (1986) *Losing Out: Sexuality and Adolescent Girls*. London: Hutchinson.
Mahony, P. (1985) *Schools for the Boys: Coeducation Reassessed*. London: Hutchinson.
Malcolm, L. and Haddock, L. (1991) Make trouble—get results: provision for girls in Southwark's support services (mimeo).
Marks, P. (1976) Femininity in the classroom: an account of changing attitudes. In J. Mitchell and A. Oakley (eds) *Rights and Wrongs of Women*. Harmondsworth: Penguin.
Miles, M. B. and Huberman, A. M. (1984) *Qualitative Data Analysis: A Source Book of New Methods*. London: Sage.
Millman, V. (1985) The new vocationalism in secondary schools: its influence on girls. In J. Whyte *et al.* (eds) *Girl Friendly Schooling*. London: Methuen.
Moses, D., Hegarty, S. and Jowett, S. (1988) *Supporting Ordinary Schools: LEA Initiatives*. Windsor: NFER-Nelson.
Ramasut, A. (ed.) (1989) *Whole School Approaches to Special Needs*. Basingstoke: Falmer Press.
Spender, D. (1982) *Invisible Women: The Schooling Scandal*. Writers and Readers Co-operative.

Spender, D. and Sarah, E. (1990) *Learning to Lose: Sexism in Education.* London: The Women's Press.

Stanworth, M. (1981) *Gender and Schooling: A Study of Sexual Divisions in the Classroom.* Pamphlet no. 7. London: Women's Research and Resources Centre.

Swann, W. (1985) Is the integration of children with special needs happening? An analysis of recent statistics of pupils in special schools. *Oxford Review of Education* 11 (1), 3–18.

Tomlinson, S. (1981) *Educational Subnormality—A Study in Decision-making.* London: Routledge and Kegan Paul.

—(1982) *The Sociology of Special Education.* London: Routledge and Kegan Paul.

—(1985) The expansion of special education. *Oxford Review of Education* 12, 157–65.

Walkerdine, V. (1985) On the regulation of speaking and silence. In C. Steedman, C. Urwin and V. Walkerdine (eds) *Language, Gender and Childhood.* London: Routledge and Kegan Paul.

Walkerdine, V. and Lucey, H. (1989) *Democracy in the Kitchen: Regulating Mothers and Socialising Daughters.* London: Virago.

Wedell, K. (1993) Special Needs Education: the next 25 years. National Commission on Education, Briefing No. 14.

Whyte, J., Deem, R., Kant, L. and Cruickshank, M. (eds) (1985) *Girl Friendly Schooling.* London: Methuen.

Winter, M. (1983) Remedial education. In J. Whyld (ed.) *Sexism in the Secondary Curriculum.* London: Harper and Row.

Wolpe, A. M. (1977) *Some Processes in Sexist Education.* London: Women's Research and Resources Centre.

Woods, J. (1984) Groping towards sexism: boys' sex talk. In A. McRobbie and M. Nava (eds) *Gender and Generation.* London: Macmillan.

Wright, C. (1986) School processes: an ethnographic note. In J. Eggleston *et al.,* *Education for Some: The Educational and Vocational Experience of 15–18 Year Old Members of Minority Ethnic Groups.* Stoke-on-Trent: Trentham Books.

Part 3   Policy in Practice

14 WHAT PROFESSIONAL RESPONSIBILITY MEANS TO TEACHERS: NATIONAL CONTEXTS AND CLASSROOM CONSTANTS

PATRICIA BROADFOOT AND MARILYN OSBORN, WITH M. GILLY AND A. PAILLET

In this article we intend to argue that the national context within which teachers work deeply influences their professional ideology, their perceptions of their professional responsibility, and the way in which they carry out their day-to-day work. By drawing upon the findings of a comparative study of primary school teachers in England and France, we shall argue that even where, as in France, teachers are deeply committed to the principle of centralized educational policy-making, they have difficulty in implementing policy changes in a way that does not disadvantage some children. Correspondingly, the chances of such a centralist approach (as embodied in current moves towards a national curriculum and assessment framework) being successful in England where teachers are unconvinced of its merits and have been unable to participate in its design are very much less, and the likelihood of further disadvantaging those children who are lagging behind in terms of life chances is considerably greater.

This article was orginally published at a time (1988) of momentous change for educational provision in England and Wales. It is doubtful whether there has ever been a more fundamental challenge to the prevailing ethos and assumptions about how public education should be delivered in this country. [. . .]

From the mid 1970s onwards there has been a series of government measures, each concerned with getting a tighter grip on just how well the education system was performing and how it might be made more closely supportive of policy priorities. [. . .] On top of a rash of documents in the 1980s setting out central government's perspective on good curriculum and administrative practice, there have been a number of more explicit initiatives designed to influence curriculum practice in a more direct way. [. . .] In

Source: Abridged from *British Journal of Sociology of Education* (1988) Vol. 9, No. 3, pp. 265–87.

addition, the Education Acts of 1981 and 1986 have been significant in working towards the increase of parental choice in education, giving more power to school governors, and correspondingly decreasing both the power of local authorities to determine their own priorities and the power of teachers who will be increasingly subject to formal appraisal and explicit pressures for accountability.

The coherent and insistent trend towards greater centralization in the provision of education in England and Wales is now well documented and its potential effects widely agreed. The traditional saying that in England 'education is a national service locally administered' is rapidly becoming untrue, since central government is engaged on a steady campaign of extending and increasing its powers.

The most recent initiatives in this respect under the auspices of the 1988 Education Reform Bill involve the establishment of a national curriculum with clearly specified attainment targets in key subject areas and the testing of levels of achievement in relation to those targets at ages 7, 11, 14 and 16. [. . .] No one can be quite clear what the precise impact on the education system will be at this stage, [. . .] but it is possible to make some informed judgements about the potential impact of current policies by engaging in a systematic study of the factors that currently influence how teachers do their work. In particular, it is important to identify the relative significance of such changes in the policy context, compared with other more perennial factors that must influence teaching, such as classroom relations, the socio-economic environment of the school, school ethos and so on. In recent years the assumption that a simple relationship exists between teaching and the subsequent learning of pupils has been challenged by studies which reveal the complex processes by which teachers' practice is assembled and the difficulties of changing it once it has become established routine and adapted to the context (Calderhead, 1987). Many studies spanning the fields of sociology, psychology, philosophy, anthropology and linguistics are now focusing on the way in which teachers see their work, with the aim of improving our understanding of what must be a key variable in educational change.

A particularly valuable perspective in this respect is that of the national context since it enables a comparison to be made of teacher populations pursuing broadly similar tasks within different traditions and policy frameworks. Such a comparison can thus reveal the relative significance of policy directives as determinants of teachers' practice as against the more generalized features of teaching and learning inherent in classroom life itself.

This article is based on such a study, using the comparative context to highlight the relative importance of national differences in educational provision and organization rather than employing more universal social and classroom determinants. [. . .] The study was concerned to explore teachers' conceptions of their professional responsibility in the very different context of the traditionally highly centralized French education system and the equally traditionally decentralized English education system. [. . .] The findings not only provide most valuable illumination of the differences between teachers in the two systems, and some explanation of the origin of these differences, they also give a sound basis for projecting some of the more likely results of current policy initiatives in England and Wales. In particular they highlight the important role of ideology and tradition as it affects the way in which teachers respond to central directives and incorporate these in their teaching. [. . .]

METHODOLOGY

The study reported here, which was carried out in close collaboration with two French researchers, Gilly and Paillet, concerns two cohorts of primary school teachers, 360 in each country, drawn from the relatively matched geographic areas of Avon in England and the Bouches-du-Rhône area of France—the former encompassing the cities of Bristol and Bath, the latter the cities of Marseille and Aix-en-Provence. The teachers were subdivided in each case into roughly equal numbers representing four defined socio-economic zones, referred to as 'rural', 'inner city', 'affluent suburban' and 'average suburban'. In order to provide for comparison intra-nationally as well as inter-nationally, in addition to the major questionnaire survey carried out in 1984/85, a programme of in-depth interviews and classroom observation has been conducted with a sub-sample of teachers in each region in each country, the mixture of quantitative and qualitative methodologies enabling us both to map the scale of difference in perspective of teachers in the two countries and begin to understand some of the origins of these differences. However, this article is based mainly on the replies to one open-ended question put to teachers in the questionnaire, in the form: 'What does professional responsibility mean for you?' The replies to this question were lengthy, often up to a page long, and posed a considerable challenge in categorizing and interpreting the data. [. . .]

Four areas of marked difference began to emerge between the professional 'perspectives' (Zeichner, Tabachnick and Densmore, 1987) which teachers in England and France typically held. We have summarized these differences in terms of four dichotomies: 'restricted as opposed to extended professionality', 'problematic as distinct from axiomatic conceptions of teaching', an emphasis on the 'process versus the product of learning', and a 'universalistic as distinct from a particularistic' approach to teaching. It should be noted, however, that our investigations also revealed substantial intra-national differences between the various socio-economic contexts studied. [. . .]

RESTRICTED VERSUS EXTENDED PROFESSIONALITY

Responsibility to pupils, parents, head and colleagues

One of the most marked areas of difference between teachers in France and England is the contrast between a narrow as against an expanded conception of role, between a 'restricted' and an 'extended' professionality (Hoyle, 1980). (Restricted professionality involves thought and practice which is largely intuitive and classroom based, while extended professionality takes account of a broader educational context and a wider range of professional activities.) Teachers' responses in France clearly indicate a more limited and more classroom-focused conception of role, while English teachers' responses encompass a more wide-ranging and diffuse set of responsibilities. This results partly, one suspects, from the greater support received from other professionals in the school in France, such as educational psychologists and remedial teachers, but largely because of tradition, the tradition of central control, and the fact that French teachers' duties are contractually defined.

Above all, the French teacher's responses concentrate on his/her role as a classroom teacher, responsible for pedagogy and for the child's academic and educational success. In contrast, the English teacher expresses widely dispersed goals which relate to responsibilities both inside and outside the classroom, encompassing extra-curricular and sometimes even community activities, all aspects of school relationships, accountability to parents, colleagues and head, and a strong consciousness of the need to justify his or her actions to others. At their most extreme, then, a French teacher's responses can be characterized as 'meeting one's contractual responsibility' and an English teacher's as a 'striving after perfection'.

Thus, while both sets of teachers attach an overwhelming priority to their responsibility to the children in their care (Table 14.1), among French teachers very little else is specifically mentioned as a focus for accountability. Teachers perceive themselves as independent professionals, carrying out instructions produced from elsewhere, but owing responsibility only to the pupils in their care. By contrast, whilst teachers in England have an equally great commitment to the children in their care, they are rather more aware of an obligation to colleagues, parents, the head teacher, and their employers. [. . .] Far from being autonomous in their classrooms, they may be conceived more as partners who, along with colleagues and relevant non-professionals, attempt to realize a very wide range of educational goals.

Responses to other parts of the questionnaire, and subsequent interviews also suggest that considerably more emphasis is placed by French teachers on the hierarchical, contractual elements of their responsibility, while greater emphasis is placed by English teachers on the more informal, 'moral' dimension of accountability to parents. This is illustrated by one rural teacher in England and by her counterpart in France. The former stated:

TABLE 14.1 Accountability to whom: percentage of teachers mentioning each of the following categories

Responsible to	England	France
Children	91.0	93.9
Colleagues	29.3	3.8
Parents	25.4	8.0
Employers	12.7	8.6
Headteacher	11.5	0.4
The school	9.4	2.3
Myself	7.6	3.1
Society	6.8	3.0
Governors	1.9	0.4
Other professionals	1.7	0.4
Senior staff	1.3	0.4
Other	0	2.2
Total no. of teachers responding	360	360

> I'm responsible to each child in my class, that he/she develops intellectually, socially and emotionally during the time in my class. Also I'm responsible to the children's parents that they are informed of the problems and needs of their child, and have some say in how their child is treated in my class. Also to the rest of the staff that I do nothing to hinder their relationships with each other and the children.
>
> (English teacher)

The teacher in France had a somewhat different view:

> For me, to be responsible is to do my job as well as I possibly can, to teach according to the curriculum laid down and to try to follow it as closely as possible. To be 'responsible' means refusing to accept carelessness. (French teacher)

Thus English teachers tended to emphasize:

> ... working with my colleagues to achieve our goals for the children ... Consultation with head and senior staff. Making myself available for consultation with parents when I/they feel it necessary. [...]

In contrast, a more typical French teacher's response was:

> To do one's work. To be present every day. To respect the curriculum objectives. [...]

Because primary schools in England have traditionally been free to determine their own curriculum and pedagogy within broad guidelines, so they have correspondingly tended to develop their own idiosyncratic ethos, centred on the institution itself and the leadership of the head teacher. The lack of any clear central prescription of content has also meant the necessity both to explain and often justify to parents and others the practices adopted.

By contrast, since it is widely known and accepted that French teachers are not in control of what is taught or even how it is taught, but for the most part are simply following centrally-prescribed guidelines which have changed very little over the years, so it is not typically necessary for French teachers to justify to parents and others their classroom practices. All parties are well aware of the system of goals laid down for each year group which must be achieved for the child to progress, and all parties are united in seeking to achieve that progression for each pupil. By the same token, the head teacher has been, in theory and in practice, a relatively unimportant figure in the French school, his/her situation of *primus inter pares* summed up in the commonly favoured title of 'instituteur-chef' rather than 'directeur' or 'directrice'. [. . .] It is significant that one of the new educational policy developments introduced in France during 1987 was the creation of new powers and conditions for primary school heads to encourage them to take more of a leadership role and to develop more of an institutional ethos. [. . .]

Responsibility for other professional activities

Central to Hoyle's concept of the 'extended professional' is 'being concerned with locating one's classroom teaching in a broader educational context, comparing one's work with that of other teachers, evaluating one's work systematically, and collaborating with other teachers'. It also involves being interested in theory and current educational developments, reading journals and educational books and 'seeing teaching as a rational activity amenable to improvement on the basis of research and development'.

In contrast, 'restricted' professionality is:

> . . . intuitive, classroom focused, and based on experience rather than theory. The good restricted professional is sensitive to the development of individual pupils, an inventive teacher, and a skilful class manager. He is unencumbered with theory, is not given to comparing his work with that of others, tends not to perceive his classroom activities in a broader context, and values his classroom autonomy.
>
> (Hoyle, 1980, p. 43)

While it would be misleading to imply that all English teachers approximate to the 'extended' ideal type and all French teachers to the 'restricted' (Isambert-Jamati, 1984), it is clear from the pattern of responses summarized

TABLE 14.2 'Being a teacher': reflections on the role (percentage of teachers mentioning each category)

Category	England	France
Fulfil role to best of one's ability	34.2	36.6
Justify actions to others	17.9	3.7
Continuing training and improving knowledge	15.0	7.4
Importance of teacher's position/ conception of role	14.7	36.2
Upholding the profession	11.4	2.8
Acting as a 'model' for children	10.4	11.8
To be committed to job	7.1	29.7
Self-evaluation	5.5	5.6
Protective role	1.6	2.1
Impossible to say	1.0	2.6
Total no. of teachers mentioning at least one of these categories	243	211
Proportion of total sample mentioning at least one of these categories	67.5%	58.5%

in Table 14.2 that a higher proportion of teachers in England *do* mention a 'reflective' dimension, a sense of teaching as problematic and subject to question. [...] French teachers, inasmuch as they focus more intensively on the importance of their classroom teaching and see themselves as having sole responsibility for the child's education, correspond more closely to the ideal type of 'restricted' professionality.

One example of this is that far more teachers in England emphasize a responsibility for improving their knowledge and training and keeping abreast of new ideas and the importance of 'upholding the profession' and acting in a professional capacity (Table 14.2). As one English deputy head put it:

> I must always be aware of new techniques by going on courses, reading educational publications etc. I try to bring these to the attention of my colleagues by discussion and, once again, example ... I need to feel satisfied with my teaching—and to do this I have to put into my work a lot of thought, planning etc. I thoroughly enjoy the interaction with other teachers I meet on courses—I find the necessary 'drug' to bring enthusiasm and enjoyment into my teaching.
>
> (English teacher)

[...] A more typical French response lacks this element:

> [My duty is] to work as carefully and as conscientiously as possible, but
> also enthusiastically, to encourage the learning of the children who are
> entrusted to us for six hours of the day.   (French teacher)

[...] While French teachers may have a more narrowly focused sense of
responsibility, often expressed in terms of 'meeting one's contractual responsibility' as against the English teacher's view that teaching is 'always trying
to do a little more than is possible', they take very seriously this perceived responsibility for children's achievement and are more likely than
English teachers to express the view that teachers *themselves* must take
responsibility for a child's failure rather than blaming it on family background, society, etc. This theme is repeated frequently in French teachers'
responses:

> To take responsibility myself, never to blame academic failure entirely
> on pupils, society, curriculum, to know how to call into question my
> own teaching methods.   (French teacher)

[...] In contrast, English teachers seem more prepared to see themselves as sharing with others the responsibility for a child's progress.
[...]

> In my work I must work closely with others to help the mental, physical,
> creative and moral development of the children in my care. These people
> will be, most importantly, parents followed by other teachers, social
> workers, psychologists, etc.   (English teacher)

The contrasts displayed in these responses almost certainly stem at least
in part from the pressures created by the centralized curriculum in France,
the objectives which teachers must ensure that their pupils attain, and the
knowledge French teachers have that every year, a proportion of their
children—the average was 29.3% in our sample—will face 'redoublement'
(children repeating the year if they do not attain the required standard).
The difference may also result from the relatively narrow focus and range
of responsibilities French teachers perceive for themselves. With more clearly
defined rather than 'diffuse' responsibilities, it is perhaps easier to feel oneself
'in control' of one's work and totally responsible, whereas the more wide-
ranging and diffuse the responsibility, the greater may be the difficulty in
feeling that one has accomplished one's role.

Such concern amongst teachers in France with successful classroom teaching
above all else has its corollary in the point made by an English teacher during
staffroom discussion:

> During the teachers' dispute, parents were very concerned about the
> effect on their children, but if only they had known, it was the one
> time I felt that I was really doing my best in the classroom—able to

concentrate entirely on classroom teaching because I wasn't stretched in
so many other directions as well.   (English teacher)

Another teacher in England put this point slightly differently:

A teacher can feel responsible to so many people, or groups of people,
that s/he may well end up feeling responsible to no one, or differently
to different people in turn, and very often it is the kids one is teaching
that can come out the worst.   (English teacher)

The implications of these differing conceptions of role for teachers' satisfaction and sense of achievement in their work will be returned to in the
concluding section.

PROBLEMATIC VERSUS AXIOMATIC CONCEPTIONS OF TEACHING

Related to the concept of 'restricted' versus 'extended' professionality is a conception of teaching as 'problematic' in England and 'axiomatic' or self-evident
in France. Partly because of the diffuse nature of the role they impose upon
themselves, and partly because of the lack of clear social consensus about what
it is appropriate for a teacher to do (even down to the content of what is to
be taught), English teachers see their role as fraught with dilemmas, not to say
contradictions, whereas French teachers take for granted, very largely, that
they know what is expected of them. These contradictions were expressed
both in terms of means and of ends—that is, pedagogy and curriculum. In
comparison with the confident commitment to 'firmness', 'rigour', the three
'Rs' and 'academic skills' which French teachers expressed, English teachers
often described their teaching style in dichotomous terms such as 'at the same
time traditional and progressive', or 'a mixture of formal and informal'! Their
responses suggested the difficulty they have in balancing competing priorities,
torn between a child-centred professional rhetoric and a wider public concern
for standards.

Part of the reason why teachers in France appear to experience a less problematic definition of their professional responsibility is simply that it is clearly
defined for them by government directives. But, at least as important is the
homogeneity of the underlying national culture, the reproduction of which
has been an informing principle of French education since the days of
Napoleon, who recognized that the state had a potentially powerful role to
play in cementing and encouraging nationalism (Barnard, 1969). Napoleon
asserted that schools must be *of*, not *in*, the state 'as the state is one, its
schools must be the same everywhere' (Liard, 1894). Thus in 1808, when
Napoleon instituted a national bureaucracy for educational provision—the
Université—this was an attempt to impose a state monopoly of educational
provision (Crozier, 1970) which included the key areas of teacher provision

and training, schools, qualifications and the curriculum. 'The development in France of a rationalized, articulated, bureaucratised educational system and the absence of such a system in England is therefore a special case of more fundamental differences in the development of institutions in both countries' (Lacqueur, 1973, p. 60).

The continued persistence, relatively unchanged, of the primary school of Jules Ferry whose 1881 law introduced mass elementary education in France is explicitly recognized by many French teachers. Such persistence is further testimony to the coherence of French culture and the power of successive generations of educational institutions to reproduce it. Both Durkheim (1977) writing at the turn of the century and Bourdieu and Passeron (1976) in recent years have pointed to the significant role of teachers in this process of reproduction. Their analyses show how the persistence of a belief in the reality and desirability of a 'national culture' have been directly instrumental in leading teachers to accept the imposition of a centrally-determined curriculum and have rendered unproblematic to teachers their role in passing on this culture to the next generation.

Thus while English teachers may experience feelings of 'anomic' stress and even 'burn out' because of the open-ended and ill-defined nature of their role, French teachers' principal source of stress is the opposite of that. The external provision of a teaching programme relieves the teacher of the need to justify or decide upon what is to be taught but the accompanying lack of professional freedom can result in some teachers in feelings of helplessness and alienation, of an impersonal machine, bound up with red tape, which has little contact with classroom reality. At a time when changes in the social context as a whole are resulting in life styles which in France, as elsewhere, have little in common with tradition, French teachers are finding themselves increasingly confronted by strains which are the product of the very homogeneity of purpose which has traditionally been their protection and rationale. French teachers' flight from schools in inner-city areas to those in rural and 'bourgeois' districts where more traditional cultural values still prevail [. . .] is in strong contrast to their English counterparts and provides clear testimony to the dilemmas confronting teachers who find themselves unable either through conviction or training, to adapt their teaching to meet the increasingly diverse needs of children in a rapidly changing society. In the light of this analysis, the move to introduce a national curriculum in England could have two possible outcomes. On the one hand, it could reduce the 'triangle of tensions at times invigorating, and at other times almost overpowering' (English teacher) that the English teacher experiences in feeling responsibility 'directed towards my pupils, their parents, my professional colleagues, my employer and to the teaching profession at "large"', by considerably reducing the scope for ambiguity in the expectations of these various groups. On the other hand, uninformed as such a national curriculum would necessarily be by any long-standing cultural consensus,

teachers may experience it as a source of arbitrary restriction and professional frustration.

PROCESS VERSUS PRODUCT OF LEARNING

Our data suggest a strong emphasis on the 'process' of learning in England and
on the 'product' of learning in France. French teachers are far more concerned with helping children to acquire basic skills and a recognized body of
academic knowledge than are their English counterparts, who in turn place
more emphasis on how children learn and on the development of desirable
long-term characteristics rather than the acquisition of a particular body of
knowledge (Table 14.3). Thus French teachers argue the importance of:

> ... making sure that pupils acquire the knowledge appropriate to the
> level of the class and doing this with commitment.

> (French teacher)

TABLE 14.3 Responsibility for what: percentage of teachers mentioning
each of the following objectives in relation to pupils

Objectives	England	France
Development of intelligence	46.0	17.6
'All-round' education	41.4	17.3
Socialization	33.8	25.9
Personal development	31.7	19.1
Desire to learn	21.8	16.6
Physical development	18.3	11.5
Academic knowledge	14.7	55.6
Basic skills, '3 Rs'	13.3	61.2
Moral education	9.8	9.3
Happiness at school	7.5	8.0
Understanding of the world	4.9	3.9
Preparation for adult life	3.6	23.2
Artistic education	3.2	2.3
Leisure activities	1.6	0.0
'Toughen' them for a difficult life/ help them succeed in spite of system	1.3	3.9
Citizenship	01	6.8
Total no. of teachers mentioning at least one of these objectives	298	260
Proportion of total sample mentioning at least one of these categories	82.7%	72.3%

By contrast, teachers in England typically stress 'development' both of the child's intelligence and personality and include more diffuse goals such as:

> ... creating an atmosphere whereby children will learn through experi-
> ence—moral and social norms, physical skills and aspects of health and
> hygiene, develop enquiring minds and creativity and generally to develop,
> progress, and fulfil their potential.   (English teacher)

Associated with this latter distinction are the strikingly different conceptions of childhood itself which the two groups hold. Where English
teachers emphasize the whole child, and therefore take responsibility for
the children's aesthetic, intellectual, physical, socio-emotional and moral
development, French teachers are much more likely to see the child as
'student', to use the term of Berlak and Berlak (1981) stressing intellectual and
cognitive development and mastery of a narrow range of school subjects.
Further, English teachers tend to see children as unique and qualitatively
different from adults in the way that they perceive the world and in their
learning, whereas French teachers clearly have a conception of the child as a
future adult, holding, in the sense of Berlak and Berlak, a view of childhood
as continuous.

Nearly a quarter of French teachers, compared with four per cent of
English teachers, four per cent stressed the importance of 'preparing children
for adult life' (Table 14.3). A typical French response mentions:

> ... ensuring that my pupils acquire the basic values necessary for adult
> life in society, the moral principles of honesty and hard work and
> respect for others.

As Acker (1987) points out, there have been a number of attempts in recent
research to delineate the particular ideologies held by primary school teachers
and to seek their sources not only in shared experiences in schools but also in
common structural positions in society, historical legacies, features of initial
teacher education and so on (Pollard, 1985; King, 1978; Alexander, 1984).
However, while all of these are of importance, it is clear from observation
and subsequent discussion with teachers that the French teachers' emphasis
on 'knowledge to be acquired' and 'objectives to be attained', in short, on
the child as 'student', must also stem more immediately from the pressure
of the centralized curriculum and of attainment targets. If, as seems likely, the
imposition of attainment targets within the National Curriculum in England
results in a parallel change of emphasis in favour of product rather than
process in English primary schools the tension between these two polarities
is likely to be a particular issue for initial teacher training in the future. While
research in the area of 'teaching quality' has moved from trying to identify
the generic qualities of the 'good' teacher in favour of efforts to equip all
teachers with the ability to be self-critical and reflective (Pollard, 1988) about
the *process* of teaching and learning, policy concerns are increasingly focused

on the assessment of the products of such learning as an indication of teaching quality.

UNIVERSALISM VERSUS PARTICULARISM

As was mentioned earlier, there is a notable difference between the goals teachers set themselves in different environments in England. [...] The child-centred ethos of English primary schools emphasizes responding to the needs and abilities of each child, in stark contrast to the French emphasis on a common entitlement of all children and on fulfilling the same goals for every child. It is readily apparent that although an individualized pedagogy makes considerable sense educationally in terms of the differential rate of development of pupils, their different backgrounds, interests and aspirations, it also has the potential for disadvantaging those pupils for whom teachers may have low expectations, or those who are not good at convincing the teacher of their interests or needs.

Our data suggest a marked difference between teachers working in disadvantaged inner-city areas in the two countries. While French inner-city teachers work towards the same 'mainstream' goals as the rest of the school system, emphasizing the acquisition of basic skills and academic knowledge by their pupils, there is some evidence from the responses examined here (Table 14.4), together with subsequent classroom observation and interviews, that English inner-city teachers set themselves goals which are alternative to the mainstream, which may define success in terms other than those of academic achievement. The inner-city teachers in our English sample, like those in Sharp and Green's (1975) study, perceived their pupils as having different needs from those in more affluent areas. Consequently they were less concerned than other teachers in England with the acquisition of basic skills and a body of knowledge, but slightly more concerned with a child's immediate happiness in school. [...]

The responses of the English inner-city teachers in our sample emphasized 'providing education relevant to children's needs and a caring, thoughtful environment', 'looking at the job in a caring way' and 'treating each child as an individual, and helping him or her with specific problems, always taking into account the considerable difficulties which many of these children experience in their home environment'. Academic achievement was often mentioned, but it was frequently modified by phrases similar to the above.

In striking contrast, French inner-city teachers were less concerned than their colleagues in more affluent areas with socialization and the development of the child's personality, but equally concerned with children acquiring academic skills and knowledge, arguing the importance of:

> ... bringing my pupils up to the highest level of knowledge and culture possible to help them to overcome the harsh realities of their future life as adults. (French teacher)

TABLE 14.4   Responsibility for what: percentage of teachers mentioning each of the following objectives in relation to pupils

| | | Socio-economic zone | | | |
| | | *Average* | *Inner* | *Affluent* | |
Objectives	*Rural*	*suburban*	*city*	*suburban*	*Mean*
France					
Basic skills '3 Rs'	68.8	73.5	55.7	46.7	61.2
Academic knowledge	62.5	69.4	54.0	36.7	55.6
Development of intelligence	20.8	8.2	18.0	23.3	17.6
Desire to learn	16.6	18.4	8.2	23.3	16.6
Physical development	10.4	12.3	1.6	21.7	11.5
Personal development	16.6	26.5	9.8	23.3	19.1
Happiness at school	2.1	8.2	6.6	15.0	8.0
Socialization	33.3	22.4	13.0	35.0	25.9
Understanding of the world	10.4	2.0	3.3	0.0	3.9
Citizenship	2.1	10.2	4.9	10.0	6.8
Moral education	6.8	20.4	3.3	6.7	9.3
Artistic education	2.1	2.0	0.0	5.0	2.3
'All-round' education	22.9	18.4	19.6	8.3	17.3
Leisure activities	0	0	0	0	0
Preparation for adult life	18.8	24.5	29.5	20.0	23.2
'Toughen' them for a difficult life	0	4.1	9.8	1.7	3.9
No. of teachers =260 *N* =	60	53	68	79	
England					
Basic skills, '3 Rs'	19.2	12.0	7.9	14.1	13.3
Academic knowledge	14.1	14.7	10.6	19.2	14.7
Development of intelligence	41.0	46.6	44.0	52.6	46.0
Desire to learn	25.6	18.7	19.7	23.0	21.8
Physical development	17.9	18.7	17.3	19.2	18.3
Personal development	29.5	38.7	26.3	32.1	31.7
Happiness at school	7.7	5.3	11.8	5.1	7.5
Socialization	35.8	37.3	31.5	30.7	33.8
Understanding of the world	11.5	5.3	0	2.6	4.9
Citizenship	0	0	0	0	0
Moral education	7.7	10.7	10.5	10.2	9.8
Artistic education	3.8	0	2.6	6.4	3.2
'All-round' education	26.9	49.3	36.8	52.5	41.4
Leisure activities	2.6	1.3	1.3	1.3	1.6
Preparation for adult life	6.4	6.7	1.3	0	3.6
'Toughen' them and help them succeed in spite of system	0	0	3.9	1.3	1.3
No. of teachers = 298 *N* =	70	74	72	82	

or

> ... working with children whom society wishes to exclude and arming them sufficiently to be able to succeed in some capacity—to refuse elitism and to give all children the know-how and ability to face up to life as a challenge. (French teacher)

This French 'universalistic' emphasis on equality and the need to treat all children in the same way on justice and educational fairness goes back even further than the Napoleonic era, to the 1789 Revolution and its emphasis on 'liberty, equality and fraternity'. This ideal, combined with the marginally later Napoleonic ideal of education as a unifying force, is the reason why the notion of a common entitlement to education regardless of place, talent or wealth is so strongly entrenched in French teachers' ideology and ensures the commitment of most teachers to centralization and the national curriculum. However, in spite of this undoubted commitment, the evidence from our sample suggests strongly that equal treatment does not produce equal results. The rate of children's 'redoublement' (that is, repeating the year as a result of failure to attain the prescribed standard) in the inner-city was well over three times the rate for children in 'affluent' areas. Thus an average of 50.3% of the inner-city pupils of teachers in our sample repeated the year *at least* once compared with an average figure of 14.7% in 'affluent' areas.

Equally, there is concern with the level of achievement of English primary school pupils in less advantaged areas. While one recent report in England (Thomas, 1985) has suggested that teachers in inner-city schools may have lower expectations of achievement for their pupils, consequently producing poorer results, our evidence from France would not appear to support the case for centralized control and a national curriculum as the solution to the problem of 'the long tail of underachievement' (Bolton, 1988).

IMPLICATIONS

The implications of the marked differences of approach that we have identified above for children's development, their educational success, their eventual competencies, their self-esteem, and their general enjoyment of education are clearly considerable, but something on which we do not as yet have data other than the statistics cited above. However, in terms of the teachers, there are a number of important implications that may be identified from these data. Hoyle (1980), for example, suggests that any extension of teachers' professionality can lead to a loss of job satisfaction and perhaps of teaching skill. He cites *Life in Classrooms,* Philip Jackson's 1968 study of teachers identified as good practitioners by their superiors, and who nearly all conformed more to the 'restricted professionality' model. Their approach to teaching was intuitive, classroom-focused and based largely on their commonsense knowledge of pupil development. Their satisfaction came from the immediacy of events and from their autonomy and their personal relationship with children. In some respects, Hoyle's suggestion of loss of job satisfaction may explain what is happening to English primary teachers who, as a result of their widely dispersed goals and their expanded conception of their role, often express feelings of being over-stretched, of conflict and confusion about their role. The replies we have already discussed suggest that some teachers feel the need to protect themselves from the demands of the job, but this fear of 'burn-out' is only one aspect of a situation in which teachers in England talk about 'compromise' and 'tension' in achieving what is expected of them. As one teacher put it:

> This means all the time being willing to work under great pressure compromising the ideal with the realistic, the useful with the expedient. It means also working to improve the working environment and to remove some of the 'ever increasing' pressures that are being placed on teachers.   (English teacher)

Sometimes the impossibility of all this results in feelings of guilt and [...] in the end it means acknowledging that:

> I also take it to be a fundamental rule of thumb that I should know I am trying to do something that is impossible to achieve (and so should try not to get disheartened), but that is so desirable to achieve that you keep trying.   (English teacher)

Other researchers have talked about English teachers 'living with contradiction' (Poppleton, 1986) or 'living with paradox' (Nias, 1986) and all those feelings are borne out in the responses of the English teachers in our sample. [...] Our study suggests that English teachers are setting themselves and being set goals they cannot possibly fulfil and at the same time they are trying to meet the conflicting demands of government, parents, head and children.

In contrast, as we have seen, French teachers are relatively sure of what they are supposed to be doing, confident that they are working towards achievable goals, and consistent in their ideology. As a result they see themselves as firmly in charge of classroom teaching and solely responsible for children's educational success. However, as some French teachers in our study are already aware, the relatively restricted role they perceive for themselves can in itself lead to a feeling of loss of autonomy, and to a mechanistic carrying out of duties which are perceived as predefined by others. 'Where there is no freedom there is no responsibility' sums up these feelings.

As one French teacher put it:

> I haven't enough margin of manoeuvre to be responsible. The school as an institution is responsible and through it the state and the society which perpetuates it. I don't have to assume responsibility if I am not given the corresponding freedom.
>
> [...]

For some French teachers, even being asked about professionalism evokes a caustic response:

> Being responsible means submitting to an impressive list of tests and rules which seek above all to preserve 'l'Institution Education Nationale'. In revenge, a teacher (after obtaining initial qualifications) doesn't any longer have to prove his competence, his effectiveness, or his aptitude for training. After his CAP (teaching qualification) he is definitely seen as possessing these qualities. Where is the responsibility in all that?
>
> (French teacher)

> The term 'professional' in the eyes of l'Education Nationale is a pejorative term. They don't think an educator needs professionalism.
>
> (French teacher)

Although it may be the case that French teachers feel that they have much less scope for exercising a degree of professionalism than their English counterparts might feel, the irony is that this perceived lack of autonomy is not entirely borne out by the evidence. While the centralized curriculum dominates what teachers perceive as possible in terms of content, the actual constraints to which French teachers are subject, and the controls which are exercised over them, are relatively limited. The existence of national pro-grammes of study certainly lends itself to a remarkable coherence of content from school to school, but the reason why such a marked similarity exists is not because its institution is rigidly policed. Inspection takes place very infre-quently (only every four or five years on average) and, within the school, French teachers are less subject to control by the head or to demands from parents than their English counterparts.

Rather, it is for two other reasons: first, it is because French teachers believe more or less passionately in the need for a national curriculum as the basis for equality and unity in their society. Secondly, and more instrumentally, teachers are aware that if their pupils are not equipped with the skills and knowledge expected from a particular year grade, they will be refused access to the following class, and thus will be disadvantaged. They therefore feel a strong sense of obligation to protect pupils by preparing them appropriately as far as they possibly can.

Neither of these reasons currently pertains in England. Arguably, though, teachers are subject to greater control in England, permeable as they are to pressure from consumers—notably parents—and a range of exhortations emanating from within the school, the local authority and at national level. The passionately held commitment of most primary teachers in England and Wales to professional autonomy in both curriculum and pedagogy, the freedom of the individual school to decide how to educate its children, and the child-centred ideology which supports a pedagogy that aspires to be individu-alistic, are all ideals that are held at the cost of a not inconsiderable personal sacrifice amongst English teachers. If they were to accept a narrower, more universal and common curriculum, they would probably find themselves with a greater sense of achievement, being less vulnerable to outside criticism, and possibly even having a higher status in society. However, as we pointed out in an article in *The Times Educational Supplement* on 7 July 1987, it is the ideology or, to put it another way, the conception of their professional role, which plays the most fundamental part in determining what teachers do. If policy changes ride roughshod over such ideologies and fail to take them into account, the result is likely to be widespread resentment, a lowering of morale and with it a reduced effectiveness.

A much more profitable strategy would be to set in motion a process of self-examination within the teaching profession itself in the light of the kind of data we have presented here. As part of this, teachers would be invited to address the assumptions underpinning the ideology of autonomy and the potential advantages for themselves of more clearly defined expectations of their role. It could even be that teachers would recognize that having a minimum structure—the framework of a national curriculum devised by teachers themselves—might provide both support and protection within which they could still work in relative professional freedom. Simply to impose a national curriculum and annual attainment targets on teachers is most unlikely to work in the same way that it does in France even if that were the desired goal. Rather, all the recognized disadvantages of the French system—its rigidity and inflexibility, its narrowness and limited relevance to much of modern life—would be likely to be added to the widespread resentment and disquiet felt by teachers who are constrained to adopt a professional role that is alien to them.

It is significant that recent French educational policy has moved towards a decentralization of educational provision and, at least in primary schools, to a considerable strengthening of the power of the headteacher. [...] This kind of carefully controlled decentralization can be seen as a response to the urgent need to overcome some of the disadvantages associated with strong central control of education. Prominent in this respect are the difficulties of promoting curriculum development and new approaches to teaching in a system where conformity has long been the norm. This lesson is an important one which current British government policy seems to be bent on ignoring.

'The National Curriculum 5–16' Consultative Document of July 1987 embodies many fallacies. It casts the curriculum in terms of 'what pupils should be able to know, do and understand' (para. 22); it assumes that to study and to learn are the same thing; that all pupils should pursue the same 'attainment targets' and at the same pace, and that the existence of universal competition will motivate, rather than demoralize, the majority of children. French experience contradicts these assumptions. As the 'redoublement' figures we cited earlier indicate, many teachers are finding it increasingly difficult to promote successful learning among children whose backgrounds offer little support for what the education system is trying to do for them. Yet the notion of a common entitlement remains strongly supported by most French teachers. How much more likely to fail is the National Curriculum in England where the teachers in primary schools at least believe their professional responsibilities ought to be exercised according to an ideology of personal need and interest?

A study of the context of teaching such as we have presented here can play a vital role in distinguishing the elements that influence the subjectivity of professionalism within the context of a particular education system. It can also reveal how complex is the relationship between making decisions about pedagogy, curriculum and assessment and that of achieving pupil outcomes and the dilemmas, even agonies, inherent in this process.

Any attempt to understand teachers' professional motivation must address the interaction between the influence of the teaching situation itself—the impact of a particular socio-psychological environment characterized by factors such as unequal authority relations, pupil coercion and group-oriented curricula and those nationally specific influences involving traditions and ideology which are mediated by the day-to-day manipulations of policy-makers and administrators. The personal influences of teachers' careers, experience and training, personalities and attitudes add a further layer of variation. The broad systematic differences we have identified above necessarily obscure a good deal of this variation. They also do not address the potentially substantial disjuncture between intention and action so well documented in other studies such as Sharp and Green (1975) and Keddie (1971), although data collected as a part of the study on which this article draws confirm that classroom practice broadly reflects the major differences in approach to teaching among teachers in the two countries reported here. Yet, this national difference in teachers' perceptions renders problematic ethnocentrically inspired notions of professionalism in teaching and underlines the relativity of what constitutes 'good' teaching in a given context.

The familiar stereotypes of the two national education systems under study are borne out by the data reported here. The French system, to use Bernstein's (1977) conceptualization, is still characterized by strong classification and strong framing, the English by weak classification and weak framing. Both systems, however, are responding to major changes in the social context of education at the present time. These changes are challenging policy-makers to address the contradiction present in both systems concerning how good teaching can be promoted without forfeiting control of educational outcomes. In recent years, the British Government has given a great deal of policy attention to measures aimed at improving the quality of teachers and teaching. The proposed institution of teacher appraisal, the provision of 'merit payments', the identification of national priority areas for INSET (In-Service Training) and the significant strengthening of consumer choice under the 1988 Education Act reflect a policy climate committed to improving educational quality through giving schools the means and the obligation to respond to market forces. Indeed the combined effect of current policy initiatives should be to reduce the ambiguity which this article shows to be the defining characteristic of English primary teachers' conceptions of their professional responsibility.

The lessons from France, however, suggest that the resolution of the strains inherent in extended professionalism, problematic goals, process orientation and a particularistic pedagogy is also likely to constitute a strong challenge to prevailing English notions of professional autonomy where 'quality' is defined in terms of the ability to respond to individual pupil needs. By the same token, much of the current content of initial teacher education which seeks to equip students with the skills to identify pupils' individual needs and how they may best provide learning experiences to meet them, will need to be replaced with an emphasis on equipping students to implement National Curriculum objectives and to be able to respond to consumer pressure rather than identifying in a more ideographic way the needs and interests of individual pupils. The assumption which is found in French education that both the means and the ends of the educational process can and should be generalized relieves teachers of the burden of choice but in so doing reduces both their ability and their willingness to respond to different local and pupil needs.

It is the recognition of this limitation that lies behind current French moves to increase personal and institutional autonomy within the education system. Both attempts at reform ignore the international evidence that now exists that educational change cannot be brought about simply by manipulating institutional structures or issuing policy directives. Furthermore the reform attempts fail to take into account the significant drop in morale that is likely to accompany any move to force teachers to change their practice. [. . .]

The evidence we have presented here suggests that any attempt at change which fails to take into account the real influences on teachers' professional motivation and practice will be unsuccessful in all respects but one. It may well succeed in eroding the professional commitment inherent in working towards self-imposed goals, which is the explicit core of the motivation of both cohorts of teachers in the study reported here. Only then, when it is too late, will the real key to effective educational change be apparent.

Acknowledgement

The research on which this paper was based was funded by the ESRC whose support is gratefully acknowledged.

Note

All the tables are summaries of qualitative analyses, therefore tests of significance were not felt to be appropriate.

In all tables it was possible for individual teachers to mention more than one category, therefore total percentages do not equal 100.

References

Acker, S. (1987) Primary school teaching as an occupation. In S. Delamont (ed.) *The Primary School Teacher*. Basingstoke: Falmer Press.

Alexander, R. (1984) *Primary Teaching*. London: Holt, Rinehart and Winston.

Barnard, H. (1969) *Education and the French Revolution*. London: Cambridge University Press.

Berlak, A. and Berlak, H. (1981) *Dilemmas of Schooling*. London: Methuen.

Bernstein, B. (1977) On the classification and framing of educational knowledge. In B. Bernstein *Class, Codes and Control, Vol. III*. London: Routledge and Kegan Paul.

Bolton, E. (1988) The National Curriculum: an overview. Paper presented to INOGOV conference, Birmingham.

Bourdieu, P. and Passeron, W. C. (1977) *Reproduction in Education, Society and Culture*. London: Sage.

Broadfoot, P.M. and Osborn, M.J. (1987) French lessons: what comparative research can teach us about plans for a national curriculum. *The Times Educational Supplement*, 7 July.

Calderhead, J. (1987) *Exploring Teachers' Thinking*. London: Cassell.

Crozier, M. (1970) *The Stalled Society*. New York: Viking.

Durkheim, E. (1977) *The Evolution of Educational Thought* (transl. P. Collins). London: Routledge and Kegan Paul.

Hoyle, E. (1980) Professionalisation and deprofessionalisation in education. In E. Hoyle and J. Megarry (eds) *World Yearbook of Education 1980: Professional Development of Teachers*, pp. 42–54. London: Kogan Page.

Isambert-Jamati, V. (1984) *Culture Technique et Critique Sociale a l'Ecole Elémentaire*. Paris: P.U.F. Pédagogie d'Aujourd'hui.

Jackson, P. W. (1968) *Life in Classrooms*. Chicago: Holt, Rinehart and Winston.

Keddie, N. (1971) Classroom knowledge. In M.F.D. Young (eds) *Knowledge and Control*. London: Collier-Macmillan.

King, R. (1978) *All Things Bright and Beautiful? A Sociological Study of Infants' Classrooms*. Chichester: Wiley.

Lacqueur, T.W. (1973) English and French education in the nineteenth century. *History of Education Quarterly* (Spring), 53–60.

Liard, L. (1894) *L'enseignement supérieur en France 1789–1893, Vol. II*. Paris: Armand Colin.

Nias, J. (1986) What it is to feel like a teacher. Paper given at a symposium on 'Becoming and Being a Teacher', BERA Conference, Bristol.

Pollard, A. (1985) *The Social World of the Primary School*. London: Holt, Rinehart and Winston.

— (1988) Social constructivism and the future of 'primary education'. Paper presented at 1st CARIERA Conference, St Lucia, April.

Poppleton, P. (1986) The experience of teaching in 'disadvantaged' areas in the UK and USA. Paper given at a symposium on 'Becoming and Being a Teacher', BERA Conference, Bristol.

Sharp, R. and Green, A. (1975) *Education and Social Control*. London: Routledge and Kegan Paul.

Thomas, N. (1985) *Improving Primary Schools: Report of the Committee on Primary Education* (The Thomas Report). London: ILEA.

Zeichner, K.M., Tabacknick, B.R. and Densmore, K. (1987) Individual, institutional and cultural influences on the development of teachers: craft knowledge. In J. Calderhead (ed.) *Exploring Teachers' Thinking*. London: Cassell.

15 RACIALIZED AND GENDERED DISCOURSES IN TEACHER EDUCATION

IRAM SIRAJ-BLATCHFORD

> The institution which many sociologists have regarded as central in perpetuating inequality—and also, crucially, central in potentially eliminating inequality—is education.
> (Thomas, 1990)

Education is clearly one site in a large number of societal institutions, such as the family, employment and the media, that plays an important role in the reproduction of inequality at both an ideological and at a material level.

In this article I will argue that, in terms of 'race' and gender policy, practice and research, education have often been defined in the limited terms of *schooling*. Within this process, secondary edu examination entry and performance has also been regarded as central. I shall explore the role and validity of state policies on 'race' and gender equality and attempt to make apparent the ideological basis of the dominant discourses associated with equality of opportunity. The role that researchers have played in promoting these conceptions will be identified. It will be argued that these perspectives have been incorporated into policy and research in the area of teacher education and into higher education more generally.

Teacher education can, however, be seen as important in its own right, as a crucial ideological site from which 15,000 teachers in schools enter employment annually. I shall therefore argue for a concerted paradigmatic shift in analyzing policy and practice and in pursuing research on inequality in teacher education in the light of:

- the limited nature of existing research that considers discrete aspects of teacher education in relation to 'race' and gender
- recent reforms in education that have been based on Conservative and 'New Right' socio-economic ideals
- the further development of school partnership approaches to initial teacher education (ITE) and the attack on 'theory' in course content
- the 'structured absence' of 'race' and gender in dominant discourses of teacher education
- the changing cultural context of teacher education.

Such a shift of analysis may provide a more progressive research approach for those wishing to promote greater equality in the process of teacher education and schooling.

Source: This article was specially commissioned for this Reader.

THE ROLE OF EDUCATION IN REPRODUCING SOCIAL STRATIFICATION BY 'RACE' AND GENDER

In order to identify any role that teacher education plays in relation to the existence and perpetuation of gender and 'race' inequality, it is necessary first to consider the role of education in general and of schooling in particular. Much of the rhetoric and debate surrounding teacher education and equality has maintained that teachers have a special role and responsibility in tackling racism and sexism. It is argued that teachers need to understand the role that education plays in the process of sustaining and reproducing racism and sexism. Two broad approaches can be identified in both the research perspectives and in the forms of provision that are advocated. Multicultural/equal opportunity approaches have tended to focus upon the negative effects that education has on the educational performance of black and ethnic minority pupils in general and on girls in some subject areas. By contrast, anti-racist/anti-sexist approaches have more often emphasized the role that education has in reproducing structural inequality through its preferential treatment of boys and ethnic majority pupils. While some anti-racist/anti-sexist writers have drawn attention to the importance of positively influencing the socialization of future adult males and ethnic majorities as potential discriminators, others have taken a more traditional Marxist approach and emphasized the role of the State and of policy.

An adequate treatment of the various conceptions of the state and of the neo-Marxist approaches that have come to inform the more recent emphasis upon masculinity, patriarchy, white supremacy and decolonialism is beyond the scope of this article. A brief review of some of the major theoretical approaches may, however, be useful.

The dominant liberal ideology of schooling in Britain has been significantly predicated upon 'meritocratic' notions of social mobility, where an individual's position in the class structure has been assumed to be, at least in part, a result of her/his own efforts (or lack of them). While this ideology has been widely contested by groups and individuals, and in particular by those involved in the various civil rights and women's movements, it remains a powerful assumption lying behind much of the popular discourse. In education, early radical theorists adopted structural functionalist frameworks to maintain an essentialist relationship between labour and schooling. They identified the role of schools in the reproduction of capitalist economic relations (Bowles and Gintis, 1976). As McCarthy and Apple (1988) have argued, 'racial' and gender divisions were also seen by structuralists as the effects of economic divisions in society and as by-products of a more fundamental conflict between the working class and their capitalist employers who adopted 'divide and rule' policies to disorganize the working class (p. 18). A major critique of this approach emphasized that it neglected, and tended to characterize negatively, the autonomous workings of racial and patriarchal structures of domination (Weis, 1988). The contributions made by earlier liberal researchers and 'policy intellectuals' to our understanding of school culture and politics were also ignored (McCarthy and Apple, 1988). In more recent years, cultural reproduction theorists such as Apple (1982) and Giroux (1983) drew upon perspectives informed by the sociology of knowledge. Writing by Bourdieu and Passeron (1977), Bernstein (1977), and Wexler (1976) contributed to what became known as 'the new sociology of education'. Theories that emphasized the relative autonomy of schools with respect to the social structure focused attention on the 'hidden curriculum' and 'invisible pedagogies' which operated to the advantage of middle-class, male and ethnic majority pupils. A growing concern with the triad of knowledge, ideology and power offered a more helpful way forward for 'race' and gender analysis without ignoring the effects of economic and social class dynamics.

Marxist feminists (Barrett, 1984; Wolpe, 1978) argued that while women's oppression is almost universal it has taken different forms at different times in different societies. Again, as Thomas effectively puts it:

> Thus under capitalism, women's oppression is not simply a question of individual men oppressing individual women nor of men in general oppressing women in general; it takes the form of exploitation in the labour market, which has become essential to maintaining capitalism—low wages, harsh working conditions, little job security—as well as exploitation in the home and family.   (Thomas, 1990)

During the 1980s a growing interest in post-structuralist theory has drawn renewed attention to the essentialism of class analysis and has led many women, black and ethnic minorities, homosexual and other marginalized groups to seek alternative theoretical models from a range of disciplines including psychoanalytic theory, literary criticism and linguistics (Irigaray, 1982; Said, 1983). This, in turn, has given voice and legitimacy to the exploration and analysis of social phenomenon at the level of agency and experience as well as structure. In education, 'critical educational theory' has been advanced by Wexler (1982), Apple and Weis (1983) and Giroux (1992) in order to look beyond class and analyze the interrelationship and dynamics of 'race', gender and class. As McCarthy and Apple remind us, the project is far from complete:

> A nonsynchronous parallelist framework remains to be fully articulated. But we also need to remember what all of these theoretical labours are about. The political, economic and cultural lives of real people—of real children, of real men and women, of real people of colour in schools and elsewhere—are subject not to theoretic but lived relations of differential power.   (McCarthy and Apple, 1988, p. 32)

Theorists such as Spender (1982) and Mahoney (1985) have thus argued that schools reflect and reproduce patriarchal relations. While Barrett's (1984) analysis may be unduly deterministic and limited, her consideration of the four levels at which gender relations are reproduced in schooling is valuable. At the *ideological* level, boys and girls are socialized into appropriate (*sic*) feminine and masculine behaviour. At the *structural and organizational* level, the gendered occupational structure of the school acts as part of the hidden curriculum. Mechanisms operate to *channel* pupils into gendered subjects reflecting gendered occupational structures outside the school, while androcentric definitions of *legitimate knowledge* are taught as objective and neutral. School subjects are, in fact, themselves defined in these terms.

In the same way, ideologies of 'race' and ethnicism act to socialize black and white pupils for *their* future roles. Research concerned with these ideological issues has tended to focus upon the alleged poor 'self-esteem' of black pupils. Black teachers and assistants occupy inferior positions within the structure and organization of the school (CRE, 1988), and researchers have been particularly concerned about the lack of positive role models. Black and white pupils are also channelled into subjects reflecting a racialized division of labour in society. Ethnocentric knowledge is equally legitimated and presented as objective and neutral.

The labour market in Britain is segregated according to 'race' and gender (Jenkins, 1986; Brennan and McGeevor, 1987, 1990). Throughout our educational system black and white minority students, teachers and lecturers are under-represented. They are also disproportionately placed in low-status sets, streams and posts within school and college hierarchies (Gillborn, 1990; Siraj-Blatchford, 1991; Troyna and Siraj-Blatchford, 1993). Women are also channelled into specific areas of the labour market and, even in those areas that they dominate such as education, they are largely to be found in the lowest positions. While in higher education, feminist theory and women have gained footholds in areas such as sociology and women's studies, and to a lesser extent black and ethnic minority academics are now represented in 'race' relations, the overall opportunities for black and ethnic minority women are even more limited (Beechey, 1986).

A CRE (1988) survey suggests that more than half of the black and ethnic minority teachers in this country experience racial discrimination, and over three-quarters feel that racial discrimination has adversely affected their careers. The research shows that ethnic minority teachers are on lower salaries, are over-represented on the lowest rungs of the professional ladder and are disproportionately concentrated in shortage subjects or where ethnic minority pupils are involved.

Further insight into the discrimination faced by black and ethnic minority teachers can be found in the reasons the Swann Report (DES, 1985) provided to explain why so few potential ethnic minority pupils aspired to be teachers. It was suggested that:

- they had experienced the racism and negative stereotyping of ethnic minority groups while at school and had no desire therefore to rejoin such an institution;
- they were disenchanted by the somewhat limited role which they felt many ethnic minority teachers were asked to play in the system—as E2L or 'mother tongue' teachers or simply as supervisors of ethnic minority pupils;
- the restricted career opportunities this presented; and
- they did not regard teaching as offering good career prospects in the current economic situation, especially since they felt their own chances in the job market would be hindered by the influence of racism.

(DES, 1985, p. 609)

Morrison and McIntyre (1976) have also suggested that suitably qualified candidates often choose not to enter the teaching profession due to the perceived monotony of teachers' work, their low pay, the discipline problems and poor promotion prospects. Raminder Singh's (1988) survey of South Asian and white ethnic majority sixth-formers' perceptions of teaching also found that well-qualified South Asian pupils cited the racism that they had experienced or witnessed among pupils and staff as a major deterrent to entering the profession.

About 15,000 new teachers are currently appointed in England and Wales each year (DFE, 1992). Overall, 2.3% of the students that are accepted into ITE are South Asian or African-Caribbean (Adelman, 1993), this compares with 5.3% of the total population made up of these groups. In many other courses the acceptance rates of South Asian or African-Caribbean students have reached 10%. Women make up the majority of students in education, taking up 81% of the places in primary courses and 47% in secondary courses (Adler, Laney and Packer, 1993). As I shall argue, to appreciate fully the nature of 'race' and gender inequality it is necessary to look more closely at the nature and status of those courses.

RESEARCH FOCUSED ON SCHOOLING AND 'CREDENTIALISM'

During the 1970s and early 1980s much of the 'race' equality research was focused on the injustice of teacher stereotyping and the prejudicial treatment of ethnic minority pupils (Brittan, 1976; Edwards, 1978; Rex and Tomlinson, 1979). Similar preoccupations dominated gender studies (Acker, 1988). At the same time anti-racist and anti-sexist perspectives were beginning to shift the emphasis beyond the adoption of policies and practices for combating racist and sexist incidents and for dealing with interpersonal discrimination, racist and sexist abuse, harassment and name calling. The emphasis began to move towards the need for *all* children to be taught about racism, even in predominantly white areas.

The dominant discourse equality of opportunity has been firmly rooted in beliefs that multicultural education is about and for black and ethnic minority children. The wider context of racism in society outside the school and the role of white ethnic majority people in the production and reproduction of it have largely been ignored. It is significant in this context that Giles and Cherrington (1981) found that the main thrust for multicultural educational development was coming from those institutions which were situated in urban multi-ethnic conurbations.

Menter's (1989) study of teaching practice focused on the triad of teacher, student and college supervisor, and described how tensions and contradictions within the triad influence students' reflective and critical development of issues concerning racism and sexism in schools. Teaching practice, he concluded:

> ... is characterized by 'stasis', a strong tendency for those most closely involved to avoid conflict or confrontation. Even mild appraisal of existing classroom practice is avoided.   (Menter, 1989, p. 459)

Given the current UK Government reforms to move ITE more firmly into schools, such stasis and reinforcement of existing practices take on even more significance. In the short term both the training of students and those teachers designated as their mentors may be compromised. In the long term we may be in danger of moving towards the further development of stasis characterizing relations at an *institutional* level, between students, school and HE.

Much of the equal opportunities provision for girls has also focused on attitudes and the 'hidden curriculum' that has influenced them. While providing important evidence of direct and indirect discrimination, much of this work has been far from anti-racist and anti-sexist in effect and has failed to address the educational needs of *all* children.

As I have argued, while 'liberal' theoretical approaches have focused on the failure of children within the education system, radical 'cultural reproduction' and 'critical education' theorists (Willis, 1977; Apple, 1982) have drawn attention to the *process* by which inequality is created and renewed and to the resistance of pupils towards the dominant 'hegemonic' ideology. Changes in the labour market have increasingly been seen by radicals as providing educational contradictions that offer real potential for change.

In the past, many feminist writers (Sharpe, 1976; Deem, 1978) argued that the occupational inequality of men and women is directly related to subject segregation in schools. Girls continue to be under-represented in mathematics, physical science and technology subjects at advanced levels. It is, however, highly questionable whether these subjects and related employment opportunities would be highly rated and rewarded if women were doing them. Millet (1983) argues that women are deliberately excluded from science and technology because these subjects have a crucial instrumental role to play in maintaining male dominance.

It has been suggested that in some respects the educational problems of girls and the issues of black underachievement are quite different. Williams (1987) argues that, while girls need to be encouraged to accept a wider range of occupations in our increasingly technological society, the underachievement of black pupils, by contrast, is usually seen as a result of a more *general* lack of academic achievement. Policy statements that refer to the need to promote 'racial harmony' and 'stability' may be traced back to assumptions regarding indiscipline of black pupils and to the 1981 inner-city uprisings (Troyna and Williams, 1986; Solomos, 1986). But what is similar in these accounts is the emphasis on the pupils themselves and on their individual educational experiences rather than any acceptance of the need to confront the hierarchical cultural and structural determinants of inequality directly. Both accounts provide theoretical models that emphasize a 'cultural deficit' on the part of girls or black children.

Both gender and 'race' are social constructions. As Thomas (1990) argues, our actions are socially constrained, although not socially determined. People make decisions based upon awareness of the potentialities and limitations of certain courses of action. Research has suggested that, when choosing courses, black students in further education place greater emphasis on the subject and the certification available, than on specific cultural or anti-racist provision (FEU, 1985; Reeves, 1986). Subject choices are determined by pupils' perceptions of the realistic options open to them. While often not passively accepted by individuals, the subject choices that are made by women and black people are limited by social expectations of femininity and 'race', both within and outside schools.

Some subjects are undoubtably regarded as gender specific (Thomas, 1990) and we have become accustomed to seeing black people in manual roles. Analysis of national data collected by the Universities Central Council on Admissions (UCCA) shows that in higher education, subjects are clearly racialized: for example, 16% of all South Asian students who apply for courses seek to enter medicine and dentistry, compared with only 4% of all ethnic majority students, while 33% of social science applicants are 'black' compared with 17% ethnic majority. Ethnic minority women are even more concentrated into particular courses than ethnic minority men.

> It is also of interest to consider subjects 'avoided'. The very low application rates for education courses are noticeable ... Also, few ethnic minority students apply for languages and humanities relative to White students. This may reflect the actual or anticipated 'Eurocentric' nature of such courses.   (Taylor, 1993)

Thomas's survey of students in three institutions shows that subject disciplines offer distinct cultures. Thomas cites Measor (1984) and Bernstein (1971) to argue that subject specialization reinforces both class and gender distinctions, however:

It is not enough ...to say more women should do science, or that domestic economy should be compulsory for both sexes; we have to get to grips with the ways in which femininity is consistently devalued, both in society generally and specifically in the education system. (Thomas, 1990)

Higher education may be relatively autonomous with respect to the state but at the same time it is not isolated from the power structures and values of society. Despite the widespread involvement of women in traditional male occupational roles during the Second World War these gains were reversed soon after the war ended. Occupational status is not simply related to skills shortages. Despite a clear shortage of linguists in industry, women's over-representation (by four to one) in A-level French classes has not resulted in their promotion to senior jobs:

... it would be wrong to assume that the balance of power between the sexes can be changed simply by persuading more girls to take 'boys' subjects: the issue is clearly too complex to justify simplistic remedies. (Thomas, 1990)

Feminist analysis that was initially focused upon the need to change schools in order to change girls' attitudes to subjects has thus moved towards a critique of the educational subject disciplines themselves (Kelly, 1985). Some feminists have emphasized the role of education in transmitting 'male' knowledge. Spender, for example, suggests that:

Men have provided us with a false picture of the world ... not just because their view is so limited, but because they have insisted that their limited view is the total view. (Spender, 1982, p. 16)

Radical feminists such as Harding (1990) have contributed significantly to the critique of patriarchal science. In the same way, writing by bel hooks (1989), Said (1985), Bernal (1987), Goonatilake (1984), Joseph (1991) and others is contributing to the 'de-colonization' of literature, history, science and mathematics. These are clearly parallel yet non-synchronous developments which have yet to be drawn together into a common theoretical framework of the sort advocated by McCarthy and Apple (1988).

STATE POLICIES ON 'RACE' AND GENDER

While some policy-makers have, in the past, considered 'race' and gender as significant cultural divisions requiring alternative curricula and pluralist forms of learning, others have focused upon students' social and educational experiences of racism and sexism as the key variables (Williams, 1987; ILEA, 1983). Both of these classifications of 'race' and gender highlight certain aspects of school experience while ignoring others and, as Williams (1987) argues, certain aspects of group unity are also emphasized while others are rejected. Crucially, both classifications have resulted in a situation where policy discussions of 'race' and gender inequality have ignored the effects of class and regional/urban inequality. 'Race', gender and class data have been largely collected and analysed in discrete categories and the connections between these categories have rarely been given more than token consideration. In recent years some efforts have been made to identify the different forms of racism and sexism experiened by different groups in different educational settings (Clarricoates, 1980; Fuller, 1982; Brah and Minhas, 1985; Mac an Ghaill, 1988).

THE IDEOLOGICAL BASIS OF DOMINANT DISCOURSES

As I have shown, a range of explantory frameworks have been used to analyze the educational problems associated with 'race' and gender (Williams, 1987). The adoption of 'cultural deficit theories' has led policy-makers towards solutions emphasizing compensatory education. Cultural difference theories have also focused on the need for teachers to 'celebrate' *other* cultures and to make them educationally relevant. Attempts have thus been made to provide 'girl friendly science' and to promote limited versions of multicultural education. At the same time, theories of teacher labelling and stereotyping have also led to attempts to remove bias and, as Williams (1987) argues, it is only within this latter framework of discrimination that the remodelling of teachers and schools may be linked to wider social and political changes.

All of these policies have operated within an ideological framework that has emphasized 'equality of opportunity', a concept 'capable of uniting diverse political and educational campaigners precisely because of its vagueness' (Williams, 1987, p. 346). Unfortunately, such apparent 'unity' may be less productive than it is often supposed; Jewson and Mason (1992) argue, for example, that the benefits of such expedients are often short lived. They also suggest a theoretical distinction between liberal and radical conceptions of equal opportunities and they argue that the invocation of the term 'equal oportunities' often generates both disappointment and distrust in the long run. Liberal equal opportunity policies aim to implement fair procedures in order to illuminate unfair distortions in the operation of market forces. Radicals, by contrast, informed by critical analysis of 'ability', 'talent' and the function of educational credentials, actually seek to overcome these 'free market processes' in order to achieve structural equality.

Jewson and Mason's research suggests that equal opportunity policies should not be taken at face value:

> Instead they must be seen as social practices, i.e. social activities which engage groups and individuals in a dynamic structure of intended and unintended actions in relation to others ... The expedient, or accidental,

adoption of items of an opponent's or a critic's conceptual armoury may lead one along a logical road quite divergent from the straight and narrow path of one's own proffered principles. In these circumstances both liberals and radicals may simultaneously be cynical manipulators and confused victims of their own manipulation.

(Jewson and Mason, 1992, pp. 229–30).

THE LIMITATIONS OF RESEARCH ON 'RACE' AND GENDER IN ITE

In the past, 'race' and gender equality research in ITE has tended to focus on the differential access provided to higher education and the teaching profession, and on aspects of discrimination in course contents and teaching practice, as well as on the experiences of ethnic minority ITE students and the attitudes of their white peers. A major assumption that has informed this approach to research has been the perceived need for black and ethnic minority pupils to be given positive role models. The suggestion has also been made that the presence of black and ethnic minorities as students in ITE and as teachers in schools would have an educational influence upon their ethnic majority peers. Unfortunately, this assumed need to increase black and ethnic minority involvement in ITE in order to improve the educational achievement of black and ethnic minority pupils is clearly contradicted by the realities of women's involvement in education. Women dominate the teaching profession yet have failed to affect radically the achievement of girls in key subject areas. The issues are more complex than they would appear at first sight.

Although it is vital to have research which documents the experiences of and gives 'voice' to black and female students, the recognition of apparent contradictions in the over-representation of women and the under-representation of black and ethnic minorities in education begs the question of why people choose to enter teacher education and focuses attention upon issues of social expectation. An associated question relates to our target groups for research—are we focusing our attention on the right groups? Should we be focusing more on structures, cultures and/or the distribution of power? How does this affect and how is it affected by the theories that we adopt? In 1993, the Higher Education Funding Council for Education (HEFCE), awarded 17 grants to institutions of teacher education as part of an initiative to increase the participation of ethnic minorities in ITE. This initiative is clearly informed by a limited conception of equal opportunities which emphasizes 'access'. An alternative approach might have included research on 'race' and the education of ethnic majority students, the formulation of equality policies, and staff development. As Thomas (1990) stresses, research on gender requires an examination of the cultural creation of male dominance as well as the creation of female subordination. Equally, research on 'race' equality requires an equivalent examination of the creation and perpetuation of white superiority.

Williams' (1987) argument that there are crucial differences in the political and professional contexts within which 'race' and gender policies are implemented is unconvincing (Williams, 1987, p. 349). She maintains that only 'middle-class' or 'academically able' girls may enjoy better initial occupational choices than their working-class and academically disabled sisters. But surely this is equally true of equivalent black groups. The crucial difference is in the number of individuals who actually fall into each of these categories. While all equality goals cannot be achieved by strategies confined to schooling, and while schools cannot be isolated from the wider structures through which inequality is created and recreated, schools and education in general do have a central, though not determining, role to play. We need to move beyond monocausal explanations and explore the multi-dimensional nature of the structures and cultures of inequality in schools and teacher education (Mac an Ghaill, 1992).

THE NEED FOR A PARADIGMATIC SHIFT

I have argued that it is essential for those involved in teacher education who are 'committed' to change in policy and practice to adopt theoretical understandings that incorporate structural, cultural and political dimensions. This is equally essential for researchers. I have argued that 'race' and gender researchers have tended to focus upon discrete and isolated aspects of policy and practice, such as student experiences and attitudes, staff promotion, course delivery and policy development. Very few research studies explore 'race' and gender together—a challenging task since 'race' and gender cannot simply be added together. Problems have arisen where this has been attempted without due regard to the specific complexities of each form of inequality and without critically analyzing actors' (and researchers') understanding of the issues (Siraj-Blatchford, 1993a).

Heward, Taylor and Vickers (1993) provide an illuminating example of the difficulties involved. These researchers explored the career progress of women and ethnic minorities in higher education, and they offer a useful and convincing critique of women's limited promotion prospects. The research identifies and critically deconstructs the specific reasons that those in power give for not promoting women. The researchers are, however, unable to provide anything approaching an equivalent deconstruction of the reasons 'elites' give for not promoting ethnic minorities. While the researchers clearly recognize that the statements are discriminatory they are unable to say *why*. The voices of 'elites' in higher education present the consensual, normalized (if oppressive) frames of the status quo and, as such, they may not have been open to scrutiny. I have argued elsewhere (Siraj-Blatchford, 1994) that this type of research would benefit from the adoption of a more 'committed', critical social research perspective. It is not enough to attempt to 'bolt-on' a 'race' dimension any more than it would be to consider the influence of inequalities of class, sexuality or disability without considering the specific form that the influence takes in the context of the study. The academic community often considers with some scepticism the products of research which seek to give 'voice' to oppressed groups (Siraj-Blatchford, 1993b). In this instance, Heward, Taylor and Vickers failed to draw on literature which examines the critical role of wider structural and cultural racial inequalities, so the voices of the discriminators are presented relatively uncritically, reifying and reproducing the 'racial' inequality that these researchers seek to identify.

COMMITMENT AND CHANGE: CRITICAL CONTEXTS

It is important that 'race' and gender discourses in teacher education do not remain marginal issues. I have argued for an increased focus of attention upon curriculum contents and powerful groups (including male and ethnic majority students) as transformative agents. This new agenda can be explored more fully if future policy, practice and research are informed by a clear recognition of the following contexts within which any developments in teacher education must be located.

Existing research

Not only researchers, but all of those committed to change in teacher education will need to adopt ways of evaluating and assessing their praxis. We can learn a great deal by critically analyzing the types of methods that activists and committed groups have used. The CRE and EOC (Equal Opportunities Commission) have often sponsored research which yields statistics that are convincing to policy-makers, but the emphasis upon gathering evidence of discrimination has resulted in very limited attention being given to the powerful change agents in teacher education. Those who have researched discrete aspects of 'race' and gender in teacher education have relied heavily upon the use of questionnaires (Siraj-Blatchford, 1991; Hannan, 1985; Menter, 1987), small-scale informal interviews (Menter, 1989; Skelton, 1989; Blair and Maylor, 1993), documentary analysis and limited action research (Spender, 1984), or observations and interviews (Flintoff, 1993). None of these techniques has offered critical insight into the wider cultures, structures and politics of the departments in which the studies took place.

The New Right

We must be fully cognizant of the agenda of the New Right in reforming teacher education to meet Conservative socio-economic priorities (Ball, 1993). In this context the macro-micro political contexts of 'image' and impression management are more important than the educational process. At the macro level we need to understand the implications of the demise of local authorities, the advance of the marketplace philosophy, changes in funding arrangements, the attack upon educational theory and the shift of power to schools in their role as teacher educators (Whitty, 1990). At another level the impact of the New Right is expressed through the move towards competency-based teacher education, the imposition of the three-year six-subject B.Ed. and the demise of courses which traditionally dealt with 'race' and gender, such as those concerned with sociological or psychological aspects of educational studies.

School and ITE partnerships

The Government reforms that aim to establish marketplace philosophies in teacher education (DFE Circulars 9/92 and 14/93) have forced ITE departments to forge even closer partnerships with schools. This shift of power over training to schools provides new challenges to teacher educators committed to equality. Research has suggested that some of the worst forms of educational discrimination are faced by students on school practice and yet this is rarely countered (Siraj-Blatchford, 1991; Menter, 1989). Competency-based learning in schools could inhibit deeper understanding of the social factors that influence learning. When coupled with the general reduction in the 'theoretical' content of courses this could potentially be a seriously retrogressive step. The responses of the Anti-Racist Teacher Education Network to the DFE have highlighted these problems. It is clear that ITE departments will need to take a leading role in this area if they are not to lose the limited progress that they have made. The training of mentors and the issues surrounding 'the whole' and 'cross-curriculum' dimensions, as well as the interpretation of competencies in practice will be key arenas or sites for future praxis.

The discourses of teacher education

Just as school curricula (Apple, 1980) are dominated by 'technicist' concerns to find the best means to reach pre-chosen educational ends, mainstream research in teacher education is effectively 'deracialized' and 'degendered' along with the dominant policies and practices that it is studying (Spender, 1984; Booth *et al.*, 1989; Day, Calderhead and Denicolo, 1993). Ideology functions as much by the *structured absence* of alternative concerns as by any inclusion. The dominant discourse of ITE is itself ideological, and the ideology serves to provide normative consensus and socio-economic adjustment to an essentially stratified and unequal society. Despite some progress in the 1970s and early 1980s, the last ten years have seen the erosion of all official efforts to incorporate issues of gender and racial equality into ITE. The emphasis has now been firmly focused upon narrowly defined school-based competencies and the '*delivery*' of the National Curriculum.

Culture of teacher education

Teacher educators are subject to the same pressures facing higher education more generally. They are expected to research, publish, teach, constantly devise new courses, develop postgraduate work, seek funding through research proposals, and they are also required to administrate as well as implement the school partnerships. Many teacher educators are suffering low morale with the perceived demise of their profession and in some cases their departments. They are anxious to salvage what is left by creating school partnerships and working within the reforms. It is no exaggeration to suggest that teacher educators are suffering 'hard times'. The shifting cultures and politics of departments, with the emphasis on quality criteria, academic auditing and a highly competitive research selectivity exercise, could hamper equality initiatives. We need to find ways of articulating equality measures within these changes, and this will require a great deal of re-evaluation of strategy by committed individuals and groups. It will also require a measure of optimism that cannot be taken for granted.

THINKING POSITIVELY AND PRAXICALLY: A WAY FORWARD

As I stated at the beginning of this article, the links between policy, practice and research in 'race' and gender equality are both overlapping and dynamic. The kind of committed intervention that I am arguing for involves teacher educators as tutors and as researchers in 'action', committed to changing the practices and policies of their own and colleagues' departments. In order to do this there are some prerequisites to be considered. I have outlined these very briefly in the previous section. 'Race' and gender equality can only be viewed together if there is a firm recognition of their different histories and related theoretical foundations, some of which do overlap. Both areas must also be informed by equivalent understandings of class seen as an additional 'non-synchronous' area that implicates both 'race' and gender inequalities without determining them (Sleeter and Grant, 1988).

I have argued that those concerned to counter 'race' and gender inequality cannot afford to ignore the dominant racial and gender groups and ideologies as sites for action and change. Indeed, such a focus may be seen as pertinent to every action. The critical tradition in education, through critical pedagogy (Friere, 1974), critical theory (Giroux, 1992) and critical social research (Harvey, 1990), may offer some of the most fruitful ways forward at a micro-level, that of agency and experience for students and staff. This requires, in the context of 'race' and gender, the application of what I have referrd to as a 'committed' perspective to each dimension of the triad of policy, practice and research.

The new agendas imposed upon teacher education have served to weaken traditional structures and, while the new competitive marketplace structures are themselves antagonistic to the equality project, this period of rapid change does offer possibilities for progressive action. Counter hegemonic equality initiatives may be developed within the structural 'spaces' that inevitably open up. The development of partnership schools, for example, offers the possibility of critical and committed practitioners informing and setting precedence for the manner in which mentors are trained and teacher competencies defined. Anti-sexist and anti-racist perspectives may be introduced to students as they themselves critically evaluate the competencies for omission and coherence.

In the area of 'race', gender and teacher education we need to be informed by critical traditions and to be aware of the cultural, political and structural contexts within which research on 'race' and gender is situated. McCarthy and Apple (1988) have usefully identified the need to develop parellelist, nonsynchronous approaches, and as they poignantly add:

> ... for this we do need conceptual advances. But one learns to see more clearly through political action as well.
>
> (McCarthy and Apple, 1988, p. 32)

References

Acker, S. (1988) Teachers, gender and resistance. *British Journal of Sociology of Education* 9 (3), 307–22.

Adelman, C. (1993) Access to teacher training and employment. In G. Verma (ed.) *Inequality and Teacher Education: An International Perspective*. London: Falmer Press.

Adler, S., Laney, J. and Packer, M. (1993) *Managing Women*. Buckingham: Open University Press.

Apple, M. (1980) *Ideology and Curriculum*. London: Routledge and Kegan Paul.

—(1982) *Education and Power*. Boston: Routledge and Kegan Paul.

Apple, M. and Weis, L. (eds) (1983) *Ideology and Practice in Schooling*. Philadelphia: Temple University Press.

Ball, S. (1993) Education policy, power relations and teachers' work. *British Journal of Educational Studies* 41 (2).

Barrett, M. (1984) *Women's Oppression Today: Problems in Marxist Feminism Analysis*. London: Verso.

Beechey, V. (1986) Womens' employment in contemporary Britain. In V. Beechey and E. Whitelegg (eds) *Women in Britain Today*. Milton Keynes: Open University Press.

Bernal, M. (1987) *Black Athena: The Afro Asiatic Roots of Classical Civilisation*. London: Free Association Books.

Bernstein, B. (1971) On the classification and framing of educational knowledge. In M. Young (ed.) *Knowledge and Control*. London: Collier-Macmillan.

—(1977) *Class, Codes and Control: Volume 3*. Boston: Routledge and Kegan Paul.

Blair, M. and Maylor, U. (1993) Issues and concerns for black women teachers in training. In I. Siraj-Blatchford (ed.) *'Race', Gender and the Education of Teachers*. Buckingham: Open University Press.

Booth, M., Furlong, J., Hargreaves, D., Reiss, M. and Ruthven, K. (1989) *Teacher Supply and Teacher Quality: Solving the Coming Crisis*. Cambridge: Cambridge Education Papers No. 1, Cambridge University.

Bourdieu, P. and Passeron, J. (1977) *Reproduction in Education, Society and Culture.* London: Sage.

Bowles, S. and Gintis, H. (1976) *Schooling in Capitalist America.* New York: Basic Books.

Brah, A. and Minhas, R. (1985) Structural racism or cultural difference: schooling for Asian girls. In G. Weiner, (ed.) *Just a Bunch of Girls.* Milton Keynes: Open University Press.

Brennan, J. and McGeevor, P. (1987) *Employment of Graduates from Ethnic Minorities.* London: CRE (Commission for Racial Equality).

— (1990) *Ethnic Minorities and the Graduate Labour Market.* London: CRE.

Brittan, E. (1976) Multicultural education 2. Teacher opinion on aspects of school life: pupils and teachers. *Education Research* 18 (3), 182–91.

Clarricoates, K. (1980) The importance of being Ernest, Emma, Tom, Jane. In R. Deem (ed.) *Schooling for Women's Work.* London: Routledge and Kegan Paul.

CRE (Commission for Racial Equality) (1988) *Ethnic Minority School Teachers.* London: CRE.

Day, C., Calderhead, J. and Denicolo, P. (1993) *Research on Teacher Thinking.* London: Falmer Press.

Deem, R. (1978) *Women and Schooling.* London: Routledge and Kegan Paul.

DES (Department of Education and Science) (1985) *Education for All* (The Swann Report). London: HMSO.

DFE (Department for Education) (1992) *Initial Teacher Training Secondary Phase.* CATE Circular No. 9/92. London: HMSO.

— (1993) *The Initial Training of Primary School Teachers.* CATE Circular No. 14/93, DFE. London: HMSO.

Edwards, V. (1978) Language attitudes and underperformance in West Indian children. *Educational Review* 30, 51–8.

FEU (Further Education Unit) (1985) *Black Perspectives of FE Provision.* London: FEU.

Flintoff, A. (1993) One of the boys? Gender identities in physical education initial teaching education. In I. Siraj-Blatchford (ed.) *'Race', Gender and the Education of Teachers.* Buckingham: Open University Press.

Freire, P. (1974) *Education for Critical Consciousness.* London: Sheed and Ward.

Fuller, M. (1982) Young, female and black. In E. Cashmore and B. Troyna (eds) *Black Youth in Crisis.* London: Allen and Unwin.

Giles, R. and Cherrington, D. (1981) *Multicultural Education in the UK: A Survey of Courses and Other Provisions in British Institutions of Higher Education.* London: CRE.

Gillborn, D. (1990) *'Race', Ethnicity and Education.* London: Unwin Hyman.

Giroux, H. (1983) *Theory and Resistance in Education.* South Hadley: Bergin and Garvey.

— (1992) *Border Crossings: Cultural Workers and the Politics of Education.* New York: Routledge.

Goonatilake, S. (1984) *Aborted Discovery: Science and Creativity in the Third World.* London: Zed Press.

Hannan, A. (1985) The education and training of teachers and the 'multicultural dimensions'. *Multiracial Education* 13 (1), 15–28.

Harding, S. (1990) Feminism, science and the anti-Enlightenment critiques. In L. Nicholson (ed.) *Feminism/Postmodernism.* New York: Routledge.

Harvey, L. (1990) *Critical Social Research.* London: Unwin Hyman.

Heward, C., Taylor, P. and Vickers, R. (1993) Gender, race and career success in the academic profession. Research paper presented 25.11.93, Department of Education, University of Warwick.

HEFCE (Higher Education Funding Council for Education) (1993) Special initiatives to encourage widening participation. Circular 22/93. London: HEFCE.

hooks, b. (1989) *Talking Back: Thinking Feminist—Thinking Black*. Boston: Sheba Feminist Publishers.

ILEA (Inner London Education Authority) (1983) *Anti-Racist Statement and Guidelines*. London: ILEA.

Irigaray, L. (1982) This sex which is not one. In A. Kuhn (ed.) *Women's Pictures*. Boston: Routledge and Kegan Paul.

Jenkins, R. (1986) *Racism and Recruitment: Managers, Organizations and Equal Opportunity in the Labour Market*. Cambridge: Cambridge University Press.

Jewson, N. and Mason, D. (1992) The theory and practice of equal opportunities policies: liberal and radical approaches. In P. Braham *et al.* (eds) *Racism and Antiracism*. London: Open University and Sage.

Joseph, G. (1991) *The Crest of the Peacock: Non-European Roots of Mathematics*. Harmondsworth: Penguin.

Kelly, A. (1985) The construction of masculine science. *British Journal of Sociology of Education* 6 (2), 133–54.

Mac an Ghaill, M. (1988) *Young, Gifted and Black*. Milton Keynes: Open University Press.

— (1992) Coming of age in 1980s England: reconceptualising black students' schooling experience. In D. Gill, B. Mayor and M. Blair (eds) *Racism and Education*. London: Open University and Sage.

McCarthy, C. and Apple, M. (1988) Race, class, and gender in American educational research: towards a nonsynchronous parellelist position. In L. Weis (ed.) *Class, Race and Gender in American Education*. Albany: State University of New York Press.

Mahoney, P. (1985) *Schools for the Boys? Coeducation Reassessed*. London: Hutchinson/Explorations in Feminism Collective.

Measor, L. (1984) Gender and the sciences: pupils' gender based conceptions of school subjects. In M. Hammersley and A. Hargreaves (eds) *Curriculum Practice*. Lewes: Falmer Press.

Menter, I. (1987) Evaluating teacher education: some notes on an antiracist programme for B.Ed. students. *Multicultural Teaching* 5 (3), 39–42.

— (1989) Teaching practice stasis: racism, sexism and school experience in initial teacher education. *British Journal of Sociology of Education* 10 (4), 459–73.

Millet, K. (1983) *Sexual Politics*. London: Virago.

Morrison, A. and McIntyre, D. (1976) *Teachers and Teaching*. Harmondsworth: Penguin.

Reeves, F. (1986) Culture, race and education. Bilston Community College, occasional paper.

Rex, J. and Tomlinson, S. (1979) *Colonial Immigrants in a British City*. London: Routledge and Kegan Paul.

Said, E. (1983) *The World, the Text and the Critic*. Cambridge, MA: Harvard University Press.

— (1985) *Orientalism: Western Conceptions of the Orient*. Harmondsworth: Penguin.

Sharpe, S. (1976) *Just Like a Girl*. Harmondsworth: Penguin.

Singh, R. (1988) Asian and white sixth formers' perceptions of the teaching profession. Bradford: Bradford and Ilkley Community College occasional paper.

Siraj-Blatchford, I. (1991) A study of black students' perceptions of racism in initial teacher education. *British Education Research Journal* 17 (1), 35–51.

— (1993a) Ethnicity and conflict in physical education: a critique of Carroll and Hollinshead's case study. *British Education Research Journal* 19 (1), 77–82.

— (ed.) (1993b) *'Race', Gender and the Education of Teachers.* Buckingham: Open University Press.

— (1994) Critical social research and the academy: the role of organic intellectuals in educational research. Unpublished paper, University of Warwick.

Skelton, C. (1989) And so the wheel turns ... gender and initial teacher education. In C. Skelton (ed.) *Whatever Happens to Little Women.* Buckingham: Open University Press.

Sleeter, C. and Grant, C. (1988) A rationale for integrating race, gender, and social class. In L. Weis (ed.) *Class, Race, Gender in American Education.* Albany: State University of New York Press.

Solomos, J. (1986) Political language and violent protest: ideological and policy responses to the 1981 and 1985 riots. *Youth and Policy* 18, 12–24.

Spender, D. (1982) *Invisible Women: The Schooling Scandal.* London: Writers and Readers Co-operative.

— (1984) Sexism in teacher education. In S. Acker and D. Warren Piper (eds) *Is Higher Education Fair to Women?* Surrey: SRHE and NFER Nelson.

Taylor, P. (1993) Ethnic group data for university entry: project report for CVCP Working Group on Ethnic Data. Coventry: CRER, University of Warwick.

Thomas, K. (1990) *Gender and the Subject in Higher Education.* Buckingham: SRHE and Open University Press.

Troyna, B. and Siraj-Blatchford, I. (1993) Providing support or denying access? the experiences of students designated as 'ESL' or 'SN' in a multi-ethnic secondary school. *Educational Review* 45 (1), 3–11.

Troyna, B. and Williams, J. (1986) *Racism, Education and the State.* London: Croom Helm.

Weis, L. (ed.) (1988) *Class, Race and Gender in American Education.* Albany: State University of New York Press.

Wexler, P. (1976) *The Sociology of Education: Beyond Equality.* Indianapolis: Bobbs-Merril.

—(1982) Structure, text, and subject: a critical sociology of school knowledge. In M. Apple (ed.) *Cultural and Economic Reproduction in Education.* London: Routledge and Kegan Paul.

Whitty, G. (1990) The New Right and the National Curriculum: state control or market forces? In M. Flude and M. Hammer (eds) *The Education Reform Act 1988.* London: Falmer Press.

Williams, J. (1987) The construction of women and black students as educational problems: re-evaluating policy on gender and 'race'. In M. Arnot and G. Weiner (eds) *Gender and the Politics of Schooling.* London: Hutchinson.

Willis, P. (1977) *Learning to Labour: How Working Class Kids get Working Class Jobs.* Farnborough: Saxon House.

Wolpe, A. (1978) Education and the sexual division of labour. In A. Kuhn and A. Wolpe (eds) *Feminism and Materialism.* London: Routledge and Kegan Paul.

16 FEMINIST CHANGE IN A PATRIARCHAL ORGANIZATION: WOMEN'S INITIATIVES IN LOCAL GOVERNMENT

SUSAN HALFORD

Over the last decade the issue of equal opportunities for women has been placed on the agenda of an ever-increasing number of British local authorities. More than half of all authorities have now devised policies that fall within the broad field of equal opportunities, whilst a smaller proportion of the authorities have chosen to set up specific structures such as Women's Committees and Equal Opportunities Committees to address equality issues (Halford, 1989a). To varying degrees all these local councils have recognized the implicitly gendered nature of existing policies and practice and appear to have made a commitment to introducing new policies and practices that promote positive alternatives for women.

This explicit intervention by local government into the field of gender politics raises some important questions, particularly concerning the extent to which feminist social change can be brought about via the institutions of the state. More specifically, how far can Women's Committees and similar initiatives actually bring about change in the policies and practices of local government? The foundation for these concerns lies with a tradition of feminist analysis that locks state institutions into a broader analysis of gender inequality, and emphasizes the ways in which state actions reflect and reinforce the dominance of men and the oppression of women. How are we to interpret a situation where these very institutions, defined as patriarchal, are apparently pursuing feminist policies?

In this article I shall argue that feminist perspectives which view 'the state' as a functional tool in the hands of patriarchal (and/or capitalist) interests paralyse our understanding of local government women's initiatives and, more widely, of the relationship between gender relations and the state in contemporary Western society. I shall argue that we must turn our attention

Source: Abridged from 'Feminist change in a patriarchal organization: the experience of women's initiatives in local government and implications for feminist perspectives on state institutions', *The Sociological Review* (1992), pp. 155–85. Oxford: Blackwell Publishers.

inwards and examine the organizational forms and social relations *within* state institutions. I will briefly summarize some feminist theoretical debates on the relationship between gender relations and state institutions, demonstrating some major weaknesses in the debate to date. I will then describe the inter-action of women's initiatives with local state organizations using empirical material from two local authorities. Women's initiatives have encountered a number of *general* features common to local government organizations which make the implementation of *any* change difficult. But there are specifi-cally *gendered* structures and relations within local government organizations which make the implementation of positive changes for women especially difficult. I will conclude by drawing out some of the wider implications for understanding the ways in which organizations are gendered and for feminist perspectives on the state.

THEORETICAL PERSPECTIVES ON THE STATE

There is a long and diverse history of theoretical perspectives concerning the nature and role of state institutions and their relationship to wider society. Despite well-debated differences between the more influential per-spectives—Liberal, Marxist, New Right—they share certain common features. First, few contain any analysis of gender. Second, most have gendered assump-tions and implications embedded firmly within them (see Franzway, Court and Connell, (1988) for an excellent review).

Feminists reject this gender-blind view of state institutions on both empirical and theoretical grounds (see Showstock-Sassoon, 1987; Franzway, Court and Connell, 1988; Walby, 1990). Historical and contemporary ana-lyses of state policies and practices demonstrate beyond question that these have had—and continue to have—gendered implications in everyday life. For example, policies on childcare, employment, policing and taxation all have different implications for men and women, reinforcing gender roles which are not only distinct but are also unequal (Wilson, 1977; Barrett, 1980). The theoretical basis for rejection of gender-blind perspectives on the state lies with rejection of the common idea that society can be divided into distinct and discrete public and private portions. Layers of connected dichotomies are embedded within this division: public/private; social/natural; political/apo-litical; male/female. Were this to be accepted, women would be confined to the private sphere, and politics and the state would have no connection with gender relations, and supposedly private matters such as sexuality, domestic violence or childrearing. Feminist theory exposes this distinction as an arti-ficial and patriarchal construction (Gamarnikow *et al.,* 1983; Elshtain, 1984).

The implications of this revelation for theoretical perspectives on the state are two-fold. First, state policies can be seen to enter the supposedly private sphere and to shape supposedly natural gender roles in this sphere. For example, the division of labour in the household whereby women are largely responsible for domestic labour and childcare is shaped, *inter alia*, by government's choice not to provide affordable childcare. State policies and practices also affect gender divisions in the public sphere. Here the child-care example is important again, as is successive governments' reluctance to set 'equal pay for equal value' or 'comparable worth' precedents for women's pay (Equal Opportunities Commission, 1988). Second, and at the same time, state policies and practices maintain a false division between public and private. A clear example of this is state policy on violence against women. Domestic violence is still widely seen as a private matter, whilst women are literally confined to the private sphere through fear of attack on the streets—in part, they are confined because of police advice to women to protect themselves by staying at home and also because of inadequate policing on the streets (Hanmer and Saunders, 1984).

Beyond this theoretical foundation, feminist perspectives on the state diverge, most commonly as a result of disagreement over theorization of gender inequality, but also because of differences in the theorization of the nature and role of state institutions themselves. [. . .]

Liberal perspectives view gender inequality as the result of individual cases of discrimination combined (sometimes) with the existence of sex-role stereotyping in education and the labour market. Through the removal of these stereotypes, and legislation outlawing discrimination, it is believed that the state will be able to fulfil its proper function as the upholder of equality between all citizens. The introduction of women's initiatives into local gov-ernment could be a prime strategy for the achievement of this objective. Once women's interests are properly represented at the level of the state the male bias will successfully be redressed. Most other perspectives reject the essen-tially atomistic conception of gender inequality in liberal theory, as well as the notion that the state is, in principle at least, a neutral arbiter over con-flicts in society. Both Marxist-feminist and radical feminist perspectives call on an analysis of socio-economic power relations and integrate the role of state institutions into the long-term survival of capitalism, or patriarchy, or both. Whilst Marxist-feminism and radical feminism differ fundamentally in their analysis of gender inequality, both perspectives view state institutions as instruments in the hands of a dominant interest, capital or men.

[. . .] Difficulties stem from the functionalism of such perspectives and the drawbacks inherent in this are well exemplified when we turn to analyze local government women's initiatives. Functionalist perspectives pay little attention to political struggle, and assume that 'the state' is a monolithic, all-seeing, all-knowing corpus, which will always act in the most advantageous way possible for existing power relations. In practice, complex and com-peting political pressures are constantly levelled at state institutions (Walby, 1990). Dualist perspectives on gender inequality point to the tension between capitalism and patriarchy, and the competing pressures which this creates on the state (Eisenstein, 1984; Walby, 1990). There are also competing pressures from within capitalism and patriarchy themselves, from trade unions and employers, from feminists and anti-feminists. All these competing pressures may, under certain circumstances, influence state policies and practices. Local government women's initiatives were set up largely as the result of pressure from feminist women organized in the Labour Party (Halford, 1989b). Thus they provide an example of successful political pressure put on the state by feminists. [. . .]

Can we hail women's initiatives as the end of the male-biased state (the liberal view) or must we reject them as a patriarchal strategy (the functionalist view)? In fact, most feminist commentators have preferred to adopt a 'wait and see' stance. This is symptomatic of the problematic nature of the state for feminists. On the one hand, the implication of state policy and practice in gender inequality is irrefutable. On the other hand, many feminist goals can only be met by state institutions. It was in recognizing the power of the state to address issues such as the provision of affordable childcare, abortion on demand, free contraception, and action on violence against women that the feminists in the Labour Party pressured for change and the setting up of women's initiatives in local government (see Halford, 1989b). [. . .]

To move on we have to accept that it is simply not credible to view the diverse set of institutions that comprise the modern democratic state as unitary or rational and in pursuit of clearly defined single strategies. State policies and actions are 'not simply a reflex response to the functional needs of a system' (Franzway, Court and Connell, 1988, p. 35) but should be seen as the outcome of specific social struggles. State institutions *themselves* are the result of social struggles. There have been some policies and laws which benefit women (for example, extension of the franchise, legalization of contraception and abortion or the Equal Pay and Sex Discrimination Acts). But overall, the modern state represents the institutionalization of male power arising from a history of social struggle. This position allows us to reject functionalism without recourse to pluralism.

To take the point further, the institutionalization of male dominance does not simply mean that state policies and practices reflect gender relations which only exist somewhere else, i.e. in society outside the state. Rather, gender relations (and those of class and race) are articulated *within* state institutions (cf. Franzway, Court and Connell, 1988). In this sense, state institutions are themselves a node in the network of gender relations (Franzway, Court and Connell, 1988).

Where does this revised perspective leave us as far as women's initiatives are concerned? We would still not expect that action by certain local governments will bring about the end of patriarchal gender relations, since gender inequality is not caused solely, or even mainly, by state actions. However, moving away from functionalism we can see that local state institutions may *in principle* bring about some positive changes for women. Whether they do or not is another question. The ability of particular women's initiatives to implement change is shaped by a variety of factors including resources, political commitment and leadership and the degree and nature of political mobilization in the local area. My research has shown the extensive and powerful influence which local government organizations have in shaping the implementation of change by women's initiatives. In part this lies with a general tendency to resist *any* change, although women's initiatives have suffered particularly from this because of the organizational form which they have taken. But beyond this there is clear evidence of powerful, pervasive and *specific* resistance to positive policies for women. This lies in the gendered dynamics of local government structures and cultures. Paradoxically however, both general and gendered dynamics in local government may, under certain circumstances, 'flip-over' from resistance to *support* for positive gender policies. This is not common, but I will discuss the possibilities as they arise.

THE PLACE OF WOMEN'S INITIATIVES IN LOCAL GOVERNMENT ORGANIZATIONS

Women's initiatives (WIs) have been set up to promote the interests and welfare of women. This means analyzing the gendered content of existing policies, devising new positive policies and implementing them. Sometimes the initiatives are restricted to looking at employment by the local authority, but more often they are charged with examining all areas of local authority activity covering both employment and service delivery. The scope which most WIs have been given clearly means that they are not able to devise and implement all the policies alone. Most commonly, WIs have been placed in central, co-ordinating locations within both councils and local authority organizations. From this position, WIs may devise policies for implementation elsewhere in the authority and/or act as co-ordinators and monitors of current practice and new policy developments across the authority. The WIs themselves have no responsibility for actual employment (beyond the handful of women's officers employed) or for service delivery (beyond the occasional administration of small grants to voluntary sector women's groups). This means that WIs have to get the *rest* of the local authority to change. The degree to which different WIs are able to achieve this varies. In what follows, I will describe the dynamics of both change and resistance to change in local government organizations, using material from case study research carried out between 1988 and 1990.

In total, ten case studies were carried out[1] and my argument below draws generally on material from all these studies. But I shall refer in detail to the two major studies: the London Borough of Haringey and Manchester City Council. These two studies were chosen to explore in detail the dynamics of policy implementation by local government WIs. [. . .]

First, I shall outline the meaning of the term 'bureaucracy' as a background for describing and analyzing the interaction of WIs with bureaucratic local states.

LOCAL AUTHORITIES AS BUREAUCRATIC ORGANIZATIONS

The emergence of the term 'bureaucracy' was closely connected to the development of modern state organizations. [. . .]

The best known and most influential account of the characteristics of bureaucracies was produced by Max Weber. Weber's model emphasized the following features:

- a specialized division of labour;
- a hierarchy of authority with a clearly demarcated system of command and responsibilities;
- a formal set of rules and procedures governing operations and activities, co-ordinating behaviour in a predictable, uniform and impersonal manner;
- a body of full-time, permanent officials, appointed according to technical competence, trained in specialized tasks, paid according to rank in the hierarchy and able to develop careers on the basis of their ability and seniority.

[. . .] Weber regarded bureaucracy as the most *efficient* and *rational* form of organization, stressing the virtues of:

> . . . precision, speed, unambiguity, knowledge, continuity, discretion, unity, strict subordination, reduction of friction and of material personal costs. (Weber, 1968, p. 973)

Weber's model identifies many significant characteristics that remain strongly associated with state organizations, including local government organizations, today. This leaves us with a problem. If local state organizations function in the efficient and rational manner identified by Weber, how can we explain the widespread yet qualitatively uneven influence that these organizations have on the implementation of positive policies for women?

Two major criticisms of Weber's account are as follows: first, the features identified by Weber do not necessarily equal 'efficiency'; second, Weber's concentration on the formal organizational characteristics of bureaucracies misses the informal dynamics which exist and without which we cannot understand the operation of bureaucratic organizations (see Albrow, 1970; Jackson, 1982). Morgan (1986) helpfully suggests that Weber's 'machine' model of bureaucracy is just one metaphor with which to approach the study of organizations. Morgan presents seven further metaphors (for example, organizations as 'organisms', as 'brains', and as 'political systems'). He argues that we cannot choose one approach and reject all others. Rather, different perspectives should be critically employed as appropriate, in order to analyze different questions and different organizations. Hence, although local authority organizations *do* undoubtedly bear a strong resemblance to Weber's ideal-type bureaucracy, it is to the criticisms and alternative metaphors that we must turn in order to analyse the processes of organizational support and resistance in the implementation of positive policies for women.

INTRODUCING CHANGE INTO BUREAUCRATIC ORGANIZATIONS

Bringing about change in bureaucratic organizations is not easy. Resistance to organizational change is endemic as empirical research on major changes in large organizations has clearly shown (Argyris, 1967; Johns, 1973). It is suggested that the more bureaucratic an organization is, particularly the finer the division of labour in it and the more hierarchical it is, the more there will be resistance to change (Crozier, 1964). The experiences of WIs provide evidence of two *general processes* of organizational resistance to change: empire building and organizational inertia.

Empire building

In both Haringey and Manchester it was widely suggested that centralized WIs have had difficulties influencing the activities of other authority departments. This is partly due to the physical distance of central policy units from other departments, and the generalized nature of WIs compared with day-to-day departmental work. Making inroads into departmental work in this context is difficult. However, these general problems are compounded by the prevalence of 'empire building'.

Functional specialism, a fine division of labour, is one of the fundamental characteristics of a Weberian bureaucracy and is a significant feature of local authority organizations today. It ' . . . creates a structure that is supposed to be a system of co-operation, but often turns out as a system of competition' (Morgan, 1986, p. 37). Empire building means competition between departments. In the context of limited funding, competition arises for resources. Individual departments naturally want to secure as many resources as possible in order to fulfil their function. However, what is sensible behaviour for one department does not necessarily benefit the whole organization, as competition for resources results in insularity and low levels of co-operation (Morgan, 1986). A further cause of empire building stems from the career strategies of managers within particular departments. The hierarchical organization of local authorities is also a career ladder for employees, and expanding the size, scope and status of a department enhances career opportunities.

Professionalization of administration is another of Weber's bureaucratic characteristics. Local authority management largely remains the province of professionals: individuals trained and awarded qualifications by major professional associations/institutes, [...] but with little training in management or public administration. The local authority professional:

> ... like all professional experts ... will tend to believe that his ability and expertise enable him to provide solutions to all the problems with which he is confronted and he will be reluctant to accept that experts in other disciplines, or for that matter councillors, have anything useful to contribute to the solution of these problems.
>
> (Elcock, 1982, p. 96)

Local authorities have therefore tended to '... remain in essence loose confederations of semi-autonomous empires' (Smith, 1966, p. 29). This makes the implementation of corporate policy rather difficult. [...]

It is likely that empire building is a common feature of most British local authorities. Certainly it was present to some extent in all the ten authorities researched by this author (Halford, 1991). But in the London Borough of Haringey the level of empire building was particularly severe and widely cited as a major problem for the WI (interviews with author, 1988–9). Departments in the organization are highly insular, with little communication between them. Indeed, an internal report into management problems in the borough concluded that the authority was suffering from a 'policy vacuum filled by bargaining and fiefdom' (Lansley, 1990, p. 115). The central position of the women's unit makes it difficult to get information. What communication there is, is distrusted since 'information is power. No-one wants to tell anyone anything else. If you *do* hear something you assume it's false' (ex-chair of Haringey Women's Committee, June 1988).[2] The WI rarely gets reliable information and its ability to analyze the situation across the authority, and what action should be taken, is severely impeded. [...]

Departments are resistant to intervention by the centrally located women's unit for several reasons. Fundamentally, where an empire is under construction, demands that it be built differently are not welcome! In Haringey the demands came from a unit with few resources and, therefore, low bureaucratic status. Women's units may be further weakened by the non-professional status of women's officers. This may undermine the respect with which professional managers regard such officers. There is also the objective problem that altering the policies and practices of particular departments may require detailed professional knowledge. [...] Arguments from the departments that women's officers do not know the details of policy implementation may simply indicate an unwillingness to co-operate. In Haringey the women's unit was deliberately located in the chief executive's department, supposedly the nerve-centre of a local authority. But in this case the department was weak and ineffectual. The problem was so bad that one chief officer remarked:

> If you have people in that location then you set them up to fail ... If
> you'd set out to chart a way to make something start out as badly as
> possible, that's how you'd do it.   (December 1989)

Empire building in Haringey has also *led* to some departmental initiatives on women's equality. Paradoxically, these developments confirm the
operation of departmentalism. In-department initiatives have taken place
unevenly in Haringey, but *always independently* of the WI. Thus women's
equality work has itself become an empire-building strategy. Whether or not
this happens depends on whether the issues are seen to enhance departmental
status. [...] The major departmental initiatives in Haringey have taken place
in the Planning and Housing Departments. Both are professional areas that
were radicalized in the 1970s and in which women's equality work may have
some status.

The take-up of women's equality work in Manchester City Council's
departments was also uneven. Most developments have taken place in the
Education Department, largely as the result of committed individuals in a
supportive professional context. Manchester experimented with departmental
equal opportunities officers for a short time, whereby extra equalities officers
were located in mainstream departments in order to encourage departmental
ownership of equal opportunities. The results are instructive. Apart from
Education (where a Women's Education Team of three officers was set up)
the results were minimal. Different explanations are suggested for this, but at
a general level these concern the inability of one isolated officer to change
a department, especially in those cases where there was open hostility to
the promotion of women's equality work. In one case opposition was
so fierce that the officer was badly harassed and resigned after a few
months. [...]

Bureaucratic inertia

The second general explanation for resistance to change within local authorities is the *inertia* that exists in large bureaucratic organizations. Some writers
suggest that organizations noted for their security and stability of work functions (which despite major upheavals still included local government in the
1980s) will attract employees

> ... motivated by the desire for security and stability, qualities clearly
> associated with personal rigidity and resistance to innovation.
>   (Johns, 1973, p. 68)

These so-called mechanistic personalities may be one explanation for bureaucratic inertia, although it seems unwise (not to mention inaccurate) to assume
that all local authority workers fall into this category!

A more satisfactory explanation lies with the problems of educating people
to change their behaviour and the fear of failure—two factors that pervade

bureaucratic structures. WIs require officers to revise the way they discharge their functions and to take the initiative in adapting policies and practices to take account of the interests of women. However, bureaucratic structures do not provide a good context for this kind of evaluation and learning process. Morgan (1986) suggests three explanations. First, in highly fragmented structures information and knowledge are restricted both horizontally (as we have seen with empire building) and hierarchically. Yet without information and knowledge people are unable to learn and re-evaluate. [...] Second, the accountability placed on individuals in the division of tasks produces defensiveness, making people unable to deal with uncertainty. Anything new is 'strange and threatening, surrounded by uncertainties' (Johns, 1973, p. 50). In a context where information and knowledge are restricted and people are uncertain as to what is actually expected of them, the tendency is to oversimplify. Thus people are 'interested in problems only if there are solutions at hand' (Morgan, 1986, p. 90). The development of women's equality work is unlikely to be compatible with this simple task orientation. Last, where there is uncertainty the impulse may be to claim action where there is none. [...]

Organizational inertia should not be accepted as inevitable, and Morgan cites practical strategies that can be employed to overcome organizational learning difficulties. [...] Morgan warns:

> ... there is a danger of overlooking important conflicts between the requirements of learning and self-organization on the one hand and the realities of power and control on the other.   (Morgan, 1986, p. 108)

Allowing officers to re-evaluate their work and initiate change threatens the power of those in control. Further, changing an organization means changing attitudes and values. This cannot be a simple technical matter. Organizational inertia is reinforced by the attitudes and values that currently prevail. An essential element of this concerns the *gendered* attitudes and values which are present in local authority organizations. Bringing about *any* change in a local authority bureaucracy is difficult. Bringing about changes that challenge the gender order of local authority organizations is far more difficult still.

GENDER RELATIONS IN BUREAUCRATIC ORGANIZATIONS

Weber suggested that impersonality, together with an emphasis on technical competence in the appointment of staff, and the presence of rules and procedures would rid organizations of social and individual biases and prejudices. [...] He stressed the removal of personal attributes, placing the emphasis instead on skills and standardized rules and procedures. This remains a common conception of how bureaucracies function and has been employed as a lever by liberal feminists in their campaigns for equal opportunities. Equal opportunities employment policies emphasize, above all, the importance of excluding personal considerations, preconceptions and prejudices based on race, gender, sexuality or physical ability, in favour of the impersonal application of uniform rules of assessment. Where it is assumed that local authorities *should* function in this impersonal way, claims for modification to iron out aberrations can be difficult to reject.

This is one of the planks of Weber's perspective that has been most thoroughly and convincingly criticized. It has been argued that the personal attributes of employees continue to shape bureaucratic organizations, and that even the most rule-bound structure allows scope for personalized actions and judgement. Despite the widespread acceptance of these points, most organizational theory continues to treat *gender* as marginal and/or incidental to the workplace (Pringle, 1989). In what follows, I will argue that gender relations and gendered interests are, in fact, thoroughly embedded in local authority organizations, and that it is only by re-conceptualizing local authority organizations in this sense that we can understand the operation of organizational resistance to implementation of positive policies for women.

Formal and informal structures

The formal structure of local authority organization is not depersonalized in the way that Weber indicated. Pringle (1989) suggests that the dominant discourse of 'rationality' in the formal structure of organizations is one important aspect of this. Weber's view of bureaucracy implicitly relies on a public—private division of society. He separates ' ... the public world of rationality and efficiency from the private sphere of emotional and personal life' (Pringle, 1989, p. 86). It is feminist exposure of the patriarchal basis of this dichotomy that provides a specific foundation on which to build a model of bureaucratic organizations that includes gender relations. [. . .]

Belief in the discourse of rationality and separation of the so-called 'private' from the supposedly 'public' local authority may be one basis for resistance to women's equality work. WIs explicitly challenge the 'public' rational image of local authority organizations, making it clear that gender is a significant dimension of all areas of organizational life. This makes people uncomfortable. WIs challenge conventional notions of what local authorities should be involved in. A common response to WIs is that it is unnecessary for them to get involved in women's equality, and not what local authorities should spend their time and money on. [. . .]

In fact it is common knowledge that all sorts of informal practices and events take place within the supposedly formal and rational structure of organizations. Indeed, it is now widely accepted that, in addition to the formal structure of bureaucracies elaborated by Weber, all organizations have *informal* structures (Selznick, 1964). [. . .] Selznick argues that in every organization, goals are modified (abandoned, deflected or elaborated) and that this is effected through the informal structure. An informal structure arises partly from the inability of *any* organization to specify rules and procedures down to the *n*th degree. Organizational rules are incomplete guidelines within which individual judgement must operate (Bendix, 1949). This element of 'individual judgement' is absent from Weber's model, but bureaucrats are not depersonalized automatons! [...]

Interests, prejudices and fears shape the actions and practices of officials in the absence of complete guidelines. [...] Once we accept that staff bring their personal interests into organizations, and that these shape the way they discharge their functions, we must also accept that *gendered* perceptions, practices and attitudes will be present too. To varying degrees, women's initiatives challenge the patriarchal gender relations within local authority bureaucracies. In the rest of this section I will consider in more detail the ways in which male interests are embedded in local authority organizations and the ways in which this affects the implementation of positive policies for women.

Individual interest in organizations

Morgan (1986) suggests that decoding the personal agendas underlying informal actions and activities in organizations depends on understanding the way in which the following three areas of interest interconnect: organizational task, career, extra-mural interests (see Figure 16.1). The implementation of women's equality work may interfere with any of these interests. The introduction of positive policies for women requires that individuals re-evaluate their actions and practices. Thus the 'organizational' task is altered, requiring new and/or extra work perhaps over a long period of time. The interests of individuals in an organization—both men and women—may well be against such alterations, particularly the need to take a long-term and overall perspective rather than just to tick off specific tasks to be carried out.

Second, there is the question of career interests. Hierarchical local authority organizations are also career ladders. The pyramid shape of the hierarchy means that the numbers of opportunities diminish towards the top. The typical pattern of men's and women's employment in local authorities displays a strong tendency for women to be concentrated towards the bottom of the hierarchy, whilst the top echelons are almost exclusively male (Stone, 1988). Normally, then, the competition for promotion up the career ladder takes place between men, and this intensifies towards the top of the ladder. Equal opportunities employment policies aim (amongst other things) to increase the number of women competing for senior jobs. Thus, a successful equal opportunities employment policy would intensify competition, diminishing opportunities for individual men even further. Men's career interests may, therefore, be served by opposing the entry of women into senior jobs. [...]

FIGURE 16.1. Individual interests in organizations. *Source:* Morgan (1986).

But the relationship between career interests and positive policies for women is not so simple. The development of women's equality work may become *part* of a career strategy. In departments where a positive attitude to women's equality work prevails, or in professions that have taken the issues on board, career mileage may actually be gained by the implementation of positive policies for women. Another complication is the attitude of those women who are already in senior positions. They do not always support equal opportunities employment policies for women, referring to their own success under the current system. There also appears to be a fear that women's credentials and skills will be undermined if they are seen to be receiving special treatment. [. . .]

The third and final area of individual interest in Morgan's model is 'extra-mural' activities. [. . .] In many ways it is the most interesting category. Equal opportunities employment policies often make direct links to 'extra-mural' activities/responsibilities, in particular childcare. It is recognized that because of the sexual division of labour in the household, women will not be able to compete in the workplace without childcare provision. So WIs promote policies that enable women to combine career and extra-mural activities as well as a variety of policies and campaigns that challenge women's inequality in all areas of life and encourage women to fight inequality. Because WIs may challenge gender relations in all areas of life, they may well also challenge the extra-mural interests of men. Johns (1973, p. 60) argues that: 'people oppose change if their social relationships, their status or their security are threatened.' Johns (1973, p. 62) goes on to state that employee reaction to organizational change will be affected by 'any perceived threat to his status in the family'. By encouraging women to fight inequality, along all dimensions of patriarchal gender relations, WIs may be perceived as a threat to male status in the family and to civil society more generally. An example of this came from one officer in Haringey who described a common male reaction to the WI as 'fine so long as their wives didn't find out about it'!

Thus we can see that WIs may run counter to the individual interests of men or women in any of the three interest categories described by Morgan. This is a useful starting point but it is rather simplistic and requires development in a number of ways.

Organized male interests in bureaucracies

There are three principal forms of organization through which collective male interests tend to be represented in local authority organizations: these are the trade unions, the professions, and the senior managers group which (supposedly) co-ordinates all authority activity.

The role which trade unions have had as representatives of organized male labour is now well documented (see Walby, 1987). Although women are increasingly unionized, they remain less likely to hold official posts and the particular interests of female-dominated occupations and of women generally remain less likely to be addressed. The response of local authority trade unions to positive policies for women varies by union and by geographical location. In general, manual unions are less supportive and white collar unions more so. Where there is a strong and recent tradition of organized male labour dominating local politics there is also likely to be more resistance to equalities policies (see Halford, 1989b, on Sheffield). Trade unions can disrupt the adoption of new policies during negotiations over changes to employment practice. [. . .] The situation appears to improve when women take on official posts, as the unions' national organizations begin to address equalities issues, and as new generations of members, particularly women and black people, begin to make new demands on the grounds of race and gender.

Professionals dominate local authority management (Elcock, 1982). The term 'professional' implies objectivity, rationality and technical occupational expertise. However, this hides a gendered reality. Professionalism is a means by which entrants to an occupation can be controlled. Witz (1990) argues convincingly that we must abandon any generic notion of profession as a state, and refer rather to professional projects. [. . .]

Witz shows how medical occupational groups dominated by women (for example, midwives) were engaged in professional projects but were denied the status by male-dominated state institutions. Furthermore, she argues, seeking professional status has often been a project of occupational exclusionary closure with gendered dimensions. For example the history of law and medicine shows clearly that professionalization deliberately excluded women. There are other informal ways in which professions effectively exclude women. Training may take many years, requiring extensive evening and weekend work, and often takes place when the trainee is in his/her twenties. Of course it is possible for women to undertake this commitment, but since women may well have children at this stage in their life cycle, the likelihood of having time for professional training is less than is the case for men who tend to bear less domestic responsibility.

Paid work typically performed by women is less likely to have achieved professional status; women have been formally excluded from occupations with professional status; and, gender divisions of labour make women less likely to be in a position to achieve professional status. Thus, it is hardly surprising that the number of women amongst local authority managers, who are overwhelmingly professionals, is low.

Professional institutions also regulate the *practice* of professionals in the field. Those professionals are trained to perform tasks in certain ways, prioritize particular factors and so on. The creation of professional practices and norms is gendered too. For example, separation of the so-called 'private' and 'public' spheres of home and (paid) work became one of the key principles of land-use planning in the postwar period. This rested on inherent assumptions about the household and the division of labour, in particular, the assumption that there would be a full-time paid worker and a full-time domestic worker. In fact this

> ... organization of urban land use tends to benefit employed men with wives, at the expense of both married and single women struggling to run homes, care for children and, in greater and greater numbers, also manage a part-time job.
>
> (Women and Geography Study Group, 1984, p. 46)

Women's employment opportunities are limited by physical accessibility and compounded by the planning of transport routes around full-time workers making simple home-to-work-and-back-again journeys, not the complex routes women perform in order to combine paid and unpaid work. There are numerous other examples of the way in which professional norms and practices institutionalize gender differences and assumptions (see, for example, MacKinnon, 1983, on law; Matrix, 1984, on architecture).

Professions are not static in terms of members or practices and norms. The number of women in professional occupations is increasing, and the nature of professions is changing. [...] It is certainly the case that some professions particularly associated with local authorities became radicalized in the 1970s. According to Gyford (1985) these professions formed a crucial element of the 'New Left' which emerged around local government in the early 1980s.

At a general level, equal opportunities developments are more likely in some local authority departments than in others. Engineering, Environmental Health and Direct Works (dominated by crafts not professions) are all unusual sites for development. By contrast, developments in Housing, Social Services and Education are far more common. There is, however, no guarantee that transformations in a profession will be uniform across all local authorities. Whether or not new professional discourses are taken up depends on whether managers have had exposure to new ideas (connected to age) as well as on personal dispositions and council politics.

A final grouping of male interests present in local authorities is rather different from the previous two. Each local authority department has a chief officer. Usually these chief officers meet on a regular basis to discuss corporate policy. The power of individual senior managers is multiplied in this group which forms the very heart of the organization. According to Michels, one of Weber's early critics, every organization is in fact run by a few leaders. Michels spoke of the 'iron law of oligarchy' and argued that this small group of leaders

> ... will put their own interests first and work to preserve the bureaucratic procedures which have all the character of efficiency and certification and which keep them at the top.   (Smith *et al.*, 1982, p. 183)

There is no rule that chief officers *have* to be men or that they must all be hostile to equality policies! In fact, the number of female chief officers is increasing. But in 1985 there were only 50 women chief officers in the whole of the UK (Stone, 1988).[3] Chief officers are usually male, white, middle-class and at the peak of their career. They are commonly older and less likely to have been affected by the new professional ideas discussed above. The chief officers' group can then represent the very bastion of organizational resistance to change. Whether this is actually the case will vary according to individuals, council politics and the ability of council politicians to control the chief officers' group.

Gendered cultures

It is not credible to suggest that all individual men consciously or explicitly pursue the patriarchal career and/or extra-mural interests described above. Some may do, but focusing on strategic individual interests will not illuminate all the gendered processes that exist in organizations. In order to understand patriarchal resistance to organizational change, we need to consider more subtle gender dynamics. One way of approaching this is to consider the way in which the culture of organizations is gendered. The masculine bias of 'rationality' as a basis for organizational culture is one aspect of this. Indeed, some have even suggested that the discourse of rationality which surrounds bureaucratic organizations makes for a more stable form of male domination than other forms of patriarchy which rely on power being vested in the hands of individual men in the household. It is the apparent neutrality of bureaucracies hiding the gendered interests served by them that bestows this potency (Pringle, 1989).

Perhaps surprisingly, a well-documented aspect of this concerns the nature of sexuality in organizations (Hearn and Parkin, 1987; Hearn *et al.*, 1989; Pringle, 1989). A Weberian perspective leads us to believe that sexuality is private and hence absent from the public workplace. This line of argument simply cannot be sustained. Brenda Jones sums this up well: 'Sex is like paper-clips in the office: commonplace, useful, underestimated, ubiquitous' (quoted in Pringle, 1989, p. 84).

Feminist exposure of the widespread occurrence of male sexual harassment of women in the workplace is the most obvious example of the gendered power of sexuality in organizations. [. . .] Sexual harassment can take place in varying degrees, and it can be argued that there is an almost seamless join with broader organizational culture as this comment from Hearn and Parkin claims:

> Male managers with female subordinates may use sexuality, harassment, joking and abuse as a routine means of maintaining authority. This may be thoroughly embedded in the taken-for-granted culture of the organi-zation.   (Hearn and Parkin, 1987, p. 93)

(Hetero) sexuality is embedded within organizations in a diversity of ways (see Cockburn, 1991; Adkins, 1992), but sexuality is not the only gendered aspect of organizational culture. We need also to consider the gendering of status, power and control both formally and informally, as well as the presence of wider ideological constructions of masculinity and femininity.

Where individuals are able to use their own judgement and make deci-sions independently of specified procedures—in the informal structure—it is likely that they will rely on informal 'norms' based on shared meanings, understandings and values (Morgan, 1986). These are shaped by the cultural context in which the organization exists, in this case, a patriarchal society. For example, where two candidates are equally qualified for a job/promotion, after the formal procedures have been exhausted the decision as to whom to appoint will depend on such nebulous factors as 'Will this person fit in?' or 'Can I work with this person?' [. . .]

A study of executive life in the Swedish public sector demonstrates clearly the way in which male norms operate at this stage, when it is men who are making the decision (Ressner, 1987). For example, in executive life the communication of information is essential but Ressner's study shows male executives to be more satisfied communicating with socially uniform people. Women, Ressner (1987, p. 48) argues, are therefore not 'legitimate and natural recipients of information'. [. . .]

Ressner's study provides an excellent basis for understanding the hidden hierarchy of gendered informal structures in organizations. In particular she illuminates the way in which the operation of the hidden hierarchy varies at different levels within organizations. In contrast to the executive example above, she shows how the lack of a career ladder and development prospects affects low-level office workers, who are almost exclusively female. This is partly a problem for the formal structure of organizations, which could be altered to provide more opportunities. However, Ressner also shows how the existing formal structure affects women's self-esteem. Lack of change makes them afraid of change, therefore less likely to apply for new jobs and therefore less likely to build successful careers. Ressner quotes one woman worker:

> The treatment you get as a clerical worker doesn't improve your self con-
> fidence, it does just the opposite ... If you're a clerical worker, you're
> marked for life—you behave like a skivvy because you're treated like one,
> and this narrows you down. It's a vicious circle.
>
> (Ressner, 1987, p. 25)

Ressner draws our attention to variations in the nature of gendered attitudes and practices throughout an organization. This point is also important
in respect of departmental differences. Both the intermediate and major case
studies described in this article showed some departments in particular local
authorities to be especially reactionary or sexist, whilst others were especially progressive or innovatory. Commenting on *sub*-corporate cultures
Morgan says:

> In organizations there are often many different and competing value
> systems that create a mosaic of organizational realities rather than a
> uniform corporate culture.   (Morgan, 1986, p. 127)

Why do differences exist in the gendered culture of different local authority
departments? One explanation may be differences in the degree of male dominance in department personnel. [...] Another reason may be the level of
staff turnover. A common reason cited for Haringey Personnel Department's
lack of interest in equal opportunities was that the same managers had been
in post for many years and had not been affected by recent changes in the
personnel profession which incorporate equal opportunities as 'good professional practice'. This suggests that the nature of professions may be important
in shaping the differences that exist between departments in the take-up of
women's equality work.

CONCLUSIONS

The story of organizational resistance and opposition to change in the two
local authorities described above is not an unusual one. Research in a further
eight local authorities *and* a national survey of all local authorities with
women's initiatives have both clearly pointed to organizational resistance
and opposition as major problems in the implementation of new policies
to address the needs and interests of women (Halford, 1989a; 1991). What
implications do the experience of women's initiatives in local government
have for broader understandings of gender, bureaucracy and the state?

[...] Impersonality, rationality, technical specialism and the dominance of

rules and procedures are characteristics still closely associated with bureaucratic organizations (especially local authorities) by the public and even by
those who work within them. Yet gender is centrally located even within
the confines of this Weberian perspective, for example within notions of
rationality and/or the definition and operation of technical expertise. Furthermore, few non-Weberian perspectives on bureaucracy recognize the
implicitly gendered nature of *all* the alternatives they suggest. Feminists
have not been blind to the gendered nature of bureaucracy. Some have
suggested that feminism and bureaucracy are inherently in opposition to
one another (Ferguson, 1984). More pragmatically, women's initiatives have
often been set up to work according to non-bureaucratic principles, following
from the women's movement, and creating a feminist space within male local
authority bureaucracies. On a day-to-day basis this objective has met with
some success—at least in the operation of women's initiatives themselves. In
challenging the broader bureaucratic structures there has been far less success.
This is not surprising. If a major obstacle to change lies with the structure and
practice of local government organizations, then trying to change those
organizations will meet with certain resistance.

Understanding the gendered nature of bureaucratic local government
organizations is essential to any consideration of the potential that local
government women's initiatives have to implement change. Dismissing
women's initiatives as a functional strategy by 'the patriarchal state' to
demobilize and disempower feminism is not credible. Some politicians and
officers may indeed behave in a tokenistic manner and/or hope that they
can 'co-opt' feminist activism into local state structures and thus silence independent criticism of policy and practice. But 'the state' as a whole has neither
clearly defined goals to this end nor the textbook strategies to achieve them as
implied by the more functionalist perspectives. Conversely, all the empirical
evidence indicates that state institutions are not monoliths blindly serving
particular interests. [. . .]

A revised organizational perspective demonstrates the operation of gendered power relations within state institutions, and it is in this sense that
those institutions can be understood as patriarchal. The historical form of
the organizations, the people who work in them, and the political structures
too, cannot be separated from the social relations of gender (and those of class,
and race and sexuality) that exist in society more generally. *But* what happens
in state organizations is not simply a *reflection* of what happens outside. The
scope of activities that concern local state institutions (for example, education,
planning and design, and health) means that policies and practices also *shape*
gender relations.

This perspective transcends the functionalism of pioneering feminist
theoretical perspectives. It allows proper consideration of the complex and
contradictory nature of political struggle and the modern democratic welfare
state, *without* rejecting the operation of gender power relations within those
institutions.

Acknowledgements

I am grateful to the ESCR for their support of this research.

Thanks are due to Simon Duncan, Tony Fielding, Mike Savage, and all the people who agreed to be interviewed during the course of my research, as well as to all who helped with finding and interpreting council minutes and official reports.

Notes

1. These were: Cambridge City Council, London Borough of Camden, Derbyshire County Council, London Borough of Haringey, Kirklees Metropolitan District Council, Manchester City Council, Nottingham City Council, Redditch District Council, Sheffield City Council and the London Borough of Wandsworth.
2. Unless otherwise specified all local authority interviews were carried out by the author.
3. There are 500 plus local authorities in the UK, each with at least six chief officers.

References

Adkins, L. (1992) Sexual work and the employment of women in the service industries. In M. Savage and A. Witz *Gender and Bureaucracy*. Sociological Review Monograph. Oxford: Blackpool.

Albrow, M. (1970) *Bureaucracy*. London: Pall Mall Press.

Argyris, C. (1967) Today's problems with tomorrow's organisations. *Journal of Management Studies*, February.

Barrett, M. (1980) *Women's Oppression Today*. London: Verso.

Bendix, R. (1949) *Higher Civil Servants In American Society*. Colorado: University of Colorado Studies.

Cockburn, C. (1991) *In the Way of Women: Men's Resistance to Sex Equality in Organisations*. London: Macmillan.

Crozier, M. (1964) *The Bureaucratic Phenomen*. London: Tavistock.

Eisenstein, Z. (1984) *Feminism and Sexual Equality*. New York: Monthly Review Press.

Elcock. H. (1982) *Local Government: Politicians, Professionals and the Public in Local Authorities*. London: Methuen.

Elshtain, J. (1984) *Public Man, Private Woman: Women in Social and Political Thought*. Oxford: Martin Robertson.

Equal Opportunities Commission (1988) *From Policy to Practice: A Strategy for the 1990s*. Manchester: EOC.

Ferguson, K. (1984) *The Feminist Case Against Bureaucracy*. Philadelphia: Temple University Press.

Franzway, S., Court, D. and Connell, R. (1988) *Staking a Claim: Feminism, Bureaucracy and the State*. Cambridge: Polity.

Gamarnikow, E., Morgan, D., Purvis, J. and Taylorson, D. (eds) (1983) *The Public and the Private*. London: Heinemann.

Gyford, J. (1985) *The Politics of Local Socialism*. London: George Allen and Unwin.

Halford, S. (1989a) Local authority women's initiatives 1982–8: the extent, origins and efficacy of positive policies for women in British local government. Urban and regional working paper 69, University of Sussex.

— (1989b) Spatial divisions and women's initiatives in British local government. *Geoforum*.

— (1991) Local politics, feminism and the local state: women's initiatives in British local government in the 1980s. Unpublished PhD thesis.

Hanmer, J. and Saunders, S. (1984) *Well Founded Fear.* London: Hutchinson.

Hearn, J. and Parkin, W. (1987) *'Sex' at 'Work': The Paradox of Organisation Sexuality.* Brighton: Wheatsheaf.

Hearn, J., Sheppard, D.L., Tancred-Sheriff, P. and Burrell, G. (1989) *The Sexuality of Organisation.* London: Sage.

Jackson, P. (1982) *The Political Economy of Bureaucracy.* London: Phillip Allen.

Johns, E. (1973) *The Sociology of Organisational Change.* Oxford: Pergamon.

Lansley, S. *et al.* (1990) *Councils in Conflict.* London: Macmillan.

MacKinnon, C. (1983) Feminism, Marxism, method and the state: towards a feminist jurisprudence. *Signs* 8 (4), 635–58.

Matrix Book Group (1984) *Making Space: Women and the Man-made Environment.* London: Pluto.

Morgan, G. (1986) *Images of Organisation.* London: Sage.

Pringle, R. (1989) *Secretaries Talk.* London: Verso.

Ressner, U. (1987) *The Hidden Hierarchy: Democracy and Equal Opportunities.* Aldershot: Avebury.

Selznick, P. (1964) An approach to a theory of bureaucracy. In L. Coser and B. Rosenberg (eds) *Sociological Theory.* New York: Macmillan.

Showstack-Sassoon, A. (ed.) (1987) *Women and the State.* London: Hutchinson.

Smith, M. *et al.* (1982) *Introducing Organisational Behaviour.* London: Macmillan.

Stone, I. (1988) *Equal Opportunities in Local Authorities.* London: HMSO.

Walby, S. (1987) *Patriarchy at Work.* Cambridge: Polity.

— (1990) *Theorising Patriarchy.* Oxford: Blackwell.

Weber, M. (1968) *Economy and Society.* Berkeley: University of California Press.

Wilson, E. (1977) *Women and the Welfare State.* London: Tavistock.

Witz, A. (1990) Professions and patriarchy: gender and the politics of occupational closure. *Sociology* 24 (4), 675–90.

Women and Geography Study Group of the IBG (1984) *Geography and Gender.* London: Hutchinson.

17 UNHOLY ALLIANCES: THE RECENT POLITICS OF SEX EDUCATION

RACHEL THOMSON

Sex education both constructs and confirms the categories of 'normal' and 'deviant' which it regulates, monitors and controls. Sex education is a particularly resonant intersection of power/knowledge

(Thoroughgood, 1992).

'Education' reflects the dominant politics of a society's institutions, and sex education reflects the sexual politics of those institutions. The debates that have surrounded the process of defining a 'national curriculum', particularly in the areas of English and history, illustrate the ways in which hegemonic definitions of education, culture and knowledge are contested. The processes that have contributed to contemporary definitions of sex education are also born of contestation.

This article is about institutional sexual politics and hegemonic discourses. It is also about activism: the processes by which the social movements of feminism, gay liberation and AIDS activism have impacted on the institutions and discourses that structure the aims and imperatives of school sex education. In particular it focuses on the intersection and shifting configuration of two institutional discourses that address sex and sexuality in the public sphere, public health pragmatism and the moral authoritarianism of conservative education philosophy.

I will argue that these two approaches—sexual health and sexual moralism—are increasingly coming into conflict, the former stressing the distinction between sexually healthy and sexually unhealthy practices, the latter between the morally legitimate and the morally illegitimate. As Jeffrey Weeks (1985, p. 4) notes, sex is a contested zone, a moral and political battlefield. School sex education is one of the key sites in which this battle is played out. State schools not only provide an environment enabling universal access to the under-16 'population', but schools are also public arenas in which hegemonic or 'official' representations of personal and public morality are expressed. As such, schools are key sites for both social engineering and social control.

The year 1992 saw the publication of two important government policy documents of relevance to personal, social and sex education in schools. On one

Source: Adapted from Bristow, J. and Wilson, A.R. (eds) (1994) *Activating Theory* (pp. 219–45). London: Lawrence and Wishart.

hand the Department of Health (1992) published *The Health of the Nation* which identified sexual health as one of five key areas to be targeted for inter-vention. On the other, the Department for Education (DFE, 1992) published *Choice and Diversity: A New Framework for Schools*. This document attempts to define the nature of the 'spiritual and moral development' of students, a quality that schools will be required to demonstrate to the newly reformed school inspectorate (OFSTED, 1992). There is a fundamental dichotomy between these two approaches to the aims of school sex education held by government departments. Should school sex education be used as an oppor-tunity to communicate knowledge and skills to enable young people to make their informed decisions, or should it be used as an opportunity to impose a prescriptive model of sexual and personal morality?

I will trace some of the recent key points in the development of public policy in the area of sex education and in doing so try to outline some of the tensions within this very public form of sexual politics. I will conclude by considering the opportunities that exist for contemporary sexual politics and activism to contribute to the politics and practice of school sex education. In particular I will argue that progressive sexual politics should be aware of the significance of 'unholy alliances' of discourse and be prepared to engage strategically in unfamiliar discursive territory.

ORIGINS

Historically the evolution of public policy around sexuality mirrors wider social anxieties concerning nationhood, social change and social stability.[1] Historians have shown that the origins of school sex education lie in mor-alist and eugenic concerns around the breakdown of the family, the changing role and expectations of women, the purity of the race and the differential birth rate between social classes (Mort, 1987; Bland, 1982; Weeks, 1981). The aims of school sex education have never been to help young people have sat-isfying and fulfilling sexual relationships.

The biological legacy identified by all major studies of sex education (Schofield, 1965; Farrell, 1978; Allen, 1987), can be seen as a product of these origins. The imperatives of sex education were two-fold, firstly, to address the negative consequences of sexual behaviour (disease, pregnancy), and secondly to reinforce normative definitions of appropriate sexuality (sex within marriage). The biological model enables the pathology of sex to be explored while leaving the broader social dimensions unquestioned. Such an approach also focuses on the girl and the woman, both in terms of reifying her reproductive capacity and by placing upon her the responsibility for policing the 'natural' sexual excesses of men (Thomson and Scott, 1991; Hudson, 1984; Fine, 1988).

EQUAL OPPORTUNITIES: THE IMPACT OF THE NEW SOCIAL MOVEMENTS

During the 1970s and early 1980s the social movements of feminism, anti-racism and gay liberation began to make an impact on education in the form of equal opportunities and anti-racist philosophies (Troyna, 1987; Arnot, 1985; Haringey Council, 1988). In the absence of any constitution or bill of rights these philosophies helped to construct the rights of minority and oppressed groups in anti-discrimination and positive images strategies. In the area of sex education this was marked by a move beyond the bio-logical model of sex education to social or rights-based interventions which attempted to educate against prejudice. During this time we saw initiatives such as the ILEA (Inner London Education Authority) sexuality project, and a number of positive image exercises in the area of lesbian and gay sexuality such as the video *A Different Story*. Research undertaken at this time by the London Lesbian and Gay Teenage Group for the first time made visible the experiences of lesbian and gay pupils at school (Trenchard and Warren, 1984). The underachievement of girls and ethnic minority students in the education system became increasingly acknowledged and tentative attempts began to be made to redress social inequality through education (Burchell and Millman, 1989; Weiner, 1985).

Participatory and consciousness-raising models of education originating in the new social movements began to influence work undertaken with young people. We find an increase in group work and experiential learning methodologies and the genesis of anti-sexist work and girls' groups in youth clubs. Teachers, influenced by the new social movements were undertaking anti-sexist and anti-racist work within the classroom. Schools, like the wider society, began to respond to some of the challenges and changes brought about by the sexual politics of the times.

During this time education about sex and personal relationships generally took place in an *ad hoc* way there being no formal curriculum framework within which sex education was taught (Farrell, 1978; Allen, 1987). Yet there was a growing consensus in educational practice and philosophy as to the value of developing young people's critical abilities and communi-cation skills, particularly those of young women. While formal 'biological' sex education usually appeared in science lessons, increasingly attempts were made to address broader decision-making skills in personal and social edu-cation (PSE) and other areas of the curriculum (see Doggett, in Allen, 1987; Reid, 1982).

THATCHERISM, PARENT POWER AND THE IMPOSITION OF A MORAL FRAMEWORK

It is impossible to understand the policy changes that affected sex edu-cation through the 1980s in isolation from the general ideological project of

Thatcherism, with its construction of new political constituencies and shifts in power from local to central government.

One of the ideological centre-pieces of Thatcherism was the identification of the family as the unit of society and the construction of parents as a mythical political constituency, a 'discourse of familialism' (Franklin, Lury and Stacey, 1991), or what in education has come to be called 'parent power'. In Margaret Thatcher's own words 'there is no such thing as society', only individuals and families. In effect, by giving mythical rights to mythical parents, real rights and powers were taken away from those who had been represented within the equal opportunities discourse. In education this meant an attack on the power and influence of local education authorities (LEAs) and the appearance of increased powers to school governors and parents. What actually took place was an unprecedented transfer of power to central government and the Department of Education (Coulby and Bash, 1991).

In many ways the Thatcherite revolution in education was expressed as a revolution against the philosophy and practice of equal opportunities which became caricatured as 'the permissive society'. Anti-sexist and anti-racist education were targeted for amplification and vilification by the media and the government in the lead-up to plans for transforming education.

The two planks of the Thatcherite assault on the state of education were: to undermine parental trust in the teaching profession and to discredit the role of local education authorities. As others (Davies, Holland and Minhas, 1992; Hardy and Vieler-Porter, 1992) have noted, an appeal to popular racism and homophobia were key elements in the process by which some LEAs acquired the stigma of Loony Left. This label in turn played a critical role in galvanizing public support for a generalized attack on the education system. The media circus that surrounded the book *Jenny Lives with Eric and Martin*, culminating in Section 28 of the Local Government Act which prohibits LEAs from 'promoting homosexuality' was essential in enabling the government to mobilize popular support for wholesale changes in the nature and organization of the education system.

Sex education has not only been deeply affected by the changes that have swept state education in the last few years, but, alongside anti-racist education, sex education has provided one of the focal points through which public support for these wider changes has been rallied. The press and the government together succeeded in convincing the public that the enemy within lay in the schools and the LEAs, and that political indoctrination if not sexual corruption was taking place in the classroom (Scruton, Ellis-Jones and O'Keefe, 1985).

SEX-TION 28: THE ENEMY WITHIN

The two most significant pieces of legislation to affect sex education during this period are the Gillick ruling on contraceptive advice to under-16s, and Section 28 of the Local Government Bill, which makes it an offence for a Local Authority to 'promote homosexuality'. Both of these pieces of legislation drew on public and parental fears concerning the sexuality of young people and questioned the degree to which teachers should be allowed professional discretion to respond to young people's needs for confidential advice and guidance. Significantly, neither Section 28 nor the Gillick restrictions on the giving of contraceptive advice to under-16s in fact apply to the teaching of sex education in schools (Children's Legal Centre, 1989). Nevertheless the media contribution to the Section 28 debate had the effect of undermining parents' confidence in the ability of teachers to undertake this task.

Section 28 in particular was a key cultural and symbolic event in the recent history of sexual politics. At a time of increasing public awareness of child sexual abuse and male violence within the home, the moral panic that surrounded the legislation helped to deflect attention from the 'health' and 'normality' of the family (Stacey, 1991). More directly it played an important role in undermining the professionalism and in policing the politics of teachers. The phrase 'the promotion of homosexuality' had the insidious effect of constructing teachers as the potential corruptors of young people. Despite the popular rhetoric of familialism and the sovereignty of the family the vast majority of parents were in fact keen for schools to provide teaching in this area.[2]

The Section 28 controversy also had a significant effect on the agenda of sex education itself. By constructing homosexuality as the symbolic 'other', a biological and reproductive model of sexual relations was reinforced. The inclusion of sexual identity in sex education potentially challenges the traditional biological approach that excludes a whole range of non-reproductive aspects of sexuality, masculinity and feminity. It could be argued that by implying that a particular sexual identity could be 'promoted' Section 28 'was an implicit response to many feminist ideas and practices which had gained a certain foothold' (Stacey, 1991, p. 296).

The net effect within education of both Section 28 and the Gillick ruling on contraceptive advice has been to create a climate of paranoia around the teaching of sex education. While neither should directly impact on the teaching of sex education they both encourage self censorship and caution. (Stears and Clift, 1990; Sex Education Forum, 1992). Progressive teachers who once took the lead in sex education and PSE have become increasingly nervous about what it is safe to teach; others see it as an opportunity to avoid discussing more challenging aspects of sex education.[3] Ironically, research with young people suggests that they are more interested in questions of sexual identity than any other areas of sex education.[4]

Neither the Gillick ruling nor Section 28 were genuine responses to the educational challenge of sex education, nor to the needs of the young people whom education should serve. Rather they are examples of the way in which school sex education has been used to address the interests and anxieties of an adult society unable to contemplate the existence of adolescent sexuality. Throughout the 1980s sex education was the subject of a disproportionate amount of parliamentary and media attention (Meredith, 1989). By utilizing the concept, if not the reality of parent power and by mobilizing parental fears concerning corruption in the classroom, sex education was effectively isolated from the rest of the curriculum. Educational professionals were no longer trusted to exercise their professional judgement in this area. By rejecting teachers' professional expertise, the educational philosophies that informed their practice were also marginalized. Equal opportunities philosophies were replaced by a 'common sense' discourse of family values, closely allied to the concept of parental choice and the centrality of the family as the unit of society. The disbanding of ILEA in 1990 sounded the death knell for equal opportunities philosophies in education. ILEA had been at the forefront of curriculum and staff development in PSE, health and sex education as well as in anti-racist and anti-sexist strategies for the classroom. With its demise the confidence and status that had slowly accrued to this area of the curriculum was dissipated. The focus and energy of activism by this point began to move away from education, and driven by the emerging crisis of HIV/AIDS, began to move towards health and the HIV/AIDS voluntary sector.

THE 1986 EDUCATION ACT: GOVERNOR CONTROL

The 1986 Education Act removed from LEAs the responsibility for, or control over, school sex education, and placed it for the first time in the hands of school governors—an explicit attempt to provide sex education with inherently conservative gatekeepers. School governors were required to consider whether sex education should form part of the curriculum, and if they decided it should, to produce a written statement on the form and content of that curriculum. This policy statement should then be made available to parents. Although parents were not granted the right to withdraw their children from sex education lessons, governors were given the discretionary power to allow students to withdraw if parents had religious objections. The 1986 Education (No. 2) Act further required teachers, governors and LEAs to ensure that: 'Where sex education is given ... it is given in a manner as to encourage those pupils to have due regard to moral considerations and the value of family life.'

Although school governors were entrusted with control over the sex education curriculum they were not trusted to develop a moral framework for that curriculum. In 1987, the Department for Education issued guidance to school governors on their new responsibilities for sex education, setting out a moral framework within which sex education should be taught.

> Teaching about the physical aspects of sexual behaviour should be set within a clear moral framework in which pupils are encouraged to consider the importance of self-restraint, dignity and respect for themselves and others, and are helped to recognise the physical, emotional and moral risks of casual and promiscuous sexual behaviour. Schools should foster a recognition that both sexes should behave responsibly in sexual matters. Pupils should be helped to appreciate the benefits of stable married life and the responsibilities of parenthood. (DES, 1987, p. 4)

This guidance went further than the requirement to encourage pupils to have 'due regard to moral considerations' laid out in the 1986 Act. Circular 11/87 (DES, 1987) gives specific directives on the way in which sex education should be taught with particular reference to the teaching of 'controversial' subjects such as abortion, AIDS, homosexuality, contraception and the use of outside speakers:

> It is important to distinguish between, on one hand, the school's function of providing education generally about sexual matters ... and, on the other, counselling and advice to individual pupils particularly if this relates to their own sexual behaviour. Good teachers have always taken a pastoral interest in the welfare and well-being of pupils. But this function should never trespass on the proper exercise of parental rights and responsibilities. On the specific question of the provision of contraceptive advice to girls under 16, the general rule must be that giving an individual pupil advice on such matters without parental knowledge or consent, would be an inappropriate exercise of a teacher's professional responsibilities, and could, depending on the circumstances amount to a criminal offence.
> (DES, 1987, p. 5)

In effect, Circular 11/87 constructed a model for the teaching of sex education which was knowledge-based, legalistic and excluded any understanding of inequality, diversity or social change. It was primarily concerned with delineating a 'traditional' model of family life and normative sexual relations and paid no attention to practical teaching methods or the reality of young people's needs and lives. By selectively defining 'controversial issues' the circular constructed sex education as inherently problematic territory and thereby provided a framework of surveillance rather than practical support. The language of the circular is deliberately exclusive, not only of lesbian and gay students or children of lesbian and gay parents, but all of those students who do not live in stable nuclear families. Speaking of homosexuality the guidance notes:

> There is no place in any school in any circumstances for teaching

which advocates homosexual behaviour, which presents it as the 'norm'
or which encourages homosexual experimentation by pupils. Indeed,
encouraging or procuring homosexual acts by pupils who are under the
age of consent is a criminal offence. It must also be recognised that for
many people, including members of religious faiths, homosexual practice
is not morally acceptable, and deep offence may be caused to them if the
subject is not handled with sensitivity by teachers if discussed in the
classroom.   (DES, 1987, p. 4)

While the guidance recognizes the rights and sensibilities of conservative
minorities it ignores the rights and opinions of those who hold more progressive and critical views as to the 'value of family life'. In contrast to the
inclusive nature of equal opportunities philosophies which aimed to embrace
and respect the diversity of society, this framework prescribes an exclusive
model of the family and sexual relationships in relation to which the majority
are seen to fail.[5] Although the guidance does not have statutory status, and
school governors are free to decide their own moral framework and policy
guidelines, in the absence of alternative interpretations this circular has had
a significant impact on the way in which school sex education is perceived
by school governors and teachers.

THE NATIONAL CURRICULUM: DISCOURSES
IN COLLISION

The public health discourse, from which school sex education partly origi-
nates, was given renewed impetus in the late 1980s by the advent of
HIV/AIDS. Although the public health discourse or the epidemiological
model of sexual health has many hidden values (Patton, 1990; Aggleton
and Norton, 1989), it is based on a pragmatic approach to the issue of sex
education. Where moral authoritarianism is primarily interested in securing
a traditional definition of sexual relations within the educational institution,
public health prgamatism is concerned to get information to students and
to affect their behaviour. The present disjuncture between the Departments
of Health and Education surrounding the implementation of *The Health of
the Nation* (with the former setting statistical targets for teenage pregnancy
reduction and the latter concerning itself with pupils' spiritual and moral
development), is testament to the differing objectives of their respective
ideologies.

These tensions can also be seen in the conflicts surrounding sex education
within the National Curriculum. The 1986 Act succeeded in isolating sex
education from the rest of the curriculum by giving school governors the
responsibility to decide whether it would appear in the curriculum, and if
so in what form. In doing so, education about sex and sexuality appeared
to be excluded from the commitment in the 1988 Education Reform Act

to provide all students the entitlement to 'a broad and balanced curriculum' and to prepare 'pupils for the opportunities, responsibilities and experiences of adult life'.

The changes brought about to sex education in the form of the 1986 Act took place before widespread public acknowledgement of the threat of HIV and AIDS. With the introduction of the National Curriculum, some aspects of sex education, particularly the reproductive and disease components, were included in the science curriculum.[6] Although school governors supposedly had control over what sex education was taught, their powers in this area were compromised. It was clearly felt that irrespective of rhetoric about parental and governor control of the sex education curriculum it was necessary to provide a safety net of basic information in the interests of public health. In 1991, the National Curriculum Science orders were revised to include HIV/AIDS at Key Stage 3 (11–14 years). The revision, made after consultation with key agencies in the field, recommended that HIV/AIDS was such a serious threat to public health that it could not be left to governors to decide whether it should be taught. Another example of public health pragmatism overriding the rhetoric of parent power and the supposed sovereignty of the family.

The contradictions in the Government's policy of governor control of sex education and the requirements of the National Curriculum had not attracted attention, but the inclusion of HIV in the National Curriculum was picked up by the right wing and religious lobbies which began a concerted campaign for the right of parents to remove their children from National Curriculum classes. In the House of Lords debate that ensued, one peer stated:

> In my view the order is yet another erosion of parental rights. It is the sacrifice of a parent's rights to guide the moral well-being of their children and it is sacrificing it to the newest politically correct attitude. Members of this House and another place then wonder why parents want to slough off their responsibilities when the state tells them they may not have a conscience about what is taught to their children in our schools on matters of sex and sexual morality. As I say it is little wonder that parents are becoming concerned about the state's attitude towards their ability to bring up their own children. The parent's charter that was put before the electorate at the last election, specifically provides that there should be choice. Where is the choice here to the parents as to whether their children should be taught in accordance with their own views and concepts? The right is being taken away from them and there is no conscience clause.
>
> (Lord Stoddard of Swindon, *Hansard*, 11 June 1992, p. 1436)

The ambiguous government response to such remarks illustrates the precarious balancing act that the DFE found itself performing in an attempt to negotiate the conflicting imperatives of public health pragmatism and moral authoritarianism. Thus Baroness Blatch, Minister of State for Education, said:

> There will occasionally be areas where those two interests, the secular and the religious, to some extent overlap. The current case is one. There are strongly held and irreconcilable views. After careful consideration of the issues, the Government have taken the line that they should follow the broad principles that parliament agreed should be enshrined in the 1988 Education Reform Act: that the curriculum should fully prepare all pupils for the challenges and problems, as well as the opportunities, which their adult lives will present; and that to this end all pupils are entitled to receive a broad, comprehensive curriculum. To create rights of exemption from the secular curriculum would not in my view be in the interests of securing an effective, broad education for every child. That must be our first concern. However I must repeat that the teaching of sex education and HIV within national curriculum science must, and I repeat must, have due regard to moral considerations and the value and promotion of family life.
>
> (Baroness Blatch, *Hansard*, 11 June 1992, p. 1460–1).

Under Thatcherism, sex education was politicized and used in an opportunistic way for broader political ends. The legacy for sex education has been that its 'recent' evolution has been determined more by the consequences of "moral panics" than rationalization' (Meredith, 1989, p. 2). The instrumental deployment of the 'discourse of familialism' also brought into being a political alliance of the moral right. With the growing public health crisis of HIV/AIDS we find the Government hoist on the petard of its own rhetoric and increasingly at the mercy of an unrepresentative moral lobby.

THE RISE OF RELIGIOUS MORALISM

The campaign to establish a parental right of withdrawal from National Curriculum sex education illustrates the conflicting and shifting forces at play in public policy on school sex education. The campaign, led by a fundamentalist Christian sect called the Plymouth Brethren, and culminating in the debate in the House of Lords quoted above also demonstrates the rising influence on the Government of a brand of religious moralism.

In the absence of a discourse of equal opportunities, religion is playing an increasingly important role in educational debate over the nature of school sex education. The impetus for this rising influence is rooted in a number of factors including developments in multi-cultural politics, the close relationship between religion and education in the British education system, and the increasing influence of American style moral lobbies. The National Curriculum Council has published guidance to schools on 'spiritual and moral development' yet refuses to publish the finding of the NCC Working Group on Multi-cultural education. Increasingly, ethnic groups are becoming identified as religious groups and we slip semantically from a commitment to multi-culturalism to an awareness of multi-faith issues.[7]

The arrival of John Patten, practising Catholic and self-avowed moralist (Patten, 1992), at the Department for Education has clearly encouraged the growth of this tendency. Secretary of State for Education Kenneth Clarke treated some 400 letters of complaint from the Plymouth Brethren with indifference: to Clarke the Brethren were just a minority group to be ignored in the face of public health pragmatism. With a change of Minister the same 400 letters came to symbolize serious political pressure. It is clear that the conservative religious lobbies were aware of a powerful ally in Mr Patten, as Baroness Phillips said:

> I was delighted when my friend mentioned Soddom and Gomorrah. If you want to see evidence of global warming and all the other events which are happening, you only have to reread the Old Testament, the literature about the fall of the Roman Empire, if you want to be a little more up to date, or the fall of the Greek Empire. Those accounts include greed, perversion and all matters which will become prevalent in our society if we are not very careful ... We do not want to become threatening, but parents feel very strongly about these matters. Rather unfashionably some of us have tried to voice these issues. I know that the Minister [Baroness Blatch] is a woman of great understanding. We hope that if she cannot give us the answers, she will at least pass on the questions to her noble friend. After all, Mr John Patten is a very good practising Catholic. How does a Minister think? Does one put one's conscience or one's job first?
>
> (Baroness Phillips, *Hansard*, 11 June 1992, p. 1440)

Baroness Phillips' hopes appear to have been well placed. The recent White Paper, now Education Bill, *Choice and Diversity: A New Framework for Education* identifies the reduction of truancy and the spiritual and moral development of students as the future direction of educational policy.[8] Significantly this document does not specifically address sex education, yet it does address the development of moral values. The development of moral autonomy, decision making and social skills had previously been the territory of that part of the curriculum known as PSE. With the introduction of the National Curriculum, PSE disappeared, to be replaced by the non-statutory cross curricular themes. In direct contrast to the child-centred methodologies characteristic of the PSE curriculum, *Choice and Diversity* argues that values should be imposed on young people and that these values are not negotiable. Where PSE aimed to enable young people to explore and define their *own* values, *Choice and Diversity* actually proposes what those values should be. This prescriptive moralism goes beyond the 'familial discourse' of Thatcherism where moral authoritarianism was tempered by radical liberalism. Parents, it appears, are no longer to be trusted to instil the correct set of values within the sphere of the family:

> In a variety of ways and across a range of subject areas, young people should always be taught that, in addition to rights and expectations, they also have important duties and responsibilities to their community. They should be encouraged to be involved members of those communities, to grow up as active citizens. They should be taught the importance of developing a strong moral code that includes a concern for others, self-respect and self-discipline, as well as basic values such as honesty and truthfulness. Schools should have and should communicate a clear vision of those things they and the community hold to be important. The transition from dependent child to independent adult, imbued with these moral codes and values, should be the aim of every school and teacher. Most do this very well and are to be warmly congratulated on it. Some struggle to do it, or fail—sometimes because of the indifference of parents or the surrounding community.   (*Choice and Diversity*, p. 6)

The tone of these passages point to a growing disjuncture between education and health philosophies in the area of teaching methods. Teaching methodologies are currently hotly contested within education. The Government has been forthright in its support for 'traditional' teaching methods despite near universal opposition from teachers and educationalists. Applied to PSE, or moral education, traditional methods will mean that students are to be *told* what is right and what is wrong. This not only flies in the face of what educational theory and practice knows of personal and social development but also of recent developments in health education which place importance on identification, participation and ownership in the learning process.

While school sex education comes under the auspices of the Department for Education it is obvious that the targets identified in *The Health of the Nation* of reducing pregnancies in the under-16s by 50% and gonorrhea rates by 20% will be impossible to meet without significantly improving provision. Yet at precisely the time that the Department of Health was looking to the Department for Education to move forward on sex education, the Department for Education withdrew funding from Health Education Co-ordinators—key figures in the local co-ordination and support of sex and HIV/AIDS education. Meanwhile, the increasing development of finances and managerial responsibility to schools under local management of schools removes from LEAs responsibility for and means to advise, support and monitor school sex education (Sex Education Forum, 1992).

A survey by the Association of County Councils (1993) into the future provision of local support in the area of health, drugs and sex education concludes:

The action of central government in withdrawing funding from this particular area of activity directly contradicts the objectives set out in central government's key strategic document *The Health of the Nation*. The action by the Department for Education in withdrawing this funding runs contrary to central government's pronounced aspirations to develop prevention for young people as one of its key themes and activities. It would appear that whilst asking local organisations to co-ordinate their activities there is significant lack of co-ordination within central government itself. (Association of County Councils, 1993)

The Department of Health may want to help schools provide effective sex education, but it is not clear how far they will cross the Department for Education in order to enable this actually to take place, or to what extent they are prepared to compromise the ethos and methodology of such interventions. It may be easier for the Departments of Health and Education to agree on abstention ('just say no') programmes rather than on interventions that aim to empower. Again, the net result of this conflict is that policy and resources are caught up around struggles over definition and control rather than in supporting teachers and improving provision.

ACTIVISM: INFLUENCING THE AGENDA

In this article I have mapped the range of official discourses that define and constrain the nature of school sex education. These discourses are not static and their changing configuration both opens and closes windows of opportunity to influence the sex education debate. They can interact to reinforce, constrain and temper one another, giving rise to both unexpected and unholy alliances. The language of policy cannot be taken simply at face value but needs to be placed in political context and in relation to other competing official discourses. When understood in the context of the reorganization of education, the moral authoritarianism of Thatcherite educational philosophy can be seen as a means to a specific political end (the destruction of the LEAs) and, to a certain extent, as tempered by the radical liberalism of 'parent power' and the pragmatism of the public health discourse. However, the contemporary conjunction of public health pragmatism and religious moralism may prove to be a more constraining configuration. In the light of this shift I will argue that the moral agenda should not be left to the domination of the religious Right, but that progressive sexual politics should engage in this increasingly dominant discourse and challenge its framework of authoritarianism.

The focus on policy and the language of the public sphere in this article may be somewhat misleading in that it obscures the degree to which these official discourses are contested from within, as well as the ways private discourses of sexuality and sexual morality may have a far greater impact on young people's lives and awareness. It could be argued that the inclusion in

TV programmes, such as the HIV/AIDS issues in *East Enders*, teenage pregnancy in *Home and Away* and lesbianism in *Brookside*, has more cultural significance than the entire legislative framework for school sex education. Those with knowledge of schools will also know that the gap between official policy and actual school practice can be enormous. Nevertheless, I hope to have shown that public discourses are significant and that the political and policy pressures on school sex education over the last ten years have been constraining and have hindered curriculum developments and innovation.

Those innovations that have taken place in sexual health education have been mainly in the field of public health and community education. The advent of HIV/AIDS created a close relationship between public health and the voluntary sector, which has spearheaded the introduction of a number of progressive health education initiatives, promoting client-centred approaches and empowerment strategies (Hamilton and Lynch, 1992; Rhodes and Hartnoll, 1991; MESMAC, 1992). Innovations in this area have also been encouraged by the contribution of social research into sexual behaviour and HIV/AIDS. Such research challenges the increasingly idealized public discourse of sexual moralism, and by bringing evidence of the rules and conduct of intimate relations into the public sphere encourages the 'personal to be made political' (Watney, 1991). The identification of a gap between knowledge of sexual risks and actual behaviour has placed issues of power, control, and sexual identity tentatively on the public health agenda. (McKeganay and Barnard, 1992; Holland *et al.*, 1991a; Weatherburn *et al.*, 1992; Wight, 1992).

The key to influencing policy-making within the discourse of public health has been effectiveness—whether an initiative works (i.e. actually affects behaviour). Moral and religious sensibilities are seen as relevant where they are factors enhancing or blocking the communication of health education messages. These factors are seen as significant as aspects of individuals' identities rather than as ideologies to be promoted in themselves. Yet clearly, this neutral pragmatism is equally open to progressive and reactionary influences. Public health support for progressive tendencies is skin deep, a support born of pragmatism rather than of principle. The recent decision by the Department of Health to veto an HEA public awareness campaign on sexual health on the grounds that it may be 'offensive to the public' suggests that the tide may have already turned (*Independent*, 29 January, 1994).

The ideological terrain of education is characterized by a concern with principle rather than pragmatism. Whether this be in the form of equal opportunities philosophies, 'parent power' or religious moralism, schools are institutions where the transmission of dominant social values is the primary aim. As the notes accompanying the DES AIDS video say, just because a sexual act is safe it 'does not mean it is morally acceptable or desirable' (Baker, 1988). Ironically, the opportunity for activism in education may now lie in turning moral rhetoric into educational practice. Although the Right controls the official moral framework for sex education, it has been unable to translate this hegemony of rhetoric into educational practice. Morals cannot simply be taught or imposed, 'morality' can only be made visible, modelled and enabled.[9]

However uncomfortable progressive sexual politics feels with the language of morality, it may be precisely this area which it is best equipped to address. The gap between knowledge and behaviour, between social and sexual identity, is also the arena of moral autonomy and empowerment. For sex education to be meaningful it needs to address and develop moral autonomy and to do this it needs to address power and interconnecting relationships of power (Holland *et al.*, 1991b). Participatory and empowerment methodologies which creatively engage young people are coming to be recognized as having greater and more lasting impact than those which are morally prescriptive. Learner-centred methodologies such as role play and peer education, where young people define and address their own agendas around sexual health, are beginning to make an impact in education. And there is an increasing awareness that social and decision-making skills can only be developed actively through participation, reflection and debate.

Yet there continues to be a gulf between the public agenda of sex education as defined by 'gatekeepers' and policy-makers and the needs and opinions of young people. Research into young people's attitudes and behaviour has uncovered widespread dissatisfaction with the approach and emphasis of school sex education (Thomson and Scott, 1991; MORI, 1990) and initiatives involving young people have found them to be forceful critics of policy-makers in their own right (National AIDS Trust, 1991). The emergent discourse of children's rights in social policy potentially challenges the paternalistic character of the current sex education agenda.[10] For progressive sexual politics to make a meaningful contribution to contemporary school sex education it is necessary to act strategically, to engage in the moral discourse but to challenge the authoritarianism that constructs sex education around the twin poles of 'just say yes' or 'just say no'. Rather than fall into a trap of fighting for the alternative, though equally prescriptive, agenda it would be more effective and more honest to champion an agenda which grows from an acknowledgement of the reality of young people's needs, centred on empowerment and skills development.

POSTSCRIPT

The 1993 Education Act: the parental right of withdrawal

In the Spring of 1993 the Department for Education issued draft guidelines on sex education for consultation. However, before the end of the consultation period, the guidelines were to be rendered redundant by an effective parliamentary ambush in the House of Lords. Amendments to the Education Bill calling for a parental right of withdrawal from sex education were introduced in the House of Lords. A combination of an absent Secretary of State for Education, the support of Baroness Blatch, the complicity of the Department of Health and the temerity of the Labour Party, led to the introduction of a government amendment to the Act at third reading.

This amendment called for all non-biological aspects of sex education (including education about contraception, STDs and HIV) to be removed from the National Curriculum, for sex education to become a compulsory requirement of secondary education and for there to be established a parental right of withdrawal. Despite widespread opposition from educationalists and the voluntary sector the amendment was passed without debate in the Commons in July 1993, to become effective from August 1994. The Department for Education is yet again consulting on guidelines to be issued to schools. Concerns that the requirement for sex education to become a compulsory part of the secondary curriculum being met by a single 'one off' lesson have been alleviated by the recommendation of the Dearing Review that sex and careers education should receive 2.5% of curriculum time (approximately one lesson per week).

Notes

1. Speeches delivered as part of the 1992 House of Lords debate on the inclusion of HIV/AIDS in the National Curriculum show how similar contemporary concerns about social stability continue to dominate public debate in this arena. Speaking of the DES booklet *HIV/AIDS: A Guide for the Education Service*, one peer observed: 'To ram some of the rest of that amoral booklet down the throats of even 14-year-olds especially girls, would be a deeply immoral act ... I have here some material which I understand is widely used in schools. The thought of forcing that material down 14-year-old Muslim girls seems to me to be asking for riots.' (Lord Pearson of Rannoch, *Hansard*, 11 June 1992, p. 1452).

2. Allen (1987) found that an overwhelming 96% of parents supported school sex education.

3. Rubin (1984) describes parallel examples of the surveillance of teachers in the United States.

4. A survey of more than 7,000 16–18 year olds found that while 87% had learnt about puberty at school and 83% pregnancy, only 18% and 14% respectively, had learnt anything about homosexuality and lesbianism. When questioned as to which subjects, they felt their schools had given them insufficient information, 8% mentioned puberty and 11% pregnancy, while 45% mentioned homosexuality (MORI, 1990).

5. The imposition of a prescriptive framework in the area of sex education is mirrored by the imposition of a prescriptive model of 'cultural and national identity' in the curriculum, in the form of the requirement of the 1986 Act for collective worship to be wholly or partly Christian.

6. Sex education also appears in the National Curriculum as part of health education, a non-statutory cross curricular theme (i.e. it is not tested and does not

have to be taught by law). Due to the non-statutory nature of cross curricular themes, it is questionable whether it will be taught.

7. This is particularly true in the area of sex education, where equal opportunities in the area of gender is increasingly being superseded by a requirement that sex and health education messages be 'culturally appropriate'. See Amin (1992); Ali (1992); Haw (1991).

8. It is worth noting that *Choice and Diversity* selectively aims to promote students' spiritual and moral development, and fails to address the full entitlement to 'spiritual, moral, social and cultural development'.

9. The production of the first 'abstinence' video on sex education by CARE, launched in February 1994, marks the beginning of the involvement of the moral lobbies in curriculum matters.

10. Article 13 of the United Nations Convention of the Rights of the Child establishes children's right of access to education about health (see Newell, 1991). The Children Act (1989) also requires that young people are consulted and involved in decisions that affect their lives. There is growing concern that much of the recent education legislation is in contradiction to the ethos of the Children Act.

References

Aggleton, P. and Norton, M. (1989) Perverts, inverts and experts: the cultural production of an AIDS research paradigm. In P. Aggleton, G. Hart and P. Davies (eds) *AIDS: Social Representations, Social Practices*. Basingstoke: Falmer Press.

Ali, Y. (1992) Muslim women and the politics of ethnicity and culture in northern England. In G. Saghal and N. Yuval-Davis (eds) *Refusing Holy Orders: Women and Fundamentalism in Britain*. London: Virago.

Allen, I. (1987) Education in sex and personal relationships. PSI Research Report No. 665.

Amin, K. (1992) Values conflicts in a plural society: the case of sex education. *The Runnymede Bulletin* 257 (July/August), 6–8.

Arnot, M. (ed.) (1985) *Race and Gender: Equal Opportunities Policies in Education*. Oxford: Pergamon Press.

Association of County Councils (1993) *Health Education Co-ordinators — LGDF Survey Results*. London: ACC.

Baker, N. (1988) Facts versus morals: guidelines on sex education. *Times Educational Supplement* 3747, 18–19.

Bland, L. (1982) 'Guardians of the race' or 'vampires upon the nation's health'? Female sexuality and its regulation in early twentieth-century Britain. In E. Whitelegg *et al.* (eds) *The Changing Experience of Women*. Oxford: Martin Robertson.

Burchell, H. and Millman, V. (eds) (1989) *Changing Perspectives on Gender: New Initiatives in Secondary Education*. Milton Keynes: Open University Press.

Children's Legal Centre (1989) *Section 28 and Sex Education: Children's Right to Know*. London: Children's Legal Centre.

Coulby, D. and Bash, L. (1991) *Contradiction and Conflict: The 1988 Education Act in Action*. London: Cassell.

Davies, A., Holland, J. and Minhas, R. (1992) *Equal Opportunities in the New ERA* (Second edition). London: Tufnell Press.

Department of Health (1992) *The Health of the Nation: A Strategy for Health in England*. London: HMSO.

DES (Department of Education and Science) (1987) Sex education at school. Circular No. 11/87.

DFE (Department for Education) (1992) *Choice and Diversity: A New Framework for Schools*. London: HMSO.

Farrell, C. (1978) *My Mother Said . . . The Way Young People Learned about Sex and Birth Control*. London: Routledge and Kegan Paul.

Fine, M. (1988) Sexuality, schooling and adolescent females: the missing discourse of desire. *Harvard Educational Review* 58 (1), 29–53.

Franklin, S., Lury, C. and Stacey, J. (1991) Feminism, Marxism and Thatcherism. In S. Franklin, C. Lury and J. Stacey (eds) *Off-Centre: Feminism and Cultural Studies*. London: HarperCollins.

Hamilton, V. and Lynch, F. (1992) Educating young people about HIV/AIDS. In P. Aggleton (ed.) *Young People and HIV/AIDS: Papers from an ESRC Sponsored Seminar*. London: ESRC and University of London.

Hardy, J. and Vieler-Porter, C. (1992) Race, schooling and the 1988 Education Reform Act. In D. Gill, B. Mayor and M. Blair (eds) *Racism and Education: Structures and Strategies*. London: Sage and The Open University.

Haringey Council (1988) *Equal Opportunities: The Lesbian and Gay Perspective*. London: Haringey Council.

Haw, K. (1991) Interactions of gender and race—a problem for teachers? A review of the emerging literature. *Educational Research* 33 (1), 12–21.

Holland, J., Ramazanoglu, C., Scott, S., Sharpe, S. and Thomson, R. (1991a) Between embarrassment and trust: young women and the diversity of condom use. In P. Aggleton, G. Hart and P. Davies (eds) *AIDS: Responses, Interventions and Care*. London: Falmer Press.

— (1991b) *Pressure, Resistance and Empowerment: Young Women and the Negotiation of Safe Sex*. London: Tufnell Press.

Hudson, B. (1984) Femininity and adolescence. In A. McRobbie and M. Nava (eds) *Gender and Generation*. London: Macmillan.

McKeganey, N. and Barnard, M. (1992) *AIDS, Drugs and Sexual Risks: Lives in the Balance*. Buckingham: Open University Press.

Meredith, P. (1989) *Sex Education: Political Issues in Britian and Europe*. London: Routledge.

MESMAC (1992) *The MESMAC Guide to Good Practice*. London: Health Education Authority.

MORI (1990) *Young Adults' Health and Lifestyle: Sexual Behaviour*. London: Health Education Authority.

Mort, F. (1987) *Dangerous Sexualities. Medico-Moral Politics in England since 1830*. London: Routledge and Kegan Paul.

National AIDS Trust (1991) *Living for Tomorrow: The National AIDS Trust Youth Initiative*. London: NAT.

Newell, P. (1991) *The UN Convention and Children's Rights in the UK*. London: National Children's Bureau.

OFSTED (1992) *A Handbook for the Inspection of Schools*. London: HMSO.

Patten, J. (1992) There is a choice: good or evil. *Spectator*, 18 April, 9–10.

Patton, C. (1990) What science knows: formations of AIDS knowledges. In P. Aggleton, P. Davies and G. Hart (eds) *AIDS: Individual, Cultural and Policy Dimensions*. London: Falmer Press.

Reid, D. (1982) School sex education and the causes of unintended pregnancy: a review. *Health Education Journal* 41 (1), 4–10.

Rhodes, T. and Hartnoll, R. (1991) Reaching the hard to reach: models of HIV outreach health education. In P. Aggleton, G. Hart and P. Davies (eds) *AIDS: Responses, Interventions and Care*. London: Falmer Press.

Rubin, G. (1984) Thinking sex: notes for a radical theory of the politics of sexuality. In C. Vance (ed.) *Pleasure and Danger: Exploring Female Sexuality*. London: Routledge and Kegan Paul.

Schofield, M. (1965) *The Sexual Behaviour of Young People*. London: Longman.

Scruton, R., Ellis-Jones, A. and O'Keefe, D. (1985) *Education and Indoctrination: An Attempt at Definition and a Review of Social and Political Implications*. Harrow: Education Research Centre.

Sex Education Forum (1992) *An Enquiry into Sex Education*. London: National Children's Bureau.

Stacey, J. (1991) Promoting normality: Section 28 and the regulation of sexuality. In S. Franklin, C. Lury and J. Stacey (eds) *Off-Centre Feminism and Cultural Studies*. London: HarperCollins.

Stears, D. and Clift, S. (1990) *A Survey of AIDS Education in Secondary Schools*. Horsham: Avert.

Thomson, R. and Scott, S. (1991) *Learning about Sex: Young Women and the Social Construction of Sexual Identity*. London: Tufnell Press.

Thoroughgood, N. (1992) Sex education as social control. *Critical Public Health* 3(2), 43–50.

Trenchard, L. and Warren, J. (1984) *Something to Tell You*. London: London Lesbian and Gay Teenage Group.

Troyna, B. (1987) A conceptual overview of strategies to combat racial inequality in education. In B. Troyna (ed.) *Racial Inequality in Education*. London: Tavistock.

Watney, S. (1991) AIDS: the second decade. In P. Aggleton, G. Hart and P. Davies (eds) *AIDS: Responses, Interventions and Care*. London: Falmer Press.

Weatherburn, P., Hunt, A., Hickson, F. and Davies, P. (1992) *The Sexual Lifestyles of Gay and Bisexual Men in England and Wales*. London: HMSO.

Weeks, J. (1981) *Sex, Politics and Society: The Regulation of Sexuality since 1800*. London: Longman.

— (1985) *Sexuality and its Discontents: Meanings, Myths and Modern Sexualities*. London: Routledge and Kegan Paul.

Weiner, G. (ed) (1985) *Just a Bunch of Girls: Feminist Approaches to Schooling*. Milton Keynes: Open University Press.

Wight, D. (1992) Impediments to safer heterosexual sex: a review of research with young people. *AIDS Care* 41 (1), 11–21.

INDEX

accountability
— in bureaucracies 269
— of schools 63, 155
— of teachers 222, 224-6
Acker, S. 113, 232
action
— affirmative 150, 152
— direct 32
action research 167, 253, 255
activism, and sex education 281, 286, 293-5
Adam Smith Institute 129
adolescence
— and boys 27
— and girls 27-8
African-Caribbean children
— and educational attainment 185, 188-90, 194
— and special educational needs xiii, 204-5
— and teacher training 246
Allan, Mary 95-6, 99-100, 104-6
Allen, I. 296 n.2
Altbach, P. 69
Amos, V. 164
androcentrism
— in curriculum 155, 171-2, 245
— and liberalism 140-1, 144, 146, 148, 154, 163
anti-racism
— and ILEA 189
— and National Curriculum xiii, 127, 136, 172
— in New Zealand 154
— and role of education 243, 246, 256, 283-4
Anti-racist Teacher Education Network 254
anti-sexism
— and equality of opportunity 113, 118, 127, 136, 284
— and Inner London Education Authority xiii, 113, 119-21, 129, 283

— and National Curriculum xiii, 172
— in New Zealand 154
— and role of education 243, 246, 256, 283-4
Apple, M. 243-4, 249, 256
appraisal of teachers 222, 239
Arends, Janny xiii, 113-21
Arnot, Madeleine xiii-xiv, 117, 159-78
Asian children
— educational attainment 185
— and special educational needs 205
— and teacher training 246
assessment
— in France 221
— student 64, 128, 131-2, 172, 208, 233
Assessment of Performance Unit 127
assimilation 182
Assistant Mistresses Association 30 n.30
assisted places scheme 63-4, 66
Association of County Councils 292-3
Association of Headmistresses 26
Association of Metropolitan Authorities (AMA) 210
Astuto, T.A. 57, 73-4
attainment
— and class 77-8, 80, 82, 85, 87
— and race 182-4
— scores 208-9
— targets 67, 127, 131, 222, 232, 238
  see also under-achievement
attendance, compulsory 7
Attlee, Clement 18-19, 23
Audit Commission 209
authoritarianism, moral, and sex education xv, 281, 287-90, 292, 293, 295
autism, and special educational needs 205
autonomy
— sexual 295
— of teachers 240, 2367-8
Avery Hill College 104